THE SAINT MAKER SERIES

DAILY MEDITATIONS OF THE WORDS OF ST. ALPHONSUS FOR PENTECOST THROUGH THE 8TH WEEK AFTER PENTECOST

ST ALPHONSUS

SENSUS FIDELIUM PRESS

Gastonia, North Carolina

DAILY PRAYERS

Morning and Evening Prayers

LATIN RITE PRAYERS

Morning Offering

O JESUS, through the Immaculate Heart of Mary, I offer Thee my prayers, works, joys
and sufferings of this day for all the intentions of Thy Sacred Heart, in union with
the Holy Sacrifice of the Mass throughout the world, in reparation for my sins, for the
intentions of all our Associates and in particular for the intention of the Apostleship of
Prayer.

Act of Faith

O MY God, I firmly believe that Thou art one God in Three Divine Persons, Father, Son
and Holy Ghost. I believe that Thy Divine Son became man, and died for our sins, and
that He will come to judge the living and the dead. I believe these and all the truths which
the Holy Catholic Church teaches, because Thou hast revealed them, Who canst neither
deceive nor be deceived.

Act of Hope

O MY God, relying on Thy almighty power and infinite mercy and promises, I hope to obtain pardon of my sins, the help of Thy grace, and life everlasting, through the merits of Jesus Christ, my Lord and Redeemer.

Act of Charity

O MY God, I love Thee above all things, with my whole heart and soul, because Thou art all-good and worthy of all love. I love my neighbour as myself for the love of Thee. I forgive all who have injured me, and ask pardon of all whom I have injured.

Prayers for the Day Ahead

Grace at Meals

Before:
BLESS us, O Lord, and these Thy gifts, which we are about to receive from Thy bounty. Through Christ our Lord. Amen.

After:
WE give Thee thanks, O almighty God, for all Thy mercies. Who livest and reignest forever and ever. Amen.

Act of Spiritual Communion

My Jesus, I believe that Thou art present in the Most Holy Sacrament. I love Thee above all things, and I desire to receive Thee into my soul. Since I cannot at this moment receive Thee sacramentally, come at least spiritually into my heart. I embrace Thee as if Thou wert already there and unite myself wholly to Thee. Never permit me to be separated from Thee. Amen.

BYZANTINE PRAYERS

OPENING PRAYERS

In the Name of the Father, + and of the Son, and of the Holy Spirit. Glory be to You, O God; glory be to You.

O Heavenly King, Comforter, Spirit of Truth, You are everywhere present and fill all things. Treasury of Blessings and Giver of Life, come and dwell within us, cleanse us of all stain, and save our souls, O gracious Lord.

Holy God, + Holy and Mighty, Holy and Immortal, have mercy on us. (3 times)

Glory be to the Father, + and of the Son, and of the Holy Spirit, now and ever, and forever. Amen.

O Most Holy Trinity, have mercy on us; O Lord, cleanse us of our sins; O Master, forgive our transgressions; O Holy One, come to us and heal our infirmities for Your Name's sake.

Lord, have mercy. (3 times)

Glory be to the Father, + and of the Son, and of the Holy Spirit, now and ever and forever. Amen.

Our Father, Who art in Heaven, hallowed be Thy name; Thy Kingdom come, Thy will be done on earth as it is in Heaven. Give us this day our daily bread; and forgive us our trespasses as we forgive those who trespass against us And lead us not into temptation, but deliver us from evil.

For Thine is the kingdom and the power and the glory, Father, + Son, and Holy Spirit, now and ever and, forever. Amen.

MORNING PRAYERS

Awakening from sleep, I worship You, O blessed God; and offer the Angelic Hymn to You, O powerful Lord: Holy, holy, holy are You, O God! Through the intercession of Your Heavenly Hosts, have mercy on me.

Glory be to the Father, + and of the Son, and of the Holy Spirit:

O Lord, You have lifted me up from my bed and from sleep; now enlighten my mind, open my heart and my lips that I may sing to You, O Holy Trinity: Holy, holy, holy are You, O God! Through the prayers of all Your Saints, have mercy on me.

Now and ever, and forever. Amen.

The Judge shall come suddenly, and the deeds of all shall be brought to light. In fear, I cry out at the break of day: Holy, holy, holy are You, O God! Through the prayers of the Mother of God, have mercy on me.Lord, have mercy. (12 times)

I give thanks to You, O Holy Trinity. Because of Your great goodness and endless patience, You did not become angry with me, a slothful and sinful being; nor did You destroy me because of my transgressions. But, as always, You have shown Your love for us; and have raised me up as I lay in despair, that I might recite these prayers and sing the praises of Your power. Enlighten the eyes of my understanding, that I may meditate upon Your Words, understand Your Commandments, and accomplish Your Will. Open my mouth that I may sing to You in sincere praise; and that I may proclaim Your Most Holy Name, Father, + Son, and Holy Spirit, now and ever and, forever. Amen.

Come, let us adore the King, our God.
Come, let us adore Christ, the King and our God.
Come, let us adore and bow down to the only Lord Jesus Christ, the King and our God.

The Psalm of Repentance (Psalm 50) or another appropriate Psalm is now recited.

PSALM 50:

O God, have mercy on me in the greatness of Your love; in the abundance of Your tender mercies wipe out my offense. Wash me thoroughly from malice and cleanse me from sin; for I am well aware of my malice, and my sins are before me always. It is You alone I have offended, I have done what is evil in Your sight; wherefore, You are just in Your deeds and triumphant in Your judgment. Behold, I was born in iniquities, and in sins my mother conceived me. But You are the Lover of Truth; You have shown me the depths and secrets of Your wisdom. Wash me with hyssop, and I shall be pure; cleanse me, and I shall be whiter than snow. Let me hear sounds of joy and feasting; the bones that were afflicted shall rejoice. Turn Your face away from my offenses, and wipe off all my sins. A spotless heart create in me, O God; renew a steadfast spirit in my breast. Cast me not afar from Your face; take not Your blessed Spirit out of me. Restore to me the joy of Your salvation, and let Your guiding Spirit dwell in me. I will teach Your ways to the sinners, and the wicked shall return to You. Deliver me from blood-guilt, O God, my saving God, and my tongue will joyfully sing Your justice. O Lord, You shall open my lips, and my mouth will declare Your praise. Had You desired sacrifice, I would have offered it, but You will not be satisfied with whole-burnt offerings. Sacrifice to God is a contrite spirit; a crushed and humbled heart God will not spurn. In Your kindness, O Lord be bountiful to Sion; may the walls of Jerusalem be restored. Then will You delight in just oblation, in sacrifice and whole-burnt offerings. Then shall they offer calves upon Your altar.

NICENE CREED:

I believe in one God, the Father Almighty, Creator of heaven and earth, and of all things visible and invisible. And in one Lord Jesus Christ, Son of God, the only-begotten, born of the Father before all ages. Light of Light, true God of true God; begotten, not made; of one substance with the Father, through Whom all things were made. Who for us men and for our salvation, came down from heaven, and was incarnate from the Holy Spirit and Mary the Virgin, and became man. He was also crucified for us under Pontius Pilate, and suffered, and was buried. And He rose again on the third day, according to the Scriptures. And He ascended into heaven, and sits at the right hand of the Father. And He will come again with glory, to judge the living and the dead; and of His kingdom there will be no end. And in the Holy Spirit, the Lord, and Giver of Life, Who proceeds from the Father; Who together with the Father and the Son is worshipped and glorified; Who spoke through the prophets. In one, holy, catholic, and apostolic Church. I profess one baptism for the remission of sins. I expect the resurrection of the dead, and the life of the world to come.

Amen.

PRAYER OF PENANCE:

Remit, pardon, and forgive, O God, our sins committed voluntarily and involuntarily, by word and deed, knowingly and in ignorance, by thought and purpose, by day and night. Forgive all these, for You are gracious and love us all.

ANGELIC SALUTATION:

Hail Mary, Full of Grace, the Lord is with thee. Blessed art thou amongst women, and blessed is the Fruit of thy womb; for thou hast borne Christ, the Savior and Deliverer of our souls.

PRAYERS FOR INTERCESSION:

We fly to your patronage, O Virgin Mother of God. Despise not our prayers in our necessities, but who are alone pure and blessed, deliver us from all danger.

O most glorious ever Virgin Mary, Mother of Christ our God, receive our prayers and offer them to your Son, our God, that He, for your sake, enlighten and save our souls.

PRAYERS TO THE ANGELS AND SAINTS:

All you heavenly powers, holy Angels and Archangels, beseech God for us sinners. O holy and glorious Apostles, Prophets, Martyrs, and Saints, beseech God for us sinners.

PRAYER OF THE PUBLICAN:

O God, + be merciful to me, a sinner.
O God, + cleanse me of my sins and have mercy on me.
O Lord, + forgive me, for I have sinned without number.

EVENING PRAYERS

Take the opening prayers up to "For Thine is the kingdom... Amen."

Have mercy on us, O God, have mercy on us. Since we have no defense, we sinners offer this supplication to You, our Master; have mercy on us.

Glory be to the Father, + and of the Son, and of the Holy Spirit:

Lord, have mercy on us; for in You we place our hope. Be not exceedingly angry with us, nor mindful of our transgressions; but look upon us even now with mercy, and deliver us from our enemies. For You are our God, and we are Your people; we are all the work of Your Hands, and we call upon Your Name.

Now and ever, and forever. Amen.

Open unto us the doors of mercy, O blessed Mother of God; that we, who place our trust in you, may not perish; but that through you we be delivered from misfortune. For you are the salvation of all Christians.

Lord, have mercy. (12 times)

O eternal God, and Ruler of all creation, You have allowed me to reach this hour. Forgive the sins I have this day committed by word, deed, or thought. Purify me from every spiritual and physical stain. Grant me to rise from this sleep to glorify You by my deeds throughout the remainder of my life, and that I be victorious over every spiritual and physical enemy which fights against me. Deliver me, O Lord, from all vain thoughts and evil desires. For Thine is the Kingdom, and the Power, and the Glory, Father, + Son, and Holy Spirit, now and ever, and forever. Amen.

O loving mother of our most gracious King, O pure and blessed Virgin Mary, pour forth into my restless soul the grace of your Son, our God. Lead me by your prayers to salutary deeds, that I might spend the remainder of my life without fault, and attain paradise through you, O Virgin Mother of God. For you are pure and blessed forever.

O Guardian Angel, protector of my soul and body, to your care I have been entrusted by Christ. Obtain for me the forgiveness of the sins committed by me this day. Pray for me, your sinful and unworthy servant, that I may become worthy of the grace and mercy of the Most Holy Trinity and the Mother of our Lord God, Jesus Christ. Amen.

We are yours, O Mother of God. Since you have delivered us from all tribulation, we give thanks to you by dedicating our songs of victory to you, O Saving Champion. In your invincible might, deliver us from all dangers that we may exclaim to you: "Hail, Full of Grace!"

O most glorious, ever-virgin Mother of Christ our God, offer up our prayers to your Son and our God, so that through you, O Mother of God, He may save our souls. I place all my hope in you, Mother of God. Do not turn away from me, a sinner, for I need your help and intercession. Have mercy on me, for my soul hopes in you.

The Father + is my hope! The Son + is my refuge! And the Holy Spirit + is my protection! O Most Holy Trinity +, glory be to You!

It is truly proper to glorify you, who have borne God; the ever-blessed, immaculate, and the Mother of our God. More honorable than the Cherubim, and beyond compare, more glorious than the Seraphim; who, a virgin, gave birth to God, the Word. You, truly the Mother of God, we magnify.

HYMN OF THE EVENING:
O Joyful Light! Light and Holy Glory of the Father immortal; the heavenly, holy, the blessed One, O Jesus Christ. Now that we have reached the setting of the sun, and see the evening light, we sing to God, Father, + Son, and Holy Spirit. It is fitting at all times to raise a song of praise in measured melody to You, O Son of God, the Giver of Life. Behold, the universe sings Your glory

Prayer to the Virgin

O spotless, unstained, incorruptible, undefiled, pure Virgin, Lady Bride of God, who through your wondrous birth-giving united God the Word with mankind, and linked the fallen nature of our human race with the heavenly; the only hope of the hopeless and the help of the persecuted; the ready support of those who seek refuge in you, and the shelter of all the Christians: do not despise me, the wretched sinner who have defiled myself with shameful thoughts and words and deeds, and through negligence of thought have become slave to the pleasures of life.
But as the Mother of our compassionate God, and a friend of man, have compassion on me the sinner and prodigal, and accept this prayer from my impure lips; and using

your motherly standing, entreat your Son and our Master and Lord to open unto me the depths of his loving goodness and, overlooking my innumerable faults, to return me to repentance and make me a worthy servant of his commandments.

Stand by me forever; in this life as a merciful and compassionate and good and lovingly warm protector and helper, by repulsing the assaults of the adversary and leading me toward salvation; and at the time of my death, by embracing my miserable soul and driving far away from it the dark fares of the evil demons; and at the awesome day of judgment by redeeming me from eternal hell, and proclaiming me an heir of the ineffable glory of your Son and our God.

May I enjoy such fate, my Lady, most-holy Theotokos, through your intercession and protection; through the grace and love for mankind of your only begotten Son, our Lord and God and Savior Jesus Christ. To whom belong all glory, honor and worship, together with his beginningless Father, and the all holy and good and life giving Spirit, now and ever, and to the ages of ages. Amen.

Prayer to our Lord Jesus Christ

And grant to us, Master, as we depart for sleep, rest of body and soul, and preserve us from the gloomy slumber of sin, and from every dark and nocturnal pleasure. Arrest the drives of passion; extinguish the burning arrows of the Evil One which insidiously fly in our direction; suppress the rebellions of our flesh, and calm our every earthly and material thought. And grant to us, O God, alert mind, prudent thinking, sober heart, light sleep free of any satanic fantasy. Awaken us at the time of prayer rooted in your commandments and having unbroken within us the remembrance of your ordinances. Grant that we may sing your glory through the night by praising and blessing and glorifying your most honorable and majestic name, of the Father and of the Son and of the Holy Spirit, now and ever, and to the ages of ages. Amen.

Final Prayer

Lord, forgive those who hate us and those who wrong us; do good to those who do good; to our brethren and relatives, grant their requests for salvation and eternal life; visit the sick and grant them healing; govern those at sea; accompany the travelers; to those who serve us and those who help us grant remission of sins; forgive those who have asked us to pray for them and have mercy on them according to Your great mercy.

Remember, Lord, all our fathers and brethren departed this life and rest them where the light of Your face shines. Remember, Lord, our brethren, the captives, and spare them from every tribulation. Remember, Lord those who labor and bring forth fruit in Your holy Churches, and grant to them all requests for salvation and eternal life. Remember us, as well, Lord, Your humble and sinful servants and illumine our mind with the light of your knowledge and guide us in the way of Your commandments; through the intercessions of Your most sacred Mother, our Lady Theotokos and ever virgin Mary, and all Your Saints; for You are blessed unto the ages of ages. Amen.

CONTENTS

PENTECOST SUNDAY

Morning Meditation

THE COMING OF THE HOLY GHOST INTO THE SOUL

The Eternal Father was not content with giving us His Son, Jesus Christ, to save us by His death, He has given us also the Holy Ghost to dwell always in our souls and keep them inflamed with His holy love. Hence, when the Holy Spirit descended upon the Apostles, He appeared in the form of tongues of fire. This is the holy fire that inflamed the Saints with the desire to do great things for God, that enabled them to love their most cruel enemies, to seek after contempt, to renounce all the riches and honors of the world, and even to embrace torments and death.

I.

The Holy Ghost is that divine bond which unites the Father with the Son; it is He Who unites our souls, through love, with God. For, as St. Augustine says, union with God is the effect of love. "Charity is a virtue which unites us with God." The chains of the world are chains of death, but the bonds of the Holy Ghost are bonds of Eternal life, because they bind us to God, Who is our true and only Life. Let us also remember that all the lights, inspirations, divine calls, all the good acts we have performed during our life, all our acts of contrition, of confidence in the divine mercy, of love, of resignation, have been the gifts of the Holy Ghost. Likewise, the Spirit also helps our infirmity; for we know not what we should pray for as we ought; but the Spirit himself asketh for us with unspeakable groanings- (Romans viii. 26). Thus, it is the Holy Ghost Who prays for us; for we know not what to ask, but the Holy Spirit teaches us what we should pray for.

O holy and divine Spirit, come into my heart and teach me to pray as I ought. Give me strength not to neglect prayer in times of weariness and dryness. I have been lost by my sins. Thou desire my sanctification and salvation, and I, too, earnestly desire to become holy. I love Thee, my sovereign Good, my Love, my All, and because I love Thee, I give myself wholly to Thee. O Blessed Virgin Mary, protect me.

II.

We know by Faith that the Holy Ghost is the Love that the Eternal Father and the Eternal Word bear one another, and therefore the gift of divine charity which the Lord infuses into our souls, and which is the greatest of all gifts, is particularly attributed to the Holy Ghost, as St. Paul teaches: The charity of God is poured forth in our hearts by the Holy Ghost who is given to us (Romans v. 5). And our Lord Himself made this great promise: If you love Me, I will pray My Father, and He will send you the Holy Spirit that He may always dwell in you. If you love me, keep my commandments. And I will ask my Father, and he will give you another Paraclete that he may abide with you forever (John xiv. 15, 16).

O Holy Spirit, divine Paraclete, Father of the poor, Consoler of the afflicted, Light of hearts, Sanctifier of souls, behold me prostrate in Thy Presence. I adore Thee with the most profound submission. I love Thee with all my affections. I have been so ungrateful as to offend Thee. I ask a thousand pardons for all my sins. I offer Thee my heart, cold as it is, and I supplicate Thee to let a ray of Thy light and a spark of Thy fire enter therein. Thou art a divine Spirit, fortify me against the wicked spirits: Thou art a Fire, enkindle in me the fire of Thy love: Thou art a Light, enlighten me that I may know the things of eternity: Thou art the Author of the heavenly gifts, I beseech Thee to grant them to me. Vivify me by Thy grace, sanctify me by Thy charity, govern me by Thy wisdom, adopt me by Thy beauty as Thy child, and save me by Thy infinite mercy. Amen.

Spiritual Reading

THANKSGIVING AFTER COMMUNION

There is no prayer more agreeable to God, or more profitable to the soul, than that which is made during the Thanksgiving after Communion. It is the opinion of many grave writers (Suarez, Cajetan, Valentia, De Lugo, and others), that the Holy Communion, as long as the Sacramental species last, constantly produces greater and greater graces in the soul, provided the soul is then constant in disposing itself by new acts of virtue. The Council of Florence, in the Decree of Eugenius IV to the Armenians, teaches that the Blessed Sacrament produces the same effect in the soul as material food, which, when it enters the body, produces effects according to the state in which it finds it. For this reason, holy souls endeavor to remain as long as possible in prayer after Communion. The Blessed John of Avila, even when he was giving his missions, used to remain for at least two hours in prayer. Father Balthazar Alvarez used to say, that we should set great value on, the time after Communion, imagining that we hear from the lips of Jesus Christ Himself the words that He addressed to His disciples: But me you have not always with you (Matthew xxvi. 11). It is not advisable, as many do, to begin to read immediately after Communion: it is better to spend at least a short time in producing holy affections, and in conversing with Jesus, who is then within us, and in repeating many times words of tenderness, or some fervent prayer. Jesus Christ repeated the same prayer in the Garden three times: And he prayed the third time, saying the self-same word (Matthew xxvi. 44). In affections and prayers, it is, then, that the soul should entertain itself with Jesus after Communion; for we must know that the acts formed in prayer after Communion are far more precious and meritorious in the sight of God than when made at another time; for the soul being then united with Jesus, the value of the acts is increased by the presence of Jesus. We should, moreover, know that after Communion Jesus Christ is more disposed to grant graces. St. Teresa says, that after Communion Jesus places Himself in the soul as on a throne of grace, and then says: What willest thou that I should do for thee? (Mark x. 51) meaning: O soul, I am come for the express purpose of granting thee graces: ask Me what thou wilt, and as much as thou wilt, and thou shalt receive all.

Oh, what treasures of grace would you receive, devout soul, if you only entertained yourself with Jesus for an hour, or at least half-an-hour, after Communion! After your thanksgiving is ended, be also careful during the whole day on which you have communicated to keep yourself united by affections and prayers with Jesus, Whom you have received.

Evening Meditation

THE PRACTICE OF THE LOVE OF JESUS CHRIST
X.-THE MEANS OF AVOIDING LUKEWARMNESS AND ATTAINING
PERFECTION

I.

The greatest evil is that without mental prayer we do not pray at all. I have spoken frequently in my spiritual works of the necessity of prayer, and more especially in a little volume entitled, On Prayer, the Great Means of Salvation and Perfection; and here also I will say a few other things. It will be sufficient, then, to quote the opinion of the Venerable Palafox, Bishop of Osma: "How can charity last, unless God grants us perseverance? How will the Lord grant us perseverance unless we ask it of Him? And how shall we ask it of Him except by prayer? Without prayer there is no communication with God for the preservation of virtue." And so it is, because he that neglects mental prayer sees very little into the wants of his soul; he knows little of the dangers of his salvation, of the means to be used to overcome temptations; and so, understanding little of the necessity of prayer, he leaves off praying, and will certainly be lost.

II.

Then as regards subjects for Meditation, nothing is more useful than to meditate on the Four Last Things: Death, Judgment, Hell, and Heaven; but it is of especial advantage to meditate on Death, and to imagine ourselves expiring on the bed of sickness, with the Crucifix in our hands, and on the point of entering eternity. But above all, to one that loves Jesus Christ, and is anxious always to increase in His love, no consideration is more efficacious than that of the Passion of the Redeemer. St Francis of Sales calls Mount Calvary "the Mountain of Lovers." All the lovers of Jesus Christ love to abide on this Mountain, where no air is breathed but the air of Divine love. When we see a God dying for our love and dying to gain our love (He loved us and delivered himself up for us), it is impossible for us not to love Him ardently. Such darts of love continually issue forth from the Wounds of Christ Crucified as pierce even hearts of stone. Oh, happy he who is ever going during life to the heights of Calvary! O blessed Mount! O lovely Mount! O beloved Mount! And who shall ever leave thee more! A Mount that sends forth flames to enkindle the souls that perseveringly abide upon thee!

WHIT MONDAY

Morning Meditation

THE LOVE OF JESUS IN THE MOST BLESSED SACRAMENT

Jesus, not wishing to separate Himself from us even in death, instituted the Most Blessed Sacrament to remain with us therein until the end of the world. Behold I am with you all days even to the consummation of the world- (Matthew xxviii. 20).

I.

Our most loving Redeemer, knowing that He must leave this earth and return to His Father as soon as He should have accomplished the work of our Redemption by His death, and seeing that His hour was near at hand– Jesus knowing that his hour was come that he should pass out of this world to his father (John xiii. l)– would not leave us orphans in this valley of tears. What, then, did He do? He instituted the Most Holy Sacrament of the Eucharist, in which He left us His whole Self. "No tongue," says St. Peter of Alcantara, "can express the greatness of the love of Jesus for our souls; and hence this Spouse, before He departed this life, in order that His absence might not be the occasion of our forgetting Him, left us as a memorial this Most Holy Sacrament, in which He might Himself remain with us, not being willing that any other pledge but Himself should remain to remind us of Him." Jesus, therefore, not wishing to separate Himself from us by His death, instituted this Sacrament of love, to remain with us until the end of the world: Behold I am with you all days, even to the consummation of the world (Matthew xxviii. 20). Let us behold Him, therefore, as Faith teaches us, residing upon numberless altars, shut up in so many prisons of love, that He may be found by all who seek Him. "But, O Lord," says St. Bernard, "this does not become Thy majesty." Jesus Christ answers: It is sufficient that it accords with My love.

O my beloved Jesus, O God Who lovest us with such great love, what more canst Thou do to make us, ungrateful sinners, love Thee? Oh, if men loved Thee, all the churches would be continually filled with devout people, prostrate on their faces, adoring and thanking Thee, burning with Thy love at beholding Thee with the eyes of Faith hidden in a tabernacle! But no, men, forgetful of Thee and of Thy love, wait indeed upon a mortal man from whom they expect some perishable good, and leave Thee, my Lord, abandoned and alone. Oh, that I were able to make Thee amends for so much ingratitude by my own devotion!

II.

Those persons are tenderly affected who go to Jerusalem, and visit the place where the Word Incarnate was born, the hall where He was scourged, the Mount on which He died, and the Sepulcher in which He was buried; but how much greater ought our tenderness to be in visiting an altar on which Jesus is present in the Most Holy Sacrament? The Blessed John of Avila was accustomed to say, that there was no sanctuary so excellent and holy as a church in which Jesus was sacramentally present.

I am grieved, O my Jesus, that I have hitherto been like unto such, careless and forgetful of Thee. But for the future I will not be one of their number. I will devote myself to Thee and visit Thee as often as I am able. Inflame my heart with Thy holy love, that for the future I may live only to love and to please Thee. Thou deserves to be loved by the hearts of all. If at one time I despised Thee, I now desire to love Thee. My Jesus, Thou art my Love and my only Good my God and my All. Most Holy Virgin Mary, obtain for me a great love of Jesus in the Holy Sacrament.

Spiritual Reading

VISITING JESUS IN THE BLESSED SACRAMENT

Our holy Faith teaches us, and we are bound to believe that in the consecrated Host Jesus Christ is really present under the species of bread. But we must also understand that He is thus present on our altars as on a throne of love and mercy, to dispense graces and to show us the love He bears us, in wishing thus to dwell night and day hidden in our midst.

It is well known that the Holy Church instituted the Festival of Corpus Christi with a solemn Octave, and that she celebrates it with many processions, and frequent Exposition of the Most Holy Sacrament, that men may thereby be moved to gratefully acknowledge and honor this loving presence and dwelling of Jesus Christ in the Sacrament of the Altar, by their devotions, thanksgivings, and the tender affections of their souls. O God, how many insults and outrages has not this admirable Redeemer had and has He not daily to endure in this Sacrament on the part of those very men for whose love He remains upon our altars! Of this He indeed complained to His dear servant, St. Margaret Mary

Alacoque, as the author of the Book of Devotion to the Heart of Jesus relates. One day, as she was in prayer before the Most Holy Sacrament, Jesus showed her His Heart on a throne of flames, crowned with thorns, and surmounted by a cross, and thus addressed her: "Behold this Heart which has loved men so much, and which has spared Itself in nothing, and has even gone so far as to consume Itself, thereby to show them Its love; but in return the greater part of men only show Me ingratitude by the irreverence, tepidity, sacrilege, and contempt, of which they make Me the object in this Sacrament of love; and that which I feel most acutely is, that hearts consecrated to Me treat Me thus." Jesus then expressed His wish, that the first Friday after the Octave of Corpus Christi should be dedicated as a particular festival in honor of His adorable Heart; and that on that day all souls who loved Him should endeavor by their homage, and by their affections to make amends for the insults men have offered Him in the Sacrament of the Altar. He at the same time promised abundant grace to all who should thus honor Him present in the Blessed Sacrament.

This Presence makes us understand what our Lord said of old by His Prophet, that His delights are to be with the children of men; for He knows not how to tear Himself from them, even when they abandon and despise Him. This also shows us how pleasing to the Heart of Jesus are all those souls who frequently visit Him and keep Him company in the churches in which He is present under the sacramental species. He desired St. Mary Magdalen de Pazzi to visit Him in the Most Blessed Sacrament thirty-three times a day; and in this His beloved spouse faithfully obeyed Him, and in all her visits she approached as near as possible to the altar, as we read in her Life.

But let all those devout souls who often go to keep company with Jesus in the Most Blessed Sacrament speak -let them tell us of the gifts and inspirations they have received, of the flames of love which are there enkindled in their souls, and the Paradise they enjoy in the presence of this hidden God.

The servant of God, and great Sicilian, missionary Father Louis La Nouza, was, even in his youth and as a layman, so enamored of Jesus Christ, that he seemed unable to tear himself from the presence of his beloved Lord. Such were the joys which he experienced here: that his director, to moderate his devotion, had to command him, in virtue of obedience, not to remain before the tabernacle for more than an hour. The time having elapsed, he showed in obeying that in tearing himself from the bosom of Jesus Christ, he had to do himself just such violence as a child that has to detach itself from its mother's breast in the very moment in which it is satiating itself with the utmost avidity. St. Aloysius also was forbidden to remain in the presence of the Most Blessed Sacrament, and as he passed before the Tabernacle, finding himself drawn, so to speak, by the sweet attractions of his Lord, and almost forced to remain there, he would with the greatest effort tear himself away, saying, in an excess of tender love: Depart from me, O Lord, depart! There it was also that St. Francis Xavier found refreshment in the midst of his many labors in India, for he employed his days in toiling for souls, and his nights he passed in the presence of the Most Blessed Sacrament.

Evening Meditation

THE PRACTICE OF THE LOVE OF JESUS CHRIST
XI.-THE MEANS OF AVOIDING LUKEWARMNESS AND ATTAINING PERFECTION

I.

The fourth means of perfection, and even of perseverance in the grace of God, is frequently to receive Holy Communion, of which we have often spoken, and often declared that a soul can do nothing more pleasing to Jesus Christ than to receive Him often in the Sacrament of the Altar. St. Teresa said: "There is no better help to perfection than frequent Communion. Oh, how admirably does the Lord bring on such a soul to perfection!" And she adds that ordinarily speaking, they who communicate most frequently are found further advanced in perfection; and that there is greater spirituality in those Religious Communities where frequent Communion is the custom. For this reason, it is that, as we find declared in a decree of Innocent XI, in 1679, the Holy Fathers have so highly extolled, and so much promoted, the practice of frequent and even of daily Communion. The Holy Communion, as the Council of Trent tells us, delivers us from daily faults, and preserves us from mortal sins. St. Bernard asserts that Communion represses the movements of anger and incontinence, which are the two passions that most frequently and most violently assail us. St. Thomas says that Communion defeats the suggestions of the devil. And finally, St. John Chrysostom says that Communion pours into our souls a great inclination to virtue, and a promptitude to practice it; and at the same time imparts to us a great peace, by which the path of perfection is made very sweet and easy to us. Besides, there is no Sacrament so capable of kindling Divine love in souls as the Holy Sacrament of the Eucharist, in which Jesus Christ bestows on us His whole Self, to unite us all to Himself by means of holy love. Wherefore Blessed John of Avila said: "Whoever deters souls from frequent Communion does the work of the devil." Yes, for the devil has a great horror of this Sacrament, from which souls derive immense strength to advance in Divine love.

II.

But a proper preparation is requisite to communicate well. The first preparation, or, in other terms, the remote preparation, to be able to go to Communion daily, or several times in the week, is,

(1) To keep free from all deliberate affection to sin, that is, to sin committed, as we say, with the eyes open.

(2) The practice of much mental prayer.

(3) The mortification of the senses and of the passions.

St. Francis of Sales teaches as follows: "Whoever has overcome the greatest part of his bad inclinations, and has arrived at a notable degree of perfection, can communicate every day." The angelic Doctor, St. Thomas, says that anyone who knows by experience that his soul derives an increase of Divine love from Holy Communion, may communicate daily. Hence Innocent XI, in the above-mentioned decree, said that the greater or less frequency of Holy Communion must rest on the decision of the Confessor, who ought to be guided in this matter by the profit which he sees accrue to the souls under his direction. In the next place, the proximate preparation for Communion is that which is made on the morning itself of Communion, for which there is need of at least half an hour's mental prayer.

To reap also more abundant fruit from Communion, we must make a good thanksgiving. Blessed John of Avila said that the time after Communion is "a time to gain treasures of graces". St. Mary Magdalen de Pazzi used to say that no time can be more calculated to inflame us with Divine love than the time immediately after our Communion. And St. Teresa says: "After Communion let us be careful not to lose so good an opportunity of negotiating with God. His Divine Majesty is not accustomed to pay badly for His lodging, if He meets with a good reception."

WHIT TUESDAY

Morning Meditation
JESUS REMAINS ON OUR ALTARS THAT HE MAY BE FOUND BY ALL

St. Teresa used to say that in this world it is impossible for all subjects to speak with their king. But everyone who wishes can find Jesus, the King of Heaven, in the Blessed Sacrament, and may speak with Him without restraint.

I.

St. Teresa used to say that in this world it is impossible for all subjects to speak with their king. The most the poor can hope for is to convey what they have to say to him by means of some third person. But to speak with Thee, O King of Heaven, there is no need of any third person. Everyone who wishes may find Thee in the Holy Sacrament and may speak to Thee without restraint. For this reason, it is, says the same Saint, that Jesus has concealed His majesty under the appearance of bread, to give us confidence, and to take away from us all fear of approaching Him. Ah, how does Jesus hourly exclaim from our altars: Come to me all you who labor and are burdened, and I will refresh you- (Matthew xi. 28). Come, He says to us-come, ye poor; come, ye infirm; come, ye afflicted; come ye just and sinners, and you shall find in Me a remedy for all your losses and afflictions. Such is the desire of Jesus Christ to console all who have recourse to Him. He remains night and day upon our altars that He may be found by all and may bestow His favors upon all.

O my Jesus, I could even die of grief when I think that hitherto I have loved creatures and my own gratification more than Thee, by turning my back upon Thee, my sovereign Good. But Thou wouldst not suffer me to be lost; Thou hast borne with me with so much patience, and, instead of chastising me, hast wounded my heart with so many darts of love that I can no longer resist Thy allurements and have now given myself to Thee. I see that Thou wouldst have me all Thine. But since Thou desires this, do Thou effect it, for it is Thou that must do it. Detach all my affections from myself and from creatures, and grant that I may seek no other but thee, nor think of any other, nor speak of any but Thee, and that I may desire and sigh only to burn with Thy love, to live and to die for Thee. O love of my Jesus, come and occupy my whole heart, and expel from it all love that is not for God. I love Thee, O Jesus, present in the Holy Sacrament. I love Thee, my Life, my Treasure, and my All. O Mary, pray for me, and make me belong entirely to Jesus.

II.

The Saints here in this world experienced such delight in remaining before Jesus in the Blessed Sacrament that days and nights appeared to them but as moments. The Countess of Feria, having become a Poor Clare was never wearied of remaining in the choir in sight of the tabernacle. Being one day asked what she was doing so long before the Blessed Sacrament, she answered with surprise: "What was I doing before the Blessed Sacrament-what was I doing? I was thanking, loving, arid asking!" St. Philip Neri, at the sight of the Blessed Sacrament, exclaimed: "Behold my Love! Behold all my Love!" Ah! if Jesus Christ were our whole love, our days and nights in His presence would also appear as moments. From this day forward, O Jesus, I hope to be able to say always of Thee, when visiting Thee on the altar: "Behold my Love! Behold all my Love!" Yes, my beloved Redeemer, I desire to love no other but Thee; I desire only Thee, Who art the only love of my soul.

Spiritual Reading

VISITING JESUS IN THE BLESSED SACRAMENT

St. John Regis was accustomed frequently to visit Jesus in the Blessed Sacrament. Sometimes, however, finding the church closed, he satisfied his longings by remaining on his knees outside the door, exposed to the rain and cold, that, at least at a distance, he might pay his homage to his Comforter concealed under the sacramental veils. St. Francis of Assisi used to converse concerning all his labors and undertakings with Jesus in the Most Holy Sacrament. But tender, perhaps, beyond all others was the devotion of St. Wenceslaus, Duke of Bohemia, towards the Most Holy Sacrament. This holy king was so enamored of the presence of Jesus that he not only gathered the wheat and grapes and made the hosts and wine with his own hands, and then gave them to be used in the Holy Sacrifice, but he used, even during the winter, to go at night to visit the church in which the Blessed Sacrament was kept. These Visits enkindled in his soul such flames of divine love that the ardor imparted itself even to his body and took from the snow on which he walked its wonted cold. It is related that the servant who accompanied him, and had to walk on the snow, suffered much from the cold. The holy king, on perceiving this, was moved to compassion, and commanded him to follow him, and to step only in his footmarks. He did so, and never afterwards felt the cold.

In the Visits, you will read other examples of the tender affection with which souls inflamed with the love of God longed to remain in the presence of the Most Blessed Sacrament. You will find that all the Saints were enamored of this most sweet devotion, and, indeed, it is not possible to find on earth a more precious gem, or a treasure more worthy of all our love, than Jesus in the Most Holy Sacrament. Certainly, amongst all devotions, that of receiving the Sacraments alone excepted, adoring Jesus in the Blessed Sacrament holds first place. It is the most pleasing to God and the most useful to us. Do not then, O devout soul, refuse to begin this devotion; leave the conversation of men, and remain each day, from this time forward, for half, or at least a quarter of an hour, in some church in the presence of Jesus Christ under the sacramental species. Taste and see how sweet the Lord is. Make a trial, and by experience you will learn the great benefit you will derive from this devotion.

Be assured that the time thus spent with devotion before this most Divine Sacrament will be the most profitable to you in life, and the source of your greatest consolation in death and for eternity. And you should know that in a quarter of an hour's prayer in the presence of the Blessed Sacrament, you may gain more than in all the other spiritual exercises of the day. It is true that in every place God hears the petitions of those who pray to Him, having promised to do so. Ask and you shall receive- (John xvi. 24}. Yet The Disciple tells us that Jesus dispenses His graces in greatest abundance to those who visit Him in the Most Blessed Sacrament. Blessed Henry Suso also used to say that Jesus Christ hears the prayers of the faithful more graciously in the Sacrament of the Altar than elsewhere. And where, indeed, did holy souls make their most beautiful resolutions, but prostrate before the Most Holy Sacrament? Who knows but that you also may one day, in the presence of the Tabernacle, make the resolution to give yourself entirely to God? In this little book I feel myself bound, at least out of gratitude to my Jesus in the Holy Sacrament, to declare, that through means of this devotion of visiting Him, which I practiced, though with so much tepidity and in so imperfect a manner, I abandoned the world, in which, unfortunately, I lived until I was six-and-twenty years of age. Fortunate indeed will you be if you can detach yourself from it at an earlier period and give yourself without reserve to that Lord Who has given Himself without reserve to you. I repeat, blessed indeed you will be, not only in eternity, but even in this life. Oh, how sweet a joy it is to remain with faith and tender devotion before an altar, and converse familiarly with

Jesus Christ, Who is there with the express purpose of listening to and graciously hearing those who come to visit Him; to ask His pardon for the displeasure we have caused Him; to put before Him our wants, as a friend to a friend in whom he places all his confidence; to ask Him for His graces, for His love, for His Kingdom. But, above all, oh, what a paradise it is there to remain making acts of love towards that Lord who is in the Tabernacle burning with love for us and praying to His Eternal Father for our welfare. In truth it is love that keeps Him there thus hidden and unknown, even though He is despised by ungrateful souls. But why say more? Taste and see.

Evening Meditation
THE PRACTICE OF THE LOVE OF JESUS CHRIST
XII.-THE MEANS OF AVOIDING LUKEWARMNESS AND ATTAINING PERFECTION

I.

There are certain pusillanimous souls, who, on being exhorted to communicate more frequently, reply: "But I am not worthy." But, my child, do you not know, that the more you refrain from Communion, the more unworthy you become? Because deprived of Holy Communion you will have less strength, and will commit many faults. Well, then, obey your director and be guided by him: faults do not forbid Holy Communion, when they are not committed with full will; besides, among your failings the greatest is not to submit to what your spiritual father says to you.

"But in my past life I was very bad." And I reply that you must know that he who is weakest has most need of the physician and of medicine. Jesus in the Blessed Sacrament is our Physician and Medicine as well. St. Ambrose said: "I, who am always sinning, have always need of medicine." You will then say, perhaps, "But my confessor does not tell me to communicate oftener." If, then, he does not tell you to do so, ask him permission to communicate oftener. Should he deny you, obey him; but in the meantime, make him the request. "It would seem pride." It would be pride if you were to wish to communicate against his will, but not when you ask his consent with humility.

II.

This heavenly Bread requires to be hungered for. Jesus loves to be desired, says a devout author, sitit sitiri, "He thirsts to be thirsted for." And what a thought is this: "Today I have communicated, and tomorrow I am to communicate." Oh, how such a reflection keeps the soul attentive to avoid all defects and to do the will of God! "But I have no devotion." If you mean sensible devotion, it is not necessary, neither does God always grant it even to

His most beloved souls: it is enough for you to have the devotion of a will determined to belong wholly to God, and to make progress in His Divine love. John Gerson says that he who abstains from Communion because he does not feel that devotion which he would like to feel, acts like a man who does not approach the fire because he does not feel warm.

WEDNESDAY EMBER DAY

Morning Meditation

THE GREAT GIFT OF JESUS IN THE BLESSED SACRAMENT

God is Omnipotent; but after He has given Himself to us in the Blessed Sacrament, He has no greater gift to give us. O wonderful prodigy of Divine love!

I.

The love of Jesus was not satisfied with His shedding His Blood and laying down His life for us in the midst of ignominies and torments, in order to make known His affection for us; but, moreover, to oblige us the more to love Him, on the night, before His death, He would leave us His whole Self to be our Food in the Holy Eucharist. God is omnipotent, but, having given Himself to us in this Sacrament, He has nothing more to give. The Council of Trent says that Jesus, in giving Himself to us in the Holy Communion, pours out upon us all the riches of His infinite love. He pours out, as it were, the riches of His love towards men.

O my dear Jesus, what more canst Thou do to make us love Thee? Oh! make us sensible of the excess of Thy love in reducing Thyself to Food to be united with us sinners. Thou, then, my Redeemer, hast had so much love for me as not to refuse to give me Thy whole Self frequently in the Holy Communion, and I have many times had the baseness to expel Thee from my soul! But Thou wilt not despise a contrite and humble heart. Thou didst become Man for my sake; Thou didst die for me; and Thou hast given me Thyself to be my Food; and what more remains for Thee to do to gain my love? Oh! that I might die with grief as often as I remember having despised Thy graces! I am sorry with my whole heart for having offended Thee. I love Thee, O infinite Goodness! I love Thee, O infinite Love!

II.

How honored would that vassal esteem himself, says St. Francis of Sales, to whom his prince at table should offer a portion from his own dish, or of his own very flesh! Jesus, in the Holy Communion, gives us for our Food, not a portion from His own table, nor a part of His sacred Flesh, but His whole Body: Take and eat this is my body. And at the same time that He gives us His Body He gives us also with it, His Soul and Divinity; so that, as St. Chrysostom says, our Lord, in giving us Himself in the Holy Eucharist, gives us all that He has, and nothing more remains that He can give to us. O wonderful prodigy of love! God, Who is the Lord of all, makes Himself entirely ours!

I desire nothing but to love Thee, O my Jesus, and I fear nothing but to live without loving Thee. My beloved Jesus, do not refuse to come again into my soul. Come, for I would rather die a thousand deaths than drive Thee from me anymore; and I will do all in my power to please Thee. Come, and inflame my whole soul with Thy holy love. Grant that I may forget all things else to think only of Thee, and to aspire after Thee alone, my sovereign and only Good. O Mary, my Mother, pray for me, and by thy holy prayers make me grateful for the great love of Jesus towards me.

Spiritual Reading

THE VISIT TO MARY

And now as to the Visit to the Most Blessed Virgin, the opinion of St. Bernard is well known and commonly accepted: namely, that God dispenses no graces otherwise than through the hands of Mary: "God wills that; we should receive nothing that does not pass through Mary's hands." Hence Father Suarez declares that it is now the sentiment of the universal Church, that the intercession of Mary is not only useful, but even necessary to obtain grace. And we may remark that the Church gives us strong grounds for this belief, by applying the words of the Sacred Scripture to Mary and making her say: In me is all hope of life and of virtue. Come over to me all ye that desire me– (Ecclesiasticus xxiv. 25, 26). Let all come to me; for I am the hope of all that you can desire.

Hence she adds: Blessed is the man that heareth me, and that watcheth daily at my gates, and waiteth at the posts of my doors- (Proverbs viii. 34). Blessed is he who is diligent in coming every day to the door of my powerful intercession, for by finding me he will find life and eternal salvation: He that shall find me shall find life and shall have salvation from the Lord- (Proverbs viii. 35). Hence it is not without reason that the Church wills that we should call Mary our common hope, by saluting her with the words: "Hail, our hope!"

"Let us then," says St. Bernard (who went so far as to style Mary "the whole ground of his hope"), "seek for graces, and seek them through Mary." For, as St. Antoninus says, if we ask for graces without her intercession, we shall be only trying to fly without wings and obtain nothing. "He who asks without her as his guide, attempts to fly without wings." In Father Auriemma's little book, Affetti Scambievoli, we read of innumerable favors granted by the Mother of God to those who practiced this most profitable devotion of often visiting her in her churches or before her image.

Do you also, then, be careful to ever join to your daily visit to the Most Blessed Sacrament a visit to the most holy Virgin Mary in some church, or at least before a devout image of her in your own house. St. Andrew of Crete says, that Mary always bestows great gifts on those who offer her even the least act of homage.

Spiritual Communion during Visit

As it is suggested in the following visits to the Most Blessed Sacrament to make a Spiritual Communion after each, it will be well to explain what a Spiritual Communion is, and the great advantages of making it. A Spiritual Communion, according to St. Thomas, consists in an ardent desire to receive Jesus in the Most Holy Sacrament, and in lovingly embracing Him as if we had actually received Him.

How pleasing Spiritual Communions are to God, and how many graces He bestows through their means, was manifested by Our Lord Himself to Sister Paula Maresca, the foundress of the Convent of St. Catherine of Sienna, in Naples. It is related in her Life that our Lord showed her two precious vessels, one of gold, another of silver. He then told her that in the gold vessel He preserved her Sacramental Communions, and in the silver her Spiritual Communions. He also told Blessed Jane of the Cross that each time she communicated spiritually she received a grace like in kind to that which she received when she really communicated. But for us it will suffice to know that the holy Council of Trent greatly praises Spiritual Communion and encourages the faithful to practice it.

Hence devout souls are accustomed often to making use of this holy exercise of Spiritual Communion. Blessed Agatha of the Cross did so two hundred times a day. Father Peter Faber, the first companion of St. Ignatius, used to say that it was of the highest utility to make Spiritual Communions, to receive the Sacramental Communion well.

All, therefore, who desire to advance in the love of Jesus Christ are exhorted to make a Spiritual Communion at least once in every visit that they pay to the Most Blessed

Sacrament, and once at every Mass that they hear. Better still on these occasions to repeat the Spiritual Communions three times; that is to say, at the beginning, in the middle, and at the end. This devotion is far more profitable than some suppose, and at the same time nothing can be easier to practice. The above-named Jane of the Cross used to say that a Spiritual Communion can be made without anyone remarking it, without fasting, without the permission of our director, and that we can make it any time we please; an act of love does all.

Evening Meditation

THE PRACTICE OF THE LOVE OF JESUS CHRIST
XIII.-THE MEANS OF AVOIDING LUKEWARMNESS AND ATTAINING PERFECTION

I.

Alas, my God, how many souls, for want of applying themselves to lead a life of greater recollection and more detachment from earthly things, care not to receive Holy Communion! And this is the true cause of their not wishing to communicate frequently. They are well aware that to wish always to appear, to dress with vanity, to be fond of nice eating and drinking, of bodily comforts, of conversations and amusements, does not harmonize with frequent Communion; they know that more prayer is required, more mortification, as well internal as external, more seclusion; and on this account they are ashamed to approach the altar more frequently. Without doubt, such souls are right to refrain from frequent Communion if they find themselves in that unhappy state of lukewarmness; but whoever is called to a more perfect life should lay aside this lukewarmness, if he would not greatly risk his eternal salvation.

II.

It will be found likewise to contribute very much to keep fervor alive in the soul often to make a Spiritual Communion, so much recommended by the Council of Trent, which exhorts all the faithful to practice it. The Spiritual Communion, as St. Thomas says, consists in an ardent desire to receive Jesus Christ in the Holy Sacrament; and therefore, the Saints were careful to make it several times in the day. The method of making it is this: "My Jesus, I believe that Thou art really present in the Most Holy Sacrament. I love Thee and I desire Thee; come into my soul. I embrace Thee; and I beseech Thee never to allow me to be separated from Thee again." Or more briefly, thus: "My Jesus, come to me; I desire Thee; I embrace Thee; let us remain ever united together." This Spiritual Communion may be practiced several times a day: when we make our prayer, when we make our Visit to the Blessed Sacrament, and especially when we assist at Mass at the moment of the priest's Communion. The Dominican Sister, Blessed Angela of the Cross, said: "If my confessor had not taught me the method of communicating spiritually several times a day, I should not have trusted myself to live."

Thursday – Whit Week

Morning Mediation

THE GREAT LOVE JESUS HAS SHOWN US IN GIVING US THE BLESSED SACRAMENT

St. Paul says that God, by becoming Man, showed the world how far His goodness and kindness towards us went. But by giving Himself to us in the Blessed Sacrament He makes us know the depths of the tenderness of His love towards us. Does it not, says St. Augustine, seem madness Jesus Christ to say to us: Eat my flesh; drink my blood?

I.

Jesus, knowing that his hour was come, that he should pass out of this world to the Father; having loved his own who were in the world, he loved them unto the end - (John xiii. I). Jesus, knowing that the time of His death was near, desired to leave us the strongest pledge of His love for us, and this was the gift of the Blessed Sacrament: He loved them to the end-which St. Chrysostom explains: "He loved them with extreme love." He, therefore, loved men with the greatest love He could possibly entertain towards them by giving them His whole Self. But when was it that Jesus instituted this great Sacrament? The night before His death. The Lord Jesus, says the Apostle, the same night in which he was betrayed, took bread, and giving thanks, broke and said: Take ye and eat-this is my body-(1 Corinthians xi. 23, 24). While men were preparing to put Him to death, He was pleased to give them this last proof of His love. O infinite love of Jesus, Thou art worthy of being loved with an infinite love! Thou, my Lord, hast loved man so much, and how is it that man loves Thee so little? What more couldst Thou do to make him love Thee? O my Jesus, Thou art most amiable and loving; make Thyself known, make Thyself loved.

When shall I ever love Thee as Thou hast loved me? Discover to me more and more the greatness of Thy bounty, that I may always burn more and more with Thy love and always seek to please Thee.

II.

The marks of affection which are shown to us by our friends at the time of their death remain more deeply impressed on our hearts; and for this reason, did Jesus choose to bestow Himself upon us in the Blessed Sacrament, a little before His death. Well, therefore, might St. Thomas call this Sacrament "the Sacrament of love and pledge of tenderest affection"; and St. Bernard, "the love of loves"- "amor amorum"-because Jesus Christ in this Sacrament unites and comprises all the other marks of His love towards us. Hence St. Mary Magdalen de Pazzi, speaking of the day on which Jesus instituted this Sacrament, calls it "the day of love."

O Beloved of my soul, oh! that I had always loved Thee! Alas! there was a time when I not only did not love Thee, but even despised Thy graces and Thy love. I am consoled with the sorrow I feel for having done so, and I hope for pardon through Thy promise to forgive those who repent. To Thee, my Savior, do I direct all my affections; help me, through the merits of Thy Passion, to love Thee with my whole strength. O that I could die for Thee, as Thou hast died for me! Holy Mary, Mother of God, obtain for me the grace of loving henceforward God alone.

Spiritual Reading

CORAM SANCTISSIMO

Introductory Prayer to be said before each Visit

My Lord Jesus Christ, Who for the love which Thou bearest to men, remainest night and day in this Sacrament full of compassion and of love, awaiting, calling, and welcoming all who come to visit Thee; I believe that Thou art present in the Sacrament of the Altar. I adore Thee from the abyss of my nothingness, and I thank Thee for all the graces Thou hast bestowed upon me, and for having given me Thyself in this Sacrament, for having given me Thy most holy Mother Mary for my advocate, and for having called me to visit Thee in this church. I now salute Thy most loving Heart: and this for three ends:

I. In thanksgiving for this great gift;

II. To make amends to Thee for all the outrages which Thou receives in this Sacrament from all Thine enemies;

III. I intend by this visit to adore Thee in all the places on earth in which Thou art present in this Sacrament, and in which Thou art the least revered and the most abandoned.

My Jesus, I love Thee with my whole heart. I grieve for having hitherto so many times offended Thine infinite Goodness. I purpose by Thy grace never more to offend Thee for the time to come; and now, miserable, and unworthy though I am, I consecrate myself to Thee without reserve; I give Thee and renounce my entire will, my affections, my desires, and all that I possess. From henceforward do Thou dispose of me and of all that I have as Thou pleases. All that I ask of Thee and desire is Thy holy love, final perseverance, and the perfect accomplishment of Thy will. I recommend to Thee the souls in Purgatory; but especially those who had the greatest devotion to the Most Blessed Sacrament and to the Most Blessed Virgin Mary. I also recommend to Thee all poor sinners. In fine, my dear Savior, I unite all my affections with the affections of Thy most loving Heart; and I offer them, thus united, to Thy Eternal Father, and beseech Him in Thy Name to vouchsafe, for Thy love, to accept and grant them.

(Indulgence of 300 days each time; Plenary once a month).

FIRST VISIT

Behold the source of every good, Jesus in the Most Holy Sacrament, Who says, If any man thirst let him come to me- (John vii. 37). Oh, what torrents of grace have the Saints drawn from the fountain of the Most Blessed Sacrament! For there Jesus dispenses all the merits of His Passion, as it was foretold by the Prophet: You shall draw waters with joy out of the Savior's fountains- (Isaiah. xii. 3). The Countess of Feria, that illustrious disciple of the Blessed John of Avila, afterwards a Poor Clare, and surnamed the spouse of the Most Blessed Sacrament, from her long and frequent visits to It, on being asked how she employed the many hours thus passed in the presence of the Holy of Holies, replied: "I could remain there for all eternity. And is not the very Essence of God, which will be the food of the blessed, there present? Good God! Am I asked what I do in His presence? Why am I not rather asked, what is not done there? We love, we praise, we give thanks, we ask. What does a poor man do in the presence of one who is rich? What does a sick man do in the presence of his physician? What does a man do who is parched with thirst in the presence of a limpid fountain? What is the occupation of one who is starving, and is placed before a well-supplied table?"

O my most amiable, most sweet, most beloved Jesus, my Life, my Hope, my Treasure, the only Love of my soul, oh, what has it cost Thee to remain thus with us in this

Sacrament! Thou hadst to die, that Thou mightest dwell amongst us on our altars; and then how many insults hast Thou not had to endure in this Sacrament, to aid us by Thy presence! Thy love, and the desire which Thou hast to be loved by us, have conquered all.

Come, then, O Lord, come and take possession of my heart; close its doors for ever, that henceforward no creature may enter to divide the love which is due to Thee, and which it is my ardent desire to bestow all on Thee. Do Thou alone, my dear Redeemer, rule me; do Thou alone possess my whole being; and if ever I do not obey Thee perfectly, chastise me with rigor that henceforward I may be more watchful to please Thee as Thou willest. Grant that I may no longer seek any other pleasure than that of giving Thee pleasure: that all my delight may be to visit Thee often on Thy altars; to entertain myself with Thee, and to receive Thee in Holy Communion. Let all who will seek other treasures: the only treasure that I love, the only one that I desire, is the Treasure of Thy love; for this only will I plead at the foot of the altar. Do Thou make me forget myself, that thus I may remember only Thy goodness. Blessed Seraphim, I envy you, not for your glory, but for the love which you bear to your God and mine; oh, do you teach me what I must do to love Him, and to please Him.

Ejaculatory Prayer. My Jesus, I will love Thee only; Thee only do I desire to please.

A Spiritual Communion here follows for which an Indulgence of 60 days is granted by the Church:

AN ACT OF SPIRITUAL COMMUNION

My Jesus, I believe that Thou art truly present in the Most Holy Sacrament. I love Thee above all things, and I desire to possess Thee within my soul. Since I am unable now to receive Thee sacramentally, come at least spiritually into my heart. I embrace Thee as already there and unite myself wholly to Thee; never permit me to be separated from Thee.

VISIT TO MARY

In our Mother Mary we have another fountain which is indeed fruitful for us. She is so rich in good things and in graces, says St. Bernard, that there is no one in the world who does not participate in them: "Of her fulness we have all received." The Most Blessed Virgin Mary was filled by God with grace, and as such was saluted by the Angel, Hail, full of grace! -(Luke i. 28), not for herself alone, but also for us. St. Peter Chrysologus adds, that she received that great abyss of grace, that she might afterwards impart it to all who were devout to her: "The Blessed Virgin received this grace, that she might give in return salvation to all."

Ejaculatory Prayer. Cause of our joy, pray for us.

Concluding Prayer

Most holy Immaculate Virgin and my Mother Mary, to thee, who art the Mother of my Lord, and Queen of the world, the advocate, the hope, the refuge of sinners, I have recourse today-I, who am the most miserable of all. I render thee my most humble homage, O great Queen, and I thank thee for all the graces thou hast conferred on me until now, particularly for having delivered me from hell, which I have so often deserved. I love thee, O most amiable Lady; and for the love which I bear thee, I promise to serve thee always, and to do all in my power to make others love thee also. I place in thee all my hopes; I confide my salvation to thy care. Accept me for thy servant, and receive me under thy mantle, O Mother of Mercy. And since thou art so powerful with God, deliver me from all temptations, or rather obtain for me the strength to triumph over them until death. Of thee I ask a perfect love of Jesus Christ. From thee I hope to die a good death. O my Mother, for the love which thou bearest to God, I beseech thee to help me at all times, but especially at the last moment of my life. Leave me not, I beseech thee, until thou seest me safe in Heaven, blessing thee, and singing thy mercies for all eternity. Amen. So I hope. So may it be.

Indulgence of 300 days for above Prayer.

Evening Meditation

THE PRACTICE OF THE LOVE OF JESUS CHRIST

XIV.-THE MEANS OF AVOIDING LUKEWARMNESS AND ATTAINING PERFECTION

I.

The fifth and most necessary means for the spiritual life, and for obtaining the love of Jesus Christ is prayer of petition. In the first place, I say that by this means God convinces us of the great love He bears us. What greater proof of affection can a person give to a friend than to say to him, "My friend, ask anything you like of me, and I will give it to you"? Now that is precisely what our Lord says to us: Ask, and it shall be given you; seek, and you shall find- (Luke xi. 9). Wherefore prayer is called all-powerful with God to obtain every blessing: "Prayer, though it is only one, can effect all things," as Theodoret says; whoever prays obtains from God whatever he chooses. The words of David are beautiful: Blessed be God who hath not turned away my prayer nor his mercy from me- (Psalm lxv. 20). Commenting on this passage, St. Augustine says, "As long as thou seest thyself not failing in prayer, be assured that the Divine mercy will not fail thee either." And St. John

Chrysostom: "We always obtain, even while we are still praying." When we pray to God, He grants us the grace we ask for, even before we have ended our petition. If, then, we are poor, let us blame only ourselves, since we are poor merely because we wish to be poor, and so we are undeserving of pity. What sympathy can there be for a beggar, who, having a very rich master, and one most desirous to provide him with everything, if he will only ask for it, nevertheless chooses still to continue in, his poverty rather than ask for what he wants? Behold, says the Apostle, our God, rich unto all that call upon him- (Romans x. 12).

II.

Humble prayer, then, obtains all from God; but we must be persuaded at the same time, that if it be useful it is no less necessary for our salvation. It is certain that we absolutely require the Divine assistance, in order to overcome temptations; and sometimes, in certain more violent assaults, the sufficient grace which God gives to all, might possibly enable us to resist them; but on account of our inclination to evil, it will not ordinarily be sufficient in these violent temptations, and we shall then stand in need of a special grace. Whoever prays obtains this grace; but whoever prays not obtains it not and is lost. And this is more especially the case with regard to the grace of final perseverance, of dying in the grace of God, which is the grace absolutely necessary for our salvation, and without which we should be lost forever. St. Augustine says of this grace, that God only bestows it on those who pray. And this is the reason why so few are saved, because few indeed are mindful to beg of God this grace of perseverance.

FRIDAY – EMBER DAY

Morning Meditation

THE UNION OF THE SOUL WITH JESUS IN HOLY COMMUNION

Jesus was not satisfied with uniting Himself to our human nature, He would, by means of the Most Blessed Sacrament, find a way of uniting Himself also to each one of us, so as to become wholly his who would receive Him. He that eateth my flesh abideth in me and I in him -(John vi. 57).

I.

St. Dionysius says that the principal effect of love is to tend to union. For this end did Jesus institute the Holy Communion, -to unite Himself entirely with our souls. He had given Himself to us as our Teacher, our Model, and Victim; it remained to Him to give Himself to us as our Food-to become one with us, as food becomes the same with the person who eats it; and this He did by instituting the Holy Sacrament of love. "The last degree of His love," says St. Bernardine of Sienna, "was His giving uniting Himself to each one of us individually, so as to become wholly his who should receive Him." Hence St. Francis of Sales says: "In no one action can our Blessed Savior be considered more tender or more loving than in this, in which He, as it were, annihilates Himself, and reduces Food; because He gave Himself to be completely united with us, as food is united with him who takes it." Thus, Jesus Christ was not satisfied with uniting Himself to our human nature, He was desirous by this Sacrament to devise a means of Himself to Food to penetrate to the hearts of all the faithful."

O my Jesus, this is what I desire and seek from Thee in the Holy Communion-to hear from Thee: "We will consider ourselves as united forever, never more to be separated." I know that Thou wilt not separate Thyself from me if I do not separate myself from Thee. But this is my fear lest I should ever again separate myself from Thee as I have done before. Permit it not, my beloved Redeemer. "Suffer me not to be separated from Thee."

II.

Because Jesus Christ ardently loved us, He was desirous of being united with us in the Holy Eucharist, that we might become the same thing with Him; thus speaks St. Chrysostom: "He mingled Himself with us, that He might become one with us; for this belongs to ardent affection." Thou wast desirous, O God of love, that our hearts and Thine should form but one heart, says St. Laurence Justinian. And Jesus Himself meant this when He said: He that eateth my flesh and drinketh my blood abideth in me and I in him– (John vi. 57). He, therefore, who communicates, abides in Jesus, and Jesus abides in him; and this union is not a mere union of affections, but a true and real union. As two pieces of wax, says St. Cyril of Alexandria, are melted together, and united together, so he who communicates and Jesus Christ, Whom he receives, become one and the same thing. Let us therefore imagine, when we communicate, that Jesus Christ says to us, as He did to His beloved servant, Margaret of Ypres: "Behold, daughter, the beautiful union that exists between us: love Me, and we will consider ourselves as united forever, and will never separate."

Through the merits of Thy death, O my Jesus, let me die now rather than ever be separated again from Thee. I repeat and give me grace ever to repeat: Suffer me not to be separated from Thee! Suffer me not to be separated from Thee! O God of my soul, I love Thee, I love Thee, and desire always to love Thee. I protest before Heaven and earth that I desire nothing but Thee.

O my Jesus hear me; I desire only Thee. O Mary, Mother of mercy, pray for me, and obtain for me never to separate myself from Jesus, and to love only Jesus.

Spiritual Reading
CORAM SANCTISSIMO
SECOND VISIT

The devout Father Nieremberg says, that bread being a food which is consumed by eating, and which keeps when preserved for use, Jesus was pleased to dwell on earth under its species, that He might thus not only be consumed by uniting Himself to the souls of His lovers, by means of the Holy Communion, but also that He might be preserved in the Tabernacle, and be present with us, and thus remind us of the love He bears us. St. Paul says: He emptied himself, taking the form of a servant- (Philippians ii. 7). But what must we say when we see Him taking the form of bread?" No tongue can suffice," says St. Peter of Alcantara, "to proclaim the greatness of the love Jesus bears to souls in the state of grace. In order, therefore, that His absence might not be to them an occasion of forgetting

Him, this most sweet Spouse, when He was pleased to quit this life, left as a memorial this Most Blessed Sacrament, in which He Himself remains. He did not wish that between these souls and Himself any other pledge but Himself should remain, whereby to keep alive their remembrance of Him."

Since, then, my Jesus, Thou art enclosed in this Tabernacle to receive the supplications of miserable creatures who come to seek an audience of Thee, listen this day to the petition addressed to Thee by the most ungrateful sinner on earth. I come repentant to Thy feet, for I know the evil which I have committed in giving Thee displeasure. My first prayer and desire, then, is that Thou wilt be pleased to pardon me all the sins I have committed against Thee. Ah, my God, would that I had never offended Thee! After this I must tell Thee my next desire. Now that I have found out Thy sovereign goodness, I have become enamored of Thee; I feel an ardent desire to love Thee and to please Thee; but I have not the strength to do this unless Thou helpest me. Manifest, O great Lord, Thy supreme power and Thine immense goodness to the whole court of Heaven; change me from a great rebel, such as I have hitherto been to Thee, into a great lover of Thee. Thou canst do it, and I know that such is Thy will; supply all that is wanting in me, that thus I may be enabled to love Thee much-at least that I may love Thee as much as I have offended Thee. I love Thee, my Jesus; I love Thee above all things; I love Thee more than my life-my God, my Love, my All!

Ejaculatory Prayer. My God and my All!

AN ACT OF SPIRITUAL COMMUNION

My Jesus, I believe that Thou art truly present in the Most Holy Sacrament. I love Thee above all things, and I desire to possess Thee within my soul. Since I am unable now to receive Thee sacramentally, come at least spiritually into my heart. I embrace Thee as already there and unite myself wholly to Thee; never permit me to be separated from Thee.

VISIT TO MARY

Let us go with confidence to the throne of grace; that we may obtain mercy, and find grace in seasonable aid -(Heb. iv. 16). St. Antoninus says that Mary is this throne, from which God dispenses all graces.

O most amiable Queen, since thou hast so great a desire to help sinners, behold a great sinner who has recourse to thee; help me much, and help me without delay.

Ejaculatory Prayer. Sole refuge of sinners, have mercy on me.

Concluding Prayer

Most holy Immaculate Virgin and my Mother Mary, to thee, who art the Mother of my Lord, and Queen of the world, the advocate, the hope, the refuge of sinners, I have recourse today-I, who am the most miserable of all. I render thee my most humble homage, O great Queen, and I thank thee for all the graces thou hast conferred on me until now, particularly for having delivered me from hell, which I have so often deserved. I love thee, O most amiable Lady; and for the love which I bear thee, I promise to serve thee always, and to do all in my power to make others love thee also. I place in thee all my hopes; I confide my salvation to thy care. Accept me for thy servant, and receive me under thy mantle, O Mother of Mercy. And since thou art so powerful with God, deliver me from all temptations, or rather obtain for me the strength to triumph over them until death. Of thee I ask a perfect love of Jesus Christ. From thee I hope to die a good death.

O my Mother, for the love which thou bearest to God, I beseech thee to help me at all times, but especially at the last moment of my life. Leave me not, I beseech thee, until thou seest me safe in Heaven, blessing thee, and singing thy mercies for all eternity. Amen. So I hope. So may it be.

Evening Meditation

THE PRACTICE OF THE LOVE OF JESUS CHRIST
XV.-THE MEANS OF AVOIDING LUKEWARMNESS AND ATTAINING PERFECTION

I.

The holy Fathers say, that prayer is necessary for us, not merely as a necessity of precept (so that divines say, that he who neglects for a month to recommend to God the affair of his salvation is not exempt from mortal sin), but also as a necessity of means, which is as much as to say, that whoever does not pray cannot possibly be saved. And the reason of it is, in short, because we cannot obtain eternal salvation without the help of Divine grace, and this grace Almighty God only accords to those who pray. And because temptations, and the dangers of falling into God's displeasure, continually beset us, so ought our prayers to be continual. Hence St. Thomas declares that continual prayer is necessary for a man to save himself: "Unceasing prayer is necessary to man that he may enter Heaven." And Jesus Christ Himself had already said the same thing: We ought always to pray, and not to faint– (Luke xviii. 1). And afterwards the Apostle: Pray without ceasing-(Thessalonians v. 17) During the interval in which we shall cease to pray, the devil will conquer us. And though the grace of perseverance can in no wise be merited by us, as the Council of Trent teaches us, nevertheless St. Augustine says, "that in a certain sense we can merit it by prayer." The Lord wishes to dispense His grace to us, but He will be entreated first; nay more, as St. Gregory remarks, He wills to be importuned, and in a manner constrained by our prayers: "God wishes to be prayed to, He wishes to be compelled, He wishes to be, as it were, vanquished by our importunity."

II.

Saint Mary Magdalen de Pazzi said: "When we ask graces of God, He not only hears us, but in a certain sense thanks us." Yes, because God, as the infinite Goodness, in wishing to pour out Himself upon others, has, so to speak, an infinite longing to distribute His gifts; but He wishes to be besought; hence it follows, that when He sees Himself entreated by a soul, He receives so much pleasure that in a certain sense He thanks the soul for it. Well, then, if we wish to preserve ourselves in the grace of God till death, we must act the mendicant, and keep our lips ever open to beg for God's help, always repeating, "My Jesus, mercy! Never let me be separated from Thee! O Lord, come to my aid! My God, assist me!" This was the unceasing prayer of the ancient Fathers of the desert: "Incline unto my aid, O God! O Lord, make haste to help me! O Lord, help me, and help me soon; for if Thou delayest Thy assistance, I shall fall and perish!" And this above all must be practiced in the moment of temptation; he who acts otherwise is lost.

SATURDAY – EMBER DAY

Morning Meditation

THE DESIRE OF JESUS CHRIST TO BE UNITED WITH US IN HOLY COMMUNION.

Oh, with what desire does Jesus Christ pant to come into our hearts in Holy Communion! With desire have I desired to eat this pasch with you before I suffer (Luke xxii. I5). "This is the voice of most ardent charity"- (St. Laurence Justinian).

I.

Jesus knowing that his hour was come- (John xiii. I}. This hour which Jesus called his hour, was the hour of that night on which He was to begin His Passion. But why did He call so dreadful an hour his hour? Because this was the hour for which He had sighed during His whole life; because He had resolved to bequeath to us in this hour the Holy Communion, by which He desired to become united with us whom He loved, and for whom He was soon to shed His Brood and lay down His life. Hear how He spoke that night to His disciples: With desire have I desired to eat this pasch with you: by which words He would signify His great wish and anxiety to unite Himself with us in the Holy Sacrament of love. With desire have I desired. "This," says St. Laurence Justinian, "is the voice of most ardent charity." Now, the same love which then burned in the Heart of Jesus burns there still: and He gives the same invitation now to all which He gave then to His disciples to receive Him: Take ye and eat, this is my body- (Matthew xxvi. 26}.

My adorable Jesus, Thou canst give no greater proof of love, to teach us how much Thou lovest us. Thou hast given Thy life for us: Thou hast bequeathed Thyself to us in the Holy Sacrament, that we may nourish ourselves. with Thy sacred Flesh, and Thou art most desirous that we should receive Thee. How can we be sensible of all these efforts of Thy love and not burn with love of Thee? Begone, all ye earthly affections from my heart; it is you who hinder me from burning with love for Jesus, as He burns with love for me. And what other pledges of Thy love can I expect, O my Redeemer, than those which Thou hast already given me? Thou hast sacrificed Thy whole life for the love of me; Thou hast embraced for my sake the most bitter and ignominious death; Thou hast reduced Thyself for me almost to annihilation by becoming my Food in the Holy Eucharist, to give me Thy whole Self. Ah, Lord, grant that I may never more live ungrateful for such great goodness.

II.

To allure us to receive Him with affection and love, He promises Heaven to us: If any man eat of this bread, he shall live forever- (John vi. 52). And if we refuse to receive Him He threatens us with death: Except you eat the flesh of the Son of man, and drink his blood you shall not have life in you- (John vi. 54}. These invitations, promises, and threats, all arise from the desire of Jesus Christ to be united with us in the Holy Communion through His love for us. Our Lord said to St. Mechtilde that the bee does not take the honey with more eagerness of delight, than He enters the souls that desire Him. Jesus because He loves us, desires that we should love Him; and because He desires us, He would have us desire Him: "God thirsts to be thirsted after," says St. Gregory. Happy the soul that approaches the Holy Communion with a great desire of being united to Jesus Christ.

I thank Thee, O God, for having given me time to bewail my past offences against Thee, and to love Thee during the remainder of my days. I am sorry, O my sovereign Good, for having hitherto so much despised Thy love. I love Thee, O infinite Goodness, I love Thee, O infinite Treasure. I love Thee, O infinite Love, Who art worthy to be loved with an infinite love. Help me, O Jesus, to cast out from my heart all affections which tend not to Thee, that from this day forward, I may neither desire, nor seek, nor love any other but Thee. My beloved Lord, grant that I may ever find Thee, grant that I may ever love Thee. Take Thou possession of my whole will, in order that I may never desire anything but what is pleasing to Thee. My God, my God, whom shall I love if I love not Thee, Who art all goodness! O Mary, my Mother, take me under thy protection, and obtain for me the purest love for Jesus.

Spiritual Reading

CORAM SANCTISSIMO

THIRD VISIT

And my delights are to be with the children of men -(Proverbs viii. 31). Behold, our Jesus, Who, not satisfied with dying on earth for our love, is pleased even after His death to dwell with us in the Holy Sacrament, declaring that He finds His delights among men. "O men," exclaims St. Teresa, "how can you offend a God Who declares that it is with you that He finds His delights!" Jesus finds His delights with us, and shall we not find ours with Jesus? And we especially who have had the honor to dwell in His palace? How greatly do those vassals esteem themselves honored to whom the king assigns an abode in his own residence! Behold the palace of the King! It is this house in which we dwell with Jesus Christ. Let us, then, learn to thank Him for it, and to avail ourselves of it to converse with Jesus Christ.

Behold me, then, O my Lord and God, before this altar, on which Thou dost reside night and day for my sake. Thou art the Source of every good; Thou art the Healer of every ill; Thou art the Treasure of every poor creature. Behold now at Thy feet a sinner, who is of all others the poorest and most infirm, and who asks Thy mercy; have pity upon me! Now that I see Thee in this Sacrament, come down from Heaven upon earth only to do me good, I will not be disheartened at the sight of my misery. I praise Thee, I thank Thee, I love Thee; and if Thou willest that I should ask Thee for an alms, I will ask for this, O listen to me: I desire never more to offend Thee and I desire that. Thou shouldst give me light and grace to love Thee with all my strength. Lord I love Thee with all my soul; I love Thee with all my affections. Do Thou grant that I may thus speak with truth; and that I may speak in the same way during life and for all eternity. Most Holy Virgin Mary, my holy Patron Saints, ye Angels, and all ye Blessed Saints of Paradise, help me to love my most amiable God.

Ejaculatory Prayer. O Good Shepherd, true Bread, Jesus, have mercy on us! Do Thou show us good things in the land of the living!

AN ACT OF SPIRITUAL COMMUNION

My Jesus, I believe that Thou art truly present in the Most Holy Sacrament. I love Thee above all things, and I desire to possess Thee within my soul. Since I am unable now to receive Thee sacramentally, come at least spiritually into my heart. I embrace Thee as already there and unite myself wholly to Thee; never permit me to be separated from Thee.

VISIT TO MARY

Her bands are a healthful binding-(Ecclesiasticus vi. 31). The devout Pelbart says that devotion to Mary is a chain of predestination. Let us beseech our sovereign Lady to bind us always more closely by the chains of love to confidence in her protection.

Ejaculatory Prayer. O clement, O pious, O sweet Virgin Mary!

Concluding Prayer

Most holy Immaculate Virgin and my Mother Mary, to thee, who art the Mother of my Lord, and Queen of the world, the advocate, the hope, the refuge of sinners, I have recourse today I, who am the most miserable of all. I render thee my most humble homage, O great Queen, and I thank thee for all the graces thou hast conferred on me until now, particularly for having delivered me from hell, which I have so often deserved. I love thee, O most amiable Lady; and for the love which I bear thee, I promise to serve thee always, and to do all in my power to make others love thee also. I place in thee all my hopes; I confide my salvation to thy care. Accept me for thy servant, and receive me under thy mantle, O Mother of Mercy. And since thou art so powerful with God, deliver me from all temptations, or rather obtain for me the strength to triumph over them until death. Of thee I ask a perfect love of Jesus Christ. From thee I hope to die a good death.

O my Mother, for the love which thou bearest to God, I beseech thee to help me at all times, but especially at the last moment of my life. Leave me not, I beseech thee, until thou seest me safe in Heaven, blessing thee, and singing thy mercies for all eternity. Amen. So I hope. So may it be.

Evening Meditation
THE PRACTICE OF THE LOVE OF JESUS CHRIST
XVI.-THE MEANS OF AVOIDING LUKEWARMNESS AND ATTAINING PERFECTION
I.

And let us have great faith in prayer. God has promised to hear him that prays: Ask, and you shall receive. How can we doubt, says St. Augustine, since God has bound Himself by express promise, and cannot fail to grant us the favors we ask of Him? "By promising He has made Himself our debtor." ... In recommending ourselves to God, we must have a sure confidence that God hears us, and then we shall obtain whatever we want. Behold what Jesus Christ says: All things, whatsoever you ask when ye pray, believe that you shall receive, and they shall come unto you – (Mark xi. 24).

"But," someone may say, "I am a sinner, and do not deserve to be heard." But Jesus Christ says: Everyone that asketh, receiveth- (Luke xi. 10). Everyone, be he just or be he a sinner. St. Thomas teaches us that the efficacy of prayer to obtain grace does not depend on our merits, but on the mercy of God, Who has promised to hear everyone who prays to Him.

II.

And our Redeemer, in order to remove from us all fear when we pray, said: Amen, amen, I say to you, if you shall ask the Father anything in my name he will give it you-(John xvi. 23). As though He would say: Sinners, you have no merits of your own to obtain graces, wherefore act in this manner; when you would obtain graces, ask them of My Father in My Name; that is, through My merits and through My love; and then ask as many as you choose, and they shall be granted to you. But let us mark well these words, "In my Name," which signify (as St. Thomas explains it), "in the Name of the Savior"; or, in other words, that the graces which we ask must be graces which regard our eternal salvation; and consequently we must remark that the promise does not regard temporal favors; these our Lord grants when they are profitable for our eternal welfare; if they would prove otherwise, He refuses them. So that we should always ask for temporal favors on condition that they will benefit our soul. But should they be spiritual graces, then they require no condition; but with confidence, and a sure confidence, we should say: "Eternal Father, in the Name of Jesus Christ, deliver me from this temptation: grant me perseverance, grant me Thy love, grant me Heaven." We can likewise ask these graces of Jesus Christ in His own Name; that is, by His merits, since we have His promise also to this effect: If you shall ask me anything in my name, that I will do– (John xiv. 14). And whilst we pray to God, let us not forget to recommend ourselves at the same time to Mary, the dispenser of graces. St. Bernard says that it is Almighty God Who bestows the graces; but He bestows them through the hands of Mary: "Let us seek grace, and let us seek it through Mary; because what she seeks she finds, and cannot be refused." If Mary prays for us, we are safe; for every petition of Mary is heard, and she can never meet with a repulse.

First Sunday After Pentecost

HOLY COMMUNION THE MEANS OF PERSEVERANCE IN DIVINE GRACE

St. Denis says that when Jesus Christ comes to a soul in Holy Communion, He brings with Him boundless treasures of grace; and therefore, after Communion, we can truly say: Now all good things come to me together with it.

I.

When Jesus comes to the soul in the Holy Communion, He brings with Him every good, every grace, and especially the grace of holy perseverance. The principal effect of the Holy Sacrament of the Altar is to nourish the soul that receives it with the Bread of Life, by imparting great strength to advance towards perfection, and to resist those enemies who seek to affect its eternal ruin. Hence Jesus Christ calls Himself in this Sacrament heavenly Bread: I am the living bread which came down from heaven; if any man eat of this bread he shall live forever- (John vi. 51, 52). As earthly bread maintains the life of the body, so this heavenly Bread maintains the life of the soul by enabling it to persevere in the state of God's grace. Hence the Council of Trent teaches that the Holy Communion is "a medicine which frees us from daily faults and preserves us from mortal sins."

Oh, how miserable I am O Lord, bewailing my weakness while at the same time I stay away from Thee! How can I resist my internal enemies without Thee, Who art my Strength? Had I approached Thee more frequently in the Holy Communion, I should not have been so frequently overcome by my enemies. For the future it shall not be so: In thee, O Lord, have I hoped; let me not be confounded forever- (Psalm xxx. 2). No, I will no longer rely on my own strength, but will place my whole confidence in Thee, my Jesus, Who will give me strength to fall no more into sin.

II.

Innocent III says that Jesus delivers us by His Passion from sins committed, and by the Holy Eucharist from those which we might otherwise commit. Hence St. Bonaventure says that sinners should not stay away from Holy Communion because they have been sinners; but for this very reason should receive it more frequently, for "the more infirm a person is, the more does he stand in need of a physician."

I am weak, O my Jesus, but Thou by the Holy Communion wilt make me strong against all temptations – I can do all things in him who strengtheneth me (Philippians iv. 13). Pardon me, O Jesus, all the injuries I have committed against Thee for which I am sorry with my whole soul; I am resolved rather to die than wilfully offend Thee anymore; and I trust in Thy Passion that Thou wilt help me to persevere in Thy grace to the end of my life. In thee, O Lord, have I hoped, let me never be confounded. And with St. Bonaventure I will say the same to Thee, O Mary, my Mother: "In thee, that is, in thy holy intercession, O Blessed Lady, have I hoped; let me never be confounded for ever!"

Spiritual Reading

CORAM SANCTISSIMO

FOURTH VISIT

Her conversation hath no bitterness, nor her company any tediousness- (Wisdom viii. 16). Friends on earth find such pleasure in being together, that they lose entire days in each other's company; with Jesus in the Most Holy Sacrament, those who love Him not, get weary. After her death, St. Teresa, who was already in Heaven, said to a nun: "Those who are in Heaven and those who are on earth should be one and the same in purity and in love; we enjoying, and you suffering; and that which we do in Heaven with the Divine Essence, you should do on earth With the Most Blessed Sacrament." Behold, then, our Paradise on earth-the Most Blessed Sacrament!

O Immaculate Lamb, sacrificed for us upon the Cross, remember that I am one of those souls Thou hast redeemed by so many sufferings and by Thy Death. Grant that Thou mayest be mine and that I may never lose Thee, since Thou has given Thyself to me, and givest Thyself every day, sacrificing Thyself for my love on the altar; and grant that I may be all Thine. I give myself to Thee without reserve, that Thou mayest dispose of me as Thou pleasest. I give Thee my will; chain it with the sweet bonds of Thy love, that it may forever be the slave of Thy most holy Will. I wish no longer to live for the satisfaction of my desires, but only to please Thy goodness. Destroy in me all that does not please Thee; grant me the grace never to have any other thought than to please Thee, any other desire than that which Thou desirest. I love Thee, O my dear Savior, with my whole heart; I love Thee because Thou desirest that I should love Thee; I love Thee because Thou art indeed worthy of my love. I grieve that I love Thee not as much as Thou deservest. I desire, Lord, to die for Thy love; accept my desire, and give me Thy love. Amen.

Ejaculatory Prayer. O good pleasure of my God, I sacrifice myself all to Thee!

AN ACT OF SPIRITUAL COMMUNION

My Jesus, I believe that Thou art truly present in the Most Holy Sacrament. I love Thee above all things, and I desire to possess Thee within my soul. Since I am unable now to receive Thee sacramentally, come at least spiritually into my heart. I embrace Thee as already there and unite myself wholly to Thee; never permit me to be separated from Thee.

VISIT TO MARY

Mary says: I am the mother of fair love- (Ecclesiasticus. xxiv. 24). That is to say, she is the Mother of that love which beautifies souls. St. Mary Magdalen de Pazzi saw the Most Blessed Virgin Mary going about dispensing a sweet liquid, which was divine love. This gift. is dispensed only by Mary; from Mary let us seek it.

Ejaculatory Prayer. My Mother, my hope, make me belong wholly to Jesus.

Concluding Prayer

Most holy Immaculate Virgin and my Mother Mary, to thee, who art the Mother of my Lord, and Queen of the world, the advocate, the hope, the refuge of sinners, I have recourse today I, who am the most miserable of all. I render thee my most humble homage, O great Queen, and I thank thee for all the graces thou hast conferred on me until now, particularly for having delivered me from hell, which I have so often deserved. I love thee, O most amiable Lady; and for the love which I bear thee, I promise to serve thee always, and to do all in my power to make others love thee also. I place in thee all my hopes; I confide my salvation to thy care. Accept me for thy servant, and receive me under thy mantle, O Mother of Mercy. And since thou art so powerful with God, deliver me from all temptations, or rather obtain for me the strength to triumph over them until death. Of thee I ask a perfect love of Jesus Christ. From thee I hope to die a good death.

O my Mother, for the love which thou bearest to God, I beseech thee to help me at all times, but especially at the last moment of my life. Leave me not, I beseech thee, until thou seest me safe in Heaven, blessing thee, and singing thy mercies for all eternity. Amen. So I hope. So may it be.

Evening Mediation

THE PRACTICE OF THE LOVE OF JESUS CHRIST

"Charity is not puffed up."

XVII.-HE THAT LOVES JESUS CHRIST IS NOT VAIN OF HIS OWN WORTH, BUT HUMBLES HIMSELF, AND IS GLAD TO BE HUMBLED

I.

A proud person is like a balloon filled with air, which seems, indeed, great; but whose greatness in reality, is nothing more than a little air; which, as soon as the balloon is opened is quickly dispersed. He who loves God is humble and is not elated at seeing any worth in himself; because he knows that whatever he possesses is the gift of God, and that of himself he has only nothingness and sin; so that his knowledge of the Divine favors bestowed on him, humbles him more, for he is conscious of being so unworthy, and yet so favored by God.

St. Teresa says, in speaking of the especial favors she received from God: "God does with me as they do with a house, which, when about to fall, they prop up with supports." When a soul receives a loving visit from God, and feels within herself an unwonted fervor of Divine love, accompanied with tears, or with a great tenderness of heart, let her beware of supposing that God so favors her in reward for some good action; but let her then humble herself the more, concluding that God caresses her in order that she may not forsake Him; otherwise, were she to make such favors the subject of vain complacency, imagining herself more privileged because she receives greater gifts from God than others, such a fault would induce God to deprive her of His favors. Two things are chiefly requisite for the stability of a house, the foundation, and the roof: the foundation in us must be humility, in acknowledging ourselves good for nothing, and capable of nothing; and the roof is the Divine assistance, in which alone we ought to put all our trust.

II.

Whenever we behold ourselves unusually favored by God, we must humble ourselves the more. When St. Teresa received any special favor, she used to strive to place before her eyes all the faults she had ever committed; and thus the Lord received her into closer union with Himself: the more a soul confesses herself undeserving of any favors, the more God enriches her with His graces. Thais, who was first a sinner and then a Saint, humbled herself so profoundly before God, that she dared not mention His Name; so that she did not dare to say, "My God," but "My Creator, have mercy on me! Plasmator meus, miserere mei." And St. Jerome writes that, in recompense for such humility, she saw a glorious throne prepared fer her in Heaven. In the Life of St. Margaret of Cortona we read how, when our Lord visited her one day with greater tokens of tenderness and love, she exclaimed: "But, O Lord, have You, then, forgotten what I have been? Is it possible that You can repay all my outrages against You with such exquisite sweetness?" And God replied that when a soul loves Him and cordially repents of having offended Him, He forgets all her past infidelities; as, indeed, He formerly spoke by the mouth of Ezechiel: But if the wicked do penance... I will not remember all his iniquities- (Ezechiel xviii. 21-22). And in proof of this, He showed her a high throne which He had prepared for her in Heaven in the midst of the Seraphim. Oh, that we could only comprehend the value of humility! A single act of humility is worth more than all the riches of the universe.

MONDAY – FIRST WEEK AFTER PENTECOST

Morning Meditation

PREPARATION AND THANKSGIVING

The Saints derived great advantage from Holy Communion because they were most careful in preparing themselves for it. Their fire immediately burns dry wood, but not green wood, because it is not fit for burning.

I.

Cardinal Bona asks how it happens that so many souls after so many Communions make such little advancement in the ways of God? And he answers. "The fault is not in the Food, but in the dispositions of those who receive it." There is nothing wanting in the Holy Communion, but preparation is wanting on the part of those who receive it. The fire immediately burns dry wood, but not green wood, because it is not fit for burning. The Saints derived great advantage from Holy Communion because they were most careful in preparing themselves for it. There are two things which we should endeavor to acquire in preparing ourselves for Holy Communion. The first is detachment from creatures, by banishing from our hearts everything that is not of God and for God. Although the soul is in the state of grace, yet if the heart be taken up by any earthly affection, the less room will there be for Divine love. One day St. Gertrude asked our Lord what preparation He required of her for the Holy Communion; and Jesus answered: "I require no other of thee but that thou come to receive Me devoid of thyself." The second thing we should endeavor to acquire, in order to be prepared to reap great fruit from the Holy Communion, is a desire to receive Jesus Christ with a view to love Him much more for the future. Gerson says that at this banquet only those are filled who feel great hunger. Hence St. Francis of Sales writes that the principal intention of the soul in communicating should be to advance in the love of God. "He," says the Saint, "should be received for love, Who for love alone gives Himself to us." And on this account our Lord once said to St. Mechtilde: "When thou art about to communicate, desire all the love that any soul ever had for Me, and I will receive thy love as though it were what thou wouldst have it to be."

O God of love, dost Thou so much desire to dispense Thy graces to us, and are we careless in seeking for them? How great will be our distress when we come to die, to think of this neglect, so pernicious to us! Forget, O Lord, what is past; for the future, with Thy holy assistance, I will prepare myself in a better manner, by being careful to detach my affections from everything that can hinder me from receiving all those graces Thou desirest to impart to me.

II.

Thanksgiving after Communion is also necessary. No prayers are so acceptable to God as those which we offer to Him after Communion. During this time, we should employ ourselves in acts of love and petitions. The holy affections in which we then exercise ourselves have greater merit before God than those we offer to Him at other times, because they come before Him inflamed by the presence of Jesus Christ, Who has united Himself to our souls. And as to petitions, St. Teresa says that Jesus Christ after Communion remains in the soul as on a throne of grace, and says to her: What wilt thou that I should do for thee? -(Mark x. 51). I am come down from Heaven to bestow My graces upon thee: ask of Me what thou wilt, and as much as thou wilt, and thou shalt be heard. Oh! what treasures of grace are lost by those who offer but few prayers to God after Communion.

After Holy Communion, dear Jesus, I will endeavor, as far as I am able, to obtain Thy help to advance in Thy love. Do Thou give me grace to accomplish this. O my Jesus, how careless have I hitherto been in loving Thee! The time of life, which in Thy mercy Thou dost allot me, is the time to prepare myself for death, and to make amends for the offences I have committed against Thee. I desire to spend it all in bewailing my sins and in loving Thee. I love Thee, O Jesus, my Love; I love Thee, my only Good; have pity on me and do not abandon me. And, O Blessed Virgin Mary, never cease to succor me by thy holy intercession.

Spiritual Reading

CORAM SANCTISSIMO
FIFTH VISIT

The sparrow hath found herself a house, and the turtle a nest for herself, where she may lay her young ones: thy altars, O Lord of hosts, my King and my God! -(Psalm lxxxiii. 4). The sparrow, says David, finds a dwelling in houses; turtledoves in nests; but Thou, my King and my God, hast made Thyself a nest and found a dwelling on earth on our altars, that we might find Thee, and that Thou mightest dwell amongst us.

Lord, we cannot but say, that Thou art too much enamored of men; Thou no longer knowest what to do to gain their love. But do Thou, my most amiable Jesus, give us the grace that we also may be passionately enamored of Thee. It would indeed be unreasonable to be cold in our love towards a God Who loves us with such affection. Draw us to Thee by the sweet attractions of Thy love; make us understand the endearing claims which Thou hast on our love.

O infinite Majesty, O infinite Goodness, Thou loves men so much, Thou hast done so much that Thou might be loved by men, how is it that amongst men there are so few who love Thee? I will no longer be as I have hitherto been, of the unhappy number of those ungrateful creatures. I am resolved to love Thee as much as I can, and to love no other than Thee. Thou deserve it, and Thou commands me with so much earnestness to do so, I am resolved to satisfy Thee.

Grant, O God of my soul, that I may fully satisfy Thee. I entreat Thee to grant me this favor by the merits of Thy Passion, and I confidently hope for it. Bestow the goods of the earth on those who desire them; I desire and seek the great treasure of Thy love alone. I love Thee, my Jesus; I love Thee, infinite Goodness. Thou art all my riches, my whole satisfaction, my entire love.

Ejaculatory Prayer. My Jesus, Thou hast given Thy whole self to me; I give my whole self to Thee!

AN ACT OF SPIRITUAL COMMUNION

My Jesus, I believe that Thou art truly present in the Most Holy Sacrament. I love Thee above all things, and I desire to possess Thee within my soul. Since I am unable now to receive Thee sacramentally, come at least spiritually into my heart. I embrace Thee as already there and unite myself wholly to Thee; never permit me to be separated from Thee.

VISIT TO MARY

My Lady, St. Bernard calls thee "the ravisher of hearts." He says that thou goest about stealing hearts by the charms of thy beauty and goodness. Also steal my heart and will, I beseech thee: I give them wholly to thee: offer them to God with thine own.

Ejaculatory Prayer. Mother most amiable, pray for me!

Concluding Prayer

Most holy Immaculate Virgin and my Mother Mary, to thee, who art the Mother of my Lord, and Queen of the world, the advocate, the hope, the refuge of sinners, I have recourse today I, who am the most miserable of all. I render thee my most humble homage, O great Queen, and I thank thee for all the graces thou hast conferred on me until now, particularly for having delivered me from hell, which I have so often deserved. I love thee, O most amiable Lady; and for the love which I bear thee, I promise to serve thee always, and to do all in my power to make others love thee also. I place in thee all my hopes; I confide my salvation to thy care. Accept me for thy servant, and receive me under thy mantle, O Mother of Mercy. And since thou art so powerful with God, deliver me from all temptations, or rather obtain for me the strength to triumph over them until death. Of thee I ask a perfect love of Jesus Christ. From thee I hope to die a good death.

O my Mother, for the love which thou bearest to God, I beseech thee to help me at all times, but especially at the last moment of my life. Leave me not, I beseech thee, until thou seest me safe in Heaven, blessing thee, and singing thy mercies for all eternity. Amen. So I hope. So may it be.

Evening Meditation

THE PRACTICE OF THE LOVE OF JESUS CHRIST
XVIII.-HE THAT LOVES JESUS CHRIST IS NOT VAIN OF HIS OWN WORTH, BUT HUMBLES HIMSELF, AND IS GLAD TO BE HUMBLED.

I.

It was the saying of St. Teresa, "Think not that thou hast advanced far in perfection till thou considerest thyself the worst of all, and desirest to be placed below all."

And on this maxim the Saint acted, and so have done all the Saints; St. Francis of Assisi, St. Mary Magdalen de Pazzi, and the rest, considered themselves the greatest sinners in the world, and were surprised that the earth sheltered them, and did not rather open under their feet to swallow them up alive; and they expressed themselves to this effect with the sincerest conviction. The Blessed John of Avila, who from his earliest infancy had led a holy life, was on his death-bed; and the priest who came to attend him said many sublime things to him, taking him for what indeed he was, a great servant of God and a learned man; but Father Avila thus spoke to him : "Father, I pray you to make the recommendation of my soul, as of a criminal condemned to death; for such I am." This is the opinion which Saints entertain of themselves in life and death.

II.

We, too, must act in this manner, if we would save our souls, and keep ourselves in the grace of God till death, reposing all our confidence in God alone. The proud man relies on his own strength and falls on that account; but the humble man, by placing all his trust in God alone, stands firm and falls not, however violent and multiplied the temptations may be; for his watchword is: I can do all things in him that strengtheneth me- (Philippians iv. 13). The devil at one time tempts us to presumption, at another time to diffidence: whenever he suggests to us that we are in no danger of falling, then we should tremble the more; for were God but for an instant to withdraw His grace from us, we are lost. When, again, he tempts us to diffidence, then let us turn to God, and thus address Him with great confidence: In thee, O Lord, have I hoped, I shall never be confounded- (Psalm xxx. 2). My God, in Thee I have put all my hopes; I hope never to meet with confusion, nor to be bereft of Thy grace. We ought to exercise ourselves continually, even to the very last moment of our life, in these acts of difference in ourselves and confidence in God, always beseeching God to grant us humility.

Tuesday – First Week After Pentecost

Morning Meditation

JESUS DELIGHTS TO COME TO US IN HOLY COMMUNION

Oh, how delighted Jesus is to be united to our souls! To excite souls to receive Him He exhorts them to do so by many invitations. Come, eat my bread, and drink the wine which I have mingled for you- (Proverbs ix. 5). Eat, O friends, and drink, -speaking of this Heavenly Bread and Wine. These invitations all proceed from the ardent desire Jesus has to come to us in this Sacrament.

I.

Eat, O friends, and drink, and be inebriated, my dearly beloved- (Canticles v. 1). The "friends," that is, beginners, who scarcely enjoy the Divine friendship, when they receive the Holy Communion, feed indeed on the Flesh of Jesus Christ, but they eat with labor; while those who are on the way to perfection eat with less difficulty. But, by the "dearly beloved" are meant the perfect, who, inebriated with holy love, live almost out of the world, forgetting all things, even themselves, and think only how they may love and please their God.

My beloved Jesus, I am not yet perfect, but Thou canst make me perfect. I am not dear to Thee, and it is my own fault, because I have been ungrateful and unfaithful; but Thou canst make me dear to Thee by inebriating me this morning with Thy love. Thy kingdom come-(Matt. vi. 10). Come, my beloved Lord. and take possession of my whole soul. Establish Thy kingdom in me; so that Thou alone mayest reign in me, that Thy love alone may command me, and that Thy love alone may I obey. Inebriate me, inebriate me entirely; make me forget all creatures, myself, my interests, and all, that I may love nothing but Thee, my God, my Treasure, all my Good, my All! May I sigh for Thee alone, seek Thee alone, think of Thee alone, and please Thee alone. Do this by the merits of Thy Passion. This only do I ask of Thee; for this I hope.

II.

I found him whom my soul loveth. I held him, and I will not let him go- (Canticles iii. 4). So ought every soul to say who is united with Jesus in the Blessed Sacrament: Creatures, depart from me! Go out altogether from my heart! I loved you once because I was blind; now I love you not, nor can I ever love you again. I have found another Good, infinitely more delightful than you. I have found in myself my Jesus, Who has enamored me of His beauty. To this Love I have given myself entirely. He has already accepted me, so that I am no longer my own. Creatures, farewell! I am not, nor shall I ever again be yours; but I am and shall always be Christ's. He, too, is mine, and will always be mine: I held him and I will not let him go. Now l have pressed Him to my heart, receiving Him in Holy Communion; for the future I will hold Him with my love, and will not let Him leave me again.

Permit me, sweet Savior, to embrace Thee so closely that I may never more be separated from Thee. Behold, I press Thee to myself, my Jesus! I love Thee! I love Thee! Oh, that I could love Thee worthily! I wish that my only happiness and repose should be to love Thee and please Thee. Do Thou command all creatures to leave me, and not to disturb me. Say to them: I adjure you, do not arouse or waken my love– (Canticles viii. 4). Ah, if I do not wish it, creatures cannot enter in to disturb and divide me from Thee. Strengthen, then, my will; unite my miserable heart to Thy Divine Heart that it may always will what Thou willest. Do this, Lord, by Thy merits.

Spiritual Reading

CORAM SANCTISSIMO

SIXTH VISIT

Where your treasure is, there will your heart be also (Luke xii. 34). Jesus Christ says that where a person esteems his treasure to be, there also he keeps his affections. Therefore, the Saints, who neither esteem nor love any other treasure than Jesus Christ, center their hearts and their love in the Most Blessed Sacrament. My most amiable Jesus, hidden under the sacramental veils, Who for the love which Thou bearest me, remainest night and day imprisoned in this Tabernacle, draw, I beseech Thee, my whole heart to Thee, that I may think of none but Thee, that I may love and seek and hope for Thee alone. Do this by the merits of Thy Passion, through which I seek and hope for it. Ah, my sacramental Lord and divine Lover, how amiable and tender are the inventions of Thy love to gain the love of souls! O Eternal Word, Thou, in becoming Man, was not satisfied with dying for us; Thou hast also given us this Sacrament as a Companion, as Food, and as a pledge of Heaven. Thou reduced Thyself so as to appear amongst us, at one time as an Infant in a stable, at another as a poor Man in a workshop, then as a Criminal on a gibbet, and now as Bread on an altar. Tell me, couldst Thou invent other means to win our love?

O infinite Goodness, when shall I really begin to correspond with such refinements of love? Lord, I will live only to love Thee alone. And of what use is life to me, if I do not spend it wholly in loving and pleasing Thee, my beloved Redeemer, Who hast poured out Thy whole life for me? And what have I to love if it is not Thee, Who art all beauty, all condescension, all goodness, all loving, all worthy of love? May I live only to love Thee! May the mere remembrance of Thy love dissolve my soul with love! May the very names of Crib and Cross and Sacrament inflame it with the desire to do great things for Thee, O my Jesus, Who hast indeed done and suffered such great things for me!

Ejaculatory Prayer. Grant, O my Lord, that before I die I may do something for Thee!

AN ACT OF SPIRITUAL COMMUNION

My Jesus, I believe that Thou art truly present in the Most Holy Sacrament. I love Thee above all things, and I desire to possess Thee within my soul. Since I am unable now to receive Thee sacramentally, come at least spiritually into my heart. I embrace Thee as already there and unite myself wholly to Thee; never permit me to be separated from Thee.

VISIT TO MARY

As a fair olive-tree in the plain- (Ecclesiasticus xxiv. 19). I am, says Mary, the beautiful olive tree from which the oil of mercy always flows. And I stand in the plain that all may see me. "Remember," let us say in the words of the prayer of St. Bernard, "O most compassionate Mary, that it has never been heard of in any age, that anyone having recourse to thy protection was abandoned by thee." Most merciful Queen, such, a thing was never heard of, that anyone having recourse to thy aid was abandoned; I will not be the first unfortunate creature who, having recourse to thee, was abandoned.

Ejaculatory Prayer. O Mary, grant me the grace always to have recourse to thee!

Concluding Prayer

Most holy Immaculate Virgin and my Mother Mary, to thee, who art the Mother of my Lord, and Queen of the world, the advocate, the hope, the refuge of sinners, I have recourse today I, who am the most miserable of all. I render thee my most humble homage, O great Queen, and I thank thee for all the graces thou hast conferred on me until now, particularly for having delivered me from hell, which I have so often deserved. I love thee, O most amiable Lady; and for the love which I bear thee, I promise to serve thee always, and to do all in my power to make others love thee also. I place in thee all my hopes; I confide my salvation to thy care. Accept me for thy servant, and receive me under thy mantle, O Mother of Mercy. And since thou art so powerful with God, deliver me from all temptations, or rather obtain for me the strength to triumph over them until death. Of thee I ask a perfect love of Jesus Christ. From thee I hope to die a good death.

O my Mother, for the love which thou bearest to God, I beseech thee to help me at all times, but especially at the last moment of my life. Leave me not, I beseech thee, until thou seest me safe in Heaven, blessing thee, and singing thy mercies for all eternity. Amen. So I hope. So may it be.

Evening Meditation

THE PRACTICE OF THE LOVE OF JESUS CHRIST

XIX.-HE THAT LOVES JESUS CHRIST IS NOT VAIN, BUT HUMBLES HIMSELF, AND IS GLAD TO BE HUMBLED

I.

But it is not enough, in order to be humble, to have a lowly opinion of ourselves, and to consider ourselves the miserable beings that we really are. The man who is truly humble, says Thomas a Kempis, despises himself, and wishes also to be despised by others. This is what Jesus Christ so earnestly recommends us to practice, after His example: Learn of me, because I am meek and humble of heart- (Matthew xi. 29). Whoever styles himself the greatest sinner in the world, and then is angry when others despise him, plainly shows humility of tongue, but not of heart. St. Thomas Aquinas says that a person who resents being slighted may be certain that he is far distant from perfection, even though he should work miracles. The Divine Mother sent St. Ignatius Loyola from Heaven to instruct St. Mary Magdalen de Pazzi in humility; and behold the lesson which the Saint gave her: "Humility is a gladness at whatever leads us to despise ourselves." Mark well, a gladness; if the feelings are stirred to resentment at the contempt we receive, let us be glad, at least, in spirit.

II.

And how is it possible for a soul not to love contempt if she loves Jesus Christ and beholds how her God was buffeted and spit upon, and how He suffered in His Passion! *Then did they spit in his face, and buffeted him; and others struck his face with the palms of their hands-* (Matthew xxvi. 67). For this purpose, our Redeemer wishes us to keep His image exposed on our altars, not indeed representing Him in glory, but nailed to the Cross, that we might have His ignominies constantly before our eyes; a sight which made the Saints rejoice at being vilified in this world. And such was the prayer which St. John of the Cross addressed to Jesus Christ, when He appeared to him with the Cross upon His shoulders: "O Lord, let me suffer, and be despised for Thee!" My Lord, on beholding Thee so reviled for my love, I only ask of Thee to let me suffer and be despised for Thy love.

WEDNESDAY – FIRST WEEK AFTER PENTECOST

Morning Meditation

HOLY COMMUNION THE GREAT GIFT OF JESUS CHRIST TO MAN

Take ye and eat, this is my body- (Matthew xxvi. 26). Let us consider how great a Gift Jesus Christ has bestowed upon us in giving us His entire Self to be our Food in Holy Communion. St. Augustine says that Jesus, though He is the Almighty God, could give us no more. "Omnipotent though He is, He could give no more."

I.

Consider how great a Gift Jesus Christ has bestowed upon us in giving us His entire Self to be our Food in the Holy Communion. St. Augustine says that Jesus, though He is the Almighty God, yet could give us no more: "Omnipotent though He is, He could give no more." And St. Bernardine of Sienna adds that no greater treasure can be in the heart of man than the Body of Christ: "What greater treasure can a soul desire or achieve than the most holy Body of Jesus Christ?" The Prophet Isaias exclaims: Make his works known among the people- (Isaiah xii. 4). Publish, O men, the loving invitations of our good God! If our Redeemer had not given us this Gift, who could ever have asked It of Him? Who could ever have dared to say to Him: Lord, if Thou wilt make us know Thy love, conceal Thyself under the species of bread, and allow us to feed on Thee? This very idea would have been reckoned folly. "Would it not have been thought madness," says St. Augustine, "to say: Eat My Flesh, drink My Blood?" When Christ announced to His disciples this gift of the Most Holy Sacrament, which He intended to leave them, they could not bring themselves to believe, and many left Him saying, how can this man give us his flesh to eat … This saying is hard, and who can hear it? - (John. vi. 53-61). But what men could never have imagined, the great love of Jesus Christ has thought of and accomplished.

St. Bernardine says that our Lord has left us this Sacrament as a Remembrance of the love He showed us in His Passion: This Sacrament is a memorial of His love." And this agrees with what St. Luke records of the words of Jesus Christ Himself: Do this for a commemoration of me- (Luke xxii. 19). St. Bernardine adds that the love of Our Lord was not satisfied in sacrificing His life for us: before He died, He was constrained by this very love to give us the very greatest of all His gifts, by giving us Himself to be our Food: "In that excess of fervor, when He was ready to die for us, He was forced by exceeding love to do a greater work than He had ever yet accomplished, to give us Himself to be our Food."

O my Jesus, what has led Thee to give Thy whole Self to be our Food? After this Gift, what hast Thou left to give us to force us to love Thee? O Lord, give us light, and make us know how excessive is the love which has made Thee reduce Thyself into Food to unite Thyself with us poor sinners. That Thou thus givest Thyself wholly to us is a reason why we should give ourselves wholly to Thee. My Redeemer, how could I have offended Thee Who hast loved me, and Who didst leave nothing undone to win my love? Thou didst become Man for me, Thou didst die for me, and didst make Thyself my Food; tell me what remains for Thee to do. I love Thee, O Infinite Goodness, Infinite Love!

II.

The Abbot Guerric says that Jesus has shown in this Sacrament the last effort of His love: "He poured forth upon His friends all the power of His love." The Council of Trent expresses it still better in saying that in the Blessed Eucharist Jesus, "as it were poured forth the riches of His love towards man."

What a proof of love it would be considered, says St. Francis of Sales, if a prince, being at table, should send a poor man a portion of his own dish; and how much more if he should send him his whole dinner! But what would be thought if he should send him a portion of his own flesh? Jesus, in the Holy Communion, gives us not only part of His table, not only part of His Body, but His whole Body: Take ye and eat, this is my body.

And with His Body, He gives us also His Soul and His Divinity. "In short," says St. John Chrysostom, "He has given Himself wholly, and for Himself He has reserved nothing." And the angelical Doctor says: "God has given us in the Holy Eucharist all that He is, and all that He has." Behold this great God, Whom the whole world cannot contain, exclaims St. Bonaventure in admiration, makes Himself our Prisoner in the Holy Sacrament: "He Whom the whole world cannot contain is our Captive!" And if our Lord gives us His whole Self in the Blessed Eucharist, how can we fear that He will ever deny us any grace we ask of Him? How hath he not also, with him, given us all things (Romans viii. 32).

Lord, come often into my soul, inflame me wholly with Thy holy love, and make me forget all else, to think of and love none but Thee. Most holy Mary, pray for me, and by thy intercession make me worthy frequently to receive Thy Son in His ever-blessed Sacrament.

Spiritual Reading

CORAM SANCTISSIMO

SEVENTH VISIT

Behold I am with you all days even to the consummation of the world–(Matt. xxviii. 20). Thus our loving Shepherd, Who has given His life for us who are His sheep, would not separate Himself from us by death. Behold me, He says, beloved sheep, I am always with you; for you I have remained on earth in this Sacrament here you find me whenever you please, to help and console you by My presence. I will never leave you until the end of the world as long as you are on earth. The Bridegroom, says St. Peter of Alcantara, wished to leave His bride company, that she might not remain alone during so long an absence; and therefore He left this Sacrament in which He Himself, the best companion He could leave her, remains.

My sweetest Lord, my most amiable Savior, I am now visiting Thee upon this altar; but Thou returnest me the visit with far other love when Thou dost enter my soul in the Holy Communion. Thou art then, not only present to me, but Thou becomes my Food; Thou unites and gives Thy whole self to me, so that I can then say with truth: My Jesus, Thou art now all mine. Since, then, Thou gives Thyself all to me, it is reasonable that I should give myself all to Thee. I am a worm, and Thou art God. O God of love! O love of my soul! When shall I find myself all Thine, in deeds, and not in words only? Thou canst do this; by the merits of Thy Blood increase my confidence, that I may at once obtain this grace of Thee, that I may find myself all Thine, and in nothing my own. Thou graciously hears, O Lord, the prayers of all: hear now the prayers of a soul that indeed desires really to love Thee. I desire to love Thee with all my strength; I desire to obey Thee in all that Thou willest, without self-interest, without consolations, without reward. I wish to serve Thee through love, only to please Thee, only to content Thy Heart, which is so passionately enamored of me. My reward will be to love Thee. O beloved Son of the Eternal Father, take possession of my liberty, of my will, of all that I possess, and of my entire self, and give me Thyself. I love Thee, I seek after Thee, I sigh after Thee; I desire Thee, I desire Thee, I desire Thee!

Ejaculatory Prayer. My Jesus, make me all Thine own.

AN ACT OF SPIRITUAL COMMUNION

My Jesus, I believe that Thou art truly present in the Most Holy Sacrament. I love Thee above all things, and I desire to possess Thee within my soul. Since I am unable now to receive Thee sacramentally, come at least spiritually into my heart. I embrace Thee as already there and unite myself wholly to Thee; never permit me to be separated from Thee.

VISIT TO MARY

Our own most amiable Lady, the whole Church proclaims and salutes thee as, "Our hope"! Thou; then, who art the hope of all, be also my hope. St. Bernard called thee "the whole ground of his hope," and said: "Let him who despairs hope in thee." Thus also will I address thee: My own Mary, thou savest even those who are in despair; in thee I place all my hope.

Ejaculatory Prayer. Mary, Mother of God, pray to Jesus for me!

Concluding Prayer

Most holy Immaculate Virgin and my Mother Mary, to thee, who art the Mother of my Lord, and Queen of the world, the advocate, the hope, the refuge of sinners, I have recourse today I, who am the most miserable of all. I render thee my most humble homage, O great Queen, and I thank thee for all the graces thou hast conferred on me until now, particularly for having delivered me from hell, which I have so often deserved. I love thee, O most amiable Lady; and for the love which I bear thee, I promise to serve thee always, and to do all in my power to make others love thee also. I place in thee all my hopes; I confide my salvation to thy care. Accept me for thy servant, and receive me under thy mantle, O Mother of Mercy. And since thou art so powerful with God, deliver me from all temptations, or rather obtain for me the strength to triumph over them until death. Of thee I ask a perfect love of Jesus Christ. From thee I hope to die a good death.

O my Mother, for the love which thou bearest to God, I beseech thee to help me at all times, but especially at the last moment of my life. Leave me not, I beseech thee, until thou seest me safe in Heaven, blessing thee, and singing thy mercies for all eternity. Amen. So I hope. So may it be.

Evening Meditation
THE PRACTICE OF THE LOVE OF JESUS CHRIST
XX.-HE WHO LOVES JESUS CHRIST IS NOT VAIN, BUT HUMBLES HIMSELF,
AND IS GLAD TO BE HUMBLED

I.

St. Francis of Sales said, "to support injury is the touchstone of humility and of true virtue." If a person aspiring to spirituality practices prayer, frequent Communion, fasts, and mortifies himself, and yet cannot put up with an affront, or a biting word, what is it a sign of? It is a sign that he is a hollow reed, without humility and without virtue. And what indeed can a soul do that loves Jesus Christ, if she is unable to endure a slight for the love of Jesus Christ, Who has endured so much for her. Thomas a Kempis, in his golden little book of the Imitation of Christ, writes as follows: "Since you have such an abhorrence of being humbled, it is a sign that you are not dead to the world, have no humility, and that you do not keep God before your eyes. He that has not God before his eyes is disturbed at every syllable of censure that he hears." Thou canst not endure cuffs and blows for God-endure at least a pass.

II.

Oh, what surprise and scandal does that person occasion, who communicates often, and then is ready to resent every little word of contempt! On the contrary, what edification does a soul give that answers contempt with words of mildness, spoken to conciliate the offender; or perhaps makes no reply at all, nor complains of it to others, but continues with placid looks and without showing the least sign of indignation! St. John Chrysostom says that a meek person is not only serviceable to himself but likewise to others, by the good example he sets them of meekness in bearing contempt: "The meek man is useful to himself and to others." Thomas a Kempis mentions, with regard to this subject, several things in which we should practice humility. He writes as follows: "What others say shall command an attentive hearing, and what you say shall be taken no notice of. Others shall make a request and obtain it; you shall ask for something and meet with a refusal. Others shall be magnified in the mouths of men, and on you no one shall bestow a word. Such and such an office shall be conferred on others, but you shall be passed by as unfit for anything. With such like trials the Lord is wont to prove His faithful servant, and to see how far he has learnt to overcome himself and to hold his peace. Nature, indeed, will at times not like it; but you will derive immense profit thereby, if you support all in silence."

FEAST OF CORPUS CHRISTI

THE LOVE OF JESUS IN GIVING US HIMSELF IN HOLY COMMUNION

The Most Holy Sacrament is the Gift of God's pure love. Jesus had already given Himself to us in many ways; as our Companion, our Master, our Father, our Light, our Example, our Victim. "It was the last effort of love when He gave Himself to be our Food." - (St. Bernardine).

I.

Let us consider the great love Jesus has shown us in giving us Himself in the Holy Eucharist. The Most Holy Sacrament is the Gift of pure love. According to the Divine decree it was necessary that our Redeemer should die to save us, and should by the sacrifice of His life, satisfy the Divine justice for our sins; but what necessity was there that Jesus Christ, after dying for us, should leave us Himself to be our Food? Yet thus His love willed. St. Laurence Justinian says His excessive charity alone led Him to institute the Most Holy Sacrament, only to make us understand the immense love He bears us; and this is precisely what St. John writes: Jesus, knowing that his hour was come that he should pass out of this world to the Father: having loved his own who were in the world, he loved them unto the end-(Jo. xiii. 1). Knowing that the time had come for Him to quit this world, Jesus would leave us the greatest possible proof of His love, which was this Gift of the Most Blessed Sacrament, as we are taught in these words, He loved them unto the end; that is, "with extreme love He loved them to the utmost," as Theophylact and St. Chrysostom explain it.

And we must observe what the Apostle mentions, that the time in which Jesus Christ was pleased to leave us this Gift was the very time of His Death: The Lord Jesus, the same night in which he was betrayed, took bread, and giving thanks, broke, and said: Take ye and eat; this is my body-(1 Corinthians xi. 23, 24). While men were preparing scourges and thorns, and a Cross to put Him to death, our loving Savior wished to leave us this last proof of His love. And why did He institute this Sacrament when He was going to die, and not before? St. Bernardine says that He did so because "the last marks of love given by dying friends remain more easily in our memory and are more dearly cherished." The Saint adds that Jesus Christ had already given Himself to us in many ways; He had made Himself our Companion, our Master, our Father. our Light, our Example, and our Victim: "It was the last effort of love when He gave Himself to be our Food; for He gave Himself to be united completely to us, as food and he who eats it are united; so that our Redeemer was not satisfied with merely uniting Himself to our human nature, but He was pleased to find in this Sacrament the means of uniting Himself to each of us in particular.

O infinite love of Jesus, worthy of infinite love! Ah! my Jesus, when shall I love Thee as Thou hast loved me? Thou couldst do nothing more to make me love Thee; and I have forsaken Thee, O infinite Good, for the sake of vile and miserable goods! Ah! enlighten me, my God, and discover to me always more and more the greatness of Thy goodness, that my whole soul may be enamored of Thee, and that I may labor to please Thee.

II.

St. Francis of Sales says: "There is no action in which we may more perfectly see the tenderness and love of our Savior than in this, in which He, as it were, annihilates Himself, and reduces Himself into Food, to penetrate our souls, and unite Himself to the hearts of His faithful." "So that," says St. John Chrysostom, "we unite ourselves, and are made one body and one flesh with that of the Lord, on Whom the Angels dare not fix their eyes." The same Saint adds, "What shepherd ever fed his sheep with his own blood? But why do I speak of shepherds? There are many mothers who give their children to others to be nursed; but He acts not thus, He feeds us with His own Blood." But why did He make Himself our Food? Because, says the Saint, He loved us ardently, and so desired to unite Himself to us and to become One and the same thing with us: "He mingled Himself with us that we might be one thing with Him: for this is the property of those who ardently love." Thus, then, did Jesus Christ will to perform the greatest of all miracles-He hath made a remembrance of his wonderful works, he hath given food to them that fear him

(Psalm cx. 4, 5)-in order to satisfy the desire He had of remaining with us and of uniting our hearts to His own Most Sacred Heart. "Oh, how wonderful is Thy love, Lord Jesus!" exclaims St. Laurence Justinian; "Thy desire is to incorporate us so entirely with Thy own Body, that our heart and soul may be inseparably united to Thine own."

The great servant of God, Father de la Colombiere, used to say: If anything could shake my faith in the mystery of the Eucharist, I should not doubt the power, but the love which God shows us in His Sacrament. If you ask me how bread becomes the Body of Jesus-how Jesus is to be found in many places-I reply, God can do all things. But if you ask me how God can love man to such an excess as to become his Food, -I can only answer that I do not understand it, and that the love of Jesus cannot be comprehended.

But, O Lord, it seems that such an excessive affection as to reduce Thyself to Food is not becoming Thy majesty. St. Bernard answers that love makes the lover forget his own dignity; and St. Chrysostom answers similarly, that love does not seek what is suitable when it wishes to make itself known to the beloved: "Love neglects reason; and goes where it is led, not where it ought." The angelical St. Thomas was, then, right in calling this the Sacrament of Love, and the Pledge of Love; and St. Bernard, in calling it "the Love of loves." So was St. Mary Magdalen de Pazzi in calling Maundy Thursday, on which day this Sacrament was instituted, "the day of love."

I love Thee and I thank Thee, O my Jesus, my Love, my All; and I wish to unite myself frequently to Thee in this Sacrament, in order to detach myself from all things, and to love Thee alone, Who art my Life. Through the merits of Thy Passion, assist me, O my Redeemer! O Mother of Jesus, and my Mother, do thou, too, assist me; beg of Jesus to inflame my whole heart with His holy love.

Spiritual Reading

CORAM SANCTISSIMO

EIGHTH VISIT

To every soul that visits Jesus in the Most Holy Sacrament, He addresses the words He said to the Sacred Spouse: Arise, make haste, my love, my dove, my beautiful one, and come- (Canticles. ii. 10). Thou, O soul, that visits Me, arise from thy miseries; I am here to enrich thee with graces. Make haste, approach, come near Me; fear not My majesty, which has humbled itself in this Sacrament to take away thy fear, and to give thee confidence. My beloved, thou art no longer My enemy, but My friend, since thou loves Me and I love thee. My beautiful one, My grace has made thee fair. And come, draw near and cast thyself into My arms, and ask Me with the greatest confidence whatever thou wills.

St. Teresa says that this great King of Glory has disguised Himself in this Sacrament under the species of bread, and that He has concealed His majesty to encourage us to approach His divine heart with greater confidence and affection; let us unite ourselves to Him, and let us ask Him for graces.

O Eternal Word made Man, and present for my sake in this Sacrament, what joy should be mine now that I am in Thy presence, Who art my God, infinite Majesty and infinite Goodness, and Who hast so tender an affection for my soul! Ye souls who love God, wherever you may be, either in Heaven or on earth, love Him for me also. Mary, my Mother, help me to love Him. And Thou, most loving Lord, make Thyself the object of all my love. Make Thyself the Lord of my entire will; possess my entire self. I consecrate my whole mind to Thee, that it may always be occupied with the thought of Thy goodness; I also consecrate my body to Thee, that it may help me to please Thee; I consecrate my whole soul to Thee, that it may be all Thine. Would, O Beloved of my soul, that all men could know the tenderness of the love Thou bearest them, that all might live to honor Thee and to please Thee, as Thou desires and deserve. Grant that, at least, I may always live enamored of Thine infinite beauty. From this day forward my desire is to do all that I can to be pleasing to Thee. I now resolve to abandon everything, be it what it may, as soon as I perceive that it displeases Thee, however much it may cost me, even should it be necessary for this purpose to lose all, or even to lay down my life. Fortunate indeed shall I be, if I lose all to gain Thee, my God, my Treasure, my Love, my All!

Ejaculatory Prayer. Jesus, my love, take all that I have; take full possession of me.

AN ACT OF SPIRITUAL COMMUNION

My Jesus, I believe that Thou art truly present in the Most Holy Sacrament. I love Thee above all things, and I desire to possess Thee within my soul. Since I am unable now to receive Thee sacramentally, come at least spiritually into my heart. I embrace Thee as already there, and unite myself wholly to Thee; never permit me to be separated from Thee.

VISIT TO MARY

Whoever is a little one, let him come to me- (Proverbs IX. 4}. Mary invites all children who need a mother to have recourse to her, as to the most loving of all mothers. The devout Nieremberg says that the love of all mothers is but a shadow in comparison with the love which Mary bears to each one of us. My Mother, Mother of my soul, thou who loves me and desires my salvation more than any other after God-O Mother, show thyself a Mother!

Ejaculatory Prayer. My Mother, grant that I may always remember thee!

Concluding Prayer

Most holy Immaculate Virgin and my Mother Mary, to thee, who art the Mother of my Lord, and Queen of the world, the advocate, the hope, the refuge of sinners, I have recourse today I, who am the most miserable of all. I render thee my most humble homage, O great Queen, and I thank thee for all the graces thou hast conferred on me until now, particularly for having delivered me from hell, which I have so often deserved. I love thee, O most amiable Lady; and for the love which I bear thee, I promise to serve thee always, and to do all in my power to make others love thee also. I place in thee all my hopes; I confide my salvation to thy care. Accept me for thy servant, and receive me under thy mantle, O Mother of Mercy. And since thou art so powerful with God, deliver me from all temptations, or rather obtain for me the strength to triumph over them until death. Of thee I ask a perfect love of Jesus Christ. From thee I hope to die a good death.

O my Mother, for the love which thou bearest to God, I beseech thee to help me at all times, but especially at the last moment of my life. Leave me not, I beseech thee, until thou see me safe in Heaven, blessing thee, and singing thy mercies for all eternity. Amen. So I hope. So may it be.

Evening Meditation

THE PRACTICE OF THE LOVE OF JESUS CHRIST

XXI.–HE THAT LOVES JESUS CHRIST IS NOT VAIN, BUT HUMBLES HIMSELF, AND IS GLAD TO BE HUMBLED

I.

It was a saying of St. Jane Frances de Chantal that "a person who is truly humble takes occasion from receiving some humiliation to humble himself the more." Yes, for he who is truly humble never supposes himself humbled as much as he deserves. Those who behave in this manner are styled blessed by Jesus Christ. They are not called blessed who are esteemed by the world, who are honored and praised as noble, as learned, as powerful; but they who are spoken ill of by the world, who are persecuted and calumniated; for it is for such that a glorious reward is prepared in Heaven, if they only bear all with patience: Blessed are you when they shall revile you and persecute you and speak all that is evil against you untruly for my sake: be glad and rejoice for your reward is very great in heaven-(Matthew v. 11, 12).

O Incarnate Word, I entreat Thee, by the merits of Thy holy humility, which led Thee to embrace so many ignominies and injuries for our love, deliver me from all pride, and grant me a share of Thy humility. And what right have I, O Jesus, to complain of any affront whatever that may be offered me, after having so often deserved hell? O my Jesus, by the merit of all the scorn and affronts endured for me in Thy Passion, grant me the grace to live and die humbled on this earth, as Thou didst live and die humbled for my sake. For Thy love I would willingly be despised and forsaken by all the world; but without Thee I can do nothing. I love Thee, O my sovereign Good; I love Thee, O Beloved of my soul!

II.

The grand occasion for practicing humility is when we receive correction for some fault from superiors or from others. Some people resemble the hedgehog; they seem all calmness and meekness as long as they are not touched; but no sooner does a superior or a friend touch them, by an observation on something which they have done imperfectly, than they forthwith become all thorns and answer warmly, that so and so is not true, or that they were right in doing so, or that such a correction is quite uncalled for: in a word, to rebuke them is to become their enemy; they behave like persons who rave at the surgeon for paining them in the cure of their wounds. "Medicanti irascitur-they are angry with their physician," writes St. Bernard. "When the virtuous and humble man is corrected for a fault," says St. John Chrysostom, "he grieves for having committed it; the proud man on the other hand, on receiving correction, grieves also; but he grieves that his fault is detected; and on this account he is troubled, gives answers, and is angry at the person who corrects him." This is the golden rule given by St. Philip Neri, to be observed with regard to receiving correction: "Whoever would really become a saint must never excuse himself, although what is laid to his charge be not true." And there is only one case to be excepted from this rule, and that is when self-defense may appear necessary to prevent scandal. Oh, what merit with God has that soul which is wrongfully reprehended, and yet keeps silence, and refrains from defending herself! St. Teresa said: "There are occasions when a soul makes more progress and acquires a greater degree of perfection by refraining from excusing herself than by listening to ten sermons; because, by not excusing herself she begins to obtain freedom of spirit, and to be heedless of whether the world speaks well or ill of her."

I love Thee, O my Jesus, and I hope, through Thee, to fulfil my promise of suffering all for Thee-affronts, betrayals, persecutions, afflictions, dryness, and desolation. Enough it is for me if Thou dost not forsake me, O sole object of the love of my soul. Suffer me never more to estrange myself from Thee. Enkindle in me the desire to please Thee. Grant me fervor in loving Thee. Give me peace of mind in suffering for Thee. Give me resignation in all contradictions. Have mercy on me. I deserve nothing; but I fix all my hopes in Thee, Who hast purchased me with Thine own Blood. And I hope all from thee, too, O my Queen and my Mother Mary, who art the refuge of sinners!

Friday – First Week After Pentecost

THE AMIABLE HEART OF JESUS

The Heart of Jesus is all pure, all holy, all full of love towards God and towards us. Every perfection, every virtue reigns in this Heart. This is the Heart in which God Himself finds all His delight. O amiable Heart of Jesus, Thou dost well deserve the love of all hearts.

I.

He who shows himself amiable in everything must necessarily make himself loved. Oh, if we only applied ourselves to discover all the good qualities by which Jesus Christ renders Himself worthy of our love, we should all be under the happy necessity of loving Him. And what heart among all hearts can be found more worthy of love than the Heart of Jesus? A Heart all pure, all holy, all full of love towards God and towards us, because all Its desires are only for the Divine glory and our good. This is the Heart in which God finds all His delight. Every perfection, every virtue reigns in this Heart; a most ardent love for God, His Father, united to the greatest humility and respect that can possibly exist; a sovereign confusion for our sins, which He has taken upon Himself, united to the extreme confidence of a most affectionate Son; a sovereign abhorrence of our sins, united to a lively compassion for our miseries; an extreme sorrow, united to a perfect conformity to the Will of God; so that in Jesus is found everything that is most amiable.

O my amiable Redeemer, what object more worthy of love could the Eternal Father command me to love than Thee? Thou art the Beauty of Paradise, Thou art the Love of Thy Father, Thy Heart is the throne of all virtues. O amiable Heart of my Jesus, Thou dost well deserve the love of all hearts; poor and wretched is that heart which loves Thee not! Thus miserable, O my God, has my heart been during all the time in which it has not loved Thee. But I will not continue to be thus wretched; I love Thee, I will always continue to love Thee, O my Jesus. O my Lord, I have hitherto forgotten Thee, and now what can I expect? That my ingratitude will oblige Thee to forget me entirely and forsake me forever? No, my Savior, do not permit it. Thou art the object of the love of God; and shalt Thou not, then, be loved by a miserable sinner such as I am, who have been so favored and loved by Thee? O lovely flames that burn in the amiable Heart of my Jesus, enkindle in my poor heart that holy fire which Jesus came down from Heaven to kindle on earth. Consume and destroy all the impure affections that dwell in my heart and prevent it from being entirely His.

II.

Some are attracted to love others by their beauty, others by their innocence, others by living with them, others by devotion. But if there were a person in whom all these and other virtues were united, who could help loving him? If we heard that there was in a distant foreign country a prince who was handsome, humble, courteous, devout, full of charity, affable to all, who rendered good to those who did him evil; then, although we knew not who he was, and though he knew not us, and though we were not acquainted with him, nor was there any possibility of our ever being so, yet we should be enamored of him, and should be constrained to love him. How is it then, possible, that Jesus Christ, Who possesses in Himself all these virtues, and in the most perfect degree, and Who loves us so tenderly, how is it possible that He should be so little loved by men, and should not be the only object of our love? O my God, how is it that Jesus, Who alone is worthy of love, and Who has given us so many proofs of the love that He bears us, should be alone, as it were, the unlucky One with us, Who cannot arrive at making us love Him; as if He were not sufficiently worthy of our love! This is what caused floods of tears to St. Rose of Lima, St. Catherine of Genoa, St. Teresa, St. Mary Magdalen de Pazzi, who, on considering the ingratitude of men, exclaimed, weeping: "Love is not loved! Love is not loved!"

O my God, grant that I may only exist to love Thee, and Thee alone, my dearest Savior. If at one time I despised Thee, Thou art now the only object of my love. I love Thee, I love Thee, I love Thee, and I will never love any but Thee! My beloved Lord, do not disdain to accept the love of a heart which has once afflicted Thee by my sins. Let it be Thy glory to exhibit to the Angels a heart now burning with the love of Thee, which hitherto shunned and despised Thee. Most Holy Virgin Mary, my hope; do thou assist me, and beseech Jesus to make me, by His grace, all that He wishes me to be.

Spiritual Reading
CORAM SANCTISSIMO
NINTH VISIT

St. John says that he saw our Lord girt up with a golden girdle, which supported His breasts: I saw the Son of Man girt about the breasts with a golden girdle – (Apocalypse i. 13). Thus also is Jesus in the Sacrament of the Altar, with His breasts all filled with milk; that is to say, with the graces which, in His mercy, He desires to bestow upon us. And as a mother whose breasts are overcharged with milk goes about seeking children who may draw it off, and relieve her of its weight, so also does He call out to us, You shall be carried at the breasts – (Isaiah lxvi. 12).

The Venerable Father Alvarez saw Jesus in the Blessed Sacrament with His hands filled with graces, and seeking to whom He might dispense them. Of St. Catharine of Sienna it is related that when she approached the Most Holy Sacrament she did so precisely with the same loving avidity with which a child flies to its mother's breast.

O most beloved and only-begotten Son of the Eternal Father, I know that Thou art the object most worthy of being loved. I desire to love Thee as much as Thou deserve to be loved, or at least as much as a soul can ever desire to love Thee. I fully understand that I, who am a traitor and so great a rebel to Thy love, deserve not to love Thee, neither do I deserve to approach so near to Thee as I now am in this church. But I feel that Thou, for all this, seekest my love. I hear Thee say: My son, give me thy heart-(Prov. xxiii. 26}. Thou shalt love the Lord thy God with thy whole heart – (Matthew xxii. 37). I understand that it is for this end Thou hast spared my life, and not sent me to hell, that I might be converted and turn all my affections to Thee. Since, then, Thou art pleased that even I should love Thee, oh, yes, my God, I will do so. Behold, here I am! To Thee I yield myself up: I give myself to Thee: I love Thee, O God! all goodness, all love, I choose Thee for the only King and Lord of my poor heart. Thou desires it, and my will is to give it to Thee: it is cold, it is loathsome; but if Thou accepts it, Thou wilt change it. Change me, my Lord, change me; I will no longer dare to live as I have hitherto lived, ungrateful, and with so little love towards Thine infinite Goodness, which loves me so much and deserves an infinite love. Enable me to supply from this day forward all the love I have hitherto failed to bear Thee.

Ejaculatory Prayer. My God, my God, I will love Thee! I will love Thee! I will love Thee!
AN ACT OF SPIRITUAL COMMUNION

My Jesus, I believe that Thou art truly present in the Most Holy Sacrament. I love Thee above all things, and I desire to possess Thee within my soul. Since I am unable now to receive Thee sacramentally, come at least spiritually into my heart. I embrace Thee as already there and unite myself wholly to Thee; never permit me to be separated from Thee.

VISIT TO MARY

In all things like to her Son Jesus, is His Mother Mary; and as she is the Mother of Mercy, she is thrice happy when she succors and consoles the miserable. So great is the desire of this Mother to bestow graces on all that Bernardine de Bustis says "she desires more to do us good and to impart to us graces than we can desire to receive them."

Ejaculatory Prayer. Hail, our hope!

Concluding Prayer

Most holy Immaculate Virgin and my Mother Mary, to thee, who art the Mother of my Lord, and Queen of the world, the advocate, the hope, the refuge of sinners, I have recourse today I, who am the most miserable of all. I render thee my most humble homage, O great Queen, and I thank thee for all the graces thou hast conferred on me until now, particularly for having delivered me from hell, which I have so often deserved. I love thee, O most amiable Lady; and for the love which I bear thee, I promise to serve thee always, and to do all in my power to make others love thee also. I place in thee all my hopes; I confide my salvation to thy care. Accept me for thy servant, and receive me under thy mantle, O Mother of Mercy. And since thou art so powerful with God, deliver me from all temptations, or rather obtain for me the strength to triumph over them until death. Of thee I ask a perfect love of Jesus Christ. From thee I hope to die a good death.

O my Mother, for the love which thou bearest to God, I beseech thee to help me at all times, but especially at the last moment of my life. Leave me not, I beseech thee, until thou see me safe in Heaven, blessing thee, and singing thy mercies for all eternity. Amen. So I hope. So may it be.

Evening Meditation
THE PRACTICE OF THE LOVE OF JESUS CHRIST
"CHARITY IS NOT AMBITIOUS."
XX.–HE THAT LOVES JESUS CHRIST DESIRES NOTHING BUT JESUS CHRIST.

I.

He that loves God does not desire to be esteemed and loved by his fellow-men: the single desire of his heart is to enjoy the favor of Almighty God, Who alone forms the object of his love. St. Hilary writes that all honor paid by the world is the business of the devil. And so it is; for the enemy traffics for hell when he infects the soul with the desire of esteem; because, by thus laying aside humility, she runs great risks of plunging into every vice. St. James writes that, as God confers His graces with open hands upon the humble, so does He close them against the proud, whom He resists. God resists the proud, and gives his grace to the humble-(James iv. 6). He says, He resists the proud, signifying that He does not even listen to their prayers. And certainly, among the acts of pride we may reckon, the desire to be honored by men, and self-exaltation at receiving honors from them.

II.

We have a frightful example of this in the history of Brother Justin the Franciscan, who had even risen to a lofty state of contemplation; but because, perhaps-and indeed without a perhaps-he nourished within himself a desire of human esteem, behold what befell him. One day Pope Eugenius IV sent for him; and on account of the great opinion he had of his sanctity, showed him peculiar marks of honor, embraced him, and made him sit by his side. Such high honors filled Brother Justin with self-conceit; on which St. John Capistran said to him, "Alas, Brother Justin, thou didst leave us an angel, and thou returns a devil!" And, in fact, the hapless Brother becoming daily more and more puffed up with arrogance, and insisting on being treated according to his own estimate of himself, he at last committed murder. Afterwards, becoming apostate, he fled into the kingdom of Naples, where he perpetrated other atrocities, and there he died in prison, an apostate to the last. Hence it is that a certain great servant of God wisely said that when we hear or read of the fall of some towering cedars of Libanus, of a Solomon, a Tertullian, an Osius, who had all the reputation of saints, it is a sign that they were not wholly given to God, but nourished inwardly some spirit of pride, and so fell away. Let us therefore tremble when we feel arise within us an ambition to appear in public, and to be esteemed by the world; and when the world pays us some tribute of honor, let us beware of taking complacency in it, which might prove the cause of our utter ruin.

Saturday- First Week After Pentecost

Morning Mediation

THE GENEROUS HEART OF JESUS

It is a characteristic of good-hearted people to desire to make everybody happy, and especially the most distressed and afflicted. But who can ever find one who has a better heart than Jesus Christ? He is infinite Goodness itself, and has therefore a sovereign desire to communicate His riches to us: With me are riches .. that I may enrich them that love me- (Proverbs viii. 18, 21).

I.

Who can ever find one who has a better heart than Jesus Christ? He is infinite Goodness itself and has therefore a sovereign desire to communicate His riches to us. With me are riches ... that I may enrich them that love me. For this purpose, Jesus made Himself poor, as the Apostle says, that He might make us rich: He became poor for your sakes, that through his poverty you might be rich-(2 Corinthians viii. 9). For this purpose, also He chose to remain with us in the Most Holy Sacrament, where He remains constantly with His hands full of graces, as was seen by Father Balthazar Alvarez, to dispense them to those who come to visit Him. For this reason also He gives Himself wholly to us in Communion, giving us to understand from this that He cannot refuse us any good gifts, since He even gives Himself entirely to us: How hath he not also, with him, given us all things? - (Romans viii. 32).

Ah, my Jesus, Thou hast not refused to give me Thy Blood and Thy life, and shall I refuse to give Thee my miserable heart? No, my dearest Redeemer, I offer it entirely to Thee. I give Thee all my will; do Thou accept it and dispose of it at Thy pleasure. I can do nothing, and have nothing of my own, but I have this heart which Thou hast given me, and of which no one can deprive me. I may be deprived of my goods, my blood, my life, but not of my heart. With this heart I can love thee; with this heart I will love Thee. I beseech Thee, O my God, teach me a perfect forgetfulness of myself. Teach me what I must do to arrive at Thy pure love, of which Thou in Thy goodness hast inspired me with the desire. I feel in myself a determination to please Thee; but to put my resolve into execution, I expect, and implore help from Thee. It depends on Thee, O loving Heart of Jesus, to make entirely Thine my poor heart, which hitherto has been so ungrateful, and through my own fault deprived of Thy love.

II.

In the Heart of Jesus we receive every good, every grace that we desire: In all things you are made rich in him . . .so that nothing is wanting to you in any grace – (1 Corinthians i. 5,7). And we must understand that we are debtors to the Heart of Jesus for all the graces we have received-graces of Redemption, of vocation, of light, of pardon; the grace to resist temptations, and to bear patiently with contradictions; for without His assistance we could not do anything good: Without me you can do nothing- (John xv. 5).

And if hitherto, says our Savior, you have not received more graces, do not complain of Me, but blame yourself, who have neglected to seek them of Me: Hitherto you have not asked anything; ... ask, and you shall receive-(Jo. xvi. 24). Oh, how rich and liberal is the Heart of Jesus towards everyone that has recourse to Him! Rich unto all that call upon him-(Rom. x. 12). Oh, what great mercies do those souls receive who are earnest in asking help of Jesus Christ. David said, For thou, O Lord, art sweet and mild, and plenteous to all who call upon thee-(Ps. lxxxv. 5). Let us therefore always go to this Heart, and ask with confidence, and we shall obtain all we want.

Oh, grant that my heart may be all on fire with the love of Thee, dear Jesus, even as Thine is on fire with the love of me. Grant that my will may be entirely united to Thine, so that I may will nothing but what Thou wills, and that from this day forth Thy holy will may be the rule of all my actions, of all my thoughts, and of all my desires. I trust, O my Savior, that Thou wilt not refuse me Thy grace to fulfil this resolution which I now make prostrate at Thy feet, to receive with submission whatever Thou mayest ordain for me and my affairs as well in life as in death. Blessed art thou, O Immaculate Mary, who hadst thy heart always and entirely united to the Heart of Jesus. Obtain for me, O my Mother, that in future I may wish and desire only what Jesus wills and what thou wills.

Spiritual Reading

CORAM SANCTISSIMO

TENTH VISIT

O foolish ones of the world, says St. Augustine, miserable creatures, whither are you going to satisfy your hearts? Come to Jesus, for by Him alone can that pleasure which you seek be bestowed. "Unhappy creatures, whither are you going? The good you seek for comes from Him." My soul, be not of the number of these foolish ones; seek God alone: "seek for that one Good in which are all good things." And if thou desires soon to find Him, behold, He is close to thee; tell Him what thou desires, since for this end it is He in the ciborium, to console thee, and to grant thy prayer St. Teresa says that all are not allowed to speak to their king; the most that can be hoped for is to communicate with him through a third person. To converse with Thee, O King of glory, no third person is needed; Thou art always ready in the Sacrament of the Altar to give audience to all. Whoever desires Thee, always finds Thee there, and converses with Thee face to face. And even if anyone at length succeeds in speaking with a king, how many difficulties has he had to overcome before he can do so! Kings grant audiences only a few times in the year; but Thou, in this Sacrament, grants an audience to all night and day, and whenever we please.

O Sacrament of love, Thou Who, whether Thou gives Thyself in the Communion, or dwellest on the altar, knowest, by the tender attractions of Thy love, how to draw so many hearts to Thyself, who, enamored with Thee, and filled with amazement at the sight of such love, burn with joy, and think always of Thee, draw also my miserable heart to Thyself; for it desires to love Thee, and to live enslaved by Thy love. For my part, I now and henceforward place all my interests, all my hopes, and all my affections, my soul, my body, I place all in the hands of Thy goodness. Accept me, O Lord, and dispose of me as Thou pleases. I will never again complain, O my Love, of Thy holy dispensations; I know that, as all take their source in Thy loving Heart, they will be full of love, and for my good. It is enough for me to know that Thou wills them; I will them also in time and eternity. Do all Thou wills in me and with me; I unite my entire self to Thy will, which is all holy, all good, all beautiful, all perfect, all loving. O will of my God, how dear art Thou to me! My will is ever to live and die united to and bound up with Thee. Thy pleasure is my pleasure. I will that Thy desires be also my desires. O my God, my God, help me; make me henceforward live for Thee alone; make me will only what Thou wills, and make me live only to love Thy amiable will. Grant that I may die for Thy love, since Thou hast died and become Food for me. I curse those days in which I did my own will, so much to Thy displeasure. I love Thee, O Will of God, as much as I love God, since Thou art one with Him. I love Thee, then, with my whole heart, and give myself all to Thee.

Ejaculatory Prayer. O will of God, Thou art my love.

AN ACT OF SPIRITUAL COMMUNION

My Jesus, I believe that Thou art truly present in the Most Holy Sacrament. I love Thee above all things, and I desire to possess Thee within my soul. Since I am unable now to receive Thee sacramentally, come at least spiritually into my heart. I embrace Thee as already there and unite myself wholly to Thee; never permit me to be separated from Thee.

VISIT TO MARY

The great Queen says, with me are riches... that I may enrich them that love me- (Proverbs viii. 18,21). Let us love Mary if we would be rich in graces. The writer who signs himself "Idiota" styles her "the treasurer of graces." Blessed is he who has recourse to Mary with love and confidence. My Mother, my hope, thou canst make me a saint; from thee I hope for this favor.

Ejaculatory Prayer. Mother most amiable, pray for me!

Concluding Prayer

Most holy Immaculate Virgin and my Mother Mary, to thee, who art the Mother of my Lord, and Queen of the world, the advocate, the hope, the refuge of sinners, I have recourse today I, who am the most miserable of all. I render thee my most humble homage, O great Queen, and I thank thee for all the graces thou hast conferred on me until now, particularly for having delivered me from hell, which I have so often deserved. I love thee, O most amiable Lady; and for the love which I bear thee, I promise to serve thee always, and to do all in my power to make others love thee also. I place in thee all my hopes; I confide my salvation to thy care. Accept me for thy servant, and receive me under thy mantle, O Mother of Mercy. And since thou art so powerful with God, deliver me from all temptations, or rather obtain for me the strength to triumph over them until death. Of thee I ask a perfect love of Jesus Christ. From thee I hope to die a good death.

O my Mother, for the love which thou bearest to God, I beseech thee to help me at all times, but especially at the last moment of my life. Leave me not, I beseech thee, until thou see me safe in Heaven, blessing thee, and singing thy mercies for all eternity. Amen. So I hope. So may it be.

Evening Mediation

THE PRACTICE OF THE LOVE OF JESUS CHRIST
XXIII.-HE THAT LOVES JESUS CHRIST DESIRES NOTHING BUT JESUS CHRIST

I.

Let us be especially on our guard against all ambitious seeking of preference, and sensibility in points of honor. St. Teresa said, "Where points of honor prevail, there spirituality will never prevail." Many people make profession of a spiritual life, but they are worshippers of self. They have the semblance of certain virtues, but they are ambitious of being praised in all their undertakings; and if nobody else praises them they praise themselves. In short, they strive to appear better than others; and if their honor be touched, they lose their peace, they leave off Holy Communion, they omit all their devotions, and find no rest till they imagine they have got back their former standing. The true lovers of God do not so behave. They not only carefully shun every word of self-complacency, but, further, they are sorry at hearing themselves commended by others, and it is their joy to see themselves held in small repute by the rest of men.

II.

That saying of St. Francis of Assisi is most true: "What I am before God, that I am." Of what use is it to pass for great in the eyes of the world, if before God we be vile and worthless? And on the contrary, what matters it to be despised by the world, provided we be dear and acceptable in the eyes of God? St. Augustine thus writes: "The approbation of him who praises, neither heals a bad conscience, nor does the reproach of him who blames wound a good conscience." As the man who praises us cannot deliver us from the chastisement of our evil doings, so neither can he who blames us rob us of the merit of our good actions. "What does it matter," says St. Teresa, "though we be condemned and reviled by creatures, if before Thee, O God, we are great and without blame?" The Saints had no other desire but to live unknown, and to pass for contemptible in the estimation of all. Thus writes St. Francis de Sales: "But what wrong do we suffer when people have a bad opinion of us, since we ought to have such of ourselves? Perhaps we know that we are bad, and yet wish to pass off for good in the estimation of others."

SECOND SUNDAY AFTER PENTECOST

Morning Meditation

THE HEART OF JESUS LONGING FOR OUR LOVE

Jesus has no need of us. He is equally happy, rich and powerful, with or without our love, and yet He loves us so intensely that He desires our love as much as if man were His God. This so filled Job with astonishment that he cried out: What is man that thou shouldst magnify him? Or why dost thou set thy heart upon him?

I.

Jesus has no need of us. He is equally happy, rich, and powerful with or without our love; and yet, as St. Thomas says He loves us so intensely that He desires our love as much as if man were His God, and His felicity depended on that of man. This so filled holy Job with astonishment that he cried out: What is man that thou shouldst magnify him? Or why dost thou set thy heart upon him? -(Job vii. 17).

What! can God desire or ask with such eagerness for the love of a worm? It would have been a great favor if God had only permitted us to love Him. If a vassal were to say to his king: "Sire, I love you!" he would be considered impertinent. But what would one say if the king were to tell his vassal, "I desire you to love me"? The princes of the earth do not humble themselves to this; but Jesus, Who is the King of Heaven, is He Who with so much earnestness demands our love: Love the Lord thy God with thy whole heart-(Matthew xxii. 37). So pressingly does He ask for our hearts: My son, give me thy heart-(Proverbs xxiii. 26). And if He is driven from a soul, He does not depart, but stands outside the door of the heart, and calls and knocks to be allowed to return: I stand at the gate and knock-(Apoc. iii. 20). Jesus beseeches the soul to open to Him, calling her sister and spouse: Open to me, my sister, my love - (Canticles v. 2). In short, He takes a delight in being loved by us, and is quite consoled when we say, arid repeat often: "My God! My God, I love Thee!"

My dearest Redeemer, I will say to Thee with St. Augustine, Thou dost command me to love Thee, and dost threaten me with hell if I do not love Thee; but what more dreadful hell, what greater misfortune, can happen to me than to be deprived of Thy love! If, therefore, Thou desirest to terrify me, Thou shouldst threaten me only that I should live without loving Thee; for this threat alone will terrify me more than a thousand hells. If, in the midst of the flames of hell, the damned could burn with Thy love, O my God, hell itself would become a Paradise; and if, on the contrary, the Blessed in Heaven could not love Thee, Paradise would become a hell.

I see, indeed, my dearest Lord, that I, on account of my sins, did deserve to be forsaken by Thy grace, and at the same time condemned to be incapable of loving Thee; but still I understand that Thou dost continue to command me to love Thee, and I also feel within me a great desire to love Thee. This my desire is the gift of Thy grace, and it comes from Thee. Oh, give me also the strength necessary to put it into execution, and make me, from this day forth, say to Thee earnestly, and from the bottom of my heart, and to repeat to Thee always: My God, I love Thee! I love Thee! I love Thee!

II.

The great desire of Jesus' Heart to be loved by us is the effect of His own great love for us. He who loves necessarily desires to be loved. The heart requires the heart; love seeks love: "Why does God love, but that He may be loved," said St. Bernard; and God Himself first said: What doth the Lord thy God require of thee, but that thou fear the Lord thy God,.. and love him? -(Deuteronomy x. 12). Therefore, He tells us that He is that Shepherd Who, having found the lost sheep, calls all the others to rejoice with Him: Rejoice with me, because I have found my sheep that was lost- (Luke xv. 6). He tells us that He is that Father Who, when His lost son returns and throws himself at His feet, not only forgives him, but embraces him tenderly. Jesus tells us he that loves Him not is condemned to death: He that loveth not abideth in death- (1 John iii. 14). And, on the contrary, that He takes him who loves Him and keeps possession of him: He that abideth in charity, abideth in God, and God in him-(1 John iv. 16). Oh, will not such invitations, such entreaties, such threats, and such promises move us to love God Who so much desires to be loved by us?

Thou, then, desirest my love, O Jesus. I also desire Thine. Blot out, therefore, from Thy remembrance, O my Jesus, the offences that in past times I have committed against Thee; let us love each other henceforth forever. I will not leave Thee, and Thou wilt not leave me. Thou wilt always love me, and I will always love Thee. My dearest Savior, in Thy merits do I place my hope; oh, do Thou make Thyself to be loved forever, and loved greatly, by a sinner who has so greatly offended Thee.

O Mary, Immaculate Virgin, do thou help me; do thou pray to Jesus for me.

Spiritual Reading

CORAM SANCTISSIMO

ELEVENTH VISIT

"Let us be careful," says St. Teresa, "never to be at a distance from Jesus, our beloved Shepherd, or to lose sight of Him: for the sheep which are near their shepherd are always more caressed and better fed, and always receive some choice morsels of that which he himself eats. If by chance the shepherd sleeps, still the lamb remains near him and either waits until his slumber ends, or itself wakens him; and it is then caressed with new favors."

My Redeemer, present in this Most Holy Sacrament, hold me near Thee. The only favor which I ask of Thee is fervor and perseverance in Thy love. I thank thee, O holy Faith, for thou teaches and assures me that in the divine Sacrament of the Altar, in that heavenly Bread, bread does not exist; but that my Lord Jesus Christ is all there, and that He is there for love of me. My Lord and my All, I believe that Thou art present in the Most Holy Sacrament; and though unknown to eyes of flesh, by the light of holy Faith I discern Thee in the consecrated Host, as the Monarch of Heaven and earth, and as the Savior of the world. Ah, my most sweet Jesus, as Thou art my hope, my salvation, my strength, my consolation, so also I will that Thou shouldst be all my love, and the only object of all my thoughts, of my desires, and of my affections. I rejoice more in the supreme happiness which Thou enjoys, and wilt enjoy forever, than in any good thing I could ever have in time or in eternity. My supreme satisfaction is that Thou, my beloved Redeemer, art supremely happy, and that Thy happiness is infinite. Reign, reign, my Lord, over my whole soul; I give it all to Thee; do Thou ever possess it. May my will, my senses, my faculties be all servants of Thy love, and may they never in this world serve anything else than to give Thee satisfaction and glory. Such was thy life, O first lover and Mother of my Jesus! Most Holy Mary, do thou help me; do thou obtain for me the grace to live henceforward, as thou didst always live, in the happiness of belonging to God alone.

Ejaculatory Prayer. My Jesus, may I be all Thine, and be Thou all mine!

AN ACT OF SPIRITUAL COMMUNION

My Jesus, I believe that Thou art truly present in the Most Holy Sacrament. I love Thee above all things, and I desire to possess Thee within my soul. Since I am unable now to receive Thee sacramentally, come at least spiritually into my heart. I embrace Thee as already there and unite myself wholly to Thee; never permit me to be separated from Thee.

VISIT TO MARY

Blessed is the man ... that watcheth daily at my gates, and waiteth at the posts of my doors-(Prov. viii. 34). Blessed is he, who, like the poor who stand before the gates of the rich, is careful to seek for the alms of graces before the doors of the mercy of Mary! And thrice blessed is he, who, moreover, seeks to imitate the virtues which he remarks in Mary, and more especially her purity and her humility.

Ejaculatory Prayer. My hope, succor me!

Concluding Prayer

Most holy Immaculate Virgin and my Mother Mary, to thee, who art the Mother of my Lord, and Queen of the world, the advocate, the hope, the refuge of sinners, I have recourse today I, who am the most miserable of all. I render thee my most humble homage, O great Queen, and I thank thee for all the graces thou hast conferred on me until now, particularly for having delivered me from hell, which I have so often deserved. I love thee, O most amiable Lady; and for the love which I bear thee, I promise to serve thee always, and to do all in my power to make others love thee also. I place in thee all my hopes; I confide my salvation to thy care. Accept me for thy servant, and receive me under thy mantle, O Mother of Mercy. And since thou art so powerful with God, deliver me from all temptations, or rather obtain for me the strength to triumph over them until death. Of thee I ask a perfect love of Jesus Christ. From thee I hope to die a good death.

O my Mother, for the love which thou bearest to God, I beseech thee to help me at all times, but especially at the last moment of my life. Leave me not, I beseech thee, until thou see me safe in Heaven, blessing thee, and singing thy mercies for all eternity. Amen. So I hope. So may it be.

Evening Mediation

THE PRACTICE OF THE LOVE OF JESUS CHRIST

XXIV.-HE THAT LOVES JESUS CHRIST DESIRES NOTHING BUT JESUS CHRIST

I.

Oh, what security is found in the hidden life for such as wish cordially to love Jesus Christ! Jesus Christ set us the example, by living hidden and despised for thirty years in a workshop. And with the same view of escaping the esteem of men, the Saints went and hid themselves in deserts and caves. It was said by St. Vincent de Paul, that love of appearing in public, and of being spoken of in terms of praise, and of hearing our conduct commended, or that people should say that we succeed admirably and work wonders, is an evil which, while it makes us unmindful of God, contaminates our best actions, and proves the most fatal drawback to the spiritual life. Whoever, therefore, would make progress in the love of Jesus Christ, must absolutely give a deathblow to self-esteem. But how shall we inflict this blow? Behold how St. Mary Magdalen de Pazzi instructs us: "That which keeps alive the appetite of self-esteem is the occupying a favorable position in the minds of all; consequently, the death of self-esteem is to keep oneself hidden so not to be known to anyone. And till we learn to die in this manner, we shall never be true servants of God."

O my Jesus, grant me a desire to please Thee, and make me forget all creatures and myself also. What will it profit me to be loved by the whole world if I be not loved by Thee, the only love of my soul! My Jesus, Thou came into the world to win our hearts; if I am unable to give Thee my heart, do Thou be pleased to take it and replenish it with Thy love, and never allow me to be separated from Thee any more. I have, alas, turned my back upon Thee in the past; but now that I am conscious of the evil I have done, I grieve over it with my whole heart, and no affliction in the world can so distress me as the remembrance of the offences I have so often committed against Thee. I am consoled to think that Thou art Infinite Goodness; that Thou dost not disdain to love a sinner who loves Thee. My beloved Redeemer, O sweetest Love of my soul, I have heretofore slighted Thee, but now at least I love Thee more than myself! I offer Thee myself and all that belongs to me.

II.

In order, then, to be pleasing in the sight of God, we must avoid all ambition of appearing and of making a parade in the eyes of men. And we must shun with still greater caution the ambition of governing others. Sooner than behold this accursed ambition set foot in her convent, St. Teresa declared she would prefer to have the whole convent burnt, and all the nuns with it. So that she signified her wish, that if ever one of her Religious should be caught aiming at superiority, she should be expelled from the community, or at least undergo perpetual confinement. St. Mary Magdalen de Pazzi says, "The honor of a spiritual person consists in being put below all, and in abhorring all superiority over others." The ambition of a soul that loves God should be to excel all others in humility, according to the counsel of St. Paul: In humility let each esteem others better than themselves- (Philippians ii. 3). In a word, he that loves God must make God the sole object of his ambition.

O my dear Jesus, I have only one wish: to love Thee and to please Thee. This forms all my ambition; accept of it, and be pleased to increase it, and exterminate in me all desire of earthly goods. Thou art indeed deserving of love, and great indeed are my obligations of loving Thee. Behold me, then, I wish to be wholly Thine; and I will suffer whatever Thou pleases, Thou who for love of me didst die of sorrow on the Cross! Thou wishes me to be a saint; in Thee I place my trust. And I also confide in thy protection, O Mary, great Mother of God!

Monday – Second Week After Pentecost

Morning Meditation

THE SORROWFUL HEART OF JESUS

My soul is sorrowful even unto death. The principal sorrow which afflicted the Heart of Jesus so much was not the sight of the torments and infamy men were preparing for Him, but the sight of their ingratitude towards His immense love. And yet the sight of all these insults did not prevent Him from leaving us this pledge of love, Himself in the Blessed Sacrament.

I.

It is impossible to consider how afflicted the Heart of Jesus was for love of us and not pity Him. He Himself tells us that His Heart was overwhelmed with such sorrow that this alone would have sufficed to take His life away, and to make Him die of pure grief, if the virtue of His Divinity had not, by a miracle, prevented His death: My soul is sorrowful unto death- (Mark xiv. 34). The principal sorrow which afflicted the Heart of Jesus so much, was not the sight of the torments and infamy men were preparing for Him, but the sight of their ingratitude towards His immense love. He distinctly foresaw all the sins we should commit after all His sufferings and such a bitter and ignominious death. He foresaw, especially, the horrible insults men would offer to His adorable Heart, which He has left us in this most Holy Sacrament as a proof of His affection.

My adorable and dearest Jesus, behold at Thy feet one who has caused so much sorrow to Thy amiable Heart. O my God, how could I grieve this Heart, which has loved me so much, and has spared nothing to make itself loved by me? But console Thyself, I will say, O my Savior, for my heart having been wounded, through Thy grace, with Thy most holy love, feels now so much regret for the offences I have committed against Thee, that it would fain die of sorrow. Oh, who will give me, my Jesus, that sorrow for my sins which Thou didst feel for them! Eternal Father, I offer Thee the sorrow and abhorrence Thy Son felt for my sins; and, for His sake, I beseech Thee to give me so great a sorrow for the offences I have committed against Thee, that I may lead an afflicted and sorrowful life at the thought of having once despised Thy friendship.

II.

O my God, what insults has not Jesus Christ received from men in this Sacrament of love! One has trampled Him under foot, another has thrown Him into the gutter, others have availed themselves of Him to pay homage to the devil! And yet the sight of all these insults did not prevent Him leaving us this great Pledge of His love. He has a sovereign hatred of sin; but still it seems as if His love towards us had overcome the hatred He bore to sin, in as much as He was content to permit these sacrileges, rather than to deprive souls that love Him of this Divine Food. Shall not all this suffice to make us love a Heart that has loved us so much? Has not Jesus Christ done enough to deserve our love? Ungrateful that we are, shall we still leave Jesus forsaken on the altar, as the majority of men do? And shall we not unite ourselves to those few souls who acknowledge Him, and melt with love even more than the torches melt away which burn round the tabernacle? The Heart of Jesus remains there, burning with love for us; and shall we not, in His Presence, burn with love for Jesus?

O my Jesus, do Thou give me from this day forth, such a horror of sin, that I may abhor even the lightest faults, considering that they displease Thee Who dost not deserve to be offended much or little, but dost deserve an infinite love. My beloved Lord, I now detest everything that displeases Thee, and in future I will love only Thee, and all that Thou lovest. Oh, help me, give me the strength, give me the grace to invoke Thee constantly, O my Jesus, and always to repeat to Thee this petition: My Jesus, give me Thy love! Give me Thy love! Give me Thy love! And thou, most holy Mary, obtain for me the grace to pray to thee continually, and to say to thee: O my Mother, make me love Jesus Christ.

Spiritual Reading

CORAM SANCTISSIMO

TWELFTH VISIT

God is charity; and he that abideth in charity abideth in God, and God in him-(1 John iv. 16). He who loves Jesus dwells with Jesus, and Jesus with him. If anyone love me ... my Father will love him; and we will come to him, and will make our abode with him- (John. xiv. 23). When St. Philip Neri received the Holy Communion as Viaticum, on seeing the Most Blessed Sacrament enter his room, he exclaimed: "Behold, my Love! Behold all my Good! Hasten and give me my Love!" Let each one of us, then, say here in the presence of Jesus in the Blessed Sacrament: Behold my Love! Behold the object of all my love for my whole life and for all eternity!

Since, then, my Lord and my God, Thou hast said in the Gospel that he who loves Thee will be beloved by Thee, and that Thou wilt come and dwell in him, and never more leave him, I love Thee above every other good. Do Thou then, also, love me: for I, indeed, esteem being loved by Thee above all the kingdoms of the world. Come and fix Thy dwelling in the poor house of my soul in such a way as Thou mayest no more depart from me. Thou dost not go, if Thou art not expelled; but as I have already done this, so I may do again. Ah, never allow such a fresh act of wickedness, such horrible ingratitude to be perpetrated in the world, as that I, who have been so specially favored by Thee, and who have received so many graces, should again drive Thee from my soul! But this might happen. I, therefore, my Lord, desire death, if it so please Thee; that by dying united to Thee, I may live united to Thee for ever. Yes, my Jesus, for this I hope. I embrace Thee; I press Thee to my poor heart; grant that I may always love Thee, and always be beloved by Thee. Yes, my most amiable Redeemer, I will always love Thee; and Thou wilt always love me. I trust that our love will ever be mutual, O God of my soul, and this for all eternity Amen.

Ejaculatory Prayer. My Jesus, I desire always to love Thee, and always to be beloved by Thee.

AN ACT OF SPIRITUAL COMMUNION

My Jesus, I believe that Thou art truly present in the Most Holy Sacrament. I love Thee above all things, and I desire to possess Thee within my soul. Since I am unable now to receive Thee sacramentally, come at least spiritually into my heart. I embrace Thee as already there and unite myself wholly to Thee; never permit me to be separated from Thee.

VISIT TO MARY

They that work by me shall not sin- (Ecclesiasticus xxiv. 30). He, says Mary, who endeavors to honor me shall persevere to the end. They that explain me shall have life everlasting- (Ecclesiasticus xxiv. 31); and those who endeavor to make me known and loved by others, will be of the number of the Elect. Promise, then, that whenever you can, be it in public or in private, you will speak of the glories of Mary, and of devotion to her.

Ejaculatory Prayer. Vouchsafe that I may praise thee, most sacred Virgin!

Concluding Prayer

Most holy Immaculate Virgin and my Mother Mary, to thee, who art the Mother of my Lord, and Queen of the world, the advocate, the hope, the refuge of sinners, I have recourse today I, who am the most miserable of all. I render thee my most humble homage, O great Queen, and I thank thee for all the graces thou hast conferred on me until now, particularly for having delivered me from hell, which I have so often deserved. I love thee, O most amiable Lady; and for the love which I bear thee, I promise to serve thee always, and to do all in my power to make others love thee also. I place in thee all my hopes; I confide my salvation to thy care. Accept me for thy servant, and receive me under thy mantle, O Mother of Mercy. And since thou art so powerful with God, deliver me from all temptations, or rather obtain for me the strength to triumph over them until death. Of thee I ask a perfect love of Jesus Christ. From thee I hope to die a good death.

O my Mother, for the love which thou bearest to God, I beseech thee to help me at all times, but especially at the last moment of my life. Leave me not, I beseech thee, until thou see me safe in Heaven, blessing thee, and singing thy mercies for all eternity. Amen. So I hope. So may it be.

Evening Meditation
THE PRACTICE OF THE LOVE OF JESUS CHRIST
"Charity seeketh not her own."
XXV.-HE THAT LOVETH JESUS CHRIST SEEKS TO DETACH HIMSELF FROM EVERY CREATURE

I.

Whoever desires to love Jesus Christ with his whole heart must banish from his heart all that is not God but is merely self-love. This is the meaning of those words, seeketh not her own; not to seek ourselves, but only what pleaseth God. And this IS what God requires of us all when He says: Thou shalt love the Lord thy God with thy whole heart- (Matthew xxii. 37). Two things are needful to love God with our whole heart: (1) To clear it of earth; (2) To fill it with holy love. It follows that a heart in which any earthly affections linger can never belong wholly to God. St. Philip Neri said, "that as much love as we bestow on the creature, is so much taken from the Creator." In the next place, how must the earth be purged away from the heart? Truly by mortification and detachment from creatures. Some souls complain that they seek God and do not find Him; let them listen to what St. Teresa says: "Wean your heart from creatures, and then seek God, and you will find Him."

II.

The mistake is, that some indeed wish to become Saints, but after their own fashion; they would love Jesus Christ, but in their own way, without forsaking those diversions, that vanity of dress, those delicacies in food: they love God, but if they do not succeed in obtaining such or such an office, they live discontented; if, too, they happen to be touched in point of esteem, they are all on fire; if they do not recover from an illness, they lose all patience. They love God; but they refuse to let go that attachment for the riches, the honors of the world, for the vainglory of being reckoned of good family, of great learning, and better than others. Such as these practice prayer and frequent Communion; but inasmuch as they take with them hearts full of earth, they derive little profit. Our Lord does not even speak to them, for He knows that it is but a waste of words. In fact, He said as much to St. Teresa on a certain occasion: "I would speak to many souls, but the world keeps up such a noise about their ears that My voice would never be heard by them. Oh, that they would retire a little from the world!" Whosoever, then, is full of earthly affections cannot even so much as hear the voice of God that speaks to him. But unhappy the man that continues attached to the sensible goods of this earth; he may easily become so blinded by them as one day to forsake the love of Jesus Christ; and because of his attachment to these transitory goods, he may lose God, the Infinite Good, forever. St. Teresa said: "It is a reasonable consequence, that he who runs after perishable goods should himself perish."

Tuesday – Second Week After Pentecost

Morning Meditation

THE COMPASSIONATE HEART OF JESUS

O my Jesus, Thou dost pardon penitent sinners, and Thou dost not refuse to give them in this world everything in Holy Communion, and in the next world everything in eternal glory. Where, then, is a heart to be found so amiable and so compassionate as Thine, O my dearest Savior?

I.

Where shall we find a heart more compassionate or tender than the Heart of Jesus, or one that has greater pity for our miseries?

This pity induced Him to descend from Heaven to this earth; it made Him say that He was that Good Shepherd Who came to give His life to save His sheep. In order to obtain the pardon of our sins, He would not spare Himself, but would sacrifice Himself on the Cross, that by His sufferings He might satisfy for the punishment due to us. This pity and compassion makes Him say even now: Why will ye die, O house of Israel? Return ye, and live– (Ezechiel xviii. 31). O men, He says, my poor children, why will you damn yourselves by flying from Me? Do you not see that by separating yourselves from Me you are hastening to eternal death? I desire not to see you lost; do not despair; as long as you wish to return, return and you shall recover your life: Return ye and live.

O compassionate Heart of my Jesus, have pity on me. Most sweet Jesus, have mercy on me. I say now and beseech Thee to give me the grace always to say to Thee: "Most Sweet Jesus, have mercy on me!" Even before I offended Thee, my Redeemer, I certainly did not deserve any of the favors Thou hast bestowed upon me. Thou hast created me, Thou hast given me so much light and knowledge; and all without any merit of mine. But after I had offended Thee, I not only did not deserve Thy favor, but I deserved to be forsaken by Thee and cast into hell. Thy compassion has made Thee wait for me and preserve my life even when I had offended Thee. Thy compassion has enlightened me and offered me pardon; it has given me sorrow for my sins, and the desire of loving Thee; and now I hope from Thy mercy to remain always in Thy grace.

II.

This compassion even makes Jesus say that He is that loving Father Who, though He sees Himself despised by His son, yet, if the son returns a penitent, He cannot reject him, but embraces him tenderly and forgets all the injuries He has received: I will not remember all his iniquities-(Ezechiel xviii. 22). It is not thus that men behave; for though they may forgive, yet they nevertheless retain the remembrance of the offence received and feel inclined to revenge themselves; and even if they do not revenge themselves, because they fear God, at least they always feel a very great repugnance to converse or entertain themselves with those persons who have injured them.

O my Jesus, Thou dost pardon penitent sinners, and dost not refuse in this world to give them everything in Holy Communion during their life, and everything in the other world in eternal glory, without retaining the slightest repugnance towards being united forever to the soul that offended Thee so often. Where, therefore is, to be found a Heart so amiable and compassionate as Thine, O my dearest Savior?

O my Jesus, cease not to show Thy compassion towards me. The mercy which I would implore of Thee is that Thou wouldst grant me light and strength to be no longer ungrateful towards Thee. No, O my Love, I do not expect that Thou shouldst again forgive me if I again turn my back against Thee; this would be presumption, and would prevent Thee from showing mercy to me anymore. For what pity, O Jesus, could I expect from Thee if I were so ungrateful as to despise Thy friendship again, and to separate myself from Thee. No, my Jesus, I love Thee and I will always love Thee; and this is the mercy which I hope for and seek from Thee: "Permit me not to be separated from Thee! Permit me not to be separated from Thee!"

And I beseech thee, also, O Mary, my Mother, permit me not to be ever again separated from my God.

Spiritual Reading

CORAM SANCTISSIMO

THIRTEENTH VISIT

My eyes and my heart shall be there always-(3 Kings ix. 3). Behold, Jesus has verified this beautiful promise in the sacrament of the altar, wherein He dwells with us night and day

My Lord, would it not have been enough hadst Thou remained in this Sacrament only during the day, when Thou couldst have had adorers of Thy presence to keep Thee company; but why remain also the whole night, when all the churches are closed, and when men retire to their homes, leaving Thee quite alone? Ah, yes! I already understand Thee: love has made Thee our Prisoner: the excessive love which Thou bearest us has so bound Thee down on earth that neither night nor day canst Thou leave us. Ah, most amiable Savior, this refinement of love alone should oblige all men ever to stay near Thee in the holy Tabernacle, and to remain with Thee until forcibly compelled to leave Thee; and when they do so, they should all leave at the foot of the altar their hearts and affections inflamed with love towards an Incarnate God who remains alone and enclosed in a Tabernacle, all eyes to see and provide for them in their necessities, and all heart to love them, and who awaits the coming day to be again visited by His beloved souls.

Yes, my Jesus, I will please Thee; I consecrate my whole will and all my affections to Thee. O infinite Majesty of God, Thou hast left Thyself in this divine Sacrament, not only that Thou mightest be present with us and near us, but principally to communicate Thyself to Thy beloved souls. But, Lord, who will presume to approach Thee to feed upon Thy Flesh? And who, on the other hand, can keep at a distance from Thee? For this purpose, Thou conceals Thyself in the consecrated Host, that Thou mayest enter into us and possess our hearts. Thou burns with the desire of being received by us, and Thou rejoices in being united with us. Come, then, my Jesus, come; I desire to receive Thee within myself, that Thou mayest be the God of my heart, and of my will. All that is within me I yield, my dear Redeemer, to thy love; satisfactions, pleasures, self-will, all I give up to Thee. O Love, O God of love, reign, triumph over my entire self; destroy and sacrifice all in me which is mine and not Thine. Permit not, O my Love, that my soul, which, having received Thee in Holy Communion, is filled with the Majesty of God, should again attach itself to creatures. I love Thee, my God I love Thee, and I will love Thee alone and forever.

Ejaculatory Prayer. Draw me by the chains of Thy love!

AN ACT OF SPIRITUAL COMMUNION

My Jesus, I believe that Thou art truly present in the Most Holy Sacrament. I love Thee above all things, and I desire to possess Thee within my soul. Since I am unable now to receive Thee sacramentally, come at least spiritually into my heart. I embrace Thee as already there and unite myself wholly to Thee; never permit me to be separated from Thee.

VISIT TO MARY

St. Bernard exhorts us, saying: "Let us seek for grace, and let us seek it through Mary." "She," says St. Peter Damian, "is the treasurer of divine graces." She can enrich us, and she desires to do so. She therefore invites and calls us, saying: Whosoever is a little one, let him come to me- (Proverbs ix. 4). Most amiable Lady, most exalted Lady, most gracious Lady, look on a poor sinner who recommends himself to thee, and who places all his confidence in thee.

Ejaculatory Prayer. We fly to thy patronage, O holy Mother of God!

Concluding Prayer

Most holy Immaculate Virgin and my Mother Mary, to thee, who art the Mother of my Lord, and Queen of the world, the advocate, the hope, the refuge of sinners, I have recourse today I, who am the most miserable of all. I render thee my most humble homage, O great Queen, and I thank thee for all the graces thou hast conferred on me until now, particularly for having delivered me from hell, which I have so often deserved. I love thee, O most amiable Lady; and for the love which I bear thee, I promise to serve thee always, and to do all in my power to make others love thee also. I place in thee all my hopes; I confide my salvation to thy care. Accept me for thy servant, and receive me under thy mantle, O Mother of Mercy. And since thou art so powerful with God, deliver me from all temptations, or rather obtain for me the strength to triumph over them until death. Of thee I ask a perfect love of Jesus Christ. From thee I hope to die a good death.

O my Mother, for the love which thou bearest to God, I beseech thee to help me at all times, but especially at the last moment of my life. Leave me not, I beseech thee, until thou see me safe in Heaven, blessing thee, and singing thy mercies for all eternity. Amen. So I hope. So may it be.

Evening Meditation
THE PRACTICE OF THE LOVE OF JESUS CHRIST

XXVI.-HE THAT LOVES JESUS CHRIST SEEKS TO DETACH HIMSELF FROM EVERY CREATURE

I.

St. Augustine informs us that Tiberius Caesar desired that the Roman Senate should enroll Jesus Christ among the rest or their gods; but the Senate refused to do so on the ground that He was too proud a God and would be worshipped alone without any companion. It is quite true; God will be alone the object of our adoration and love; not indeed from pride, but because it is His just due, and because too, of the love He bears us. For as He Himself loves us exceedingly, He desires in return all our love; and He is therefore jealous of anyone else sharing the affections of our hearts, of which He desires to be the sole possessor: "Jesus is a jealous lover," says St. Jerome; and He is unwilling, therefore, that we should fix our affections on anything but Himself. And whenever He beholds any created object taking a share of our hearts, He looks on it, as it were with jealousy, as the Apostle St. James says, because He will not endure a rival, but will remain the sole object of all our love: Do you think that the Scripture saith in vain: To envy doth the Spirit covet which dwelleth in you -(James iv. 5). The Lord, in the sacred Canticles, praises His spouse, saying: My sister, my spouse, is a garden enclosed- (Canticles iv. 12). He calls her a garden enclosed because the soul which is His spouse keeps her heart shut against every earthly love, to preserve all for Jesus Christ alone. And does Jesus Christ, perchance, not deserve all our love? Ah, too much, too much has He deserved it, both for His own goodness and for His love towards us. The Saints knew this well, and for this reason St. Francis de Sales said: "Were I conscious of one fiber in my heart that did not belong to God, I would forthwith tear it out."

II.

David longed to have wings free from all lime of worldly affections, to flyaway and repose in God: Who will give me wings like a dove, and I will fly and be at rest? - (Psalm liv. 7). Many souls would wish to see themselves released from every earthly trammel to fly to God, and would in reality make lofty flights in the way of sanctity, if they would but detach themselves from everything in this world; but whereas they retain some little inordinate affection, and will not use violence with themselves to get rid of it, they remain always languishing in their misery, without ever so much as taking a single forward step. St. John of the Cross said: "The soul that remains with her affections attached to anything, however small, will, notwithstanding the many virtues she may possess, never arrive at Divine union; for it signifies little whether the bird be tied by a slight thread or a thick one;

since, however slight it may be, provided she does not break it, she remains always bound, unable to fly. Oh, what a pitiful thing it is to see certain souls, rich in spiritual exercises, in virtues and Divine favors yet, because they are not bold enough to break off some trifling attachment, they cannot attain to Divine union. For this union there is needed only one strong and resolute flight to break effectually that fatal thread, for when once the soul is emptied of all affections to creatures, God cannot help communicating Himself wholly to her."

WEDNESDAY – SECOND WEEK AFTER PENTECOST

Morning Meditation

THE GRATEFUL HEART OF JESUS

Jesus has offered for us all His merits, all His sufferings, all His ignominies, all His Blood and His very life; so that we are under not one, but infinite obligations to love Him. Alas, we are grateful towards the very animals. How can it be that we are so ungrateful towards God?

I.

The Heart of Jesus is so grateful, that our Lord cannot behold the most trifling works done for His love—our smallest word spoken for His glory, a single good thought directed towards pleasing Him-without giving to each its own reward. He is, besides, so grateful that he always returns a hundredfold for one: You shall receive a hundredfold- (Matthew xix. 29).

Men, when they are grateful and recompense any benefit done to them, recompense it only once; they, as it were, divest themselves of all the obligation, and then they think no more of it. Jesus Christ does not act thus with us, for He not only recompenses a hundredfold in this life every action that we perform to please Him, but in the next life He recompenses it an infinite number of times throughout eternity. And who will be so negligent as not to do as much as he can to please this most grateful Heart?

Tell me, O Jesus, what Thou wishest me to do, for I am ready to do everything with Thy help. I believe that Thou hast created me. Thou hast given Thy Blood and Thy life for the love of me. I believe also that for my sake Thou dost remain in the Blessed Sacrament; I thank Thee for it, O my Love. Oh, permit me not to be ungrateful in future for so many benefits and proofs of Thy love. Oh, bind me, unite me to Thy Heart, and permit me not, during the years that remain to me, to offend Thee or grieve Thee anymore. I have displeased Thee too much, O my Jesus, it is time that I should love Thee now. Oh, that those many years I have lost would return! But they will return no more, and the life that remains for me may be short; but whether it be short or long, my God, I desire to spend it all in loving Thee, my sovereign Good, Who dost deserve an eternal and infinite love.

O Mary, my Mother, let me never again be ungrateful to thy Son. Pray to Jesus for me.

II.

But, O my God, how do men try to please Jesus Christ? Or rather, I will say, how can we be so ungrateful towards this our Savior? If He had shed only a single drop of Blood, or one tear for our salvation, we should be under infinite obligation to Him; because this drop and this tear would have been of infinite value in the sight of God towards obtaining for us every grace. But Jesus would employ for us every moment of His life. He has offered for us all His merits, all His sufferings, all His ignominies, all His Blood, and His life; so that we are under not one, but infinite, obligations to love Him.

But, alas, we are grateful even towards animals: if a little dog shows us any sign of affection, it seems to constrain us to love it. How, then, can we be so ungrateful towards God? It would seem as if God's benefits to men change their nature, and become ill-usage; for, instead of gratitude and love, they earn only offences and injuries. Do Thou, O Lord, enlighten these ungrateful ones, to know the love Thou bearest them.

O beloved Jesus, behold at Thy feet an ungrateful sinner. I have been grateful, indeed, towards creatures; but to Thee alone I have been ungrateful to Thee, Who hast died for me, and hast done the utmost that Thou couldst do to oblige me to love Thee. But the thought that I have to do with a Heart full of goodness and infinite in mercy, of One Who proclaims that He forgives all the offences of the sinner who repents and loves Him, consoles me and gives me courage. My dearest Jesus, I have in times past offended Thee and despised Thee; but now I love Thee more than everything more than myself.

Spiritual Reading

CORAM SANCTISSIMO

FOURTEENTH VISIT

Most amiable Jesus, I hear Thee say from this Tabernacle, in which Thou art present, This is my rest for ever and ever; here will I dwell for I have chosen it - (Psalm cxxxi. 14). Since then, Thou hast chosen Thy dwelling on our altars in the midst of us, remaining there in the most Holy Sacrament, and since Thy love for us makes Thee there find Thy repose, it is but just that our hearts also should ever dwell with Thee in affection, and should find all pleasure and repose in Thee. Blessed are you, O loving souls, who can find no sweeter repose in the world than in remaining near to your Jesus in the Most Holy Sacrament! And blessed shall I be, my Lord, if from this time forward I find no greater delight than in remaining always in Thy presence, or in always thinking of Thee, Who in the Most Holy Sacrament art always thinking of me and of my welfare.

Ah, my Lord, and why have I lost so many years in which I have not loved Thee? O miserable years, I curse you; and I bless thee, O infinite patience of my God, for having for so many years borne with me, though so ungrateful to Thy love. And still, notwithstanding this ingratitude, Thou waitest for me; and why, my God, why? It is, that one day, overcome by Thy mercies and by Thy love, I may yield wholly to Thee. Lord, I will no longer resist, I will no longer be ungrateful. It is but just that I should consecrate to Thee the time, be it long or short, which I have still to live. I hope for Thy help, O my Jesus, to become entirely Thine. Thou didst favor me so much when I fled from Thee and despised Thy love; how much more may I hope that Thou wilt favor me, now that I seek and desire to love Thee? Give me, then, the grace to love Thee, O God worthy of infinite love. I love Thee with my whole heart; I love Thee above all things: I love Thee more than myself, more than my life. I am sorry for having offended Thee, O infinite Goodness. Pardon me, and with Thy pardon grant me the grace to love Thee much in this life until death, and in the next life for all eternity. O Almighty God, show the world the greatness of Thy power, in the prodigy of a soul ungrateful as mine has been, becoming one of Thy greatest lovers. Do this by Thy merits, my Jesus. It is my ardent desire, and I resolve thus to love Thee during my whole life. Do Thou, Who inspires me with this desire, give me also the strength to accomplish it.

Ejaculatory Prayer. My Jesus, I thank Thee for having waited for me until now.

AN ACT OF SPIRITUAL COMMUNION

My Jesus, I believe that Thou art truly present in the Most Holy Sacrament. I love Thee above all things, and I desire to possess Thee within my soul. Since I am unable now to receive Thee sacramentally, come at least spiritually into my heart. I embrace Thee as already there and unite myself wholly to Thee; never permit me to be separated from Thee.

VISIT TO MARY

St. Germanus, addressing the Most Blessed Virgin Mary, says: "No one is saved but through thee; no one is delivered from evils but through thee; there is no one on whom any gift is bestowed but through thee." Therefore, my Lady and my hope, if thou dost not help me I am lost, and shall be unable to bless thee in Heaven. But Lady, I hear all the Saints say that thou never abandon those who have recourse to thee. He only is lost who has not recourse to thee. I, then, miserable creature that I am, have recourse to thee, and in thee place all my hopes.

Ejaculatory Prayer. Mary is my whole confidence; she is the whole ground of my hope!

Concluding Prayer

Most holy Immaculate Virgin and my Mother Mary, to thee, who art the Mother of my Lord, and Queen of the world, the advocate, the hope, the refuge of sinners, I have recourse today I, who am the most miserable of all. I render thee my most humble homage, O great Queen, and I thank thee for all the graces thou hast conferred on me until now, particularly for having delivered me from hell, which I have so often deserved. I love thee, O most amiable Lady; and for the love which I bear thee, I promise to serve thee always, and to do all in my power to make others love thee also. I place in thee all my hopes; I confide my salvation to thy care. Accept me for thy servant, and receive me under thy mantle, O Mother of Mercy. And since thou art so powerful with God, deliver me from all temptations, or rather obtain for me the strength to triumph over them until death. Of thee I ask a perfect love of Jesus Christ. From thee I hope to die a good death.

O my Mother, for the love which thou bearest to God, I beseech thee to help me at all times, but especially at the last moment of my life. Leave me not, I beseech thee, until thou see me safe in Heaven, blessing thee, and singing thy mercies for all eternity. Amen. So I hope. So may it be.

Evening Meditation

THE PRACTICE OF THE LOVE OF JESUS CHRIST

XXVII.-HE THAT LOVES JESUS CHRIST SEEKS TO DETACH HIMSELF FROM EVERY CREATURE

I.

He who would possess God entirely must give himself up entirely to God: My beloved to me, and I to him - (Canticles ii. 16), says the Sacred Spouse. My beloved has given

Himself entirely to me, and I give myself entirely to Him. The love which Jesus Christ bears us causes Him to desire all our love; and without all He is not satisfied. On this account we find St. Teresa thus writing to the prioress of one of her convents: "Endeavour to train souls to total detachment from everything created, because they are to be trained for the spouses of a King so jealous that He would have them even forget themselves." St. Mary Magdalen de Pazzi took a little book of devotion from one of her novices, merely because she observed that she was too much attached to it. Many souls acquit themselves of the duty of prayer, of visiting the Blessed Sacrament, of frequenting Holy Communion; but nevertheless they make little or no progress in perfection, and all because they keep some fondness for something in their heart; and if they persist in living thus, they will not only be always miserable, but run the risk of losing all.

II.

We must, therefore, beseech Almighty God, with David, to rid our heart of all earthly attachments: Create a clean heart in me, O God- (Psalm 1. 12). Otherwise we can never be wholly His. He has given us to understand very plainly that whoever will not renounce everything in this world cannot be His disciple: Every one of you that doth not renounce all that he possesses, cannot be my disciple-(Luke xiv. 33). For this reason the ancient Fathers of the Desert were accustomed first to put this question to any youth who desired to associate himself with them: "Dost thou bring an empty heart that the Holy Spirit may fill it?" Our Lord said the same thing to St. Gertrude when she besought Him to signify what He wished of her: "I wish nothing else He said, but to find a heart devoid of creatures." We must therefore say to God with great resolution and courage: O Lord, I prefer Thee to all; to health, to riches, to honors and dignities, to applause, to learning, to consolations, to high hopes, to desires, and even to the very graces and gifts which I may receive of Thee! In short, I prefer Thee to every good which is not Thee, O my God! Whatever benefit Thou grantest me, O my God, nothing besides Thyself will satisfy me. I desire Thee alone, and nothing else.

Thursday – Second Week After Pentecost

Morning Mediation

THE DESPISED HEART OF JESUS

There is no greater sorrow for a heart that loves than to see its love despised; and all the more when on one side the love has been great, and on the other the ingratitude has been great. Jesus Christ has offered for us His sufferings, His Blood, His very life, and we have returned Him ill-treatment, contempt, and injuries.

I.

There is no greater sorrow for a heart that loves than to see its love despised; and so much the more when the proofs given of this love have been great, and, on the other hand, the ingratitude great. If every human being were to renounce all his goods, and to go and live in the desert, to live on herbs, to sleep on the bare earth, to macerate himself with penances, and at last give himself up to be martyred for Christ's sake, what recompense could he render for the sufferings, the Blood, the life that this great Son of God has given for his sake? If we were to sacrifice ourselves every moment unto death, we should certainly not recompense in the smallest degree the love Jesus Christ has shown us by giving Himself to us in the Most Holy Sacrament. Only conceive that God should conceal Himself under the species of bread to become the Food of one of His creatures! But, O my God, what recompense and gratitude do men render to Jesus Christ? What but ill-treatment, contempt of His laws and His maxims, injuries such as they would not commit against their enemy, or their slave, or the greatest villain upon earth.

O Heart of Jesus, abyss of mercy and love, how is it that, at the sight of the goodness Thou has shown me, and of my ingratitude, I do not die of sorrow? Thou, O my Savior, after having given me my being, hast given me all Thy Blood and Thy life, offering Thyself up for my sake to ignominy and death; and, not content with this, Thou hast invented the mode of sacrificing Thyself every day for me in the Holy Eucharist, not refusing to expose Thyself to the injuries Thou dost receive, and which Thou didst foresee in this Sacrament of love. O my God, how can I see myself so ungrateful to Thee without dying with confusion! O Lord, put an end, I pray Thee, to my ingratitude, by wounding my heart with Thy love, and making me entirely Thine.

II.

And can we think upon all the Injuries which Jesus Christ has received, and still receives every day, and not feel sorrow for them, and not endeavor by our love to recompense the infinite love of His Divine Heart-this Divine Heart which ever remains with us in the Most Holy Sacrament, inflamed with the same love towards us, and anxious to communicate every good gift to us, and to give Itself entirely to us, ever ready to receive and pardon us whenever we return? Him that cometh to me, I will not cast out- (John. vi. 37). We have been accustomed to hear of the Creation, Incarnation, Redemption, of Jesus born in a stable, of Jesus dead on the Cross. O God, if we knew that another man had conferred on us any of these benefits, we could not help loving him! It seems that God alone has, so to say? this misfortune amongst men? that though He has done His utmost to make them love Him, yet He cannot attain this end, and, instead of being loved, He sees Himself despised and neglected. All this arises from the forgetfulness of men for the love of God.

Ah, dear Jesus, remember the Blood and tears Thou hast shed for me, and forgive me. Let not all Thy sufferings be lost upon me. But though Thou didst see how ungrateful and unworthy of Thy love I have been, yet Thou didst not cease to love me even when I did not love Thee, nor even desire that Thou shouldst love me; how much more, then, may I not hope for Thy love, now that I desire and sigh after nothing but to love Thee, and to be loved by Thee. Oh, do Thou fully satisfy this my desire; or rather, this Thy desire, for it is Thou that hast given it to me. Grant that this day may be the day of my thorough conversion; so that I may begin to love Thee, and may never cease to love Thee, my sovereign Good. Make me in everything die to myself in order that I may live only to

Thee, and that I may always burn with Thy love. O Mary, thy heart was the blessed altar that was always on fire with Divine love: my dearest Mother, make me like to thee; obtain this from thy Son, Who delights in honoring thee, by denying thee nothing that Thou askest of Him.

Spiritual Reading

CORAM SANCTISSIMO

FIFTEENTH VISIT

I am come to cast fire on the earth; and what will I but that it be kindled? -(Luke xii. 49). Father Francis Olimpio, the Theatine, used to say that there was nothing on earth which enkindled such ardent flames of Divine love in the hearts of men as the Most Holy Sacrament of the Altar. Hence our Lord showed Himself to St. Catherine of Sienna, in the Blessed Sacrament, as a furnace of love, from which issued forth torrents of divine flames, spreading themselves over the whole earth; so much so, indeed, that the Saint, in perfect astonishment, wondered how it was possible that men could live without burning with love for such love on the part of God towards them.

My Jesus, make me burn with the desire of Thee; grant that all my thoughts, and sighs, and desires, and seekings may be for Thee alone. Oh, happy should I be did this Thy heavenly fire fully possess me, and as I advance in years, gradually consume all earthly affections in me!

O, Divine Word! O, my own Jesus! I see Thee all sacrificed, all annihilated, and so to say, destroyed on the Altar, for my love. It is, then, but right that, as Thou sacrificest Thyself as a Victim for love of me, I at least should consecrate myself wholly to Thee. Yes, my God and my sovereign Lord, I now sacrifice to Thee my whole soul, my entire self, my whole will and my whole life. I unite this poor sacrifice of mine, O Eternal Father, to the infinite Sacrifice of Himself which Jesus, Thy Son and my Savior, once offered to Thee on the Cross, and which He now offers to Thee so many times every day on our Altars. Accept it, then, through the merits of Jesus Christ; and grant me the grace to renew it every day of my life, and to die sacrificing my whole self to Thy honor. I desire the grace granted to so many Martyrs, to die for Thy love. But if I am unworthy of so great a grace, grant, at least, my Lord, that I may sacrifice my life to Thee, together with my entire will, by accepting the death which Thou sends me. Lord, I desire this grace; I desire to die with the intention of honoring and pleasing Thee thereby; and from this moment I sacrifice my life to Thee; and I offer Thee my death, when or wheresoever it may take place.

AN ACT OF SPIRITUAL COMMUNION

My Jesus, I believe that Thou art truly present in the Most Holy Sacrament. I love Thee above all things, and I desire to possess Thee within my soul. Since I am unable now to receive Thee sacramentally, come at least spiritually into my heart. I embrace Thee as already there and unite myself wholly to Thee; never permit me to be separated from Thee.

VISIT TO MARY

Allow me also, my most sweet Queen, to call thee, with thine own St. Bernard, "the whole ground of my hope," and to say with St. John Damascene, "I have placed my whole hope in thee." Thou hast to obtain for me the forgiveness of my sins; thou, perseverance until death; thou, deliverance from Purgatory. All who are saved obtain salvation through thee: thou, then, O Mary, hast to save me: "He will be saved whom thou willest," says St. Bonaventure. Will, then, my salvation, and I shall be saved. But thou savest all who invoke thee; behold, then, I invoke thee, and say:

Ejaculatory Prayer. O salvation of those who invoke thee, save me!

Concluding Prayer

Most holy Immaculate Virgin and my Mother Mary, to thee, who art the Mother of my Lord, and Queen of the world, the advocate, the hope, the refuge of sinners, I have recourse today I, who am the most miserable of all. I render thee my most humble homage, O great Queen, and I thank thee for all the graces thou hast conferred on me until now, particularly for having delivered me from hell, which I have so often deserved. I love thee, O most amiable Lady; and for the love which I bear thee, I promise to serve thee always, and to do all in my power to make others love thee also. I place in thee all my hopes; I confide my salvation to thy care. Accept me for thy servant, and receive me under thy mantle, O Mother of Mercy. And since thou art so powerful with God, deliver me from all temptations, or rather obtain for me the strength to triumph over them until death. Of thee I ask a perfect love of Jesus Christ. From thee I hope to die a good death.

O my Mother, for the love which thou bearest to God, I beseech thee to help me at all times, but especially at the last moment of my life. Leave me not, I beseech thee, until thou see me safe in Heaven, blessing thee, and singing thy mercies for all eternity. Amen. So I hope. So may it be.

Evening Mediation
THE PRACTICE OF THE LOVE OF JESUS CHRIST
XXVIII.-HE THAT LOVES JESUS CHRIST SEEKS TO DETACH HIMSELF FROM EVERY CREATURE

I.

When the heart is detached from creatures, Divine love immediately enters and fills it. Moreover, St. Teresa said: "As soon as the evil occasions are removed, the heart forthwith turns herself to love God." Yes, for the human heart cannot exist without loving; it must either love the Creator or creatures: if it does not love creatures, then assuredly it will love God. In short, we must leave all to gain all. "All for all," says Thomas a Kempis. As long as St. Teresa cherished a certain affection, though pure, towards one of her relations, she did not wholly belong to God; but when afterwards she summoned courage, and resolutely cut off the attachment, then she deserved to hear these words from Jesus: "Now, Teresa, thou art all Mine, and I am all thine." One heart is quite too small to love this God, so loving and so lovely, and Who merits an infinite love; and shall we then think of dividing this one little heart of ours between creatures and God? The Venerable Lewis da Ponte felt ashamed to speak thus to God: "O Lord, I love Thee above all things, above riches, above honors, friends, relations!" for it seemed to him as much as to say: "O Lord, I love Thee more than dust and smoke and the worms of the earth!"

II.

The Prophet Jeremias says that the Lord is all goodness towards him who seeks Him: The Lord is good to the soul that seeks him– (Lamentations iii. 25). But he understands it of a soul that seeks God alone! O blessed loss! O blessed gain! To lose worldly goods, which cannot satisfy the heart and are soon gone, in order to gain the sovereign and eternal Good, which is God! It is related that a pious hermit, one day while a king was hunting through the woods, began to run to and fro as if in search of something. The king, observing him thus occupied, inquired of him who he was and what he was doing; the hermit replied: "And may I ask your majesty what you are engaged about in this desert?" The king made answer: "I am going in pursuit of game." And the hermit replied: "I, too, am going in pursuit of God." With these words he went his way. During the present life this must likewise be our only thought, our only purpose, to go in search of God to love Him, and in search of His will to fulfil it, ridding our heart of all love of creatures. And whenever some worldly good presents itself to our imaginations to solicit our affection, let us be ready with this answer: "I have despised the kingdom of this world, and all the charms of this life for the sake of the love of my Lord Jesus Christ." And what else are all the dignities and grandeurs of this world but smoke, filth, and vanity, which all disappear at death? Blessed he who can say: "My Jesus, I have left all for Thy love; Thou art my only Love; Thou alone art sufficient for me."

Friday – Second Week After Pentecost

Feast of the Sacred Heart of Jesus

Morning Meditation

THE FAITHFUL HEART OF JESUS

The faithfulness of the Heart of Jesus gives us confidence to hope for all things although we deserve nothing. God is faithful, says St. Paul. Oh, how faithful is the beautiful Heart of Jesus towards those He calls to His love!

I.

Oh, how faithful is the beautiful Heart of Jesus: towards those He calls to His love: He is faithful who hath called you, who also will perform– (1 Thessalonians v. 24). The faithfulness of God gives us confidence to hope all things, although we deserve nothing. If we have driven God from our heart, let us open the door to Him and He will immediately enter, according to the promise He has made: If anyone open to me the door, I will come into him, and will sup with him-(Apocalypse iii. 20). If we wish for graces, let us ask for them of God, in the Name of Jesus Christ, and He has promised us that we shall obtain them: If you shall ask the Father anything in my name, He will give it you- (John xvi. 23). If We are tempted, let us trust in His merits, and He will not permit our enemies to strive with us beyond our strength: God is faithful, who will not suffer you to be tempted above that which you are able-(1 Corinthians x. 13). Oh, how much better is it to have to do with God than with men! How often do men promise and then fail, either because they tell lies in making their promises, or because, after having made the promise, they change their minds: "God is not as man," says the Holy Spirit, "that he should lie; or as the son of man, that he should be changed" (Numbers xxiii. 19).

I know my ingratitude, O my Jesus, and I abhor it. I know that Thou art infinite Goodness, Who deserves an infinite love, especially from me, whom Thou hast so much loved, even after all the offences I have committed against Thee. Unhappy me if I should damn myself; the graces Thou hast vouchsafed to me, and the proofs of the singular affection which Thou hast shown me, would be, O God, the hell of hells to me. Ah, no, my Love, have pity on me; suffer me not to forsake Thee again, and then by damning myself, as I should deserve, continue to repay in hell with injuries and hatred the love that Thou hast borne me. O loving and faithful Heart of Jesus, inflame, I beseech Thee, my miserable heart, so that it may burn with love for Thee, as Thine does. for me. My Jesus, it seems to me that now I love Thee, but I love Thee but little. Make me love Thee exceedingly and remain faithful to Thee until death. I ask of Thee this grace, together with that of always praying to Thee for it. Grant that I may die rather than ever betray Thee again. O Mary, my Mother, help me to be faithful to thy Son.

II.

God cannot be unfaithful to His promises, because, being Truth itself, He cannot lie; nor can He change His mind, because all that He wills is just and right. He has promised to receive all that come to Him, to give help to him that asks it, to love him that loves Him; and shall He, then, not do it? Hath he said, then, and will he not do it? Oh, that we were as faithful with God as He is with us! Oh, how often have we, in times past, promised Him to be His, to serve Him and to love Him, and then have betrayed Him, and, renouncing His service, have sold ourselves as slaves to the devil! Oh, let us beseech Him to give us strength to be faithful to Him for the future! Oh, how blessed shall we be if we are faithful to Jesus Christ in the few things that He commands us to do; He will, indeed, be faithful in remunerating us with infinitely great rewards; and He will declare to us what He has promised to His faithful servants: Well done, good and faithful servant; because thou hast been faithful over a few things, I will place thee over many things; enter thou into the joy of thy Lord-(Matthew xxv. 21).

Oh, that I had been as faithful towards Thee, my dearest Redeemer, as Thou hast been faithful to me. Whenever I have opened my heart to Thee, Thou hast entered in, to forgive me and to receive me into Thy favor; whenever I have called Thee, Thou hast hastened to my assistance. Thou hast been faithful with me, but I have been exceedingly unfaithful towards Thee. I have promised Thee my love, and then have many times refused it to Thee; as if Thou, my God, Who hast created and redeemed me, wert less worthy of being loved than Thy creatures and those miserable pleasures for which I have forsaken Thee. Forgive me, O my Jesus.

Spiritual Reading

CORAM SANCTISSIMO

SIXTEENTH VISIT

Had men but always recourse to the Most Blessed Sacrament to seek from it the remedy of their ills, they certainly would not be as miserable as they are. The Prophet Jeremias, lamenting, exclaimed: Is there no balm in Galaad, or is there no physician there? - (Jeremiah viii. 22). Galaad, a mountain of Arabia, rich in aromatical spices, according to the Venerable Bede, is a figure of Jesus Christ, Who, in this Sacrament, keeps in readiness all the remedies of our woes. Why, then, our Redeemer seems to ask, do you complain of your misfortunes, O ye sons of Adam, when you have the physician and the remedy for them all in this Sacrament? Come to me, and I will refresh you - (Matthew xi. 28). I will, then, address Thee, O Lord, in the words of the sisters of Lazarus: Behold, he whom thou lovest is sick- (John xi. 3). Lord, I am that miserable creature whom Thou lovest; my soul is all wounded by the sins I have committed; my divine Physician, I come to Thee that Thou mayest heal me; if Thou wilt, Thou canst cure me; Heal my soul, for I have sinned against thee. Draw me wholly to Thyself, my most sweet Jesus, by the all-winning attractions of Thy love. Far rather would I be bound to Thee than become the lord of the whole earth. I desire nothing else in the world but to love Thee. I have but little to give Thee; but could I gain possession of all the kingdoms of the world, I would do so, that I might renounce them all for Thy love. For Thee, then, I renounce what I can; I give up all relatives, all comforts, all pleasures, and even spiritual consolations; for Thee I renounce my liberty and my will. On Thee I desire to bestow all my love. I love Thee, infinite Goodness; I love Thee more than myself, and I hope to love Thee for all eternity.

Ejaculatory Prayer. My Jesus, I give myself to Thee; do Thou accept me!

AN ACT OF SPIRITUAL COMMUNION

My Jesus, I believe that Thou art truly present in the Most Holy Sacrament. I love Thee above all things, and I desire to possess Thee within my soul. Since I am unable now to receive Thee sacramentally, come at least spiritually into my heart. I embrace Thee as already there and unite myself wholly to Thee; never permit me to be separated from Thee.

VISIT TO MARY

My Lady, thou didst say to St. Bridget: "However much a man sins, if he returns to me with a real purpose of amendment, I am instantly ready to welcome him; neither do I pay attention to the greatness of his sins, but to the intention alone with which he comes. I do not disdain to anoint and heal his wounds; for I am called, and truly am, the Mother of Mercy." Since, then, thou hast both the power and the will to heal me, behold I have recourse to thee, O heavenly physician; heal the many wounds of my soul; with a single word addressed by thee to thy Son I shall be restored.

Ejaculatory Prayer. O Mary, have pity on me!

Concluding Prayer

Most holy Immaculate Virgin and my Mother Mary, to thee, who art the Mother of my Lord, and Queen of the world, the advocate, the hope, the refuge of sinners, I have recourse today I, who am the most miserable of all. I render thee my most humble homage, O great Queen, and I thank thee for all the graces thou hast conferred on me until now, particularly for having delivered me from hell, which I have so often deserved. I love thee, O most amiable Lady; and for the love which I bear thee, I promise to serve thee always, and to do all in my power to make others love thee also. I place in thee all my hopes; I confide my salvation to thy care. Accept me for thy servant, and receive me under thy mantle, O Mother of Mercy. And since thou art so powerful with God, deliver me from all temptations, or rather obtain for me the strength to triumph over them until death. Of thee I ask a perfect love of Jesus Christ. From thee I hope to die a good death.

O my Mother, for the love which thou bearest to God, I beseech thee to help me at all times, but especially at the last moment of my life. Leave me not, I beseech thee, until thou see me safe in Heaven, blessing thee, and singing thy mercies for all eternity. Amen. So I hope. So may it be.

Evening Meditation

THE PRACTICE OF THE LOVE OF JESUS CHRIST

XXIX.-HE THAT LOVES JESUS CHRIST SEEKS TO DETACH HIMSELF FROM EVERY CREATURE

I.

When once the love of God takes full possession of a soul, she of her own accord (supposing always, of course, the assistance of Divine grace) strives to divest herself of everything that could prove a hindrance to her belonging wholly to God. St Francis de Sales remarks that when a house catches fire all the furniture is thrown out of the window;

meaning thereby, that when a person gives himself entirely to God, he needs no persuasion of preachers or confessors, but of his own accord seeks to get rid of every earthly affection. Father Segneri the Younger called Divine love a robber, which happily despoils us of all, that we may come into the possession of God alone. A certain man, of respectable position in life, having renounced everything to become poor for the love of Jesus Christ was questioned by a friend how he fell into such a state of poverty; he took from his pocket a small volume of the Gospels, and said: "Behold, this is what has stripped me of all." The Holy Spirit says: If a man shall give all the substance of his house for love, he shall despise it as nothing - (Canticles viii. 7). And when a soul fixes her whole love in God, she despises all, wealth, pleasures, dignities, territories, kingdoms, and all her longing is after God alone; she says again and again: "My God. I wish for Thee only, and nothing more." St. Francis de Sales writes: "The pure love of God consumes everything which is not God, to convert all into itself; for whatever we do for the love of God is love."

II.

The Sacred Spouse said: He brought me into the cellar of wine, he set in order charity in me- (Canticles ii. 4). This cellar of wine, writes St. Teresa, is Divine love, which, on taking possession of a soul, so perfectly inebriates it, as to make it forgetful of everything created. A person intoxicated is as it were dead in his senses; he neither sees, nor hears, nor speaks: and so it happens to the soul inebriated with Divine love. She has no longer any sense of the things of the world; she wishes to think only of God, to speak only of God; she recognizes no other motive in all her actions but to love and to please God. In the Sacred Canticles the Lord forbids them to awake His beloved, who sleeps: Stir not up, nor make the beloved to awake, till she please (Canticles ii. 7). This blessed sleep, enjoyed by souls espoused to Jesus Christ, says St. Basil, is nothing else than "the utter oblivion of all things," a virtuous and voluntary forgetfulness of every created thing, to be occupied solely with God, and to able to exclaim with St. Francis: "Deus meus et omnia-My God and my All!" My God, what are riches, and dignities, and the goods of this world, compared with Thee! Thou art my All, and my every Good. "My God and my All!" Thomas a Kempis writes: "Oh, sweet word! It speaks enough for him who understands it; and to him who loves, it is most delicious to repeat again and again: My God and my All! My God and my All!"

Saturday – Second Week after Pentecost

MARY IS OUR MOTHER OF PERPETUAL SUCCOUR

Morning Meditation

St. Paul wrote of our Lord Jesus Christ: For in that he himself hath suffered and been tempted he is able to succor them also that are tempted- (Hebrews ii. 18). So, too, had the Mother of Jesus to be tried with many and terrible sufferings in order that, as St. Alphonsus says, she might be in all things like to her Son, and be able to succor and console the miserable.

I.

The Blessed Mother of God well deserves the glorious and beautiful title of Perpetual Succor. She has earned this title because of her great sufferings for our sake. "In all things like to her Divine Son is His Mother Mary; and as she is the Mother of Mercy, she rejoices when she succors and consoles the miserable." - (St. Alphonsus). But here she could rejoice as the Consoler and Perpetual Succor of men, she had, like her Divine Son, to be tried, to be tempted, and to suffer. St. Paul wrote of Our Lord Jesus Christ: For in that he himself hath suffered and been tempted he is able to succor them also that are tempted. To win for Himself the glorious Name of Jesus, and to succor and save mankind, our Divine Lord underwent great sufferings, even to the shedding of the last drop of His precious Blood. So, too, had the Divine Mother to be tried with many and terrible sufferings in order to share with her Son in the work of the Redemption of the human race, and win for herself the glorious name and title of the world's Perpetual Succor.

The Divine Mother suffered in her Child. It is in the sufferings of the child every true and loving mother suffers most keenly. Mary knew the Scriptures well, and from her earliest days of childhood in the Temple kept pondering them in her heart, especially all that concerned the coming of the Redeemer, His life and death. She knew better than Prophet and Priest what the Messias would have to do and to suffer that He might enter into His glory, and so from the hour the Archangel saluted her: Hail, full of grace! and she was overshadowed by Holy Ghost and the Word was made Flesh in her womb, sorrows, too, overshadowed her, and filled her with the saddest forebodings. The Angel of her joys soon became the messenger of woe to carry the awful vision of the Cross and Nails before the eyes of Child and Mother from the manger of Bethlehem to the Hill of Calvary.

O my afflicted Mother, thou didst weep bitterly over thy Son Who died for my salvation; but what will thy tears avail me if I am lost? By thy merits, then, obtain for me true contrition for my sins and a real amendment of life. If Jesus and thou, being so innocent, have suffered so much for love of me, obtain that at least I may suffer something for your love. "O Lady," I will say with St. Bonaventure, "if I have offended thee, in justice wound my heart: if I have served thee I ask for wounds as my reward. It is shameful to see my Lord wounded, and thee wounded, and myself without a wound! Ah, cease not, O Advocate of sinners, to assist my soul in the midst of the combat. I invoke thy Son and thee to succor me in life and in death. O Jesus and Mary, to you I recommend my soul."

II.

How plainly and eloquently does the Picture of the Mother of Perpetual Succor tell of the Mother's sufferings in her Child. There we see only one sufferer as it were, so united and identified are both in their sorrows. The horrid visions that afflict His eyes afflict her soul, and every quiver of pain in the limbs of the Divine Lamb in her arms makes her heart tremble and agonize. The loving St. Alphonsus says: "From the beginning of His life Jesus had always before His eyes the sad vision of all the torments He would have to endure before He left this earth, as He predicted by the mouth of the Prophet: My sorrow is continually before me- (Psalm xxxvii. 18). So, then, my Redeemer, throughout Thy life, I shall find Thee nowhere but on the Cross! Even while sleeping, says Bellarmine, the vision of the Cross was present to the Heart of Jesus. "Christ had His Cross always before His eyes. When He slept, His Heart watched; nor was it ever free from the vision of the Cross."

So likewise had the Divine Mother to endure her perpetual agony that in all things, she, the Co-Redemptrix of the world, might be like to her Divine Son, the Redeemer. Mary revealed to St. Bridget that when she suckled her Child she thought of the vinegar and gall; when swathing Him, she thought of the cords with which He was to be bound; when bearing Him in her arms, of the Cross to which He would be nailed; when He was sleeping, of His Death. As often as she put on Him His garments, she reflected how they would be torn from His bleeding body one day; and when she beheld His feet and hands, she thought of the nails that would one day pierce them, and then, as Mary said to St. Bridget, "my eyes filled with tears and my heart was tortured with grief." Thus truly had Mary to suffer and to be tempted. like her Divine Son, so as to be able to succor them also that are tempted, and to merit the glorious title of the world's Perpetual Succor. Mary is now all-powerful in Heaven, ever acting as our Advocate and interceding for us, says Blessed Amadeus, with her most powerful prayers, for she well sees our miseries and our dangers, and, as our most clement and sweet Lady, compassionates and succors us with a Mother's love.

O Mother of Perpetual Succor, grant that I may always invoke thy most powerful name, for thy name is help in life, salvation in death. I thank the Lord for having given thee for my good this name so sweet, so amiable, and so powerful. But merely pronouncing thy name is not enough for me. I wish to do so out of love. I wish that love may remind me to call thee always Mother of Perpetual Succor.

Spiritual Reading

CORAM SANCTISSIMO

SEVENTEENTH VISIT

Loving souls can find no greater delight than to be in the company of those whom they love. If we, then, love Jesus Christ much, behold we are now in His presence. Jesus in the Blessed Sacrament sees us and hears us: shall we, then, say nothing to Him? Let us console ourselves in His company; let us rejoice in His glory, and in the love which so many enamored souls bear Him in the Most Holy Sacrament. Let us desire that all should love Jesus in the Holy Sacrament and consecrate their hearts to Him; at least let us consecrate all our affections to Him. He should be all our love and our whole desire. Father Salesius, of the Society of Jesus, felt consolation in only speaking of the Most Blessed Sacrament; he could never visit It enough. When called to the parlor, or on returning to his room, or going about the house, he always profited by these occasions to repeat his visits to his beloved Lord; so much so, that it was remarked that scarcely an hour of the day passed without his visiting Him. At length he obtained the favor of dying by the hands of heretics while defending the truth of the Real Presence in the Blessed Sacrament.

Oh, had I but the happiness to die for so noble a cause as the defense of this Sacrament, in which, O most amiable Jesus, Thou hast taught us the tenderness of the love which Thou bearest us! But since, my Lord, Thou workest so many miracles in this Sacrament, work this one also; draw my entire self to Thee. Thou indeed desires that I should be all Thine, and Thou dost also, indeed, deserve that I should be so. Give me the strength to love Thee with all the affection of my soul. Give the goods of this world to whomsoever Thou willest. I renounce them all. I sigh after and desire Thy love alone; this alone do I now and will always seek. I love Thee, my Jesus; grant me the grace always to love Thee and grant me this alone.

Ejaculatory Prayer. My Jesus, when shall I really love Thee?

AN ACT OF SPIRITUAL COMMUNION

My Jesus, I believe that Thou art truly present in the Most Holy Sacrament. I love Thee above all things, and I desire to possess Thee within my soul. Since I am unable now to receive Thee sacramentally, come at least spiritually into my heart. I embrace Thee as already there and unite myself wholly to Thee; never permit me to be separated from Thee.

VISIT TO MARY

My most sweet Queen, how pleasing to me is that beautiful name by which thy devout clients address thee: "Mater amabilis, Most Amiable Mother!" Yes, my Lady, thou art truly and indeed amiable. Thy beauty has captivated thy Lord Himself: And the king shall greatly desire thy beauty- (Psalm xliv. 12). St. Bernard says that thy very name is so amiable to thy lovers that when they pronounce it, or hear it, they are inflamed with a fresh desire to love thee: "O sweet, O pious, O exceedingly amiable Mary! Thou canst not be named without inflaming, neither can thy name be heard without enkindling the affections of those who love thee." It is, then, reasonable, my most amiable Mother, that I should love thee. But I am not satisfied with only loving thee; I desire in the first place on earth, and then in Heaven, to be, after God, thy greatest lover. If my desire is presumptuous, it is thou thyself who art to blame, on account of thy amiability and the special love which thou hast shown me. If thou wert less amiable, my desire to love thee would be less. Accept, then, O Lady, this my desire, and in token thou hast accepted it, do thou obtain for me from God this love for which I ask thee, since He is so well pleased with the love which is borne thee.

Ejaculatory Prayer. My most amiable Mother, I love thee much!

Concluding Prayer

Most holy Immaculate Virgin and my Mother Mary, to thee, who art the Mother of my Lord, and Queen of the world, the advocate, the hope, the refuge of sinners, I have recourse today I, who am the most miserable of all. I render thee my most humble homage, O great Queen, and I thank thee for all the graces thou hast conferred on me until now, particularly for having delivered me from hell, which I have so often deserved. I love thee, O most amiable Lady; and for the love which I bear thee, I promise to serve thee always, and to do all in my power to make others love thee also. I place in thee all my hopes; I confide my salvation to thy care. Accept me for thy servant, and receive me under thy mantle, O Mother of Mercy. And since thou art so powerful with God, deliver me from all temptations, or rather obtain for me the strength to triumph over them until death. Of thee I ask a perfect love of Jesus Christ. From thee I hope to die a good death.

O my Mother, for the love which thou bearest to God, I beseech thee to help me at all times, but especially at the last moment of my life. Leave me not, I beseech thee, until thou see me safe in Heaven, blessing thee, and singing thy mercies for all eternity. Amen. So I hope. So may it be.

Evening Meditation

THE PRACTICE OF THE LOVE OF JESUS CHRIST

XXX.-HE THAT LOVES JESUS CHRIST SEEKS TO DETACH HIMSELF FROM EVERY CREATURE

I.

To arrive at a perfect union with God, a total detachment from creatures is of absolute necessity. And to come to particulars, we must divest ourselves of all inordinate affection towards relations. Jesus Christ said: If any man come to me, and hate not his father and mother, and wife and children, and brethren and sisters, yea and his own life also, he cannot be my disciple -(Luke xiv. 26). And wherefore this hatred to relations? Because, generally, as regards the interests of the soul, we cannot have greater enemies than our own kindred: And a man's enemies shall be those of his own household-(Matthew x. 36). St. Charles Borromeo declared that he never went to pay a visit to his own family without returning cooled in fervor. And when Father Antony Mendoza was asked why he refused to enter the house of his parents, he replied, "Because I know, by experience, that nowhere is the devotion of a Religious so dissipated as in the house of his parents."

When, moreover, the choice of a state of life is concerned, it is certain that we are not obliged to obey our parents, according to the doctrine of St. Thomas Aquinas. Should a young man be called to the Religious life, and find opposition from his parents, he is bound to obey God, and not his parents, who, as the same St. Thomas says, with a view to their own interests and private ends, stand in the way of our spiritual welfare. "Friends of flesh and blood are oftentimes opposed to our spiritual profit." And they are content, says St. Bernard, to have their children go to eternal perdition rather than that they should leave home.

II.

It is surprising, in this matter, to see some fathers and mothers, even though God-fearing, yet so blinded by mistaken fondness, that they use every effort and exhaust every means to hinder the vocation of a child who wishes to become a Religious. This conduct, however (except in very rare cases), cannot be excused from grievous sin. But someone may say: What, then, and if such a youth does not become a Religious can he not be saved? Are, then, all who remain in the world cast away? I answer: Those whom God does not call into Religion may be saved in the world by fulfilling the duties of their state; but those who are called from the world and do not obey God may, indeed, possibly be saved; but they will be saved with difficulty, because they will be deprived of those helps which God had destined for them in Religion, and for want of which they will not accomplish their salvation. The theologian Habert writes that he who disobeys his vocation remains in the Church like a member out of joint, and cannot discharge his duty without the greatest pain; and so will hardly effect his salvation. Whence he draws this conclusion: "Although, absolutely speaking, he can be saved, yet he will enter on the way, and employ the means of salvation, with difficulty."

The choice of a state of life is compared by Father Lewis of Granada to "the main-spring" of a watch: if the main-spring be broken, the whole watch is out of order; and the same holds good with regard to our salvation, if the state of life be out of order, the whole life is out of order too. Alas, how many poor youths have lost their vocation through their parents, and have afterwards come to a bad end, and have themselves proved the ruin of their family!

THIRD SUNDAY AFTER PENTECOST

(THE FEAST OF THE MOTHER OF PERPETUAL SUCCOR)

Morning Meditation
FEAST OF THE MOTHER OF PERPETUAL SUCCOUR
(The Feast of the Mother of Perpetual Succor is celebrated on the Sunday before the Feast of St. John the Baptist)

The Blessed Virgin Mary has earned the beautiful and glorious title of Perpetual Succor, not only by her valiant deeds, but also by her great sufferings. Truly Mary was that valiant woman who put forth her hands to strong things, even to be the helper, the consoler, the Perpetual Succor of the Man-God Himself. To her the divine Child ever turned for sympathy, succor, and a sweet refuge, and never did He do so in vain. Surely, she who was able to help and succor and comfort the Omnipotent God Himself when He became weak for our sakes, will be able to comfort and succor His poor creatures.

I.

Truly Mary, God's great Mother, performed valiant deeds. She was the valiant woman who put forth her hands to strong things to help even Him Who made the world, to assist Him Who sustains all creation, to succor and console Him Who was the joy of Heaven and earth, and to save Him Who was the world's Savior-this was holy Mary's work, these were her valiant deeds to which she put forth her hands, and therefore it was she received from the Lord the fruit of her glorious deeds, and became for man what she had been for God Himself, a helper, a consoler, a Mother of Perpetual Succor. The Sacred Picture itself speaks better than words. In that awful representation of suffering and sorrow the Mother's breast is the Child's perpetual succor, for there we see He clings, clasping her hand with His trembling fingers, and finding comfort and succor in her sheltering arms. She clasps Him to her bosom, kisses away the tears, hushes Him to sleep in her arms to drown if possible, by sweet lullabies, the horrid sounds and sights of His Passion that in vision haunt and scare Him. It was to her, and to her alone, He ever and always turned for succor and sweet refuge, and never did He turn in vain. Thus, we may well say, did God place in Mary's keeping Him in Whom were all human infirmities, that Child of Sorrows, so that she might learn from experience how to compassionate and succor poor humanity in us. And when she had proved her fitness, her skill, her tenderness in succoring and comforting the suffering Head, she was left to the suffering members of His mystical Body, to be to us what she had ever been to Him, a most sweet Comforter, a Mother of Perpetual Succor.

II.

Consider what conditions are required in us that Mary may be our Mother of Perpetual Succor. We must be her children that she may be our Mother. An enemy or a stranger will not dare to claim or hope to expect what is bestowed only on faithful, loving children -a mother's affection, tender care and succor. As Mary's true and faithful children, we should love her very much, and above all we should sympathize with her, remembering the bitter sorrows she had to undergo to become our Perpetual Succor. The very rocks of Calvary were rent asunder and melted to pity for Mother and Son. But it was our sins inflicted all those wounds and sorrows. For the sins of my people have I struck him- (Isaiah liii. 8). "Each one of our sins," says St. Alphonsus, "afflicted the soul of Jesus Christ more than Crucifixion and Death afflicted His body." What, then, asks the Saint, must have been the sufferings of Jesus, as yet in His Mother's arms, when He saw before Him the immense array of all the crimes of men for which He was to make satisfaction! As by our sins we had part in inflicting life-long sorrow on the Mother of the Savior, we should offer her life-long sympathy and pity.

We should have a child's confidence in our heavenly Mother, such indeed as her Child Jesus Himself had. As represented in the holy Picture, what childlike trust does Jesus repose in His holy Mother! In all His wants, and in the midst of the sorrows that were continually before Him, the Child Jesus ever turned to His Mother for comfort and succor. With the arms of His Mother guarding Him, and resting on her bosom, the weak and helpless Child becomes strong and valiant, and turning resolutely gazes on the awful vision of the instruments of His Crucifixion and Death, exclaiming with the Prophet: I am prepared for scourges.

All Mary's children should have the same unfailing, childlike trust in her power. However weak we may be of ourselves, we shall be made strong and resolute against the attacks of hell; patient, generous, and victorious in the midst of temptations and sufferings, provided only we fail not in our confidence in our Mother of Perpetual Succor. "She well understands our miseries and dangers," says St. Alphonsus, "and this most clement and sweet Lady, compassionates and succors us with a Mother's love."

Let us, then, have perpetual recourse to Mary to make sure of her Perpetual Succor. Constant recourse to Mary is a pledge of eternal salvation, but yet, alas! too often in past times have we fallen because we had not recourse to her. Sinners though we are, let us turn to Mary in spite of our unworthiness. "O sinner," says St. Alphonsus, "whoever you are, do not despair, but have recourse to this Lady with the assurance of being succored," for, he says, "she is all eyes to pity and succor us in our necessities."

Behold, then, I have recourse to thee, most holy Mary. I have lost my Father, but thou art my Mother who must enable me to find Him. In this my so great misfortune I call thee to my aid: do thou succor me. And this is the grace I now ask of thee, and I conjure thee as far as I know how and can to obtain it for me-namely, in the assaults of hell always to have recourse to thee and to say to thee: O Mary, help me! Mother of Perpetual Succor, suffer me not to lose my God! Amen.

Spiritual Reading

CORAM SANCTISSIMO

EIGHTEENTH VISIT

One day Jesus will be seated on a throne of majesty in the Valley of Josaphat; but now, in the Most Blessed Sacrament, He is seated on a throne of love. Did a king, to show his love for a poor shepherd, go and live in his village, how great would be the ingratitude of this peasant did he not go often to visit him, knowing the king's wish to see him, and that for this purpose he had come to reside there!

Ah, my Jesus, for love of me Thou dwellest in the Sacrament of the Altar. Could I, then, do so, my desire would be to remain night and day in Thy presence. If the Angels, O my Lord, filled with astonishment at the love Thou bearest us, remain always around Thee, it is but reasonable that I, seeing Thee for my sake on this altar, should endeavor to please Thee, at least by remaining in Thy presence to praise the love and goodness Thou hast for me: I will sing praise to thee in the sight of the angels; I will worship towards thy holy temple, and I will give glory to thy name; for thy mercy and for thy truth- (Psalm cxxxvii. 1, 2).

O God, present in this Most Holy Sacrament, O Bread of Angels, O heavenly Food, I love Thee, but Thou art not, neither am I, satisfied with my love. I love Thee; but I love Thee too little. Do Thou, my Jesus, make known to me the beauty, the immense goodness which I love; make my heart banish from itself all earthly affections, and give place to Thy divine love. To fill me with Thy love, and to unite Thyself all to me, Thou descends every day from Heaven on our altars; it is, then, but just that I should think of nothing else but of loving, adoring, and pleasing Thee. I love Thee with my whole soul, I love Thee with all my affections. If Thou be graciously pleased to make me a return for this love, increase my love, render its flames more ardent; that thus I may always love Thee more, and desire more and more to please Thee.

Ejaculatory Prayer. Jesus, my Love, give me love!

AN ACT OF SPIRITUAL COMMUNION

My Jesus, I believe that Thou art truly present in the Most Holy Sacrament. I love Thee above all things, and I desire to possess Thee within my soul. Since I am unable now to receive Thee sacramentally, come at least spiritually into my heart. I embrace Thee as already there and unite myself wholly to Thee; never permit me to be separated from Thee.

VISIT TO MARY

As poor sick persons, who on account of their miseries are abandoned by all, find shelter in the public hospitals, so also the most miserable sinners, although discarded by all, find protection in the mercy of Mary, by whom they are never rejected; for God has placed her in the world as a receptacle and, as St. Basil says, a public hospital for sinners. Hence St. Ephrem also calls her "the asylum of sinners." Therefore, my Queen, if I have recourse to thee, thou canst not reject me on account of my sins; nay, even the more wretched I am, the greater is the claim which I have upon thy protection, since God has created thee as the refuge of the most miserable. Therefore, to thee I have recourse, O Mary; I place myself under thy mantle. Thou art the refuge of sinners; thou art, then, my refuge, the hope of my salvation. If thou reject me, to whom shall I have recourse?

Ejaculatory Prayer. Mary, my refuge, save me!

Concluding Prayer

Most holy Immaculate Virgin and my Mother Mary, to thee, who art the Mother of my Lord, and Queen of the world, the advocate, the hope, the refuge of sinners, I have recourse today I, who am the most miserable of all. I render thee my most humble homage, O great Queen, and I thank thee for all the graces thou hast conferred on me until now,

particularly for having delivered me from hell, which I have so often deserved. I love thee, O most amiable Lady; and for the love which I bear thee, I promise to serve thee always, and to do all in my power to make others love thee also. I place in thee all my hopes; I confide my salvation to thy care. Accept me for thy servant, and receive me under thy mantle, O Mother of Mercy. And since thou art so powerful with God, deliver me from all temptations, or rather obtain for me the strength to triumph over them until death. Of thee I ask a perfect love of Jesus Christ. From thee I hope to die a good death.

O my Mother, for the love which thou bearest to God, I beseech thee to help me at all times, but especially at the last moment of my life. Leave me not, I beseech thee, until thou see me safe in Heaven, blessing thee, and singing thy mercies for all eternity. Amen. So I hope. So may it be.

Evening Meditation
THE PRACTICE OF THE LOVE OF JESUS CHRIST
XXXI.-HE THAT LOVES JESUS CHRIST SEEKS TO DETACH HIMSELF FROM EVERY CREATURE

I.

Anyone who would belong wholly to God must be free of all human respect. Oh, how many souls does this accursed respect keep far from God, and even separate them from Him forever! For instance, if they hear mention made of some or other of their failings, oh, what do they not do to justify themselves, and to convince the world that it is a calumny! If they perform some good work, how industrious are they to circulate it everywhere! They would have it known to the whole world in order to be universally applauded. The Saints behave in a very different way; they would rather publish their defects to the whole world, in order to pass in the eyes of all for the miserable creatures which they really are in their own eyes; and, on the contrary, in practicing any acts of virtue, they prefer to have God alone know of it; for their only care is to be acceptable to Him. It is on this account that so many of them were enchanted with solitude, mindful, as they were, of the words of Jesus Christ: But when thou dost alms, let not thy left hand know what thy right hand doth- (Matthew vi. 3-5). And again: But thou, when thou shalt pray, enter into thy chamber; and having shut the door, pray to thy Father in secret- (Matthew v. 6). But of all things, self-detachment is most needful; that is, detachment from self-will. Only once succeed in subduing yourself, and you will easily triumph in every other combat. "Vince teipsum -Conquer thyself," was the maxim which St. Francis Xavier inculcated on all. And Jesus Christ said: If anyone will come after me, let him deny himself - (Matthew xvi.

24). Behold in a few words all that we need practice to become saints; to deny ourselves, and not to follow our own will: Go not after thy lusts, but turn away from thy own will- (Ecclesiasticus xviii. 30). And this is the greatest grace, said St. Francis of Assisi, that we can receive from God: the power, namely, to conquer ourselves by denying self-will.

II.

St. Bernard writes that if all men would resist self-will, none would ever be damned: "Let self-will cease, and there will be no hell." The same Saint writes that it is the baneful effect of self-will to contaminate even our good works: "Self-will is a great evil, since it renders thy good works no longer good." As, for instance, were a penitent obstinately bent on mortifying himself, or on fasting, or on taking the discipline against the will of his director, we see that this act of penance, done at the instigation of self-will, becomes very defective. Unhappy the man that lives the slave of self-will, for he shall have a yearning for many things and shall not possess them; while, on the other hand, he will be forced to undergo many things distasteful and bitter to his inclinations: From whence are wars and contentions among you? Are they not hence, from your concupiscences which war in your members? You covet and have not- (James iv. 1, 2). The first war springs from the appetite for sensual delights. Let us take away the occasion; let us mortify the eyes; let us recommend ourselves to God, and the war will be over. The second war arises from the covetousness of riches: let us cultivate a love of poverty, and this war will cease. The third war has its source in ambitiously seeking after honors: let us love humility and the hidden life, and this war, too, will be no more. The fourth war, and the most ruinous of all, comes from self-will. Let us practice resignation in all that happens to us, and the war will cease. St. Bernard tells us that whenever we see a person troubled, the origin of his trouble is nothing else than his inability to gratify self-will. "Whence comes disquiet," says the Saint," except that we follow self-will?" Our Blessed Lord once complained of this to St. Mary Magdalen de Pazzi, in these words: "Certain souls desire My Spirit, but after their own fancy; and so they become incapable of receiving it."

MONDAY – THIRD WEEK AFTER PENTECOST

JUNE 25TH

Morning Meditation
"HE WAS SUBJECT TO THEM."

God created Adam and enriched him with gifts, but ungrateful man offended Him by rebelling, and thus both he and all his posterity remained deprived of divine grace and Paradise. What did the Eternal Father do to save lost man? He sent His own Son to become Man, and to die for man, in order that by His death He might pay man's debts to divine justice and so restore him to divine grace. O God, what a subject of astonishment to the Angels, this great love of God to rebellious man!

I.

God created Adam and enriched him with gifts, but ungrateful man offended Him by rebelling, and thus he and all his posterity were deprived of divine grace and Paradise. Thus, then, all mankind was lost and without a remedy. Man had offended God, and therefore was incapable of giving Him an adequate satisfaction; it was necessary, then, that Divine Person should satisfy for man. What did the Eternal Father do to save lost man? He sent His own Son to become Man and clothe Himself with the same flesh as sinful men, in order that by His death He might pay man's debts to divine Justice, and thus obtain for man a restoration to divine grace.

O my God, if Thy infinite bounty had not discovered this remedy, who of us could ever have asked it or even imagined it?

O God, what a subject of wonder must not this great love which God showed to
rebellious man have been to the Angels! What must they have said when they saw the
Eternal Word become Man, and assume the same flesh as sinful man, insomuch that this
Word Incarnate appeared to the whole world in the form of sinful man, as were all others.
O my Jesus, how much do we not owe Thee, and how much more than others am I not
indebted to Thee, who have offended Thee so much more than others! If Thou hadst not
come to save me, what would have become of me for all eternity? Who could have saved
me from the pains that I deserve? Mayest Thou be ever blessed and praised for so great
love!

II.

But, O God, how few there are who show themselves grateful for so immense a love
by faithfully loving their Redeemer! Alas! the greater part of men, after so incomparable
a benefit, after so many great mercies and so much love, still say to God: Lord, we will not
serve Thee; we choose rather to be the slaves of the devil and condemned to hell than be
Thy servants. Listen to how God upbraids such thankless wretches: Thou hast burst my
bands, and thou saidst: I will not serve- (Jeremiah ii. 20).

What say you? Have you too been one of these? And. tell me, whilst living far from
God and the slave of the devil, have you felt really happy? Have you been at peace? Ah,
no, the divine words can never fail: Because thou didst not serve the Lord thy God with
joy and gladness of heart, thou shalt serve thy enemy in hunger and thirst and nakedness,
and in want of all things- (Deuteronomy xxviii. 47). Since thou hast preferred to serve thy
enemy rather than serve thy God, behold how that tyrant has treated thee. He has made
thee groan as a slave in chains, poor, afflicted, and deprived of every interior consolation.
But come, rise up; God speaks to thee whilst thou mayest still be freed from the fetters
of death which bind thee: Loose the bonds from off thy neck, O captive daughters of
Sion- (Isaiah lii. 2). Make haste while time is left. Unbind thyself, poor soul, who hast
become the voluntary slave of hell; strike off these cursed chains that hold thee fast as a
prey for hell, and bind thyself instead with My chains of gold, chains of love, chains of
peace, chains of salvation: Her bands are a healthful binding- (Ecclesiasticus vi. 31). But
in what manner are souls bound to God? By love: Have charity, which is the bond of
perfection- (Colossians iii. 14). A soul that always walks by the single way of the fear of
punishment, and from this single motive avoids sin, is always in danger of making a relapse
before long into sin; but he that attaches himself to God by love is sure not to lose God
as long as he loves Him.

O my Jesus, Thou hast been pleased to become a Servant for love of me, and in order to release me from the chains of hell; and not only the Servant of Thy Father, but of men and of executioners, even to the laying down of Thy life: and I, for the love of some wretched and poisonous pleasure, have so often forsaken Thy service, and have become the slave of the devil. A thousand times over I curse those moments in which, by a wicked abuse of my free-will, I despised Thy grace, O infinite Majesty! In pity pardon me and bind me to Thyself with those delightful chains of love with which Thou keepest Thy chosen souls in closest union with Thee. I love Thee, O Incarnate Word; I love Thee, O my sovereign Good!

Spiritual Reading

CORAM SANCTISSIMO

NINETEENTH VISIT

It is sweet to everyone to be in the company of a dear friend; and shall we not find it sweet in this valley of tears to remain in the company of the best Friend we have, and Who can do us every kind of good: Who loves us with the most tender affection, and therefore dwell always with us? Behold, in the Most Blessed Sacrament we can converse at pleasure with Jesus, we can open our hearts to Him, we can lay our wants before Him, and we can ask Him for His graces; in a word, in this Sacrament we can treat with the King of Heaven in all confidence and without restraint. Joseph was only too happy when, as the Sacred Scripture tells us, God descended by His grace into His prison to comfort Him: She went down with him into the pit, and in bands she left him not- (Wisdom x. 13). But we are yet more highly favored; for we have always with us in this land of miseries our God made Man, Who by His real presence, is with us all the days of our life, and comforts and helps us with the greatest affection and compassion. What a consolation it is to a poor prisoner to have an affectionate friend, who keeps him company, consoles him, gives him hope, succors him, and thinks of relieving him in his misery! Behold our Good Friend, Jesus Christ, Who in this Sacrament encourages us, saying: Behold, I am with you all days-(Matt. xxviii. 20). Behold Me, He says, I am all thine: I am come from Heaven into thy prison expressly to console thee, to help thee, to deliver thee. Welcome Me, and do so always; cling to Me, and thus thou wilt never feel thy miseries; and afterwards thou wilt, come with Me to My Kingdom, where I shall make thee perfectly happy.

O God, O incomprehensible ocean of love, since Thy condescension towards us is so great, that in order to dwell near us Thou descends upon our altars, I resolve often to visit Thee; I am determined, as often as I possibly can, to enjoy Thy most sweet presence, which is the beatitude of the Saints in Heaven. Oh, could I but always remain in Thy presence, to adore Thee and to make Thee acts of love! Arouse, I beseech Thee, my soul, when through tepidity or worldly affairs it neglects to visit Thee. Enkindle in me a great desire always to remain near Thee in this Sacrament. Ah, my loving Jesus, would that I had always loved Thee! Would that I had always pleased Thee! I console myself that I still have time to do so, not only in the next life, but also in this. I am determined to do so; I am determined to love Thee indeed, my sovereign Good, my Love, my Treasure, my All. I will love Thee with all my strength.

Ejaculatory Prayer. My God, help me to love Thee!

AN ACT OF SPIRITUAL COMMUNION

My Jesus, I believe that Thou art truly present in the Most Holy Sacrament. I love Thee above all things, and I desire to possess Thee within my soul. Since I am unable now to receive Thee sacramentally, come at least spiritually into my heart. I embrace Thee as already there and unite myself wholly to Thee; never permit me to be separated from Thee.

VISIT TO MARY

The devout Bernardine de Bustis says: "O sinner, whoever you may be, despair not; but with confidence have recourse to this Lady; you will find her hands filled with mercies and graces." And know also, that this most compassionate Queen has a greater desire to do you good than you can have to be succored by her. I will ever, O my Lady, thank God for having taught me to know thee. Unfortunate indeed should I be did I not know thee, or did I forget thee; ill would it fare with my salvation. But, my Mother, I bless thee, I love thee and so great is my confidence in thee, that I place my whole soul in thy hands.

Ejaculatory Prayer. O Mary, blessed is he who knows thee, and puts his trust in thee!

Concluding Prayer

Most holy Immaculate Virgin and my Mother Mary, to thee, who art the Mother of my Lord, and Queen of the world, the advocate, the hope, the refuge of sinners, I have recourse today I, who am the most miserable of all. I render thee my most humble homage, O great Queen, and I thank thee for all the graces thou hast conferred on me until now, particularly for having delivered me from hell, which I have so often deserved. I love thee, O most amiable Lady; and for the love which I bear thee, I promise to serve thee always, and to do all in my power to make others love thee also. I place in thee all my hopes; I confide my salvation to thy care. Accept me for thy servant, and receive me under thy mantle, O Mother of Mercy. And since thou art so powerful with God, deliver me from

all temptations, or rather obtain for me the strength to triumph over them until death. Of thee I ask a perfect love of Jesus Christ. From thee I hope to die a good death.

O my Mother, for the love which thou bearest to God, I beseech thee to help me at all times, but especially at the last moment of my life. Leave me not, I beseech thee, until thou see me safe in Heaven, blessing thee, and singing thy mercies for all eternity. Amen. So I hope. So may it be.

Evening Meditation

THE PRACTICE OF THE LOVE OF JESUS CHRIST
XXXII.-HE THAT LOVES JESUS CHRIST SEEKS TO DETACH HIMSELF FROM EVERY CREATURE

I.

We must love God in the way that pleases God, and not that pleases ourselves. God will have us divested of all, to be united to Himself, and to be replenished with His Divine love. St. Teresa writes as follows: "The prayer of union appears to me to be nothing more than to die utterly, as it were, to all things in this world, for the enjoyment of God alone. One thing is certain, that the more completely we empty ourselves of creatures by detaching ourselves from them for the love of God, the more abundantly will He fill us with Himself, and the more closely shall we be united with Him." Many spiritual persons would attain to union with God; but then they accept not the contradictions which God sends them: they fret at having to suffer from ill-health, from poverty, from affronts; but, for want of resignation, they will never come to a perfect union with God. Let us hear what St. Catherine of Genoa says: "To arrive at union with God, the contrarieties which God sends us are absolutely necessary: His purpose is to consume in us, by means of them, all irregular movements, both within and without. And hence all contempt, ailments, poverty, temptations, and other trials, are all indispensable, to give us the opportunity of fighting; that so, by the way of victory, we may eventually extinguish all inordinate movements, so as to be no longer sensible of them; furthermore, until we begin to find contradictions sweet for God's sake, instead of bitter, we shall never arrive at divine union."

O Jesus, my Love, my Hope, my Courage, and my Consolation, give me strength to be faithful to Thee! Grant me light and make known to me from what I ought to detach myself; supply me too with a strong will to obey Thee in all things. O Love of my soul, I offer myself, and deliver myself up entirely, to satisfy the desire Thou hast to unite Thyself with me, that I may be wholly united with Thee, my God and my All. Come, then, my

Jesus; come and take possession of my whole self and occupy all my thoughts and all my affections. I renounce all my desires, all my comforts, and all created things; Thou alone art sufficient for me. Grant me the grace to think only of Thee, to desire only Thee, to seek only Thee, my Beloved and my only Good! O Mary, Mother of God, obtain for me holy perseverance!

II.

I will here subjoin the teaching of St. John of the Cross. The Saint says that to acquire a perfect union, "a thorough mortification of the senses and of the appetites is necessary. On the part of the senses, every single liking that presents itself to them, if it be not purely for the glory of God, should forthwith be rejected for the love of Jesus Christ; for example, should you have a desire to see or hear something in no wise conducive to the greater glory of God, then refrain from it. As to the appetites also, we should endeavor to force ourselves always to choose the worst, the most disagreeable or the poorest without fostering any other wish than to suffer and to be despised." In a word, he that truly loves Jesus Christ loses all affection for things of earth, and seeks to strip himself of all, to keep himself united with Jesus Christ alone. Jesus is the object of all his desires, Jesus the subject of all his thoughts; for Jesus he continually sighs; in every place, at every time, on every occasion, his sole-aim is to give pleasure to Jesus. But to reach this point we must strive unceasingly to rid the heart of every affection which is not for God. And, I ask, what is meant by giving the soul entirely to God? It means, firstly, to shun whatever may be displeasing to God, and to do what is most pleasing to Him; secondly, it means to accept unreservedly all that comes from His hands, how hard or disagreeable soever it may be; it means, thirdly, to give the preference in all things to the will of God over our own: this is what is meant by belonging wholly to God.

Ah, my God and my All! I cannot help feeling that, in spite of all my ingratitude and remissness in Thy service, Thou still invites me to love Thee. Behold me, then, I will resist Thee no longer. I will leave all to be wholly Thine. I will no more live for myself: Thy claims on my love are too strong. My soul is enamored of Thee; my Jesus, it sighs after Thee. And how can I possibly love anything else, after seeing Thee die of suffering on a Cross to save me! How can I behold Thee dead, all worn out with torments, and not love Thee with my whole heart? Yes, I love Thee indeed with all my soul; and I have no other desire but to love Thee in this life and for all eternity.

Tuesday – Third Week After Pentecost

Morning Meditation

I.-HOW TO CONVERSE CONTINUALLY AND FAMILIARLY WITH GOD

Holy Job was struck with wonder when he considered how our God was so devoted to benefiting man and showing the chief concern of His Heart to be to love man and to make Himself beloved by man. What is man that thou shouldst magnify him? Or why dost thou set thy heart upon him? -(Job vii. 17). Surely, then, it would be a great mistake to think that great confidence and familiarity in treating with God is a want of reverence for His Infinite Majesty.

I.

Holy Job was struck with wonder when he considered our God so devoted to benefiting man and showing the chief concern of His Heart to be to love man and to make Himself beloved by man. Speaking to the Lord, Job exclaims, What is man, that thou shouldst magnify him, or why dost thou set thy heart upon him? -(Job vii. 17). Surely, then, it would be a great mistake to think that great confidence and familiarity in treating with God is a want of reverence for His Infinite Majesty. You ought indeed, O devout soul, to revere Him in all humility, and abase yourself before Him; especially when you call to mind the unthankfulness and the outrages whereof, in past times, you have been guilty. Yet this should not hinder you treating Him with the most tender love and all the confidence in your power. He is Infinite Majesty; but at the same time, He is Infinite

Goodness, Infinite Love. In God you possess the Lord most exalted and supreme; but you have also Him Who loves you with the greatest possible love. He disdains not, but delights that you should use towards Him that confidence, that freedom and tenderness, which children use towards their mothers. Hear how He invites us to come to His feet, and the caresses He promises to bestow on us: You shall be carried at the breasts, and upon the knees they shall caress you: as one whom the mother caresseth, so will I comfort you - (Isaiah lxvi. 12). As a mother delights to place her little child upon her knees, and so to feed or to caress him; with like tenderness does our gracious God delight to treat souls whom He loves, who have given themselves wholly to Him, and placed all their hopes in His goodness.

II.

Consider you have no friend or brother, or father or mother, or spouse or lover, who loves you more than your God. Divine grace is that great treasure whereby we vilest of creatures, we servants, become the dear friends of our Creator Himself: For she is an infinite treasure to men, which they that use become the friends of God- (Wisdom vii. 14). For this purpose He increases our confidence; He emptied himself- (Philippians ii. 7), and brought Himself to nought, so to speak; abasing Himself even to becoming Man and conversing familiarly with us: He conversed with men-(Baruch iii. 38). He went so far as to become an Infant; to become poor; even so far as openly to die the death of a malefactor upon the Cross. He went yet farther, even to hide Himself under the appearance of bread, in order to become our constant Companion and unite Himself intimately to us: He that eateth my flesh and drinketh my blood abideth in me, and I in him- (John vi. 57). In a word, He loves you as much as though He had no love but towards yourself alone. For which reason you ought to have no love for any but God alone. Of Him, therefore, you may say, and you ought to say. My beloved to me, and I to him- (Canticles ii. 16). My God has given Himself all to me, and I give myself all to Him; He has chosen me for His beloved, and I choose Him, of all others, for my only Love: My beloved is white and ruddy, chosen out of thousands- (Canticles v. 10).

Say, then, to Him often: "Oh, my Lord, wherefore dost Thou love me thus? What good thing dost Thou see in me? Hast Thou forgotten the injuries I have done Thee? But since Thou hast treated me so lovingly and, instead of casting me into hell, hast granted me so many favors, whom can I desire to love from this day forward but Thee, my God and my All? Ah, most gracious God, if in time past I have offended Thee, it is not so much the punishment I have deserved that now grieves me, as the displeasure I have given Thee,

Who art worthy of infinite love. But Thou knowest not how to despise a heart that repents and humbles itself: A contrite and humble heart, O God, thou wilt not despise -(Psalm 1. 19). Ah, now, indeed, neither in this life nor in the other do I desire aught but Thee alone: What have I in heaven, and besides thee what do I desire upon earth? Thou art the God of my heart, and the God that is my portion forever- (Psalm lxxii. 25). Thou alone art and shalt be forever the only Lord of my heart, of my will. Thou art my only Good, my Heaven, my Hope, my Love, my All: The God of my heart, and the God that is my portion forever!

Spiritual Reading

CORAM SANCTISSIMO

TWENTIETH VISIT

The Prophet Zacharias says: In that day there shall be a fountain open to the house of David, and to the inhabitants of Jerusalem, for the washing of the sinner - (Zachariah xiii. 1). Jesus in the Holy Sacrament is the Fountain foretold by the Prophet as open to all, and to which we can go whenever we please, to wash our souls from all the stains of sin which are daily contracted. When anyone falls into some fault, what more beautiful remedy than to have immediate recourse to the Most Blessed Sacrament!

Yes, my Jesus, I resolve always to do this: for I know that the waters of this Fountain of Thine not only cleanse me, but also give me light, and strenghen me not to fall, and enable me cheerfully to bear contradictions, and also inflame me with Thy love. I know that for this end it is that Thou awaitest visits, and recompensest those of Thy lovers with so many graces. My Jesus, delay not, but wash me now from all the defects I have committed this day, and for which I am grieved because they have displeased Thee; strengthen me against relapse by giving me a great desire to love Thee much. Oh, could I but always dwell near Thee, as did Thy faithful servant Mary Diaz. She lived in the time of St. Teresa and had permission from the Bishop of Avila to inhabit the tribune of a church, where she remained almost always in the presence of the Most Blessed Sacrament, which she called her Neighbor, and which she only left to go to Confession and Communion. When the Venerable Brother Francis of the Infant Jesus, of the Order of the Discalced Carmelites, passed before a church in which the Blessed Sacrament was kept, he could not refrain from entering to pay a visit to our Lord, saying that: "it was not becoming for a friend to pass before the door of a friend without entering at least to salute him and exchange a word." But a word did not satisfy him; he always remained as long as obedience allowed him in the presence of his beloved Lord.

My only and infinite Good, I see that Thou hast instituted this Sacrament, and that Thou remainest on this altar to be loved by me; and that for this end Thou hast given me a heart capable of loving Thee much. Why is it, then, that I am so ungrateful as not to love Thee, or that I love Thee so little? Now it is not just that such goodness as Thou art should be so little loved. The love, at least, which Thou bearest me deserves other and greater love on my part. Thou art an infinite God and I am a miserable worm. It would be little did I die for Thee, or wear myself out for Thee, Who didst die for me, and dost still sacrifice Thyself for me every day on the altar. Thou deservest to be much loved; I will love Thee much; help me, my Jesus, help me to love Thee, help me to do that which pleases Thee so much, and which Thou so earnestly seeks of me.

Ejaculatory Prayer. My Beloved to me, and I to my Beloved! - (Canticles ii. 16).

AN ACT OF SPIRITUAL COMMUNION

My Jesus, I believe that Thou art truly present in the Most Holy Sacrament. I love Thee above all things, and I desire to possess Thee within my soul. Since I am unable now to receive Thee sacramentally, come at least spiritually into my heart. I embrace Thee as already there and unite myself wholly to Thee; never permit me to be separated from Thee.

VISIT TO MARY

O my most sweet, most compassionate most amiable Queen, how great is the confidence with which St. Bernard inspires me when I have recourse to thee! He says that thou dost not examine the merits of those who have recourse to thy compassion, but that thou offerest thyself to help all who pray to thee: "Mary does not discuss merits but shows herself ready to hear and welcome all." Therefore, I pray to thee thou dost graciously hear me. Well, then, listen to what I have to ask: I am a poor sinner, deserving of a thousand hells. I wish to change my life; I wish to love my God, Whom I have so greatly offended. I dedicate myself to thee as thy slave; to thee I give myself, miserable as I am; save, then, a poor creature who is no longer his own but thine. My Lady, dost thou understand me? Yes, I trust that thou hast understood me, and graciously heard my prayer.

Ejaculatory Prayer. O Mary, I am thine, save me!

Concluding Prayer

Most holy Immaculate Virgin and my Mother Mary, to thee, who art the Mother of my Lord, and Queen of the world, the advocate, the hope, the refuge of sinners, I have recourse today I, who am the most miserable of all. I render thee my most humble homage, O great Queen, and I thank thee for all the graces thou hast conferred on me until now,

particularly for having delivered me from hell, which I have so often deserved. I love thee, O most amiable Lady; and for the love which I bear thee, I promise to serve thee always, and to do all in my power to make others love thee also. I place in thee all my hopes; I confide my salvation to thy care. Accept me for thy servant, and receive me under thy mantle, O Mother of Mercy. And since thou art so powerful with God, deliver me from all temptations, or rather obtain for me the strength to triumph over them until death. Of thee I ask a perfect love of Jesus Christ. From thee I hope to die a good death.

O my Mother, for the love which thou bearest to God, I beseech thee to help me at all times, but especially at the last moment of my life. Leave me not, I beseech thee, until thou see me safe in Heaven, blessing thee, and singing thy mercies for all eternity. Amen. So I hope. So may it be.

Evening Meditation

THE PRACTICE OF THE LOVE OF JESUS CHRIST

"Charity is not provoked to anger."

XXXIII.-HE THAT LOVES JESUS CHRIST IS NEVER ANGRY WITH HIS NEIGHBOUR

I.

The virtue not to be angry at the contrarieties that happen to us is the daughter of meekness. We have already spoken at length on the acts that belong to meekness; but since this is a virtue that requires to be constantly practiced by everyone living among his fellow men, we will here make some remarks on the same subject more in particular, and more adapted for practice.

Humility and meekness were the favorite virtues of Jesus Christ; so that He bade His disciples learn of Him to be meek and humble: Learn of me, for I am meek and humble of heart-(Matt. xi. 29}. Our Redeemer was called the Lamb-Behold the Lamb of God-as well in consideration of His having to be offered in sacrifice on the Cross for our sins, as in consideration of the meekness exhibited by Him during His entire life, but more especially at the time of His Passion. When in the house of Caiphas He received a blow from that servant, who at the same time upbraided Him with presumption in those words: Answerest thou the high-priest so? Jesus only answered: If I have spoken evil, give testimony of the evil; but if well, why strikest thou me? - (John xviii. 23}. He observed the same invariable meekness of conduct till death. While on the Cross, and made the object of universal scorn and blasphemy, He only besought the Eternal Father to forgive His enemies: Father, forgive them; for they know not what they do- (Luke xxiii. 34}.

II.

Oh, how dear to Jesus Christ are those meek souls who, in suffering affronts, derision, calumnies, persecution, and even chastisement and blows, are not irritated against the person that thus injures or strikes them: The prayer of the meek hath always pleased thee (Judith ix. 16). God is always pleased with the prayers of the meek; that is to say, their prayers are always heard. Heaven is expressly promised to the meek: Blessed are the meek, for they shall possess the land – (Matthew v. 4). Father Alvarez said that Paradise is the country of those who are despised and persecuted and trodden under foot here. Yes, for it is for them that the possession of the eternal Kingdom is reserved, and not for the haughty who are honored and esteemed by the world. David declares that the meek shall not only inherit eternal happiness, but shall likewise enjoy great peace in the present life: The meek shall inherit the land, and shall delight in abundance of peace- (Psalm xxxvi. 11). It is so, because the Saints harbor no malice against those who ill-treat them, but rather love them the more; and the Lord, in reward for their patience, gives them an increase of interior peace. St. Teresa said: "I seem to experience a renewed love towards those persons who speak ill of me." This gave occasion to the Sacred Congregation to say of the Saint, that "even affronts themselves supplied her with the food of charity." Offences became a fresh reason for her to love the person who had offended her. No one can have such meekness as this, if he has not a great humility and a low opinion of himself, so as to consider himself worthy of every kind of contempt; and hence we see, on the contrary, that the proud are always irritable and vindictive, because they have a high conceit of themselves, and esteem themselves worthy of all honor.

WEDNESDAY – THIRD WEEK AFTER PENTECOST

Morning Meditation

II.-HOW TO CONVERSE CONTINUALLY AND FAMILIARLY WITH GOD

If you desire to please the loving Heart of Jesus, converse with Him from this day forward with the greatest possible confidence and tenderness. Beloved soul, says God, I have written thee in my hands: thy walls are always before me- (Isaiah xlix. 16). What do you fear? I have written you in My hands so as never to forget to do you service.

I.

In order the more to strengthen your confidence in God, often call to mind His loving treatment of you, and the gracious means He has used to draw you from the disorders of your life and your attachments to earth, in order to attract you to His holy love; and therefore fear lest you have too little confidence in treating with your God, now that you have a resolute will to love and please Him with all your power. The mercies He has granted you are most sure pledges of the love He bears you. God is displeased with a want of trust on the part of souls that heartily love Him, and whom He loves. If, then, you desire to please His loving Heart, converse with Him from this day forward with the greatest possible confidence and tenderness.

I have graven thee in my hands: thy walls are always before my eyes-(Isaiah xlix. 16). Beloved soul, says the Lord, why do you fear or mistrust? I have you written in My hands, so as never to forget to do you service. Are you afraid of your enemies? Know that the care of your defense is always before Me, so that I cannot lose sight of it. David rejoiced, saying to God: Thou hast crowned us as with a shield of thy good will -(Psalm v. 13). Who, 0 Lord, can ever harm us, if Thou with Thy goodness and love dost defend and encompass us round about? Above all, animate your confidence at the thought of the gift that God has given us the Gift of Jesus Christ: God so loved the world as to give his only-begotten Son- (John iii. 16). How can we ever fear, exclaims the Apostle, that God will refuse us any good, after He has vouchsafed to give us His own Son? He delivered him up for us all; how hath he not also, with him, given us all things? -(Romans viii. 32).

My delights are to be with the children of men-(Proverbs viii. 31). The paradise of God, so to speak, is the heart of man. Does God love you? Love Him. His delights are to be with you; let you delight to be with Him; to pass all your lifetime with Him, in the delight of whose company you hope to spend a blissful eternity. Accustom yourself to speak with Him alone, familiarly, with confidence and love, as to the dearest Friend you have, and Who loves you best.

II.

If it be a great mistake, as has been already said, to deal mistrustfully with God,-to be always coming before Him, as a slave, full of fear and confusion, comes before his prince, trembling with dread,-it would be a greater error to think that conversing with God is but weariness and bitterness. No, it is not so: Her conversation hath no bitterness, nor her company any tediousness- (Wisdom viii. 16). Ask those souls who love God with a true love, and they will tell you that in the sorrows of their life they find no greater, no truer relief, than in loving converse with Him.

Now this does not require that you should continually apply your mind to it, so as to forget all your various employments and recreations. It only requires of you, without putting these aside, to act towards God as you yourself act towards those who love you and whom you love.

Your God is ever near you, nay, within you: In him we live, and move, and have our being-(Acts xvii. 28). There is no barrier at the door against any who desire to speak with Him; nay, God delights that you should treat with Him confidently. Treat with Him of your business, your plans, your griefs, your fears,-of all that concerns you. Above all, do so with confidence, with an open heart. For God is not wont to speak to the soul that speaks not to Him; forasmuch as, if it be not used to converse with Him, it would little understand His voice were He to speak to it. And this is what the Lord complains of: Our sister is little: what shall we do to our sister in the day when she is to be spoken to? -

(Canticles viii. 8). Our sister is but a child in my love; what shall we do to speak to her if she understand me not? God will have Himself regarded as the Lord of surpassing power and terribleness, when we despise His grace; but, on the contrary, He will have Himself treated with the most affectionate friend when we love Him; and to this end He would have us often speak with Him familiarly and without restraint.

It is true that God ought always to be revered in the highest degree; but when He favors you by making you feel His presence and know His desire that you should speak to Him as to one who more than all loves all, then express to Him your feelings with freedom and confidence. She preventeth them that covet her, so that she first showeth herself unto them- (Wisdom vi. 14). When you desire God's love, He takes the first step, without waiting till you come to Him; and presents Himself to you, bringing with Him the graces and the remedies you stand in need of. He only waits for you to speak to Him, to show you that He is near to you, ready to hear and to comfort you: And his ears are unto their prayers- (Psalm xxxiii. 16).

Spiritual Reading

CORAM SANCTISSIMO

TWENTY-FIRST VISIT

Wheresoever the body shall be, thither will the eagles also be gathered together- (Matthew xxiv. 28). The Saints generally understand by this body that of Jesus Christ; and by the eagles, souls who, being detached from creatures, rise above the things of the earth and fly towards heaven, after which they always sigh in thought and affection, and where they constantly dwell. These eagles also find their Paradise on earth wherever they find Jesus in the Most Holy Sacrament; so much so, indeed, that they seem never to tire hovering around Him. If eagles, says St. Jerome, on scenting a dead body go afar to seek it, how much more should we run and fly to Jesus in the Most Blessed Sacrament, as to the most delicious food of our hearts! Hence the Saints in this valley of tears have always, as parched hearts, run to this Fountain of Paradise. Father Balthazar Alvarez, of the Society of Jesus, in whatever occupation he was engaged, used often to cast his eyes towards the place where he knew our Lord was present in the Blessed Sacrament; he often visited Him, and even spent entire nights in His presence. He used to weep when he saw the palaces of the great ones of this world filled with people, who paid court to a man from whom they hoped for some miserable earthly good, and the churches so abandoned in which the supreme Sovereign of the world dwells, and remains with us on a throne of love, rich in immense and eternal treasures. He used also to say that Religious were indeed fortunate, because in the very houses in which they reside they can, whenever they please, either night or day, visit this great Lord in the Most Blessed Sacrament, and this lay people cannot do.

Since, then, my most loving Lord, notwithstanding that Thou see me as a leper, and so ungrateful to Thy love, Thou invites me to approach Thee, I will not be discouraged at the sight of my miseries: I come and approach Thee; but do Thou wholly change me. Drive from me every love which is not for Thee, every desire which displeases Thee, every thought which does not tend towards Thee. My Jesus, my Love, my Treasure, my All, I am determined to please Thee alone. I will give pleasure only to Thee. Thou alone deserves all my love; Thee only will I love with my whole heart. Detach me from everything, my Lord, and bind me to Thyself alone; but bind me so firmly that I may never more be able to separate myself from Thee, either in this life or in the next.

Ejaculatory Prayer. My most sweet Jesus, never allow me to be separated from Thee!

AN ACT OF SPIRITUAL COMMUNION

My Jesus, I believe that Thou art truly present in the Most Holy Sacrament. I love Thee above all things, and I desire to possess Thee within my soul. Since I am unable now to receive Thee sacramentally, come at least spiritually into my heart. I embrace Thee as already there and unite myself wholly to Thee; never permit me to be separated from Thee.

VISIT TO MARY

Denis the Carthusian called the Most Blessed Virgin "the advocate of all the wicked who have recourse to her." Since, then, O great Mother of God, thy office is to defend the cause of the guiltiest criminals who have recourse to thee, behold me now at thy feet; to thee I have recourse, and I address thee in the words of St. Thomas of Villanova: "Now, therefore, O gracious advocate, fulfil thy charge." Now quickly enter upon thy office, undertake my cause. It is true that I have indeed been guilty before my Lord, having offended Him, after the many benefits and graces He has conferred upon me; but the evil is done. Thou canst save me. Thou hast only to tell thy God that thou defend me, and then I shall be forgiven and shall be saved.

Ejaculatory Prayer. My dear Mother, thou hast to save me.

Concluding Prayer

Most holy Immaculate Virgin and my Mother Mary, to thee, who art the Mother of my Lord, and Queen of the world, the advocate, the hope, the refuge of sinners, I have recourse today I, who am the most miserable of all. I render thee my most humble homage, O great Queen, and I thank thee for all the graces thou hast conferred on me until now,

particularly for having delivered me from hell, which I have so often deserved. I love thee, O most amiable Lady; and for the love which I bear thee, I promise to serve thee always, and to do all in my power to make others love thee also. I place in thee all my hopes; I confide my salvation to thy care. Accept me for thy servant, and receive me under thy mantle, O Mother of Mercy. And since thou art so powerful with God, deliver me from all temptations, or rather obtain for me the strength to triumph over them until death. Of thee I ask a perfect love of Jesus Christ. From thee I hope to die a good death.

O my Mother, for the love which thou bearest to God, I beseech thee to help me at all times, but especially at the last moment of my life. Leave me not, I beseech thee, until thou see me safe in Heaven, blessing thee, and singing thy mercies for all eternity. Amen. So I hope. So may it be.

Evening Prayer

THE PRACTICE OF THE LOVE OF JESUS CHRIST
XXXIV.–HE THAT LOVES JESUS CHRIST IS NEVER ANGRY WITH HIS NEIGHBOUR

I.

Blessed are the dead who die in the Lord- (Apocalypse xiv. 13). We must, indeed, die in the Lord to be blessed, and to enjoy that blessedness here in the present life: we mean, such blessedness as can be had before entering Heaven, which, though certainly much below that of Heaven, yet far surpasses all the pleasures of sense in this world: And the peace of God, which surpasses all understanding, keep your hearts-(Philippians iv. 7); so wrote the Apostle to his disciples. But to gain this peace, even in the midst of affronts and calumnies, we must be dead in the Lord: a dead person, how much soever he may be ill-treated and trampled on by others, resents it not. In like manner, he who is meek, like a dead body, which no longer sees or feels, should endure all the outrages committed against him. Whoever loves Jesus Christ from his heart easily attains to this; because, as he is conformed in all things to God's will, he accepts with equal composure and peace of mind prosperous and adverse occurrences, consolations and afflictions, injuries, and courtesies. Such was the conduct of the Apostle; and he says, therefore: I exceedingly abound with joy in all our tribulation-(2 Corinthians vii. 4). Oh, happy the man who reaches this point of virtue! He enjoys continual peace, which is a treasure precious beyond all other goods of this world. St. Francis of Sales said: "Of what value is the whole universe in comparison with peace of heart?" And in truth, of what avail are all riches and all the honors of the world to a man that lives in disquiet, and whose heart is not at peace?

II.

In short, to remain constantly united with Jesus Christ, we must do all with tranquility and not be troubled at any contradiction that we may encounter. The Lord is not in the earthquake-(3 Kings xix. II). The Lord does not abide in troubled hearts. Let us listen to the beautiful lessons given on this subject by that master of meekness St. Francis of Sales: "Never put yourself in a passion, nor open the door to anger on any pretext whatever; because, when once it has gained an entrance, it is no longer in our power to banish it, or moderate it, when we wish to do so. The remedies against it are: (1) To check it immediately, by diverting the mind to some other object, and not to speak a word; (2) To imitate the Apostles when they beheld the tempest at sea, and to have recourse to God, to Whom it belongs to restore peace to the soul; (3) If you feel that, owing to your weakness, anger has already got footing in your breast, in that case do yourself violence to regain your composure, and then try to make acts of humility and of sweetness towards the person against whom you are irritated; but all this must be done with sweetness and without violence, for it is of the utmost importance not to irritate the wounds." The Saint said that he himself was obliged to labor much during his life to overcome two passions which predominated in him, namely, anger and love; to subdue the passion of anger, he avowed it had cost him twenty-two years hard struggle. As to the passion of love, he had succeeded in changing its object by leaving creatures and turning all his affections to God. And in this manner the Saint acquired so great an interior peace that it was visible even in his exterior; for he was invariably seen with a serene countenance and a smile on his features.

Thursday – Third Week after Pentecost

(Feast of the Eucharistic Heart of Jesus)

Morning Meditation

THE LOVING HEART OF JESUS

Oh, if we could but understand the love that burns in the Heart of Jesus for us! Jesus has loved us more than His honor, more than His repose, more than His life. Yea, love has induced Him even to become the very Food of our souls so as to unite and make His Heart and ours but one.

I.

Oh, if we could but understand the love that burns in the Heart of Jesus for us! He has loved us so much, that if all men, all the Angels, and all the Saints were to unite all their energies, they could never arrive at the thousandth part of the love that Jesus bears us. He loves us infinitely more than we love ourselves.

He has loved us even to excess: They spoke of his decease (excess) which he was to accomplish in Jerusalem - (Luke ix. 31). And what greater excess of love could there be than for God to die for His creatures? He has loved us to the greatest degree: Having loved his own ... he loved them unto the end- (John xiii. I), since, after having loved us from eternity,-for there never was a moment from eternity when God did not think of us and did not love each one of us : I have loved thee with an everlasting love- (Jeremiah xxxi. 3)-for the love of us He made Himself Man and chose a life of sufferings and the death of the Cross for our sake. Therefore, He has loved us more than His honor, more than

His repose, and more than His life; for He has sacrificed everything to show us the love He bears us. And is not this an excess of love sufficient to stupefy with astonishment the Angels of Paradise for all eternity?

This love induced Him also to remain with us in the Holy Sacrament as on a throne of love; for He remains there under the appearance of a small piece of bread, shut up in the tabernacle, where He seems to remain in a perfect annihilation of His majesty, without movement and without the use of His senses; so that it seems that He performs no other office there than that of loving men. Love makes us desire the constant presence of the object of our love. It is this love and this desire that makes Jesus Christ reside with us in the Most Holy Sacrament.

O adorable Heart of my Jesus, Heart inflamed with love of men, Heart created on purpose to love them, how is it possible that Thou canst be despised, and Thy love so ill-requited by most men? Oh, miserable that I am, I also have been one of those ungrateful ones who have not loved Thee. Forgive me, my Jesus, this great sin of not having loved Thee, Who art so amiable, and Who hast loved me so much that Thou canst do nothing more to oblige me to love Thee. I feel that I deserve to be condemned not to be able to love Thee, for having renounced Thy love, as I have hitherto done. But no, my dearest Savior, give me any chastisement, but do not inflict this one upon me. Grant me the grace to love Thee, and then give me any infliction Thou pleasest. But how can I fear such chastisement, whilst I feel that Thou continuest to give me the sweet, the pleasing precept of loving Thee, my Lord and my God?

II.

It seemed too short a time to this loving Savior to spend only thirty-three years with men on earth; therefore, in order to show His desire of being constantly with us, He thought right to perform the greatest of all miracles, in the institution of the Holy Eucharist. But the work of Redemption was already completed, men had already become reconciled to God; for what purpose, then, did Jesus remain on earth in this Sacrament? Ah, He remains there because He could not bear to separate Himself from us, for, as He Himself said, He takes a delight in us.

Again, this love has induced Him even to become the Food of our souls, so to unite Himself to us, and to make His Heart and ours as one: He that eateth my flesh and drinketh my blood, abideth in me and I in him- (John vi. 57). O wonder! O excess of divine love!

It was said by a servant of God: If anything could shake my faith in the Eucharist, it would not be the doubt as to how the bread could become flesh, or how Jesus could be in several places at once and confined in so small a space, because I would answer that God can do all things; but if I were asked how He could love men so much as to make Himself their Food, I have nothing else to answer but that this is a Mystery of Faith above my comprehension, and that the love of Jesus cannot be understood. O love of Jesus, do Thou make Thyself known to men and do Thou make Thyself loved!

Love the Lord thy God with thy whole heart- (Matthew xxii. 37). Yes, O my God, Thou wouldst be loved by me, and I will love Thee; indeed I will love none but Thee, Who hast loved me so much. O Love of my Jesus, Thou art my Love. O burning Heart of my Jesus, do Thou inflame my heart also. Do not permit me in future, even for a single moment, to live without Thy love; rather kill me, destroy me; do not let the world behold the spectacle of such horrid ingratitude as that I, who have been so beloved by Thee, and received so many favors and lights from Thee, should begin again to despise Thy love. No, my Jesus, do not permit this. I trust in the Blood Thou hast shed for me that I shall always love Thee, and that Thou wilt always love me, and that this love between Thee and me will not cease for all eternity.

O Mary, Mother of fair love, thou who desirest so much to see Jesus loved, bind me, unite me to thy Son; but bind me to Him, so that we may never again be separated.

Spiritual Reading
CORAM SANCTISSIMO
TVVENTY-SECOND VISIT

The Spouse in the Sacred Canticles went about seeking for her Beloved; and, not finding Him, she asked all whom she met: Have you seen him whom my soul loveth? -(Canticles iii. 3). Jesus was not then on earth; but now, if a soul that loves Him seeks Him, she can always find Him in the Most Blessed Sacrament. Blessed John of Avila was accustomed to say that amongst all sanctuaries he could neither find nor desire a more delightful one than a church in which the Most Blessed Sacrament was reserved.

O infinite love of my God, worthy of infinite love! And how couldst Thou, my Jesus, to dwell amongst men, and to unite Thyself to their hearts, humble Thyself so as to conceal Thyself under the species of bread? O incarnate Word, Thou art supreme in Thy humility because Thou art supreme in Thy love! How can I do otherwise than love Thee with my entire self, knowing as I do how much Thou hast done to captivate my love? I love Thee much; and therefore I give Thy good pleasure the preference above every interest and every satisfaction of my own. My pleasure is to give Thee pleasure, my Jesus, my God, my Love, my All. Make me hunger to be continually in Thy presence in the Blessed Sacrament, to receive Thee into my heart, and to keep Thee company. I should be indeed ungrateful did I not accept so sweet and gracious an invitation. Ah, Lord, annihilate in me all affection for created things! Thou willest that Thou alone, my Creator, shouldst be the object of all my sighs, of all my love. I love Thee, most amiable goodness of my God. I ask nothing of Thee but Thyself. I desire not my own pleasure; Thy pleasure is all my desire, and sufficient for me. Accept, my Jesus, this good desire of a sinner who wishes to love Thee. Help me by Thy grace. Grant that I, a miserable slave of hell, may from this day forward be the happy slave of Thy love!

Ejaculatory Prayer. I love Thee, Jesus, my Treasure, above every other treasure!

AN ACT OF SPIRITUAL COMMUNION

My Jesus, I believe that Thou art truly present in the Most Holy Sacrament. I love Thee above all things, and I desire to possess Thee within my soul. Since I am unable now to receive Thee sacramentally, come at least spiritually into my heart. I embrace Thee as already there and unite myself wholly to Thee; never permit me to be separated from Thee.

VISIT TO MARY

My most sweet Lady and Mother, I am a rebel to thy great Son; but I come repentant to thy mercy, that thou mayst obtain me pardon. Say not that thou canst not do so, for St. Bernard calls thee "the minister of propitiation." To thee also it belongs to succor those who are in danger, St. Ephrem calling thee "the helper of those in peril." My Lady, who is in greater danger than I am? I have lost God; it is certain that I have been condemned to hell. I know not whether God has yet pardoned me. I may again lose Him. But thou canst obtain me all; and from thee I hope for every good, for forgiveness, perseverance, and Heaven. I hope to be one of those who, in the kingdom of the blessed, will most praise thy mercies, O Mary, for having saved me by thy intercession.

Ejaculatory Prayer. I will sing the mercies of Mary for all eternity. I will sing them for ever and ever! Amen, amen.

Concluding Prayer

Most holy Immaculate Virgin and my Mother Mary, to thee, who art the Mother of my Lord, and Queen of the world, the advocate, the hope, the refuge of sinners, I have recourse today I, who am the most miserable of all. I render thee my most humble homage, O great Queen, and I thank thee for all the graces thou hast conferred on me until now,

particularly for having delivered me from hell, which I have so often deserved. I love thee, O most amiable Lady; and for the love which I bear thee, I promise to serve thee always, and to do all in my power to make others love thee also. I place in thee all my hopes; I confide my salvation to thy care. Accept me for thy servant, and receive me under thy mantle, O Mother of Mercy. And since thou art so powerful with God, deliver me from all temptations, or rather obtain for me the strength to triumph over them until death. Of thee I ask a perfect love of Jesus Christ. From thee I hope to die a good death.

O my Mother, for the love which thou bearest to God, I beseech thee to help me at all times, but especially at the last moment of my life. Leave me not, I beseech thee, until thou see me safe in Heaven, blessing thee, and singing thy mercies for all eternity. Amen. So I hope. So may it be.

Evening Meditation

THE PRACTICE OF THE LOVE OF JESUS CHRIST
XXXV.–HE THAT LOVES JESUS CHRIST IS NEVER ANGRY WITH HIS NEIGHBOUR

I.

From whence are wars? ... Are they not from your concupiscences? –(James iv. 1, 2). When we are made angry by some contradiction, we fancy we shall find relief and quiet by giving vent to our anger in actions, or at least in words: but we are mistaken, it is not so; for after having done so, we shall find that we are much more disturbed than before. Whoever desires to persevere in uninterrupted peace must beware of ever yielding to ill-humor. And whenever anyone feels himself attacked by this ill-humor, he must do his utmost to banish it immediately; and he must not go to rest with it in his heart but must divert himself from it by the perusal of some book, by singing some devout canticle, or by conversing on some pleasant subject with a friend. The Holy Spirit says: Anger resteth in the bosom of a fool–(Ecclesiastes vii. 10). Anger remains a long time in the hearts of fools, who have little love for Jesus Christ; but if by stealth it should ever enter into the hearts of the true lovers of Jesus Christ, it is quickly dislodged, and does not remain. A soul that cordially loves the Redeemer never feels in a bad humor, because, as she desires only what God desires, she has all she wishes for, and consequently is ever tranquil and well-balanced. The Divine will tranquilizes her in every misfortune that occurs; and thus she is able at all times to observe meekness towards all. But we cannot acquire this meekness without a great love for Jesus Christ. In fact, we know by experience that we are not meeker and gentler towards others, except when we feel an increased tenderness towards Jesus Christ.

II.

But since we cannot constantly experience this tenderness, we must prepare ourselves, in our mental prayer, to bear the crosses that may befall us. This was the practice of the Saints; and so they were ever ready to receive with patience and meekness, injuries, blows, and chastisements. When we meet with an insult from our neighbor, unless we are well practiced in self-restraint, we shall find it extremely difficult to know what course to take in order not to yield to the force of anger. At the time, our passion will make it appear but reasonable for us to make an angry retort to the person who affronts us; but St. John Chrysostom says that it is not the right way to quench the fire which is raging in the mind of our neighbor by the fire of all indignant reply; to do so will only enkindle it the more: "One fire is not extinguished by another." Someone may say: But why should I use courtesy and gentleness towards an impertinent fellow that insults me without cause? But St. Francis de Sales replies: "We must practice meekness, not only with reason, but against reason."

We must therefore endeavor, on such occasions, to make a kind answer; and in this way we shall check the fire: A mild answer breaketh wrath-(Proverbs xv. 1). But when the mind is troubled, the best expedient will be to keep silence. St. Bernard writes: "The eye troubled by anger sees not straight." When the eye is dimmed with passion, it no longer distinguishes between what is, and what is not, unjust; anger is like a veil drawn over the eyes, so that we can no longer discern between right and wrong; wherefore we must, like St. Francis de Sales, make a compact with our tongue: "I have made a compact with my tongue," he wrote, "never to speak while my heart is disturbed."

Friday – Third Week after Pentecost

III.-HOW TO CONVERSE CONTINUALLY AND FAMILIARLY WITH GOD.

Oh, taste and see that the Lord is sweet! Our God dwelleth in the heights of Heaven, and yet He disdains not to occupy Himself day and night with His faithful servants in their cottages or their cells. There He bestows on them His Divine consolations which surpass all the delights the world can give. Never, then, forget God's sweet presence.

I.

By reason of His immensity, our God is in every place; but there are two places above all where He has His own peculiar dwelling. One is the highest Heaven, where He is present by that glory which He communicates to the Blessed; the other is upon earth, within the humble soul that loves Him: Who dwelleth with a contrite and humble spirit- (Isaiah lvii. 15). He, then, our God, dwelleth in the heights of Heaven; and yet He disdains not to occupy Himself day and night with His faithful servants in their cottages or their cells. And there He bestows on them His divine consolations, each one of which surpasses all the delights the world can give, and which he only does not desire who has no experience of them: Oh, taste and see that the Lord is sweet- (Psalm xxxiii. 9).

Friends in this world have hours in which they converse together, and other times during which they are apart; but between God and you, if you wish, there shall never be one hour of separation: Thou shalt rest, and thy sleep shall be sweet ... the Lord will be at thy side - (Proverbs iii. 24). You may sleep, and God will place Himself at your side, and watch with you continually: I will repose myself with him, and he shall be a comfort in my cares and grief- (Wisdom viii. 9-16). When you take your rest the Lord departs not from your pillow; He continues thinking always of you, that when you wake in the night He may speak to you by His inspirations, and receive from you some act of love, of oblation, of thanksgiving; so as to keep up even in those hours His gracious and sweet converse with you. Sometimes also He will speak to you in your sleep, and cause you to hear His voice, that on waking you may put in practice what He has spoken: I will speak to him in a dream - (Numbers xii. 6).

He is there also in the morning, to hear from you some word of affection, of confidence; to be the depository of your first thoughts, and of all the actions which you promise to perform that day to please Him; of all the griefs, too, which you offer to endure willingly for His glory and love. But as He fails not to present Himself to you at the moment of your waking, fail not you, on your part, to give Him immediately a look of love, and to rejoice when your God announces to you the glad tidings that He is not far from you, as once He was by reason of your sins; but that He loves you, and would be beloved by you: and at that same moment He gives you the gracious precept, Thou shalt love the Lord thy God with thy whole heart-(Deuteronomy vi. 5).

II.

Never, then, forget God's sweet presence, as do the greater part of men. Speak to Him as often as you can; for He does not grow weary of this or disdain it, as do the lords of the earth. If you love Him, you will not be at a loss what to say to Him. Tell Him all that occurs to you about yourself and your affairs, as you would tell it to a dear friend. Look not upon Him as a haughty sovereign who will only converse with the great, and on great matters. He, our God, delights to abase Himself to converse with us, loves to have us communicate to Him our smallest daily concerns. He loves you as much, and has as much care for you, as if He had no others to think of but yourself. He is as entirely devoted to your interests as though the only end of His providence were to succor you, of His almighty power to aid you, of His mercy and goodness to take pity on you, to do you good, and gain by the delicate touches of His kindness your confidence and love. Manifest, then, to Him freely all your state of mind, and pray to Him to guide you to accomplish perfectly His holy will. And let all your desires and plans be simply bent to discover His good pleasure and do what is agreeable to His divine Heart: Commit thy way to the Lord- (Psalm xxxvi. v.).

And desire of him to direct thy ways, and that all thy counsels may abide in him- (Tobit iv. 20).

Say not: But where is the need of disclosing to God all my wants, if He already sees and knows them better than I? True, He knows them; but God makes as if He knew not the necessities about which you do not speak to Him, and for which you seek not His aid. Our Savior knew well that Lazarus was dead, and yet He acted as if He knew it not, until Mary Magdalen had told Him of it, and then He comforted her by raising her brother to life again.

Spiritual Reading

CORAM SANCTISSIMO

TWENTY-THIRD VISIT

Many Christians submit to great fatigue, and expose themselves to many dangers, to visit the places in the Holy Land where our most loving Savior was born, suffered, and died. We need not undertake so long a journey, nor expose ourselves to so many dangers; the same Lord is near us, and dwells in the church, only a few steps distant from our homes. If pilgrims, says St. Paulinus, consider it a great thing to bring back a little dust from the Crib, or from the Holy Sepulcher in which Jesus was buried, with what ardor should we not visit the Blessed Sacrament, where the same Jesus is in person, and where we can go without encountering so much fatigue and so many dangers! A religious person, to whom God had given great love for the Most Blessed Sacrament, amongst other things wrote as follows in a letter: "I see that every good thing I have comes to me from the Most Blessed Sacrament. I have given and consecrated my whole self to Jesus in this Sacrament. I see innumerable graces which are not granted because people do not go to this divine Sacrament. I see the great desire that our Lord has to dispense His graces in this Sacrament. O holy Mystery! O Sacred Host! Where is it that God best displays His power, if it is not in this Host? For this Host contains all that God has ever done for us. Let us not envy the Blessed in Heaven, since on earth we have the same Lord, but with greater wonders of His love. Induce all with whom you speak to devote themselves to the Most Blessed Sacrament. I speak thus because this Sacrament enraptures my soul. Nor can I cease to speak of the Most Blessed Sacrament, which deserves so greatly to be loved. I know not what to do for Jesus in this Sacrament." Thus the letter ends.

O ye Seraphim, who remain sweetly burning with love around your and my Lord, though it is not indeed for love of you, but of me, that this King of Heaven is pleased to be present in this Sacrament-O loving Angels, let me also burn with love; and do you enkindle your love in me that with you I also may burn! O my Jesus, teach me to know the greatness of the love Thou bearest to men, that at the sight of so great love my desire to love Thee and please Thee may go on always increasing! I love Thee, most amiable Lord, and I will always love Thee; and this only to please Thee.

Ejaculatory Prayer. My Jesus, I believe in Thee, I hope in Thee, I love Thee, and I give myself to Thee!

AN ACT OF SPIRITUAL COMMUNION

My Jesus, I believe that Thou art truly present in the Most Holy Sacrament. I love Thee above all things, and I desire to possess Thee within my soul. Since I am unable now to receive Thee sacramentally, come at least spiritually into my heart. I embrace Thee as already there, and unite myself wholly to Thee; never permit me to be separated from Thee.

VISIT TO MARY

Most amiable Virgin, St. Bonaventure calls thee "the Mother of orphans"; and St. Ephrem, moreover, calls thee "the receiver of orphans." Alas, these wretched orphans are no other than poor sinners who have lost God! Behold, then, I have recourse to thee, Most Holy Mary. I have lost my Father; but thou art my Mother, who must enable me to recover Him. In this my so great misfortune I call thee to my aid; do thou succor me. Shall I remain disconsolate? No; for Innocent III, speaking of thee, says: "Who ever called upon her and was not graciously heard by her?" And who ever prayed to thee, and was not heard and helped by thee? Who was ever lost who had recourse to thee? He alone is lost who has not recourse to thee. Then, my Queen, if thou desirest my salvation, enable me always to invoke and confide in thee.

Ejaculatory Prayer. My own most Holy Mary, give me confidence in thee!

Concluding Prayer

Most holy Immaculate Virgin and my Mother Mary, to thee, who art the Mother of my Lord, and Queen of the world, the advocate, the hope, the refuge of sinners, I have recourse today I, who am the most miserable of all. I render thee my most humble homage, O great Queen, and I thank thee for all the graces thou hast conferred on me until now, particularly for having delivered me from hell, which I have so often deserved. I love thee, O most amiable Lady; and for the love which I bear thee, I promise to serve thee always, and to do all in my power to make others love thee also. I place in thee all my hopes; I confide my salvation to thy care. Accept me for thy servant, and receive me under thy mantle, O Mother of Mercy. And since thou art so powerful with God, deliver me from

all temptations, or rather obtain for me the strength to triumph over them until death. Of thee I ask a perfect love of Jesus Christ. From thee I hope to die a good death.

O my Mother, for the love which thou bearest to God, I beseech thee to help me at all times, but especially at the last moment of my life. Leave me not, I beseech thee, until thou see me safe in Heaven, blessing thee, and singing thy mercies for all eternity. Amen. So I hope. So may it be.

Evening Meditation

THE PRACTICE OF THE LOVE OF JESUS CHRIST

XXXVI.–HE THAT LOVES JESUS CHRIST IS NEVER ANGRY WITH HIS NEIGHBOUR

I.

But there are moments when it seems absolutely necessary to check insolence with severe words. David said: Be angry, and sin not– (Psalm iv. 5). Occasions do exist, therefore, when we may be lawfully angry, provided it be without sin. But here is just the difficulty: speculatively speaking, it seems expedient at times to speak and reply to some people in terms of severity, in order to make an impression on them; but in practice it is very difficult to do this without some fault on our part; so that the sure way is always to admonish, or to reply, with gentleness, and to scrupulously guard against all resentment. St. Francis de Sales said: "I have never been angry without afterwards repenting of it." And when, for some reason or other, we still feel angered, the safest way, as I said before, is to keep silence, and reserve the remonstrance till a more convenient moment, when the heart is cooled down.

We ought particularly to observe this meekness when we are corrected by our superiors or friends. St. Francis de Sales again writes: "To receive a reprimand willingly, shows that we love the virtue opposed to the fault for which we are corrected; and consequently, this is a great sign of progress in perfection."

Ah, my Jesus, grant that all my thoughts may be occupied in avoiding whatever may offend Thee, and in promoting whatever may contribute to Thy good pleasure. Ward off every occasion that may draw me from Thy love. I strip myself of my liberty and consecrate it entirely to Thy good will. I love Thee, O Infinite Goodness! I love Thee, O my Delight! O Word Incarnate, I love Thee more than myself! Take pity on me, and heal whatever wounds remain in my poor soul from her past disloyalties towards Thee. I resign myself wholly into Thy arms, O my Jesus; I will be wholly Thine; I will suffer everything for love of Thee; and I ask of Thee nothing but Thyself! O Holy Virgin and my Mother Mary, I love thee, and I rely on thee; succor me by thy powerful intercession!

II.

We must besides practice meekness towards ourselves. It is a delusion of the devil to make us consider it a virtue to be angry with ourselves for committing some fault; far from it, it is a trick of the enemy to keep us in a state of trouble, that so we may be unfit for the performance of any good. St. Francis de Sales said: "Hold for certain that all such thoughts as create disquiet are not from God, Who is the Prince of peace, but proceed either from the devil, or from self-love, or from the good opinion we have of ourselves. These are the three sources from which all our troubles spring. When, therefore, any thoughts arise which throw us into trouble, we must immediately reject and despise them."

Meekness is also especially necessary when we have to correct others. Corrections made with a bitter zeal often do more harm than good, especially when he who must be corrected is himself excited; in such cases the correction should be put off, and we must wait until he is cool. And we ourselves ought no less to refrain from correcting while we are under the influence of ill-temper; for then our admonition will always be accompanied with harshness; and the person in fault, when he sees that he is corrected in such away, will take no heed of the admonition, considering it the mere effect of passion. This holds good as far as concerns the good of our neighbor; as concerns our personal advantage, let us show how dearly we love Jesus Christ, by patiently and gladly supporting every ill-treatment, injury, and contempt.

O my despised Jesus, O Love, O Joy of my soul, Thou hast by Thy example made contempt most acceptable to Thy lovers! I promise Thee, from this day forward, to submit to every affront for the love of Thee, Who for love of me didst submit on earth to every species of revilement from men. Do Thou grant me strength to keep this promise. Enable me to know and to perform whatever Thou desirest at my hands. My God and my All, I crave no other good than Thyself, Who art Infinite Good! O Thou Who takest my interests so much to heart, grant that my only care may be to gratify Thee!

Saturday -Third Week After Pentecost

Morning Meditation

IV.–HOW TO CONVERSE CONTINUALLY AND FAMILIARLY WITH GOD

When you are afflicted with sickness, temptation, persecution, or any other trouble, go at once to God, and beseech Him that His hand may help you. He will not, indeed, be displeased if in your desolation you go to your friends and find some relief. But after you have applied to creatures, and they have been unable to comfort your heart, have recourse to your Creator, and say to Him: Lord, men are full of words. They cannot comfort me. Thou art all my Hope and all my Love!

I.

When you are afflicted with sickness, temptation, persecution, or other trouble, go at once to God, and beseech Him that His hand may help you. It is enough for you to present the affliction before Him; to come and say: Behold, O Lord, I am in distress– (Lamentations i. 20). He will not fail to comfort you, or at least to give you strength to suffer that grief with patience; and it will turn out a greater good to you than if He had altogether freed you from it. Tell Him all the thoughts of fear or of sadness that torment you; and say to Him: My God, in Thee are all my hopes; I offer Thee this affliction, and resign myself to Thy will; but do Thou take pity on me,-either deliver me out of it, or give me strength to bear it. And He will truly keep with you that promise made in the Gospel to all those who are in trouble, to console and comfort them as often as they have recourse to Him: Come to me, all you that labor and are burdened, and I will refresh you--(Matthew xi. 28).

He will not be displeased if in your desolation you go to your friends to find some relief; but He wills you chiefly to have recourse to Himself. At all events, therefore, after you have applied to creatures, and they have been unable to comfort your heart, have recourse to your Creator, and say to Him: Lord, men have only words for me; My friends are full of words– (Job xvi. 21); they cannot comfort me, nor do I any more desire to be comforted by them; Thou art all my hope, all my love. From Thee only will I receive comfort; and let my comfort be, on this occasion, to do what pleaseth Thee. Behold me ready to endure this grief through my whole life, through all eternity, if such be Thy good pleasure. Only do Thou help me.

II.

Fear not that God will be offended if you sometimes gently complain, and say to Him: Why, O Lord, hast Thou retired afar off? -(Psalm ix. 1). Thou knowest, Lord, that I love Thee, and desire nothing but Thy love; in pity help me and forsake me not. And when the desolation lasts long, and troubles you exceedingly, unite your voice to that of Jesus in agony and dying on the Cross, and beseech His mercy: My God, my God, why hast thou forsaken me? - (Matthew xxvii. 46). But let the effect of this be to humble you yet more at the thought that he deserves no consolation who has offended God; and yet all the more to enliven your confidence, knowing that God does all things, and permits all, for your good: All things work together unto good-(Romans viii. 28). Say with great courage, even when you feel most troubled and disconsolate: The Lord is my light and my salvation; whom shall I fear? -(Psalm xxvi. I). Lord, it is Thine to enlighten me; it is Thine to save me; in Thee do I trust: In thee, O Lord, have I hoped; let me never be confounded- (Psalm xxx. 2). And thus keep yourself in peace, knowing there never was anyone who placed his hopes in God and was lost: No one hath hoped in the Lord and hath been confounded- (Ecclesiasticus ii. 11). When you consider your God loves you more than you can love yourself, what do you fear? David comforted himself, saying: The Lord is careful for me- (Psalm xxxix. 18). Say to Him: therefore: Lord, into Thy arms I cast myself; I desire to have no thought but of loving and pleasing Thee; behold me ready to do what Thou requires of me. Thou dost not only will my good, Thou art careful for it; unto Thee, then, do I leave the care of my salvation. In Thee do I rest, and will rest for evermore, since Thou willest that in Thee I should place all my hopes: In peace, in the self-same, I will sleep and I will rest; for thou, O Lord, hast singularly settled me in hope- (Psalm iv. 9).

Spiritual Reading
CORAM SANCTISSIMO
TWENTY-FOURTH VISIT

Verily thou art a hidden God- (Isaiah xlv. 15). In no other work of divine love are these words so fully verified as in this adorable mystery of the Most Holy Sacrament, where our God is entirely hidden. When the Eternal Word took Flesh, He hid His divinity, and appeared as a Man on earth; but remaining with us in this Sacrament, He hides even His humanity, and, as remarks St. Bernard, appears only under the form of bread, to show thereby the tenderness of the love He bears us: "The divinity is hid, the humanity is hid: the bowels of charity alone appear." O my beloved Redeemer, at the sight of the excessive tenderness Thou hast for men, I am beside myself, O Lord, and know not what to say. In this Sacrament Thou goest so far for their love as to hide Thy majesty and lower Thy glory; Thou goest so far as even to consume and annihilate Thy divine life. And whilst Thou art on the altar Thou seemest to have nothing else to do than to love men, and to show them the affection Thou bearest them. And what gratitude do they show Thee in return, O great Son of God?

O Jesus, O too great Lover of men, allow me so to speak, for I see that Thou preferrest their advantage to Thine own glory. And didst Thou not know to how much contempt this loving design of Thine would expose Thee? I see, and before me Thou didst see it full well Thyself, that the greater part of men adore Thee not; neither will they acknowledge Thee in this Sacrament.

I know that these very men have gone so far as to trample on the consecrated Hosts, that they have thrown them on the ground, into water, and into fire. And I see the greater part even of those who believe in Thee, O my God, so far from repairing so many outrages by the homage of their devotion, either come to the church to offend Thee still more by their irreverence, or else abandon Thee on Thy altar, and sometimes even leave it unprovided with a lamp or the necessary ornaments!

Oh, that I could, my most sweet Savior, but wash with my tears, or even with my blood, those unhappy places in which, in this Sacrament, Thy love and Thy enamored Heart have been so greatly outraged! But if so much is not granted me, I desire at least, my Lord, and determine, to visit Thee often, in order to adore Thee as I now adore Thee, and this in compensation for the insults Thou receives in this most divine Mystery. Accept, O Eternal Father, this scanty honor, which I, the most miserable of men, now offer Thee in reparation of the outrages offered to Thy Son in the Most Holy Sacrament; accept it in union with that infinite honor which Jesus Christ gave Thee on the Cross, and which He daily gives Thee in the Most Blessed Sacrament. O my Sacramental Jesus, would that I could fill all men with love for the Most Blessed Sacrament!

Ejaculatory Prayer. O amiable Jesus, make Thyself known, make Thyself loved!

AN ACT OF SPIRITUAL COMMUNION

My Jesus, I believe that Thou art truly present in the Most Holy Sacrament. I love Thee above all things, and I desire to possess Thee within my soul. Since I am unable now to receive Thee sacramentally, come at least spiritually into my heart. I embrace Thee as already there, and unite myself wholly to Thee; never permit me to be separated from Thee.

VISIT TO MARY

My most powerful Lady, in the midst of my misgivings as to my eternal salvation, how great is the confidence I feel when I have recourse to thee; and when I think that thou, my Mother, art, on the one hand, so rich in graces that St. John Damascene calls thee "a sea of graces"; St. Bonaventure, "the assemblage of graces," that is, the source in which all graces are congregated; St. Ephrem, "a fountain of grace and of all consolation"; and St. Bernard, "the fullness of every good"-and on the other hand, I reflect that thy desire to do us good is so great that thou esteemest thyself offended, as St. Bonaventure says, by him who does not ask thee for graces: "They sin against thee, O Lady," he says, "who do not ask of thee." O most rich, O most wise, and most merciful Queen, I see that thou knowest far better than I do the wants of my soul and that thou lovest me far more than I can love thee! Know, then, the grace for which I now ask thee; obtain me the grace which thou knowest to be the most expedient for my soul. Ask this favor from God and I am satisfied.

Ejaculatory Prayer. My God, grant me the graces which Mary asks Thee for me.

Concluding Prayer

Most holy Immaculate Virgin and my Mother Mary, to thee, who art the Mother of my Lord, and Queen of the world, the advocate, the hope, the refuge of sinners, I have recourse today I, who am the most miserable of all. I render thee my most humble homage, O great Queen, and I thank thee for all the graces thou hast conferred on me until now, particularly for having delivered me from hell, which I have so often deserved. I love thee, O most amiable Lady; and for the love which I bear thee, I promise to serve thee always, and to do all in my power to make others love thee also. I place in thee all my hopes; I confide my salvation to thy care. Accept me for thy servant, and receive me under thy mantle, O Mother of Mercy. And since thou art so powerful with God, deliver me from

all temptations, or rather obtain for me the strength to triumph over them until death. Of thee I ask a perfect love of Jesus Christ. From thee I hope to die a good death.

O my Mother, for the love which thou bearest to God, I beseech thee to help me at all times, but especially at the last moment of my life. Leave me not, I beseech thee, until thou see me safe in Heaven, blessing thee, and singing thy mercies for all eternity. Amen. So I hope. So may it be.

Evening Meditation
THE PRACTICE OF THE LOVE OF JESUS CHRIST
"Charity thinketh no evil, rejoiceth not in iniquity, but rejoiceth with the truth."
XXXVII.-HE THAT LOVES JESUS CHRIST ONLY WISHES WHAT JESUS CHRIST WISHES

I.

Charity and truth always go together; so that charity, conscious that God is the only and the true Good, detests iniquity, which is directly opposed to the Divine will, and takes no satisfaction but in what pleases Almighty God. Hence the soul that loves God is heedless of what people say of her, and only aims at pleasing God. The Blessed Henry Suso says: "That man stands well with God who strives to conform himself to the truth, and for the rest is utterly indifferent to the opinion or treatment of mankind."

And as we have already more than once asserted, the sanctity and perfection of a soul consists in renouncement of self and in submission to the will of God; but now it will be well to descend more into detail. If, then, we would become saints, our whole endeavor must be, never to follow our own will, but always the will of God; the substance of all the precepts and Divine counsels is comprised in doing and suffering what God wills, and in the manner He wills it. Let us, therefore, entreat the Lord to bestow on us a holy liberty of spirit: that liberty of spirit which leads us to embrace whatever is pleasing to Jesus Christ, regardless of all feelings of repugnance arising from self-love and human respect. The love of Jesus Christ, makes those who love Him utterly indifferent; so that all things are alike to them, whether bitter or sweet. They do not wish for anything that pleases themselves, but only for that which is pleasing to God; they employ themselves in little and great things, be they pleasant or unpleasant, with the same peace of mind. It is enough for them if they please God.

II.

St. Augustine says: "Ama, et fac quod vis: Love, and do what you like." Whoever really loves God seeks only to do what pleases Him; and in this is all his pleasure. St. Teresa says:

"He that seeks but the gratification of one he loves, is gratified with all that pleases that person. Love in its perfection produces this result; it makes a person heedless of all private interests and self-satisfaction, and concentrates all his thoughts on endeavoring to please the person beloved, and to do all he can to honor him himself, and to make him honored by others. O Lord, all our ills come from not keeping our eyes fixed on Thee! Were we solely intent on advancing, we should soon come to the end of our journey; but we fall and stumble a thousand times, and we even lose our way, for want of looking attentively to the right path." Here we may see what should be the single aim of all our thoughts, actions, desires, and prayers, namely, the pleasure of God; our way to perfection must be this, to walk according to the will of God.

FOURTH SUNDAY AFTER PENTECOST

Morning Meditation

V.-HOW TO CONVERSE CONTINUALLY AND FAMILIARLY WITH GOD

Think of the Lord in goodness. In these words the Wise Man exhorts us to have more confidence in God's Mercy than dread of His divine Justice, for God is immeasurably more inclined to bestow favors than to punish. Mercy exalteth itself above judgment.

I.

Think of the Lord in goodness-(Wisdom i. I). In these words the Wise Man exhorts us to have more confidence in the divine mercy than dread of the divine justice; since God is immeasurably more inclined to bestow favors than to punish; as St. James says, Mercy exalteth itself above judgment-(James ii. 13). Hence the Apostle St. Peter tells us that in all fears, whether about our interests for time or for eternity, we should commit ourselves altogether to the goodness of our God, Who has the greatest care of our safety: Casting all your care upon him, for he hath care of you-(1 Peter v. 7). Oh, what a beautiful meaning does this lend to the title which David gives to the Lord, when he says that our God is the God Who makes it His care to save: Our God is the God of salvation-(Ps. lxvii. 21), which signifies, as Bellarmine explains it, that the office peculiar to the Lord is, not to condemn, but to save all. For while He threatens with His displeasure those who disregard Him, He promises, on the other hand, His assured mercies to those who fear Him, as the divine Mother said in her Canticle: And his mercy is to them that fear him-(Luke i. 50). I set before you, devout soul, all these passages of Scripture, that when the thought disquiets you-Am I to be saved or not? Am I predestined or not? -You may take courage, and understand from the promises He makes you what desire God has to save you, if only you are resolved to serve Him and to love Him as He commands.

II.

When you receive pleasant news, do not act like those unfaithful, thankless souls who have recourse to God in time of trouble, but in time of prosperity forget and forsake Him. Be as faithful to Him as you would to a friend who loves you and rejoices in your good; and go therefore, at once and tell Him of your gladness, and praise Him and give Him thanks, acknowledging it all as a gift from His hands; and rejoice in that happiness because it comes to you of His good pleasure. Rejoice, therefore, and comfort yourself in Him alone: I will receive in the Lord and I will joy in God my Jesus-(Habacuc ii. 18). Say to Him: My Jesus, I bless, and will ever bless Thee, for granting me so many favors, when I deserved at Thy hands not favors, but chastisements for the affronts I have offered Thee. All fruits, the new and the old, my Beloved, I have kept for thee-(Cant. vii. 13). Lord, I give Thee thanks; I keep in memory all Thy bounties, past and present, to render Thee praise and glory for them for ever and ever.

But if you love your God, you ought to rejoice more in His blessedness than in your own. He who loves a friend very much, sometimes takes more delight in that friend's good name than if it were his own. Comfort yourself, then, in the knowledge that your God is infinitely blessed. Often say to Him: My beloved Lord, I rejoice more in Thy blessedness than in any good of mine; yes, for I love Thee more than I love myself.

Another mark of confidence highly pleasing to your most loving God is this: that when you have committed any fault, you be not ashamed to go at once to His feet and seek His pardon. Consider that God is so greatly inclined to pardon sinners that He laments their perdition when they depart far from Him and live as dead to His grace. Therefore, does He lovingly call them, saying: Why will you die, O house of Israel? Return ye, and live-(Ezechiel xviii. 31, 32). He promises to receive the soul that has forsaken Him, as soon as she returns to His arms: Turn ye to me, ... and I will turn to you-(Zacharias i. 3). Oh, if sinners did but know with what tender mercy the Lord stands waiting to forgive them! The Lord waiteth, that he may have mercy on you-(Isaiah xxx. 18). Oh, did they but know the desire He has, not to chastise, but to see them converted, that He may embrace them, that He may press them to His Heart! He declares: As I live, saith the Lord God, I desire not the death of the wicked, but that the wicked turn from his way and live-(Ezechiel xxxiii. 11). He even says: And then come and accuse me, saith the Lord: if your sins be as scarlet, they shall be made as white as snow-(Isaiah i. 18). As though He had said: Sinners, repent of having offended Me; if I do not pardon you, accuse me; upbraid Me, and treat Me as one unfaithful. But no, I will not be wanting to My promise. If you come, know this: that though your consciences are dyed deep as crimson by your sins, I will make them by My grace as white as snow. In a word, God has declared that when a soul repents of having offended Him, He forgets all its sins: I will not remember all his iniquities-(Ezechiel xviii., 22).

Spiritual Reading

CORAM SANCTISSIMO

TWENTY-FIFTH VISIT

St. Paul praises the obedience of Jesus Christ, saying that He obeyed His Eternal Father even unto death: becoming obedient even unto death-(Philippians ii. 8). But in this Sacrament He has gone still farther; for here He has been pleased to become obedient, not only to His Eternal Father, but also to man; and not only unto death, but as long as the world shall last; so that we can say: "He has become obedient even unto the consummation of the world." He, the King of Heaven, comes down from Heaven in obedience to man, and then seems to dwell and converse there, to obey men: And I do not resist. There He remains without moving Himself; He allows Himself to be placed where men will, be it for exposition in the Monstrance, or to be enclosed in the Tabernacle. He allows Himself to be carried wheresoever He is borne, be it into houses or through the streets; He allows Himself to be given in Communion to whomsoever He is administered, be they just or sinners. St. Luke says that whilst He dwelt on earth, He obeyed the Most Blessed Virgin Mary and St. Joseph; but in this Sacrament He obeys as many creatures as there are priests on earth: and I do not resist-(Isaiah 1. 5).

Permit me now to address Thee, O most loving Heart of my Jesus, from which indeed all the Sacraments flowed forth, but principally this Sacrament of love. I would gladly give Thee as much glory and honor as Thou gives in the Holy Sacrament to the Eternal Father. I know that on this altar Thou still loves me with that same love with which Thou didst love me when Thou didst close Thy divine life in the midst of so much anguish on the Cross. O Divine Heart, enlighten all those who know Thee not with the knowledge of Thyself! Through Thy merits deliver from Purgatory, or at least relieve, the afflicted souls, who are already Thy spouses for all eternity. I adore Thee, I thank Thee, I love Thee, in union with all souls who at this moment love Thee, be they on earth or in Heaven.

O most pure Heart, purify my heart from all attachment to creatures, and fill it with Thy holy love! O sweetest Heart of Jesus, possess my heart, so that henceforward it may be all Thine, and may be always able to say: Who, then, shall separate us from the love of God, ... which is in Christ Jesus, our Lord?-(Romans viii. 38). Write, O Most Sacred Heart of Jesus, upon my heart all the bitter sorrows which for so many years Thou didst endure on earth with so much love for me, that, on seeing them, I may henceforward desire, or at least endure with patience, all the sorrows of this life. Most humble Heart of Jesus, give me a share of Thy humility. Most meek Heart, impart Thy sweetness to me. Take from my heart all that displeases Thee; convert it wholly to Thee, so that I may no longer will or desire other than what Thou wills. In a word, grant that I may live only to obey Thee, only to love Thee, only to give Thee pleasure. I know that I, indeed, owe Thee much; and that Thou hast indeed placed me under great obligations: it will be but little if I consume and wear myself out for Thee.

Ejaculatory Prayer. O Heart of Jesus, Thou art the sole Lord of my heart!

AN ACT OF SPIRITUAL COMMUNION.

My Jesus, I believe that Thou art truly present in the Most Holy Sacrament. I love Thee above all things, and I desire to possess Thee within my soul. Since I am unable now to receive Thee sacramentally, come at least spiritually into my heart. I embrace Thee as already there, and unite myself wholly to Thee; never permit me to be separated from Thee.

VISIT TO MARY

St. Bernard says that Mary is that heavenly Ark in which, if we take refuge, we shall certainly be delivered from the shipwreck of eternal damnation: "She is the ark in which we escape shipwreck." The Ark In which Noe escaped from the general wreck of the world was indeed a type of Mary. But Hesychius says that Mary is a more spacious, a stronger, and a more compassionate Ark. Only a few men and a few beasts were received into and saved by the Ark of Noe; but Mary, our Ark, receives all who take refuge under her mantle, and with certainty saves them. Unfortunate should we be had we not Mary! But still, my Queen, how many are lost! And why? Because they have not recourse to thee. And who would ever be lost had he recourse to thee?

Ejaculatory Prayer. Grant, most holy Mary, that we may always have recourse to thee!

Concluding Prayer

Most holy Immaculate Virgin and my Mother Mary, to thee, who art the Mother of my Lord, and Queen of the world, the advocate, the hope, the refuge of sinners, I have recourse today I, who am the most miserable of all. I render thee my most humble homage, O great Queen, and I thank thee for all the graces thou hast conferred on me until now,

particularly for having delivered me from hell, which I have so often deserved. I love thee, O most amiable Lady; and for the love which I bear thee, I promise to serve thee always, and to do all in my power to make others love thee also. I place in thee all my hopes; I confide my salvation to thy care. Accept me for thy servant, and receive me under thy mantle, O Mother of Mercy. And since thou art so powerful with God, deliver me from all temptations, or rather obtain for me the strength to triumph over them until death. Of thee I ask a perfect love of Jesus Christ. From thee I hope to die a good death.

O my Mother, for the love which thou bearest to God, I beseech thee to help me at all times, but especially at the last moment of my life. Leave me not, I beseech thee, until thou see me safe in Heaven, blessing thee, and singing thy mercies for all eternity. Amen. So I hope. So may it be.

Evening Meditation

THE PRACTICE OF THE LOVE OF JESUS CHRIST.
XXXVIII.-HE THAT LOVES JESUS CHRIST WISHES WHAT JESUS CHRIST WISHES

I.

God wishes us to love Him with our whole heart: Thou shalt love the Lord thy God with thy whole heart -(Matthew xxii. 37). That person loves Jesus Christ with his whole heart who says to Him with the Apostle: Lord, what wilt thou have me to do?-(Acts ix. 6). Lord, signify to me what Thou wilt have me do; for I desire to perform all. And let us be persuaded that whilst we desire what God desires, we desire what is best for ourselves; for assuredly God only wishes what is best for us. St. Vincent de Paul said: "Conformity with the will of God is the treasure of a Christian and the remedy for all evils; since it comprises abnegation of self and union with God and all virtues." In this, then, is all perfection: Lord, what wilt thou have me to do? Jesus Christ promises us that not a hair of your head shall perish-(Luke xxi. 18), which is as much as to say, that the Lord rewards us for every good thought we have of pleasing Him, and for every tribulation embraced with patience in conformity to His holy will. St. Teresa says: "The Lord never sends a trial without remunerating it with some favor as often as we accept it with resignation. "

II.

But our conformity to the Divine will must be entire, without any reserve, and constant, without withdrawal. In this consists the height of perfection; and to this, I repeat, all our thoughts, all our desires, all our works, and all our prayers ought to tend. Some souls given to prayer, on reading of the ecstasies of St. Teresa and St. Philip

Neri, come to wish to enjoy themselves these supernatural unions. Such wishes must be banished as contrary to humility; if we really desire to be saints, we must aspire after true union with God, which is to unite our will entirely to the will of God. St. Teresa said: "Those persons are deceived who fancy that union with God consists in ecstasies, raptures, and sensible enjoyments of Him. It consists in nothing else than submitting our will to the will of God; and this submission is perfect when our will is detached from everything, and so completely united with that of God that all its movements depend solely on the will of God. This is the real and essential union which I have always sought after, and continually beg of the Lord." And then she adds: "Oh, how many of us say this, and seem to ourselves to desire nothing besides this; but, miserable creatures that we are, how few of us attain to it." Such, indeed, is the undeniable truth; many of us say: O Lord! I give Thee my will, I desire nothing but what Thou desires,-but, in the event of some trying occurrence, we know not how to yield calmly to the Divine will. And this is the source of our continually complaining that we are unfortunate in the world, and that we are the butt of every misfortune, and so of our dragging on an unhappy life.

MONDAY – FOURTH WEEK AFTER PENTECOST

Morning Meditation

VI.-HOW TO CONVERSE CONTINUALLY AND FAMILIARLY WITH GOD

As soon as you fall into any fault, raise your eyes to God, make an act of love, and with a humble confession of your fault, hope most assuredly for His pardon, saying to Him : Lord, behold he whom thou lovest is sick. Between friends who sincerely love, it often happens that when one has displeased the other and then humbles himself and seeks pardon, their friendship becomes thereby stronger than ever.

I.

As soon as you fall into any fault, raise your eyes to God, make an act of love, and with humble confession of your fault, hope assuredly for His pardon, and say to Him: Lord, behold he whom thou lovest is sick -(John xi. 3), that heart which Thou dost love is sick, is full of sores: heal my soul; for I have sinned against thee-(Psalm xl. 5). Thou seekest after penitent sinners; behold, here is one at Thy feet, who has come in search of Thee. The evil is done already; what have I now to do? Thou wilt not have me lose courage: after this my sin Thou dost still love me, and I too love Thee. Yes, my God, I love Thee with all my heart; I repent of the displeasure I have given Thee; I purpose never to offend any more. Thou Who art that God, merciful and gracious, patient and of much compassion-(Psalm lxxxv. 5), forgive me; make me to hear what Thou didst say to Magdalen: Thy sins are forgiven thee-(Luke vii. 48) and give me strength to be faithful unto Thee for the time to come.

That you may not lose courage at such a moment, cast a glance at Jesus on the Cross; offer His merits to the Eternal Father; and thus hope with certainty for pardon, since for your sake He spared not even his own Son-(Romans viii. 32). Say to Him with confidence: Look on the face of thy Christ-(Psalm lxxxiii. 10). My God, behold Thy Son, dead for my sake; and for the love of that Son forgive me! Attend well, devout soul, to the instruction commonly given by masters of the spiritual life. After unfaithful conduct you must at once have recourse to God, though you may have repeated your unfaithfulness a hundred times in a day. But after having recourse to the Lord, be at once in peace. Otherwise, whilst you remain cast down and disturbed at the fault you have committed, your converse with God will be small; your trust in Him will fail; your desire to love Him grow cold; and you will be little able to go forward in the way of the Lord. On the other hand, by having immediate recourse to God to ask forgiveness, and to promise Him amendment, your very faults will serve to advance you further in the divine love. Between friends who sincerely love, it often happens that when one has displeased the other and then humbles himself and asks pardon, their friendship thereby becomes stronger than ever. Do you likewise; see to it that your very faults serve to bind you yet closer in love to your God.

II.

In any kind of doubt, either on your own account or that of others, never cease to act towards your God with a confidence like to that of faithful friends, who consult together on every matter. So should you take counsel with Him, and beseech Him to enlighten you that you may decide on what will be most pleasing to Him: Put those words in my mouth, and strengthen the resolution in my heart-(Judith ix. 18). Lord, tell me what Thou wouldst have me to do or to answer; and thus will I act. Speak, Lord; for thy servant heareth-(1 Kings iii. 10).

Use towards God also the freedom of recommending not only your own needs, but also those of others. How agreeable will it be to God that sometimes you forget even your own interests to speak to Him of the advancement of His glory, of the miseries of others, especially of those who groan in affliction, of those souls, His spouses, who in Purgatory sigh after the vision of Himself, and of poor sinners who are living destitute of His grace. For these especially say to Him: Lord, Thou Who art so amiable and worthy of infinite love, how dost Thou, then, endure to see such a number of souls in the world, on whom Thou hast bestowed so many favors, and who yet will not know Thee? Ah, my God, object of all love, make Thyself known, make Thyself loved! Hallowed be thy name! Thy Kingdom come! May Thy Name be adored and loved by all! May Thy love reign in all hearts! Ah, let me not depart without granting me some grace for those unfaithful souls for whom I pray.

Spiritual Reading

CORAM SANCTISSIMO

TWENTY-SIXTH VISIT

Rejoice, and praise, O thou habitation of Sion; for great is he that is in the midst of thee, the Holy One of Israel-(Isaiah xii. 6). O God, and what joy ought not we men to conceive, what hopes and affections, in knowing that in the midst of our land, in our churches, near our homes, the Holy of Holies, the true God, dwells and lives in the Most Holy Sacrament of the Altar! He Who by His presence alone renders the Saints in Heaven blessed! He Who is Love itself! "It is not so much that He has love, as that He is Love itself," says St. Bernard. This Sacrament is not only a Sacrament of love, but is Love itself, it is God Himself, Who for the immense love He bears His creatures calls Himself, and is, Love itself; God is Love-(1 John iv. 16).

But I hear Thee complain, O my Sacramental Jesus: I was a stranger and you took me not in-(Matthew xxv. 43); that Thou camest on earth to be our Guest for our good, and that we have not welcomed Thee. Thou art right, Lord, Thou art right; and I am one of those ungrateful creatures who have left Thee alone, without even visiting Thee. Chastise me as Thou pleases; but not by depriving me of Thy presence, which is the chastisement I deserve; no, I will repair my fault, and the indignities which I have heaped upon Thee. From this day forward I will not only visit Thee often but will remain with Thee as long a time as I can. O most compassionate Savior, be pleased to make me faithful to Thee; and grant that I may also, by my example, excite others to keep Thee company in the Most Blessed Sacrament. I hear the Eternal Father Who says: This is my beloved Son, in whom I am well pleased. A God, then, finds all His complacency in Thee: and shall not I, a miserable worm, find mine in dwelling with Thee in this valley of tears! O consuming Fire, destroy in me all affection for earthly things; for they alone can render me unfaithful and take me away from Thee. Thou canst do it if Thou wilt: Lord, if thou wilt, thou canst make me clean. Thou hast already done so much for me, do this also: banish from my heart all love which does not tend towards Thee. Behold, I give myself all to Thee; I now dedicate all the remainder of my life to the love of the Most Blessed Sacrament. Thou, O Sacramental Jesus, hast to be my comfort, my love in life, and at the hour of my death, when Thou wilt come to be my Viaticum and my Guide to Thy blessed kingdom. Amen, amen. So do I hope; so may it be!

Ejaculatory Prayer. When, O my Jesus, shall I behold Thy beautiful Face!

AN ACT OF SPIRITUAL COMMUNION

My Jesus, I believe that Thou art truly present in the Most Holy Sacrament. I love Thee above all things, and I desire to possess Thee within my soul. Since I am unable now to receive Thee sacramentally, come at least spiritually into my heart. I embrace Thee as already there and unite myself wholly to Thee; never permit me to be separated from Thee.

VISIT TO MARY

In thee, our own most holy Mother, we find the remedy for all our woes; in thee we find strength in our weakness; for St. Germanus calls thee, the "strength itself of our weakness;" in thee we find a door by which to make our exit from the slavery of sin; for St. Bonaventure calls thee "the gate of liberty." In thee we find our certain peace: for the same Saint calls thee, "the safe repose of men." In thee we find relief in our miserable life, for thou art "the solace of our pilgrimage," as St. Laurence Justinian calls thee. In thee, in a word, we find divine grace and God Himself, for St. Bonaventure calls thee "the throne of God's grace"; and St. Proclus, "the bridge by which God descends to men"; that happy bridge by which God, Who had been driven to a distance by our sins, returns to dwell by His grace in our souls.

Ejaculatory Prayer. O Mary, thou art my strength, my deliverance, my peace and salvation!

Concluding Prayer

Most holy Immaculate Virgin and my Mother Mary, to thee, who art the Mother of my Lord, and Queen of the world, the advocate, the hope, the refuge of sinners, I have recourse today I, who am the most miserable of all. I render thee my most humble homage, O great Queen, and I thank thee for all the graces thou hast conferred on me until now, particularly for having delivered me from hell, which I have so often deserved. I love thee, O most amiable Lady; and for the love which I bear thee, I promise to serve thee always, and to do all in my power to make others love thee also. I place in thee all my hopes; I confide my salvation to thy care. Accept me for thy servant, and receive me under thy mantle, O Mother of Mercy. And since thou art so powerful with God, deliver me from all temptations, or rather obtain for me the strength to triumph over them until death. Of thee I ask a perfect love of Jesus Christ. From thee I hope to die a good death.

O my Mother, for the love which thou bearest to God, I beseech thee to help me at all times, but especially at the last moment of my life. Leave me not, I beseech thee, until thou see me safe in Heaven, blessing thee, and singing thy mercies for all eternity. Amen. So I hope. So may it be.

Evening Meditation

THE PRACTICE OF THE LOVE OF JESUS CHRIST

XXXIX.-HE THAT LOVES JESUS CHRIST WISHES WHAT JESUS CHRIST WISHES

I.

If we were conformed to the Divine will in every trouble, we would undoubtedly become saints, and be the happiest of mankind. This, then, should form the chief object of our attention, to keep our will in unbroken union with the will of God in every occurrence of life, be it pleasant or unpleasant. It is the admonition of the Holy Spirit: Winnow not with every wind-(Ecclesiasticus v. 11). Some people resemble the weathercock, which turns about with every wind that blows. If the wind is fair and favorable to their desires, they are all gladness and condescension; but if there blow a contrary wind, and things fall out against their desires, they are all sadness and impatience; this is why they never become saints; and this is why their life is unhappy, for in the present life adversity will always befall us in a greater measure than prosperity. St. Dorotheus said that to receive from the hands of God whatever happens is a great means to keep ourselves in continual peace and tranquility of soul. And the Saint relates that on this account the Ancient Fathers of the Desert were never seen angry or melancholy, for they accepted whatever happened to them joyfully, as coming from the hands of God. Oh, happy the man who lives wholly united and abandoned to the Divine will! He is neither puffed up by success nor depressed by reverses; for he well knows that all alike comes from the self-same hand of God. The will of God is the single rule of his own will; thus, he only does what God wishes him to do, and he only desires what God does. He is not anxious to do many things, but to accomplish with perfection what he knows to be acceptable to God. Accordingly, he prefers the minutest obligations of his state of life to the most glorious and important actions, well aware that in the latter self-love may find a great share, whereas in the former there is certainly the will of God.

II.

Thus we, too, shall be happy when we receive from God all the dispositions of His Providence in the spirit of perfect conformity to His Divine will, utterly regardless of whether or not they coincide with our private inclinations. The saintly Mother de Chantal said: "When shall we come to relish the Divine will in every event that happens, without paying attention to anything else but the good pleasure of God, from Whom it is certain that prosperity and adversity proceed alike from motives of love and for our best interests? When shall we resign ourselves unreservedly into the arms of our most loving heavenly Father, entrusting to Him the care of our persons and our affairs, and reserving nothing for ourselves but the sole desire of pleasing God?" The friends of St. Vincent de Paul said of him while he was still on earth: "Vincent is always Vincent." By which they meant to say that the Saint was ever to be seen with the same smiling face, whether in prosperity or in adversity. He was always himself, because, as he lived in total abandonment of himself to God, he feared nothing and desired nothing but what was pleasing to God. St. Teresa said: "By this holy abandonment that admirable liberty of spirit is generated which those who are perfect possess, wherein they find all the happiness in this life which they can possibly desire; inasmuch as, fearful of nothing, and desirous or wanting for nothing in the things of this world, they possess all."

TUESDAY – FOURTH WEEK AFTER PENTECOST

VII.–HOW TO CONVERSE CONTINUALLY AND FAMILIARLY WITH GOD

To long but little for Heaven is to set small value on the great good of the eternal Kingdom our Redeemer purchased for us by His death. St. Teresa so greatly desired death in order to see God, that she was dying with the desire to die, and so composed that loving Canticle of hers: I die because I do not die.

I.

It is said that in Purgatory those souls who in this life have had but little longing for Heaven are punished with a particular suffering, called the pain of languor; and with reason; because to long but little for Heaven is to set small value on the great good of the eternal Kingdom our Redeemer purchased for us by His death. Forget not, therefore, devout soul, frequently to sigh after Heaven. Say to your God that it seems to you an endless time till you go and see Him and love Him face to face. Long ardently to depart out of this banishment, this scene of sinning, and danger of losing His grace, that you may arrive in that land of love where you may love Him with all your powers. Say to Him again and again: Lord, so long as I live on this earth, I am always in danger of forsaking Thee and losing Thy love. When will it be that I quit this life, wherein I am ever offending Thee, and come to love Thee with all my soul, and unite myself to Thee, with no danger of losing Thee again? Saint Teresa was ever sighing in this way, and used to rejoice when she heard the clock strike, because another hour of life, and of the danger of losing God, was past and gone. For she so greatly desired death in order to see God that she was dying with the desire to die; and so she composed that loving Canticle of hers, I die, because I do not die.

II.

In a word, if you desire to delight the loving Heart of your God, be careful to speak to Him as often as you are able, and with fullest confidence that He will not disdain to answer and speak with you in return. He does not, indeed, make Himself heard in a voice that reaches your ears, but in a voice that your heart can well perceive, when you withdraw from converse with creatures, to occupy yourself in conversing with your God alone: I will lead her into the wilderness, and I will speak to her heart-(Osee ii. 14). He will then speak to you by such inspirations, such interior lights, such manifestations of His goodness, such sweet touches of your heart, such tokens of forgiveness, such experience of peace, such hopes of Heaven, such rejoicings within you, such sweetness of His grace, such loving and close embraces-in a word, such voices of love-as are well understood by those souls whom He loves, and who seek for nothing but God alone.

Spiritual Reading

CORAM SANCTISSIMO

TWENTY-SEVENTH VISIT

The holy Church sings in the Office of the Most Blessed Sacrament: There is no other country, however great, whose gods are nigh as our God is nigh to us -(Deuteronomy iv. 7). When the Gentiles heard how far our God carried His works of love, they exclaimed: "Oh, how good a God is the God of the Christians! And, indeed, although the Gentiles imagined their gods according to their own caprices-yet, if you read history, you will never find in all their fables, and among the many gods they invented, that they went so far as even to imagine a god so enamored of men as is our true God, Who, to show His love for His adorers, and to enrich them with graces, has worked such a prodigy of love as to become their constant Companion, and to remain night and day concealed on their altars, seeming as if He knew not how to separate Himself from them, even for a moment: He hath made a remembrance of his wonderful works-(Psalm cx. 4).

Thou, then, my most sweet Jesus, hast been pleased to work the greatest of Thy miracles in order to satisfy the excessive desire Thou hast to remain always near and present to us. Why, then, do men fly from Thy presence? And how can they live for so long a time at a distance from Thee, or visit Thee So seldom? How is it that when in Thy presence they get so weary that a quarter of an hour appears an age? Oh, patience of my Jesus, how great art thou! Yes, my Lord, I understand Thee; Thy patience is great, because the love Thou bearest to men is great: and this it is which, so to say, forces Thee to dwell always in the midst of such ungrateful creatures.

Ah, my God, Who, because Thou art infinite in perfections art also infinite in love, permit not that I should for the future be, as I have hitherto been, of the number of those ungrateful ones. Grant me a love equal to Thy merits and to my own obligations. At one time I also was weary of Thy presence, either because I loved Thee not, or because I loved Thee too little; but if by Thy grace I am enabled to love Thee much, I shall no longer find it tedious to remain even for whole days and nights at Thy feet in the Most Holy Sacrament. O Eternal Father, I offer Thee Thine own Son Himself; accept Him for me, and through His merits give me so ardent and tender a love towards the Most Blessed Sacrament that, constantly turning towards some church in which Jesus dwells, I may think of, and desire with loving anxiety, the time when I may be able to go and entertain myself in His presence.

Ejaculatory Prayer. My God, for the love of Jesus, give me a great love for the Most Blessed Sacrament.

AN ACT OF SPIRITUAL COMMUNION

My Jesus, I believe that Thou art truly present in the Most Holy Sacrament. I love Thee above all things, and I desire to possess Thee within my soul. Since I am unable now to receive Thee sacramentally, come at least spiritually into my heart. I embrace Thee as already there and unite myself wholly to Thee; never permit me to be separated from Thee.

VISIT TO MARY

Mary is that Tower of David, of which the Holy Ghost says in the sacred Canticles: It is built with bulwarks; a thousand bucklers hang upon it, all the armor of valiant men-(Canticles iv. 4). A tower built with a thousand fortresses, and containing a thousand shields and weapons, for the benefit of those who have recourse to it. Thou art, then, according to an expression of St. Ignatius the Martyr, O most holy Mary, a most powerful defense for all those who are engaged in battle. Oh, how constantly are my enemies attacking me to deprive me of the grace of God and of thy protection, my most dear Lady! But thou art my strength. Thou, indeed, dost not disdain to battle for those who trust in thee; for St. Ephrem calls thee "the bulwark of all who confide in thee." Do thou, then, defend me and fight for me who have such great hope and confidence in thee.

Ejaculatory Prayer. Mary, Mary, thy name is my defense!

Concluding Prayer

Most holy Immaculate Virgin and my Mother Mary, to thee, who art the Mother of my Lord, and Queen of the world, the advocate, the hope, the refuge of sinners, I have recourse today I, who am the most miserable of all. I render thee my most humble homage, O great Queen, and I thank thee for all the graces thou hast conferred on me until now, particularly for having delivered me from hell, which I have so often deserved. I love thee, O most amiable Lady; and for the love which I bear thee, I promise to serve thee always, and to do all in my power to make others love thee also. I place in thee all my hopes; I confide my salvation to thy care. Accept me for thy servant, and receive me under thy mantle, O Mother of Mercy. And since thou art so powerful with God, deliver me from all temptations, or rather obtain for me the strength to triumph over them until death. Of thee I ask a perfect love of Jesus Christ. From thee I hope to die a good death.

O my Mother, for the love which thou bearest to God, I beseech thee to help me at all times, but especially at the last moment of my life. Leave me not, I beseech thee, until thou see me safe in Heaven, blessing thee, and singing thy mercies for all eternity. Amen. So I hope. So may it be.

Evening Meditation

THE PRACTICE OF THE LOVE OF JESUS CHRIST

XL.-HE THAT LOVES JESUS CHRIST WISHES WHAT JESUS CHRIST WISHES

I.

Many fabricate a sort of sanctity according to their own inclinations; some, inclined to melancholy, make sanctity consist in living in seclusion; others, of a busy temperament, in preaching and in making up quarrels; some, of an austere nature, make sanctity consist in penitential inflictions and macerations; others, who are naturally generous, in distributing alms; some in saying many vocal prayers; others in visiting Sanctuaries; and all their sanctity consists in such or the like practices. External acts are the fruit of the love of Jesus Christ; and true love itself consists in a complete conformity to the will of God; and as a consequence of this, in denying ourselves and preferring what is most pleasing to God, and solely because He deserves it.

II.

Others wish to serve God, but it must be in that employment, in that place, with those companions, and in such circumstances; or else they either neglect their duty, or at least do it with a bad grace: such as these are not free in spirit, but are slaves of self-love, and on that account reap little merit even from what they perform; moreover, they live in perpetual disquiet, since their attachment to self-will makes the yoke of Jesus Christ become heavy to them. The true lovers of Jesus Christ love only that which is pleasing to Jesus Christ, and for the sole reason that it does please Him; and they love it when it pleases Jesus Christ, where it pleases Him, and how it pleases Him; whether He chooses to employ them in honorable functions, or in the mean and lowly occupations; in a life of fame in the world, or in one hidden and despised. This is what is meant by the pure love of Jesus Christ; hence we must labor to overcome the cravings of our self-love, which seeks to be employed in those works only that are glorious, or that are according to our own inclinations. And what will it profit us to be the most honored, the wealthiest, the greatest in the world, without the will of God? The Blessed Henry Suso said, "I would rather be the vilest insect on earth by the will of God than a Seraph in Heaven by my own will."

WEDNESDAY – FOURTH WEEK AFTER PENTECOST

Morning Meditation

VIII.-HOW TO CONVERSE CONTINUALLY AND FAMILIARLY WITH GOD

Be assured that though in the fulfilment of your daily duties you should be employed in the meanest occupations, the faithful discharge of them will certainly make you a saint. The Lord does not require of you lofty flights of contemplation, or formidable penances: all that He does demand is that you perform all your actions well.

I.

To make a brief summary of what has already been said at large, I shall not omit to suggest a devout practice whereby you may fulfil all your daily actions in a manner pleasing to God.

When you wake in the morning let it be your first thought to raise your mind to God, offering to His glory all that you will do or suffer the day, praying Him to assist you by His grace. Then make your other morning acts of devotion, acts of thanksgiving and of love, prayers, and resolutions to live that day as though it were to be the last day of your life. Father St. Jure recommends the making in the morning of a compact with the Lord that every time you make a certain sign, as placing your hand upon your heart, or raising your eyes to Heaven or to the Crucifix, and the like, you wish thereby to make an act of love, of desire to see God loved by all, of oblation of yourself, and other acts of the same kind. When you have made these acts and placed your soul in the Heart of Jesus and under the mantle of Mary, and have prayed the Eternal Father that for the love of Jesus and Mary He would protect you during the day, be careful, before you engage in anything else, to make your mental prayer, or Meditation, at least for half an hour; and let your specially chosen Meditation be the sorrow and the shame which Jesus Christ suffered in His Passion. This is the subject dearest to loving souls, and the one that most enkindles divine love within them. If you would make spiritual progress, let three devotions be especially dear to you: devotion to the Passion of Jesus Christ, to the Most Holy Sacrament; and to the ever-blessed Virgin. In mental prayer, make again and again acts of contrition, of love to God and oblation of yourself. The Venerable Father Charles Carafia, Founder of the Pious Workers, said that one fervent act of the love of God made in the morning is sufficient to maintain the soul in fervor throughout the whole day.

II.

Besides the more specific acts of devotion, such as Confession, Communion, recitation of the Divine Office, etc., whenever you are engaged in external occupations, as in study, labor, or in any other employment that may be proper to your condition in life, never forget, when commencing your work to offer it up to God, praying for His assistance to enable you to perform it in a perfect manner; and do not omit to retire frequently into the cell of your heart, in order to unite yourself to God, according to the practice of St. Catherine of Sienna. In short, whatever you do, do it with God and for God.

In going out of your room or house, and on returning again, always commend yourself to the divine Mother by saying a Hail Mary. When sitting down to meals, make an offering to God of the distaste or gratification you may find in what you eat and drink; and, on rising from table, return thanks to Him and say: Lord, how great is Thy goodness to one who has offended Thee so much! In the course of the day be careful to make your Spiritual Reading, to make a Visit to the Most Holy Sacrament and to Most Holy Mary; and in the evening to say the Rosary and to make an examination of conscience, together with the Christian acts of Faith, Hope, Charity, Contrition, resolutions of amendment, and of receiving the Holy Sacraments during life and at the hour of death, forming also the intention of gaining all the indulgences that you can gain. And again, on going to bed, reflect that if you had your deserts, you would be lying down in the flames of hell. Then, with the Crucifix in your arms, compose yourself to sleep, saying: In peace, in the self-same, I will sleep and take my rest-(Psalm iv. 9).

I would wish briefly to point out to you the many Indulgences that are attached to the various prayers or acts of devotion. Whence it is desirable for you in the morning to make the intention of gaining all the indulgences in your power during the day. To him who makes acts of the three Theological Virtues mentioned above-of Faith, etc.-there are granted Seven Years and Seven Quarantines each day; and by continuing them for a month a Plenary Indulgence may be gained, provided he confesses, communicates, and prays for the intentions of the Pope. This indulgence is in articulo mortis. In like manner, you should form the intention of gaining also all the Indulgences granted for saying the Rosary on Beads properly blessed; the Angelus Domini three times a day; the Litany of our Blessed Lady; the Salve Regina; the Ave Maria, and the Gloria Patri; also for saying: "Blessed be the holy and immaculate and most pure Conception of the Blessed Virgin Mary!"; "Praised now and forever be the Most Holy Sacrament!"; for reciting the prayer, Anima Christi, etc.; for bowing the head at the Gloria Patri, and at the most Holy Names of Jesus and Mary; as also for hearing Mass; for making half an hour's mental prayer, to which besides a partial, there is also a Plenary Indulgence attached, provided it be continued for a month, on condition of Confession and Communion, and prayers for the Church; for genuflecting before the Most Holy Sacrament, and for kissing the Crucifix. Always have the intention formed of gaining every such indulgence.

Spiritual Reading

CORAM SANCTISSIMO

TWENTY-EIGHTH VISIT

God, having given us His own Son, says St. Paul, what good thing is there we can fear He might deny us? How hath he not also with him given us all things?-(Romans viii. 32). We know, indeed, that all the Eternal Father has, He has given to Jesus Christ: The Father has given him all things into his hands-(John xiii. 2). Let us, then, ever thank the goodness, the mercy, the liberality of our most loving God, Who has been pleased to make us rich in all good things, and in every grace, by giving us Jesus in the Sacrament of the Altar: In all things you are made rich in him . . .so that nothing is wanting to you in any grace-(I Corinthians i. 5, 7).

Therefore, O Savior of the world, O Incarnate Word, if I desire to possess Thee, I can consider Thee as mine and all mine. But can I at the same time say I am all Thine, as Thou desires? Ah, my Lord, prevent it; and never let the world witness such disorder and ingratitude as that I should not be Thine when Thou desires me! Ah, no; let it never be! If it has been so hitherto, let it never be so again. I now, with the utmost determination, consecrate myself entirely to Thee; for time and eternity I consecrate to Thee my life, my will, my thoughts, my actions, my sufferings. Behold me Thine; as a victim consecrated to Thee I bid farewell to all creatures, and offer my whole self to Thee. Consume me with the flames of Thy divine love. No, I am determined that creatures shall no longer share my heart. The proofs Thou hast given me of the love Thou bearest me, even at a time when I did not love Thee, make me hope that Thou certainly accept me now that I love Thee, and out of love give myself to Thee.

Eternal Father, I now offer Thee all the virtues, the actions, the affections of the Heart of Thy dear Jesus. Accept them, and by His merits, which are all mine for He has given them to me-grant me the graces Jesus asks Thee for me. With these merits I thank Thee for the many mercies Thou hast shown me; with these I satisfy for what I owe Thee for my sins; through these I hope for every grace from Thee-pardon, perseverance, Paradise, and, above all, the crowning gift of Thy pure love. I well see that to all these gifts I myself place impediments; but do Thou also remedy this. I ask it of Thee in the Name of Jesus Christ, Who has promised: Whatsoever you shall ask the Father in my name that will I do-(John xiv. 13). Then Thou canst not refuse me. Lord, my only desire is to love Thee, to give myself to Thee without reserve, and no longer to be ungrateful to Thee, as I have hitherto been. Behold me, and graciously hear me; grant that this may be the day of my entire conversion to Thee, so that I may never more cease to love Thee. I love Thee, my God! I love Thee, Infinite Goodness! I love Thee, my Love, my Paradise, my Good, my Life, my All!

Ejaculatory Prayer. My Jesus Who art all mine, Thou desires me, and I desire Thee!

AN ACT OF SPIRITUAL COMMUNION

My Jesus, I believe that Thou art truly present in the Most Holy Sacrament. I love Thee above all things, and I desire to possess Thee within my soul. Since I am unable now to receive Thee sacramentally, come at least spiritually into my heart. I embrace Thee as already there, and unite myself wholly to Thee; never permit me to be separated from Thee.

VISIT TO MARY

What relief do I not feel in my miseries, and what consolation in my tribulations, what strength do I not find in the midst of temptations, when I remember and call thee to my aid, O my most sweet and most holy Mother Mary! Yes, indeed, you were right, O ye Saints, in calling my Lady, "the haven of those who are in tribulation," with St. Ephrem; "the repairer of our calamities," and "the solace of the miserable," with St. Bonaventure; and "the rest from our mournings," with St. Germanus. My own Mary, do thou console me. I see myself loaded with sins, and surrounded by enemies, without virtue, and cold in my love towards God. Comfort me, comfort me, and let my consolation be to begin a new life-a life which will be really pleasing to thy Son and to thee.

Ejaculatory Prayer. Change me, O Mary my Mother, change me; thou canst do it.

Concluding Prayer

Most holy Immaculate Virgin and my Mother Mary, to thee, who art the Mother of my Lord, and Queen of the world, the advocate, the hope, the refuge of sinners, I have recourse today I, who am the most miserable of all. I render thee my most humble homage, O great Queen, and I thank thee for all the graces thou hast conferred on me until now, particularly for having delivered me from hell, which I have so often deserved. I love thee, O most amiable Lady; and for the love which I bear thee, I promise to serve thee always, and to do all in my power to make others love thee also. I place in thee all my hopes; I confide my salvation to thy care. Accept me for thy servant, and receive me under thy mantle, O Mother of Mercy. And since thou art so powerful with God, deliver me from all temptations, or rather obtain for me the strength to triumph over them until death. Of thee I ask a perfect love of Jesus Christ. From thee I hope to die a good death.

O my Mother, for the love which thou bearest to God, I beseech thee to help me at all times, but especially at the last moment of my life. Leave me not, I beseech thee, until thou see me safe in Heaven, blessing thee, and singing thy mercies for all eternity. Amen. So I hope. So may it be.

Evening Meditation

THE PRACTICE OF THE LOVE OF JESUS CHRIST

XLI.-HE THAT LOVES JESUS CHRIST WISHES WHAT JESUS CHRIST WISHES

I.

Jesus Christ said: Many will say to me: 'Lord, Lord, have we not prophesied in thy name, and cast out devils in thy name, and done many miracles in thy name?' But the Lord will answer them: I never knew you! depart from me, you that work iniquity-(Matthew vii. 22, 28). Depart from Me; I never acknowledged you for My disciples, because you preferred to follow your own inclinations rather than My will. And this is especially applicable to those who labor much for the salvation or perfection of others, while they themselves continue to, live on in the mire of their imperfections. Perfection, consists: Firstly, in a true contempt of oneself. Secondly, in a thorough mortification of our own appetites. Thirdly, in a perfect conformity to the will of God; whosoever is wanting in one of these virtues is out: of the way of perfection. On this account a great servant of God said: It was better for us in our actions to have the will of God rather than His glory as their sole motive; for, in doing the will of God, we at the same time promote His glory; whereas in proposing to ourselves the glory of God, we frequently deceive ourselves; and follow our own will under pretext of glorifying God. St. Francis of Sales said: "There are many who say to the Lord: I give myself wholly to Thee without reserve; but few indeed, in point of fact, practically embrace this abandonment, which consists in a certain indifference in accepting all kinds of events, just as they fall out according to the order of Divine Providence, afflictions as well as consolations, slights and injuries as well as honor and glory."

II.

It is therefore in suffering and in embracing with cheerfulness whatever cuts against the grain of our own inclinations, that we can discover who is a true lover of Jesus Christ. Thomas a Kempis says that "he is not deserving of the name of lover who is not ready to endure all things for his Beloved, and to follow in all things the will of his Beloved." On the contrary, Father Balthazar Alvarez says that whoever quietly resigns himself to the Divine will in troubles "travels to God post-haste." And the saintly Mother Teresa said: "What greater acquisition can we make, than to have some proof that we are pleasing God?" And to this I add that we cannot have a more certain proof of this than, by peacefully embracing the crosses which God send us. We please God by thanking Him for His benefits on earth; but, says Father John of Avila, one 'Blessed be God!' uttered in adversity is worth six thousand acts of thanksgiving in our prosperity.

Thursday – Fourth Week after Pentecost

IX.-HOW TO CONVERSE CONTINUALLY AND FAMILIARLY WITH GOD

That you may be able ever to keep yourself in a state of recollection and union with God, turn everything you see or hear into an occasion for raising your mind to God. Running water will remind you how your life is running on and carrying you nearer and nearer to death; and the lamp going out for want of oil will warn you that thus also shall you one day see your life come to an end.

I.

That you may be able to keep yourself ever in a state of recollection and union with God, as long as you live, and as far as may be possible, turn everything that you may see or hear into an occasion for raising your mind to God, or for taking a glance into eternity. For example, when you see running water reflect that your life is also in like manner running on and carrying you nearer and nearer to death. When you see a lamp going out for want of oil, reflect that thus also one day you will have to see your life come to its end. When you see the graves or remains of the dead, consider that you too will one day be buried in a grave. When you see the great ones of this world rejoicing in their wealth or distinction, pity their folly, and say: For me God is sufficient: Some trust in chariots, some in horses, but we in the name of the Lord-(Psalm xix. 8). Let them glory in such vanity; I will make nothing my glory but the grace and the love of my God. When you behold the pompous funerals, or the fine sepulchral monuments of the great ones that are dead, say: If these are damned what is the good of all this pomp to them?

II.

When you behold the sea in a calm or in storm, consider the difference there is between a soul in, and a soul out of, the grace of God. When you see a tree that is withered, consider that a soul without God is serviceable for nothing but to be cast into fire. If you ever happen to see one who has been guilty of some great crime, trembling with shame and fright in the presence of his judge, or of his father, or of his bishop, consider what the terror of a sinner will be in the presence of Christ, his Judge. When it thunders, and you become alarmed, reflect how those miserable ones who are damned tremble as they hear continually in hell the thunders of the divine wrath. If you ever see one who has been condemned to suffer a painful death, and who says: Is there, then, no longer any means for my escaping death? consider what will be the despair of a soul when it is condemned to hell, as it says, Is there, then, no longer any means for escaping from eternal ruin?

Spiritual Reading

CORAM SANCTISSIMO

TWENTY-NINTH VISIT

Behold I stand at the gate and knock-(Apocalypse iii. 20)

O most loving Shepherd, Who, not satisfied with sacrificing Thyself once to death on the altar of the Cross for the love of Thy flock, hast moreover been pleased to hide Thyself in this divine Sacrament on the altars of our churches, to be always near, and to knock at the doors of our hearts, and thus obtain admission! Ah, did I but know how to enjoy Thy nearness to me as did the sacred Spouse in the Canticles, who says: I sat down under his shadow, whom I desired-(Canticles ii. 3). Ah, did I but love Thee, did I but really love Thee, my most amiable Jesus, I also should never wish to leave the foot of a Tabernacle, night or day; and fixing myself near Thy Majesty, concealed under the apparent shadow of the sacred species, I also should find that divine sweetness and that happiness which souls enamored of Thee find in Thy Presence. Ah, do Thou be graciously pleased to draw me by the odor of Thy beauties, and of the immense love which Thou dost manifest in this Sacrament: Draw me, we will run after thee to the odor of thine ointments-(Canticles i. 3). Yes, my Savior, I will leave creatures and all earthly pleasures, to run after Thee in this Sacrament: As olive plants round about thy table -(Psalm cxxvii. 3). Oh, what abundant fruits of virtues do those happy souls, like olive plants, bring forth to God, who assist with love before the sacred Tabernacle! But I am ashamed to appear before Thee, O my Jesus, so naked and so devoid of virtue. Thou hast commanded that all who approach the altar to honor Thee should present a gift: Thou shalt not appear empty before me -(Exodus xxiii. 15). What, then, am I to do? Am I no more to appear before Thee? Ah, no; this would not please Thee. Poor as I am, I will approach Thee; and do Thou provide me with the gifts Thou desires. I see that Thou dwellest in this Sacrament, not only to reward Thy lovers, but also to provide for the poor out of Thy riches.

Be it so, then, let us now begin. I adore Thee, O King of my heart, and true Lover of men. O Shepherd, loving Thy sheep beyond all bounds, to this throne of Thy love I now approach; and having nothing else to present Thee, I offer Thee my miserable heart, that it may be entirely consecrated to Thy love and to Thy good pleasure. With this heart I can love Thee, and I will love Thee as much as I am able. Draw it, then, to Thyself, and bind it wholly to Thy will, so that, filled with consolation, I may be able from henceforth to say, as Thy dear disciple said, that I am bound by the chains of Thy love: I, Paul, the prisoner of Jesus Christ-(Ephesians iii. 1). Unite me, O my Lord, entirely to Thyself, and make me forget myself, that I may have the happiness one day to lose all things and even myself, to find Thee alone, and to love Thee forever. I love Thee, my Sacramental Lord. To Thee do I bind myself, to Thee do I unite myself. Make me find Thee; make me love Thee, and do Thou never more separate Thyself from me.

Ejaculatory Prayer. My Jesus, Thou alone art sufficient for me!

AN ACT OF SPIRITUAL COMMUNION

My Jesus, I believe that Thou art truly present in the Most Holy Sacrament. I love Thee above all things, and I desire to possess Thee within my soul. Since I am unable now to receive Thee sacramentally, come at least spiritually into my heart. I embrace Thee as already there and unite myself wholly to Thee; never permit me to be separated from Thee.

VISIT TO MARY

St. Bernard calls Mary "the royal road of the Savior"; the safe road by which to find the Savior and salvation. Since, then, it is true, O Queen, that thou art, as the same Saint says, "the chariot in which our souls go to God"-the one who guides us to Him, ah, Lady, thou must not suppose that I shall advance towards God if thou dost not carry me in thine arms! Carry me, carry me; and if I resist, carry me by main force. Do all the violence thou canst by the sweet attractions of thy charity to my soul and to my rebellious will, that they may leave creatures, to seek God alone and His divine will. Show the court of Heaven the greatness of thy power. After so many wonders of thy mercy, show this one more; make a poor creature who is far from God wholly His.

Ejaculatory Prayer. O Mary, thou canst make me a saint; I hope for this grace from thee!

Concluding Prayer

Most holy Immaculate Virgin and my Mother Mary, to thee, who art the Mother of my Lord, and Queen of the world, the advocate, the hope, the refuge of sinners, I have recourse today I, who am the most miserable of all. I render thee my most humble homage, O great Queen, and I thank thee for all the graces thou hast conferred on me until now, particularly for having delivered me from hell, which I have so often deserved. I love thee, O most amiable Lady; and for the love which I bear thee, I promise to serve thee always, and to do all in my power to make others love thee also. I place in thee all my hopes; I confide my salvation to thy care. Accept me for thy servant, and receive me under thy mantle, O Mother of Mercy. And since thou art so powerful with God, deliver me from all temptations, or rather obtain for me the strength to triumph over them until death. Of thee I ask a perfect love of Jesus Christ. From thee I hope to die a good death.

O my Mother, for the love which thou bearest to God, I beseech thee to help me at all times, but especially at the last moment of my life. Leave me not, I beseech thee, until thou see me safe in Heaven, blessing thee, and singing thy mercies for all eternity. Amen. So I hope. So may it be.

Evening Meditation
THE PRACTICE OF THE LOVE OF JESUS CHRIST
XLII.-HE THAT LOVES JESUS CHRIST WISHES WHAT JESUS CHRIST WISHES

I.

We must receive with resignation, not merely the crosses which come directly from God; for instance, ill-health, scanty talents, accidental reverses of fortune; but such, moreover, as come indirectly from God, and directly from our fellow-men; for instance, persecutions, thefts, injuries; for all, in reality, come from God. David was one day insulted by one of his vassals called Semei, who not only upbraided him with words of contumely, but even threw stones at him. One of the courtiers would have forthwith avenged the insult by cutting off the head of the offender, but David replied: Let him alone, and let him curse; for the Lord hath bid him curse David-(2 Kings xvi. 10); or, in other words, God makes use of him to chastise me for my sins, and therefore He allowed him to pursue me with injuries.

II.

Wherefore St. Mary Magdalen de Pazzi says that all our prayers should have for their end to obtain from God the grace to follow His holy will in all things. Certain souls, greedy of spiritual dainties in prayer, go in search of these banquets of sweet and tender feelings; but courageous souls who seek sincerely to belong wholly to God ask Him only for light to understand His will, and for strength to put it into execution. In order to attain to purity of love, it is necessary to submit our will in all things to the will of God: "Never consider yourselves," said St. Francis de Sales," to have arrived at the purity which you ought to have, as long as your will is not cheerfully obedient, even in things the most repulsive, to the will of God." "Because," as St. Teresa remarks, "the giving up of our will to God draws Him to unite Himself with our lowliness." But this can never be obtained except by means of mental prayer and of continual petitions addressed to the Divine Majesty, nor without a cordial desire to belong entirely to Jesus Christ without reserve.

O most amiable Heart of my Divine Savior, Heart enamored of mankind, since Thou loves me with such a depth of tenderness; O Heart, in fine, worthy to rule over and possess all our hearts, would that I could make all men comprehend the love Thou bearest them, and the tender caresses Thou dost lavish on those who love Thee without reserve! O Jesus, my Love, be pleased to accept the offering and the sacrifice which I this day make to Thee of entire will! Only make known what Thou wouldst have me to do; for I am determined to do all by the help of Thy grace.

FRIDAY – FOURTH WEEK AFTER PENTECOST

X.-HOW TO CONVERSE CONTINUALLY AND FAMILIARLY WITH GOD

The heavens and the earth and all things in them, says St. Augustine, tell me to love Thee, O my God! St. Teresa used to say that when she saw beautiful hills and slopes, they seemed to reproach her for her ingratitude to God.

I.

When your eye rests on scenes in the country or along the sea-shore, on flowers or fruits, and you are delighted by the sight and scent of all, say: Behold, how many are the beautiful creatures that God has created for me in this world, in order that I may love Him; and what further enjoyments does He not keep prepared for me in Paradise? St. Teresa used to say that when she saw any beautiful hills or slopes, they seemed to reproach her for her own ingratitude to God. And the Abbot de Rance, Founder of La Trappe, said that the beautiful creatures around him reminded him of his own obligation to love God. St. Augustine also said the same thing, crying out aloud: "Heaven and earth and all things tell me to love Thee." It is related of a certain holy man that in passing through the fields he would strike with a little stick the flowers and plants along his way, saying: "Be silent! Do not reproach me any longer for my ingratitude to God. I have understood you; be silent I say no more!" When St. Mary Magdalen de Pazzi held in her hand any beautiful fruit or flower, she used to feel herself smitten by divine love, saying to herself: "Behold, my God has thought from eternity of creating this fruit, this flower, in order to give it me as a token of the love He bears towards me."

II.

When you see the rivers and brooks, reflect that as the water which you behold keeps running on to the ocean without ever stopping, so ought you to be ever hastening on to God, Who is your only Good. When you happen to be in a vehicle drawn by beasts of burden, say: See what labor these innocent animals go through for my service; and how much pains do I myself take in order to serve and please my God? When you see a little dog, which for a miserable morsel of bread is so faithful to its master, reflect how much greater reason you must be faithful to God Who has created and preserved and provided for you, and heaps upon you so many blessings. When you hear the birds sing, say: Hearken, O my soul, to the praise these little creatures are giving to their Creator; and what are you doing? Then do you also praise Him with acts of love. On the other hand, when you hear the cock crow, recall to your memory that there once was a time when you also, like Peter, denied your God; and then renew your contrition and your tears. So, likewise, when you see the house or place where you have sinned, turn yourself to God and say: The sins of my youth and my ignorance remember not, O Lord-(Psalm xxiv. 7).

When you behold the valleys, consider that their fertility is due to the waters that run down from the mountains, so from Heaven do graces descend upon the souls of the humble, and pass by the proud. When you see a beautifully ornamented church, consider the beauty of a soul in a state of grace, which is a real temple of God. When you behold the sea, consider the immensity and the greatness of God. When you see fire, or candles lighted on an altar, say: How many years is it since I ought to have been cast into hell to burn! But since Thou, O Lord, hast not sent me there, make this heart of mine burn with love for Thee, as that wood and those candles burn. When you look up at the sky, all studded with stars, say with St. Andrew of Avellino: "O my feet, you will one day have those stars beneath you."

In order frequently to recall to mind the Mysteries of our Savior's love, when you see hay, a manger, or a cave, let the Infant Jesus in the Stable of Bethlehem be present in your recollection. When you see a saw, a hammer, a plane, or an axe, remember how Jesus labored like a mere working boy in the shop at Nazareth. Then if you see ropes, thorns, nails, or pieces of wood, reflect on the Passion and death of our Redeemer. St. Francis of Assisi, on seeing a lamb, would begin to weep, saying, "My Lord, like a lamb, was led to death for me." Again, when you see altars, chalices, or patens, recall to mind the greatness of the love which Jesus Christ has borne us in giving us the Most Holy Sacrament of the Eucharist.

Spiritual Meditation

CORAM SANCTISSIMO

THIRTIETH VISIT

Why hidest thou thy face?–(Job xiii. 24). Job feared when he saw that God hid His face: but to know that Jesus Christ veils His majesty in the Most Blessed Sacrament should not inspire us with fear, but rather with greater love and confidence; since it is precisely to increase our confidence, and with greater evidence to manifest His love, that He remains on our altars concealed under the appearance of bread. Novarinus says: "God in hiding His face in this Sacrament discloses His love." And who would ever dare to approach Him with confidence, and lay bare before Him his affections and desires, did this King of Heaven appear on our altars in the splendors of His glory?

Ah, my Jesus, what a loving invention was this of the Most Blessed Sacrament, in which Thou hides Thyself under the appearance of bread, in order to make Thyself loved and that Thou mayest be found on earth by all who desire Thee! The Prophet was right in saying that men should speak and raise their voices throughout the world, in order to make known to all men, to what an excess the inventions of the love of our good God go for us. Make his works known among the people-(Is. xii. 4). O most loving Heart of my Jesus, worthy to possess the hearts of all creatures-Heart all and ever full of flames of most pure love! O consuming Fire, consume my whole being, and give me a new life of love and grace! Unite me to Thyself in such a way that I may never more be separated from Thee. O Heart open to be the refuge of souls, receive me! O Heart, which on the Cross was so agonized for the sins of the world, give me true sorrow for my sins! I know that in this Sacrament Thou preserves the same sentiments of love for me which Thou hadst when dying on Calvary; and therefore Thou hast an ardent desire to unite me wholly to Thyself. And is it possible that I should any longer resist yielding up my entire self to Thy love and to Thy desire? Ah, by Thy merits, my beloved Jesus, be pleased Thyself to wound me, to bind me, to force me, to unite me in all things to Thy Heart. I am now determined by Thy grace to give Thee all the pleasure I possibly can, by trampling under foot all human respect, my inclinations, repugnances, all my tastes and conveniences, which may prevent me from entirely pleasing Thee. Do Thou, my Lord, so help me, that I may execute this determination in such a way that henceforth all my works, opinions, and affections may be in conformity with Thy good pleasure. O love of God, do Thou drive all other loves from my heart! O Mary, my hope, thou art all-powerful with God, obtain for me the grace to be a faithful servant of the pure love of Jesus until death. Amen, amen. So I hope; so may it be in time and eternity!

Ejaculatory Prayer. Who shall separate us from the love of Christ? -(Romans viii. 85).

AN ACT OF SPIRITUAL COMMUNION

My Jesus, I believe that Thou art truly present in the Most Holy Sacrament. I love Thee above all things, and I desire to possess Thee within my soul. Since I am unable now to receive Thee sacramentally, come at least spiritually into my heart. I embrace Thee as already there, and unite myself wholly to Thee; never permit me to be separated from Thee.

VISIT TO MARY

St. Bernard affirms that the love of Mary towards us cannot be greater or more powerful than it is; hence by her affection she is always abundant in her compassion for us, and by her power she is plentiful in the relief she affords us: "The most powerful and compassionate charity of the Mother of God abounds in tender compassion and in kind relief; she is equally rich in both." So that, my most pure Queen, thou art rich in power, and rich in compassion; thou art able and desires to save all. I therefore beseech thee now, and I will do so always, in the words of the devout Blosius: "O Lady, protect me in my combats, and strengthen me when I am wavering." O most holy Mary, in this great battle in which I am engaged with hell, do thou always succor me; but when thou see me wavering and likely to fall, O Lady, do thou then extend thy hand with greater promptitude, and sustain me with greater vigor. O God, how many temptations have I still to overcome before my death! Mary, my hope, my refuge, my strength, do thou protect me, and never allow me to lose the grace of God. And On my part I resolve always and instantly to have recourse to thee in all temptations, saying:

Ejaculatory Prayer. Help me, Mary! Mary, help me.

Concluding Prayer

Most holy Immaculate Virgin and my Mother Mary, to thee, who art the Mother of my Lord, and Queen of the world, the advocate, the hope, the refuge of sinners, I have recourse today I, who am the most miserable of all. I render thee my most humble homage, O great Queen, and I thank thee for all the graces thou hast conferred on me until now, particularly for having delivered me from hell, which I have so often deserved. I love thee, O most amiable Lady; and for the love which I bear thee, I promise to serve thee always, and to do all in my power to make others love thee also. I place in thee all my hopes; I confide my salvation to thy care. Accept me for thy servant, and receive me under thy mantle, O Mother of Mercy. And since thou art so powerful with God, deliver me from all temptations, or rather obtain for me the strength to triumph over them until death. Of thee I ask a perfect love of Jesus Christ. From thee I hope to die a good death.

O my Mother, for the love which thou bearest to God, I beseech thee to help me at all times, but especially at the last moment of my life. Leave me not, I beseech thee, until thou see me safe in Heaven, blessing thee, and singing thy mercies for all eternity. Amen. So I hope. So may it be.

Evening Mediation
THE PRACTICE OF THE LOVE OF JESUS CHRIST
XLIII.-HE THAT LOVES JESUS CHRIST WISHES WHAT JESUS CHRIST WISHES

I.

Now what is the surest way to know and ascertain what God requires of us? There is no surer way than to practice obedience to our superiors and directors. St. Vincent de Paul said the will of God is never better complied with than when we obey our superiors. The Holy Ghost says: Much better is obedience than the victims of fools-(Eccles. iv. 17}. God is more pleased with the sacrifice we make to Him of our own will, by submitting it to obedience, than with all other sacrifices which we can offer Him; because in other things, as in alms-deeds, fastings, mortifications, and the like, we give of what is ours to God, but in giving Him our will, we give Him everything. So that when we say to God: O Lord, make me know by means of obedience what Thou requires of me, for I wish to comply with all, we have nothing more to offer Him.

Whoever, therefore, gives himself up to obedience, must detach himself totally from his own opinion. "What though each one," says St. Francis de Sales, "has his own opinions, virtue is not thereby violated; but virtue is violated by the attachment we have to our own opinions." But alas! this attachment is the hardest thing to part with; and hence there are so few persons wholly given to God, because few render a thorough submission to obedience. There are some persons so fondly attached to their own opinion that, on receiving an obedience, although the thing enjoined suits their inclination, yet, from the very fact of its being commanded, they lose all fancy for it, all wish to discharge it; for they find no relish in anything but in following the dictates of their individual will. How different is the conduct of Saints! Their only happiness flows from the execution of what obedience imposes on them. The saintly Jane Frances de Chantal once told her daughters that they might spend the Recreation-day in any manner they chose. When the evening came, they all went to her, to beg most earnestly that she would never again grant them such a permission; for they had never spent such a wearisome day as that on which they had been set free from obedience.

II.

It is a delusion to think that anyone can be possibly better employed than in the discharge of what obedience has imposed. St. Francis de Sales says: "To desert an occupation given by obedience in order to unite ourselves with God by prayer, by reading, or by recollection, would be to withdraw from God to unite ourselves with our own self-love." St. Teresa adds, moreover, that whoever performs any work, even though it be spiritual, yet against obedience, assuredly works by the instigation of the devil, and not by Divine inspiration, as he perhaps flatters himself; "because," says the Saint, "the inspirations of God always come in company with obedience." To the same effect she says elsewhere: "God requires nothing more of a soul that is determined to love Him than obedience." "A work done out of obedience," says Father Rodriguez, "outweighs every other that we can imagine." To gather a straw off the ground from obedience is of greater merit than a protracted prayer, or a discipline to blood, done out of our own head. This caused St. Mary Magdalen de Pazzi to say that she would rather be engaged in some exercise from obedience than in prayer; "because in obedience I am certain of the will of God, whereas I am by no means so certain of it in any other exercise." According to all spiritual masters, it is better to leave off any devout exercise through obedience than to continue it without obedience. The Most Blessed Virgin Mary revealed once to St. Bridget that he who relinquishes some mortification through obedience reaps a twofold profit; since he has already obtained the merit of the mortification by the good-will to do it, and he also gains the merit of obedience by foregoing it. One day the famous Father Francis Arias went to see the Blessed John of Avila, his intimate friend, and he found him pensive and sad; he asked him the reason of it, and received this answer: "Oh, happy you who live under obedience, and are sure of doing the will of God. As for me, who shall warrant me whether I do a thing more pleasing to God in going from village to village, catechizing the poor peasants, or in remaining stationary in the confessional to hear every one that presents himself? Whereas he that is living under obedience is always sure that whatever he performs by obedience is according to the will of God, or rather that it is what is most acceptable to God." Let this serve as a consolation for all those who live under obedience.

SATURDAY – FOURTH WEEK AFTER PENTECOST

Morning Mediation

XI.-HOW TO CONVERSE CONTINUALLY AND FAMILIARLY WITH GOD

During the day make frequently an offering of yourself to God, as St. Teresa used to do, saying: Lord, here I am! Do with me what pleaseth Thee! She used to say that all he who practices prayer should seek is to conform his will to the divine will; and let him be assured that in this consists the highest perfection.

I.

During the day make frequently an offering of yourself to God, as St. Teresa used to do, saying: "Lord, here am I! Do with me what pleases Thee! Declare to me Thy will, that I may do it for Thee; I wish to do it thoroughly." Then repeat, as often as you can, acts of love towards God. St. Teresa used also to say that acts of love are the fuel by which the holy love of God is to be kept on fire within the heart. When the Venerable Sister Seraphine of Capri was one day considering that the mule belonging to the convent had not the power of loving God, she expressed her compassion for it thus: "Poor brute; thou neither knowest nor canst love thy God"; and the mule commenced to weep so that the tears fell in streams from its eyes; so likewise do you, when beholding any animal which has not the capacity for knowing or loving God, animate yourself, who can love Him, to make more frequent act of holy love. Whenever you fall into any fault, humble yourself for it immediately; and, with an act of more fervent love, endeavor to rise again. When anything adverse happens, immediately make an offering to God of what you have to suffer, bringing your will into conformity with God's will; and ever accustom yourself under all adverse circumstances to repeat these words: "Thus does God will; thus, I will too." Acts of resignation are the acts of love that are most precious and acceptable to the Heart of God.

II.

When you have to decide upon anything, or to give any counsel of importance, first commend yourself to God, and then set about your undertaking, or give your opinion. As often as you can during the day, after the example of St. Rose of Lima, repeat the prayer, Deus, in adjutorium meum intende: "Lord, come to my assistance! Do not leave me in my own hands!" And for this end frequently turn to the Image of the Crucified, or to that of the Most Holy Mary, which is in your room; and do not omit to make frequent invocations of the Names of Jesus and Mary, especially in time of temptation. Since God is infinite goodness, His desire of communicating His graces to us is perfect. The Venerable Father Alvarez one day saw our Savior with His hands full of graces, and going about in search of those to whom He might dispense them. But it is His will that we should ask them of Him. Ask, and ye shall receive-(John xvi. 24), otherwise He will draw back His hands, whereas, on the contrary, He will willingly open them to those who call upon Him. And who is there that hath called upon Him and God despised him by not answering his prayer? Who hath called upon him and he hath despised him?-(Ecclesiasticus ii. 12). And David tells us that the Lord shows not merely mercy, but great mercy, to those who call upon Him: For thou, O Lord, art sweet and mild and plenteous in mercy to all that call upon thee-(Psalm lxxxv. 5).

Oh, how good and bountiful is the Lord to him who seeks Him lovingly! The Lord is good to the soul that seeks him-(Lamentations iii. 25). If He lets Himself be found even by him who seeks Him not-I was found by them that did not seek me (Romans x. 20)-how much more willingly will He let Himself be found by one who does seek Him-and seeks Him, too, to serve and to love Him!

To conclude: St. Teresa says that holy souls in this world have to conform themselves by love to what the souls of the Blessed do in Heaven. As the Saints in Heaven occupy themselves only with God, and have no other thought or joy than in His glory and in His love, so also must this be the case with you. While you are in this world, let God be your only happiness, the only object of your affections, the only end of your actions and desires, until you come to that Eternal Kingdom where your love will be in all things perpetual and complete, and your desires will be perfectly fulfilled and satisfied.

Spiritual Reading

CORAM SANCTISSIMO

THIRTY-FIRST VISIT

Oh, how beautiful a sight it was to behold our sweet Redeemer on that day, when, fatigued by His journey, He sat down, all engaging and loving, beside the well to await the Samaritan woman that He might convert and save her! Jesus, therefore, sat thus on the well–(John iv. 6). It is precisely thus that this same Lord seems sweetly to dwell with us all day long, having come down from Heaven upon our altars, which are as so many Fountains of grace, whereat He waits and invites souls to keep Him company, at least for a while, that He may in this way draw them to His perfect love. From every altar on which Jesus remains in the Most Holy Sacrament He seems to address all, saying: O men! why do you fly from my Presence? Why do you not come and draw near to One Who loves you so much, and Who remains thus annihilated for your sake? Why do you fear? I am not now come on earth to sit in judgment, but I have hidden Myself in this Sacrament of love only to do good, and to save all who have recourse to Me: I came not to judge the world but to save the world-(John xii. 47).

Let us, then, understand that as Jesus Christ in Heaven is always living to make intercession for us -(Hebrews vii. 25), so in the Sacrament of the Altar He is continually, night and day, exercising the compassionate office of Advocate; offering Himself as a Victim for us to the Eternal Father, thus, to obtain for us His mercy and innumerable graces. Therefore, the devout Thomas a Kempis says that we ought to approach Jesus to converse with Him in the Blessed Sacrament without fear of chastisement, and unrestrained, as with a beloved friend, "as one who loves speaking to his beloved; as a friend to a friend."

Since, then, Thou thus gives me permission, let me, O my hidden King and Lord, now open my heart to Thee with confidence, and say: "O my Jesus! O Enamored of souls, I well know the injustice men do Thee. Thou loves them, and art not loved by them; Thou does good to them, and receives insults; Thou desires to make them hear Thy voice, and they give Thee no ear; Thou offers them graces, and they refuse them. Ah, my Jesus, and is it true that I also at one time joined these ungrateful creatures in thus displeasing Thee? O God, it is but too true! But I am determined to amend and to endeavor, during the time that I have to live, to make up for the displeasure I have caused Thee, by doing all that I possibly can to please Thee and to give Thee consolation. Tell me, O Lord, what Thou dost wish from me, and I will execute all without reserve: make known Thy will to me by means of holy obedience, and I hope to accomplish it. My God, I now resolutely promise Thee that I will never, from this day forward, omit what I know to be the more pleasing to Thee, even were it to cost me the loss of all-relatives, friends, esteem, health, yea life itself. Let all perish, provided Thou art pleased. Happy loss, indeed, when all is lost and sacrificed to satisfy Thy Heart, O God of my soul! I love Thee, O sovereign Good, worthy of love above every other good; and in loving Thee I unite my poor heart to all the hearts with which the Seraphim love Thee; I unite it to the heart of Mary, to the Heart of Jesus. I love Thee with my entire self; Thee alone will I love, and Thee alone will I always love.

Ejaculatory Prayer. My God, my God, I am Thine, and Thou art mine!

AN ACT OF SPIRITUAL COMMUNION

My Jesus, I believe that Thou art truly present in the Most Holy Sacrament. I love Thee above all things, and I desire to possess Thee within my soul. Since I am unable now to receive Thee sacramentally, come at least spiritually into my heart. I embrace Thee as already there and unite myself wholly to Thee; never permit me to be separated from Thee.

VISIT TO MARY

Blessed Amadeus says that our most blessed Queen Mary is always in the divine Presence, acting as our advocate, and interposing with God by her prayers, which are most powerful: "The most blessed Virgin stands before the face of her Creator, interceding with her most powerful prayers for us." "For," he adds, "she well sees our miseries and our dangers, and as our most clement and sweet Lady compassionates and succors us with a mother's love." Thou, my advocate and my most loving Mother, thou even now see the miseries of my soul; thou see my dangers and prayer for me. Pray, pray, and cease not to pray, until thou see me saved and thanking thee in Heaven. The devout Blosius tells me that thou, O sweet Mary, art, after Jesus, the certain salvation of those who are thy faithful servants. Ah! this grace I now ask of thee: grant me the happy lot of being thy faithful servant until death; that after death I may go to bless thee in Heaven, where I shall be certain never more, as long as God is God, to leave thy sacred feet.

Ejaculatory Prayer. O Mary, my Mother, grant that I may be ever thine.

Concluding Prayer

Most holy Immaculate Virgin and my Mother Mary, to thee, who art the Mother of my Lord, and Queen of the world, the advocate, the hope, the refuge of sinners, I have recourse today I, who am the most miserable of all. I render thee my most humble homage, O great Queen, and I thank thee for all the graces thou hast conferred on me until now, particularly for having delivered me from hell, which I have so often deserved. I love thee, O most amiable Lady; and for the love which I bear thee, I promise to serve thee always, and to do all in my power to make others love thee also. I place in thee all my hopes; I confide my salvation to thy care. Accept me for thy servant, and receive me under thy mantle, O Mother of Mercy. And since thou art so powerful with God, deliver me from all temptations, or rather obtain for me the strength to triumph over them until death. Of thee I ask a perfect love of Jesus Christ. From thee I hope to die a good death.

O my Mother, for the love which thou bearest to God, I beseech thee to help me at all times, but especially at the last moment of my life. Leave me not, I beseech thee, until thou see me safe in Heaven, blessing thee, and singing thy mercies for all eternity. Amen. So I hope. So may it be.

Evening Meditation

THE PRACTICE OF THE LOVE OF JESUS CHRIST

XLIV.-HE THAT LOVES JESUS CHRIST WISHES WHAT JESUS CHRIST WISHES

I.

For obedience to be perfect, we must obey with the will and with the judgment. To obey with the will signifies to obey willingly, and not by constraint, in the fashion of slaves; to obey with the judgment means to conform our judgment to that of the superior, without examining what is commanded. St. Mary Magdalen de Pazzi remarks on this: "Perfect obedience demands a soul without judgment." To the like purpose, St. Philip Neri said that, to obey with perfection, it was not enough to execute the thing commanded, but it must be done without reasoning on it; taking it for certain that what is commanded us is for us the most perfect thing we can do, although the opposite may be better before God.

This holds good not merely for Religious, but likewise for seculars living under obedience to their spiritual directors. Let them request their director to prescribe them rules for the guidance of their affairs, both spiritual and temporal; and so they will make sure of doing what is best. St. Philip Neri said: "Let those who are desirous of progressing in the way of God submit themselves to a prudent confessor, whom they should obey as in God's place. By so doing, we are certain of not having to render an account to God of the actions we perform." He said, moreover, that we must place faith in the confessor, because the Lord will not permit him to err; that nothing is so sure of cutting off all the snares of the devil as to do the will of others in the performance of good; and that there is nothing more dangerous than to wish to direct ourselves according to our private fancy. In like manner St. Francis de Sales says, in speaking of the direction of the spiritual father as a means of walking securely in the path of perfection: "This is the maxim of all maxims."

O Jesus, I give Thee my whole heart and all my will. It was at one time, alas! rebellious against Thee; but now I dedicate it wholly to Thee. "Lord, what wilt Thou have me to do?" Tell me what Thou requires of me, and lend me Thy assistance; for I will leave nothing undone. Dispose of me and of all that concerns me, as Thou pleases; I accept of all, and resign myself to all.

O Love deserving of infinite love, Thou hast loved me so as even to die for me; I love Thee with my whole heart, I love Thee more than myself, and into Thy hands I abandon my soul. On this very day I bid farewell to every worldly affection, I take leave of everything created, and I give myself without reserve to Thee; through the merits of Thy Passion receive me and make me faithful unto death. My Jesus, my Jesus, from this day forward I will live only for Thee, I will love none but Thee, I will seek nothing else than to do Thy blessed will. Aid me by Thy grace, and aid me, too, by thy protection, O Mary, my hope.

II.

"Seek as ye will," says the devout Avila, "you will never so surely find the will of God as in the way of this humble obedience, so much recommended and so practiced by all the ancient servants of God." The same thing is affirmed by St. Bernard, St. Bernardine of Sienna, St. Antoninus, St. John of the Cross, St. Teresa, John Gerson, and all theologians and masters of the spiritual life; and St. John of the Cross said that to call this truth in question is almost to doubt of the Faith. The words of the Saint are: "Not to be satisfied with what the confessor says is arrogance and a want of faith." Among the maxims of St. Francis de Sales are the two following, most consolatory for scrupulous souls: Firstly, a truly obedient soul was never yet lost. Secondly, we ought to be satisfied on being told by our spiritual director that we are going on well, without seeking to be convinced of it ourselves. It is the teaching of many doctors, as of Gerson, St. Antoninus, Cajetanus, Navarrus, Sanchez, Bonacina, Cordovius, Castropalao, and the doctors of Salamanca, with others, that the scrupulous person is bound, under strict obligation, to act in opposition to scruples, when from such scruples there is reason to apprehend grievous harm happening to soul or body, such as the loss of health, or of intellect; wherefore scrupulous persons ought to have greater scruple at not obeying the confessor than at acting in opposition to their scruples. To sum up, therefore, all that has been said in this chapter, our salvation and perfection consist of: (1) In denying ourselves; (2) In following the will of God; (3) In praying Him always to give us strength to do both one and the other.

What have I in heaven, and besides thee what do I desire upon earth? Thou art the God of my heart and the God that is my portion forever-(Ps. lxxii. 26). My beloved Redeemer, infinitely amiable, since Thou hast come down from Heaven to give Thyself wholly to me, what else shall I seek for on earth or in Heaven besides Thee, Who art the Sovereign Good, the only Good worthy to be loved? Be Thou then, the sole Lord of my heart, do Thou possess it entirely; may my soul love Thee alone, obey Thee alone, and seek to please no other than Thee. Let others enjoy the riches of this world, I wish only for Thee: Thou art and shalt ever be my Treasure in this life and in eternity.

I will not despair of becoming a saint on account of the sins of my past life; for I know, my Jesus, that Thou didst die in order to pardon the truly penitent. I love Thee now with my whole heart, with my whole soul; I love Thee more than myself, and I bewail, above every other evil, ever having had the misfortune to despise Thee, my Sovereign Good. Now I am no longer my own, I am Thine; O God of my heart, dispose of me as Thou pleases. In order to please Thee, I accept of all the tribulations Thou mayest choose to send me- sickness, sorrow, troubles, ignominies, poverty, persecution, desolation-I accept all to please Thee: in like manner I accept of the death Thou hast decreed for me, with all the anguish and crosses which may accompany it : it is enough if Thou grants me the grace to love Thee exceedingly. Lend me Thy assistance; give me strength henceforth to compensate, by my love, for all the bitterness I have caused Thee in past time, O only Love of my soul! O Queen of Heaven, O Mother of God, O great advocate of sinners, I trust in thee!

Fifth Sunday after Pentecost

Morning Meditation

SALVATION IS OUR ONLY BUSINESS IN THIS WORLD

One thing is necessary (Luke x 42). It is not necessary we should be rich, or honored, or in the enjoyment of good health, but it is necessary we should be saved. For this end alone has God placed us in this world, and woe to us if we do not attain it!

I.

Of all our affairs there is non more important than that of our eternal salvation, on which depends our happiness or misery for eternity.

One thing is necessary. It is not necessary that we should be rich, honored, or in the enjoyment of good health, but it is necessary that we should be saved. For this end alone has God placed us in the world; and woe to us if we do not attain it!

St. Francis Xavier said that the only good to be obtained in this world is salvation; and the only evil to be dreaded, damnation. What matters if we are poor, or despised, or infirm? If we are saved, we shall be happy forever. On the contrary, what does it avail to be great, or to be monarchs? If we are lost, we shall be miserable for all eternity.

O god, what will become of me? I may be saved, and I may also be lost! And if I may be lost, why do I not resolve to adhere more closely to Thee?

My Jesus, have pity on me. I will amend my life. Give me Thy assistance. Thou hast died to save me, and shall I, notwithstanding, forfeit my salvation?

II.

Have we already done enough to secure salvation? Are we already secure of not falling into hell?

What exchange shall a man give for his soul? (Matthew xvi. 26). If he loses his soul, what will compensate him for his loss?

What have not the Saints done to secure their salvation? How many kings and queens have renounced their kingdoms and shut themselves up in cloisters! How many young men have left their country and have gone to live in deserts! How many young virgins have renounced marriage with the great ones of the world, to go and give their lives for Jesus Christ! And what are we doing?

O my God, how much has Jesus Christ done for our salvation! He spent thirty-three years in toil and labor; He have His Blood and His Life; and shall we, through our own fault, be lost?

O Lord, I give Thee thanks for not having called me out of the world when I had forfeited Thy grace. Had I died then, what would have become of me for all eternity?

God desires that all should be saved: He will have all men to be saved (1 Timothy ii. 4). If we are lost, it will be entirely our own fault. And this will be our greatest torment in hell.

St. Teresa says that even the loss of a trifle, of an ornament, of a ring, when it has happened through our own carelessness, occasions, us the greatest uneasiness. What a torment, then, will it be to the damned to have willfully lost all – their souls, Heaven, and God!

Alas! death approaches; and what have I done for life eternal?

O my God, for how many years have I deserved to dwell in hell, where I could not repent, nor love Thee! Now that I can repent and love Thee, I will repent, and I will love Thee.

Spiritual Reading

I.—THE ADVANTAGE OF A RETREAT MADE IN SOLITUDE AND SILENCE

I have received your last letter in which you tell me you are still undecided as to the state of life you should choose, and that having communicated to your Pastor the advice I gave you – namely, to go for that purpose to perform the Spiritual Exercises in the house you father owns in the country – the said Pastor answered you it was not necessary to go there to torture your brains for eight days in solitude, but that it was enough for you to attend the Retreat he would soon have for the people in his own church. Now, as on this point of making the Exercises you again ask my advice, it is necessary I should answer you more at length, and show you how much greater the fruit of the Spiritual Exercises is when they are performed in silence, in some retired place, than in public, when one is obliged during the time to live in one's own house and converse with relatives and friends: and the more so in your case, for, as you write to me, you have in your own home no quiet room to which you can retire.

Besides, I am very much in favor of a Retreat performed in solitude, closed away from the world, as I know it is to such a Retreat I owe my own conversion and my resolution to give up the world. I will later suggest to you the means and precautions to be taken during the Spiritual Exercises to reap from them the fruit you desire. I beg of you, when you have read this letter yourself, to give it to your Rev. Parish Priest that he may read it also.

Let us, then, speak first of the great benefit of the Spiritual Exercises when performed in solitude, where one converses with God alone, and let us see the reason for this.

The truths of eternal life, such as the great affair of our salvation, the value of the time God gives us that we may amass merits for a happy Eternity, the obligations under which we are to love God for His infinite goodness and the immense love He has for us,– these and similar things are not seen with the eyes of the flesh, but only with the eyes of the mind. It is, on the contrary, certain that, unless our understanding represents to the will the value of a good or the greatness of an evil, we shall never embrace that good nor reject that evil. And this is the ruin of those who are attached to this world. They live in darkness, and not seeing the greatness of eternal good and eternal evil, and allured by the senses, they give themselves up to forbidden pleasure and thus miserably perish.

Wherefore the Holy Ghost admonishes us that in order to avoid sin we must keep before our eyes the Last Things which are to come upon us; that is, Death, with which all the goods of this earth will come to an end for us, and the Divine Judgment, in which we shall have to give to God an account of our whole life. Remember thy last end and thou shalt never sin (Ecclesiasticus vii. 40). And in another place God says: Oh that they would be wise and would understand and would provide for their last end (Deuteronomy xxxii. 29). By which words He wishes us to understand that if men would consider the things of the next life, they would all certainly take care to sanctify themselves, and would not expose themselves to the danger of an unhappy life in Eternity. But they shut their eyes to the light and thus, remaining blind, precipitate themselves into an abyss of evil. This is why the Saints always prayed the Lord to give them light. Enlighten my eyes, that I never sleep in death (Psalm xii. 4). May God cause the light of his countenance to shine upon us (Psalm. lxvi. 2). Make the way known to me wherein I should walk (Psalm cxlii. 8). Give me understanding and I will learn thy commandments (Psalm cxviii. 78).

Now in order to obtain this Divine light we must come close to God. Come ye to him and be enlightened (Psalm xxxiii. 6). For, as St. Augustine tells us, that as we cannot see the sun without the light of the sun itself, so we cannot see the light of God but by the light of God Himself. This light is obtained in the Spiritual Exercises; by them we come close to God, and God enlightens us with His light. The Spiritual Exercises mean nothing else than that we retire for a time from intercourse with the world, and go to converse with God alone, where God speaks to us by His inspirations, and we speak to God in our meditations by acts of love, by repenting of the sins by which we have displeased Him, by offering ourselves to serve Him for the future with all our heart, and by beseeching Him to make known to us His will, and give us strength to accomplish it.

Holy Job says: Now I should have rest in my sleep with kings and consuls of the earth who build themselves solitudes (Job iii. 18). Who are these kings that build themselves solitudes? They are, as St. Gregory says, those who rise above this world, and withdraw from its tumults to render themselves fit to talk alone with God. "They build solitudes, that is, they separate themselves far as possible from the tumult of the world, in order to be alone and to become fit to speak with God."

One day as St. Arsenius was reflecting on the means that he should take to become a saint, God caused him to hear these words: Fuge! Tace! Quiesce! "Fly! Be silent! And Rest!" Fly from the world, be silent, cease to talk with men, and speak only with Me, and thus rest in peace and solitude. In conformity with this, St. Anselm wrote to one worried by many worldly occupations, who complained that he had not a moment of peace, and gave the following advice: "Leave your occupations for a while; hide yourself for a time to contemplate God and rest in Him: Say to God: Now teach my heart where and how I may seek Thee; where and how I may find Thee." Words that are applicable, each and all, to yourself. Fly, says he, for a short time from those earthly occupations which render you so unquiet, and rest in solitude with God. Say to Him: O Lord, show me where and how I may find Thee, that I may speak alone with Thee, and at the same time hear Thy words.

God speaks indeed to those who seek Him, but He does not speak in the midst of the tumult of the world. The Lord is not in the commotion of the earthquake, as was said to Elias when God called him to solitude. The voice of God, as it is said in the same place, is as the breath of a gentle air, which is scarcely heard, and then not by the ear of the body, but by that of the heart, without noise and in a sweet retreat. This is exactly what the Lord says through Osee: I will lead her into solitude; far from the embarrassment of the world and intercourse with men, and there speaks to it in words of fire. The word of God is said to it in words of fire, because it melts a soul, as the sacred Spouse says: *My soul melted when he (my beloved) spoke* (Canticles v. 6). It prepares the soul to submit readily to the direction of God, and to embrace the manner of life which God wishes. The word of God is so exceedingly efficacious that at the very time it is heard it operates in the soul all that God requires.

Evening Meditation

THE PRACTICE OF THE LOVE OF JESUS CHRIST

"Charity beareth all things."

HE THAT LOVES JESUS CHRIST BEARS ALL THINGS FOR HIM, AND ESPECIALLY ILLNESS, POVERTY, AND CONTEMPT.

I.

Father Balthazar Alvarez said that a Christian must not imagine himself to have made any progress in perfection until he has succeeded in penetrating his heart with a lasting sense of the sorrows, poverty, and ignominies of Jesus Christ, to be able to support with loving patience every sorrow, privation, and contempt, for the sake of Jesus Christ.

In the first place, let us speak of bodily infirmities, which, when borne with patience, merit for us a beautiful crown.

St. Vincent de Paul said: "Did we but know how precious a treasure is contained in infirmities, we would accept them with joy as the greatest of all possible blessings." Hence the Saint himself, though constantly afflicted with ailments that often let him no rest day or night, bore them with so much peace and serenity of countenance that no one could guess that anything ailed him at all. Oh, how edifying to see a sick person bear his illness with a peaceful countenance, as did St. Francis de Sales! When he was ill, he simply made known his complaint to the physician, obeyed him exactly by taking the prescribed medicines, however nauseous; and for the rest, he remained at peace, never uttering a single complaint in all his sufferings. What a contrast to this is the conduct of those who do nothing but complain even for the most trifling indisposition, and who would like to have around them all their relatives and friends to have their sympathy! Far different was the instruction of St. Teresa to her nuns: "My sisters, learn to suffer something for the love of Jesus Christ, without letting all the world know of it." One Good Friday Jesus Christ favored the Venerable Father Louis da Ponte with so much bodily suffering that no part of him was exempt from its particular pain; he mentioned his severe sufferings to a friend, but he was afterwards so sorry at having done so that he made a vow never again to reveal to anybody whatever he might afterwards have to suffer. I say "he was favored"; for, to the Saints, the illnesses and pains which God sends them are real favors.

II.

One day as St. Francis of Assisi lay on his bed in excruciating torments, a companion said to him: "Father, beg of God to ease your pains, and not to lay so heavy a hand upon you." On hearing this the Saint instantly leaped from his bed, and going down on his knees, thanked God for his sufferings; then, turning to his companion he said: "Listen; did I not know that you so spoke from simplicity, I would refuse ever to see you again."

Someone who is sick will say it is not so much the infirmity itself that afflicts me as that it prevents me from going to church to perform my devotions, to communicate, and to hear Holy Mass; I cannot go to choir to recite the Divine Office with my brethren; I cannot celebrate Mass; I cannot pray; for my head is aching with pain, and light almost to fainting. But tell me now, if you please, why do you wish to go to church or to choir? Why would you communicate and say or hear Holy Mass? Is it to please God? but it is not now the pleasure of God that you say Office; that you communicate or hear Mass; but that you remain patiently on this bed, and support the pains of this infirmity. But you are not pleased with my speaking thus; then you are not seeking to do what is pleasing to God, but what is pleasing to yourself. The Blessed John of Avila wrote as follows to a priest who so complained to him: "My friend, busy not yourself with what you would do if you were well but be content to remain ill as long as God thinks fit. If you seek the will of God, what matters it to you whether you be well or ill?"

Monday – Fifth Week after Pentecost

Morning Meditation

LOSS OF THE SOUL, AN IRREPARABLE EVIL

How long shall we delay? Until we have to weep with the damned, saying: Ergo erravimus! We therefore have erred! (Wis. v. 6), and there is now no longer, or ever shall be, any remedy for us? For every other misfortune in this world there is some remedy, but for the loss of the soul, there is none.

I.

How long shall we delay? Until we have to weep with the damned, saying: Ergo erravimus! We therefore have erred! — and there is now no longer, or ever shall be, any remedy for us?

For every other misfortune in this world there is some remedy, but for the loss of the soul, there is none.

What pains and trouble men take to obtain wealth, dignities, pleasures! But what are they doing to save their souls? Nothing, as though the loss of the soul were but of little consequence!

How much diligence in preserving bodily health! The best physicians, the best remedies, the best climate, are sought after. And as regards the health of the soul, what great negligence!

O my God, I will no longer resist Thy calls! Who knows but that the words which I am now reading may be my last call from God!

Can we be sensible of the danger of being lost forever and not tremble? And do we delay to apply a remedy to the disorders of our consciences?

My soul, how many graces has not God bestowed upon you that you may be saved! He has caused you to be born in the bosom of the true Church. How many advantages for becoming a Saint. Sermons, confessions, the good example of companions. How many lights, how many loving calls in Spiritual Exercises, in Meditation, in Holy Communion! How many mercies has He not shown you! How long has He not waited for you! How many times has He not pardoned you! – graces which He has not bestowed on so many others.

II.

What is there that I ought to do more to my vineyard that I have not done to it? (Is. v. 4). What more, says Almighty God, ought I to do for you soul? for how many years have you been in the world and what fruit have you hitherto brought forth?

If we had been allowed to choose the means of salvation, what more easy and effectual means could we have chosen?

Alas! if we do not avail ourselves of so many graces, they will serve only to render our death the more miserable.

To become a saint, it is not necessary to have ecstasies and visions; sufficient for you are the ordinary means which you possess. Meditate, communicate frequently, read spiritual books, fly all sinful occasions, and you will become a saint.

O God, already have I lived many years in the world, and what have I hitherto gained? O Jesus! Thy precious Blood, Thy death upon the Cross, are my hope!

If this night I were to die, should I be satisfied with my past life? No; and why do I delay? Death may come, and I may have to lament and say: Alas! my life is now at an end, and I have done nothing!

What a grace would it be for a sick man, already despaired of by his physicians, to be allowed another year, or even another month! And God grants me this time; and how shall I employ it for the future?

O Lord, since Thou hast waited for me until now, I will no longer disregard Thee. Here I am! Tell me what Thou requires of me, and I will do it. I will not wait to give myself to Thee until time for me be no more. O Jesus! I will never more offend Thee. I will spend the remainder of my life in bewailing my past sins, and in loving Thee, the God of my soul.

Spiritual Reading

II. THE ADVANTAGES OF A RETREAT MADE IN SOLITUDE AND SILENCE

One day the Lord said to St. Teresa: "There are many souls to whom I would willingly speak, but the world makes so great a noise in their hearts that My voice cannot be heard. Oh, if they would but separate themselves a little from the world!" Thus, then, my very dear friend, the Lord wishes to speak to you, but alone and in solitude; since if He would speak to you in your own house, your relations, your friends, and your domestic occupations would continue to make a noise in your heart, and you would be unable to hear His voice. The Saints have for this reason left their homes and their country, and gone to hide themselves in caverns or deserts, or at least in a cell in some Religious house, there to find God and hear His voice. St. Eucherius relates that a certain person seeking a place in which he could find God, went for this purpose to ask counsel from a master of the spiritual life. The man of God led him to a solitary place and then said: "Behold, here God may be found!" adding nothing more. By this he wished him to understand that God is not to be found in the midst of the noise of the world, but in solitude. St. Bernard says that he learned to know God better amongst the beaches and oaks than in all the learned books he had ever studied.

Worldlings love to be in company with friends, to talk and divert themselves; but the desire of the Saints is to live in solitary places, in the midst of forests, or in caverns, there to converse alone with God Who in solitude familiarly converses with souls as a friend with his friend. "Oh, Solitude," exclaims St. Jerome, "in which God familiarly converses with His servants!" The Venerable Vincent Caraffa said that if it had been free to him to wish for anything in this world, he would have asked for nothing but a little grotto with a piece of bread and a spiritual book, there always to live far from men, and conversing alone with God. The Spouse of the Canticles, praising the beauty of a soul living in solitude, compares it to the beauty of the turtledove: Thy cheeks are beautiful as the turtledove's (Canticles i. 9), precisely because the turtledove avoids the company of other birds, and always lives in the most solitary places. Hence it is that the holy Angels are filled with admiration and joy at the beauty and splendor of a soul ascending into Heaven after a life hidden and solitary as in a desert: Who is this that cometh up from the desert, flowing with delights? (Canticles viii. 5).

Now I have written all these things in order to inspire you with a love for holy solitude, for I hope that in the Exercises you are going to perform you will not have to torture your brains, as your pastor said, but that the Lord will make you taste so great a spiritual delight, that you will come out of your Retreat with such an affection for the Spiritual Exercises that you will not fail hereafter to go through them every year. This will be of immense advantage to your soul, whatever state of life you may choose, because in the midst of the world, its various occupations, disturbances, and distractions always produce dryness of spirit, so that it is necessary from time to time to refresh and renew it, as St. Paul exhorts: Be ye renewed in the spirit of your mind (Ephesians iv. 23).

King David, troubled by earthly cares, wished to have wings and to fly from the bustle of the world to find rest: Who will give me wings ... and I will fly away and be at rest? (Psalm liv. 7). But being unable to leave the world in body, he at least sought from time to time to withdraw himself from the affairs of the realm he governed and dwelt in solitude conversing with God, and thus his spirit found peace. I have gone far off, flying away, and I abode in the wilderness (Psalm v. 8).

Evening Meditation

THE PRACTICE OF THE LOVE OF JESUS CHRIST

"Charity beareth all things"

HE THAT LOVES JESUS CHRIST BEARS ALL THINGS FOR HIM, AND ESPECIALLY ILLNESS, POVERTY, AND CONTEMPT

I.

You say you are unable to pray because your head is so weak. Be it so: you cannot meditate; but why cannot you make acts of resignation to the will of God? If you would only make these acts, you could not make a better prayer, welcoming with love all the torments that assail you. Thus did St. Vincent de Paul act. When attacked by a serious illness, he was wont to keep himself tranquilly in the presence of God, without forcing his mind to dwell on any subject; his sole exercise was to elicit some short acts from time to time, as of love, of confidence, of thanksgiving, and more frequently of resignation, especially in the crisis of his sufferings. St. Francis de Sales made this remark: "Considered in themselves tribulations are terrifying; but considered in the will of God, they are lovely and delightful." You cannot make meditation, you say, and what more exquisite prayer than to cast a look from time to time on your crucified Lord, and to offer Him your pains, uniting the little that you endure with the overwhelming torments that afflicted Jesus on the Cross!

II.

There was a certain pious lady lying bed-ridden with many ailments, and on the servant putting the Crucifix into her hands and telling her to pray to God to deliver her from her miseries, she made answer: "But how can you desire me to seek to descend from the Cross, whilst I hold in my hands a God crucified? God forbid that I should do so! I will suffer for Him Who chose to suffer torments for me incomparably greater than mine." This was, indeed, precisely what Jesus Christ said to St. Teresa when she was laboring under serious illness: He appeared to her all covered with Wounds, and then said to her: "Behold, My daughter, the bitterness of My sufferings, and consider if yours equal Mine." Hence the Saint was accustomed to say in the midst of all her infirmities: "When I remember in how many ways my Savior suffered, though He was innocence itself, I know not how it could enter my head to complain of my sufferings." During a period of thirty-eight years St. Lidwina was afflicted with numberless diseases – fevers, gout in the feet and hands, and sores, all her lifetime; nevertheless, from never losing sight of the sufferings of Jesus Christ, she maintained an unbroken cheerfulness and joy. In like manner, St. Joseph of Leonessa, a Capuchin, when the surgeon was about to amputate his arm, and his brethren would have bound him to prevent his stirring from vehemence of pain, seized hold of the Crucifix and exclaimed: "Wherefore bind me? Wherefore bind me? Behold Who it is that binds me to support every suffering patiently for love of Him!" And so he bore the operation without a murmur. St. Jonas the Martyr, after passing the entire night immersed in ice water by order of the tyrant, declared next morning that he had never spent a happier night, because he had pictured to himself Jesus hanging on the Cross; and thus, compared with the torments of Jesus, his own had seemed rather caresses than sufferings.

Tuesday – Fifth Week after Pentecost

Morning Meditation

WE MUST BEFORE ALL THINGS SECURE THE SALVATION OF OUR SOULS

Let us proceed at once with the work of our soul's salvation, for death is at hand. What we can do today let us not put off till tomorrow. Time passes and returns no more.

I.

Let us proceed at once with the work of our soul's salvation, for death is at hand. What we can do today let us not put off till tomorrow. Time passes and returns no more.

Everyone says, at the hour of death: Oh, that I had been a saint! But of what avail will such regrets be when the oil fails, and the lamp will soon be extinguished?

We shall say when death comes: What would it have cost me to have avoided that occasion, to have borne with that person, to have broken off that correspondence, to have yielded that point of honor? But I did not do so; and now what will become of me?

Let us not think that we can do too much to gain eternal salvation. "No security can be too great," says St. Bernard, "where Eternity is at stake."

To secure our salvation, we must resolve to adopt the means. Inclination will not be sufficient; nor will it serve us to say, I will do it by and by. Hell is filled with souls who said: By and by! By and by! Death came in the meantime, and they were lost.

O Lord, help me! I will say to Thee, with St. Catherine of Genoa: "My Jesus, no more sins, no more sins!" I renounce all things to please Thee.

II.

The Apostle says, with fear and trembling work out your salvation (Philippians ii. 12). He who trembles at the thought of being lost, always recommends himself to God, avoids the occasions of sin, and will be saved.

To be saved we must use violence. Heaven is not given to indolent cowards. The violent bear it away (Matthew xi. 12).

O Lord, how many promises have I not made Thee! But my promises have all been treasons. I will never betray Thee more; help me, grant that I may die rather than offend Thee.

Ask, says our Lord, and you shall receive (John xvi. 24), by which He manifests to us His great desire that we should be saved. If anyone should say to his friend: Ask me what you please, he could say nothing more. Let us, then, ever pray to God, and we shall be enriched with graces, and secure of salvation.

My dear Jesus, cast Thine eyes on my miseries and have pity on me. I have been forgetful of Thee, but Thou hast not forgotten me. I love Thee, my Love, with all my soul; I detest all the offences I have committed against Thee above every evil. Pardon me, my God, and forget my many acts of ingratitude. And since Thou knowest my weakness, do not abandon me; enlighten me, and strengthen me to conquer all things to please Thee. Grant that I may forget all, that I may think only of Thy love and mercies by which Thou hast so powerfully obliged me to love Thee. Mary, Mother of God, pray to Jesus for me.

Spiritual Reading

III. THE ADVANTAGE OF A RETREAT MADE IN SOLITUDE AND SILENCE

Jesus Christ, Who had no need of solitude to be recollected and united with God, in order to set us an example, often retired from intercourse with men and withdrew to mountains or into deserts to pray: Having dismissed the multitude he went into a mountain alone to pray (Matthew xiv. 23); and He retired into the desert and prayed (Luke v. 16). He also desired His disciples, after the fatigue of their missions, to retire to some solitary place to rest in spirit: Come apart into a desert place and rest a little (Mark vi. 31), declaring by this that the spirit, even amidst spiritual occupations, being obliged to treat with men, becomes somewhat relaxed, whence it is very necessary to renew it in solitude and retreat.

Worldlings, who are accustomed to divert themselves in conversations, at banquets and plays, imagine that in solitude, where no such things are found, one must suffer insupportable tediousness. This is indeed the case with those who have a conscience defiled by sin. As long as they are occupied in the affairs of this world they do not think of the things of the soul; but when they are disengaged and in solitude where they do not seek God, they feel all at once remorse of conscience, and thus they find nothing but tediousness and pain. But in the case of one who seeks God, he will find in solitude not tediousness, but contentment and joy. Of this the Wise Man assures us: For her (wisdom's) conversation hath no bitterness, nor her company any tediousness, but joy and gladness (Wisdom viii. 16). Oh no, to converse with God causes no bitterness, no tediousness, no, nothing but peace and joy.

The Blessed Cardinal Bellarmine, during the season when the other Cardinals went to pass their holidays in country seats and villas, used to go to some quiet house to make the Exercises for a month, and these be called his holiday, and certainly his heart found more delight in them than others did in their pastimes.

St. Charles Borromeo made the Exercises every year and found them his paradise on earth; and it was while he was one year engaged in these Exercises on Mount Varalle that his last illness and death came. Hence it is that St. Jerome says that solitude was his paradise on earth: "Solitude is a paradise to me."

But, perhaps, someone will ask: What contentment can a person find, being alone and having no one with whom to converse? St. Bernard answers: "He who seeks God is by no means alone in solitude, for God Himself is there with him, and renders him happier than if he had the company of the first princes of the world." "I am never less alone," wrote the holy Abbot, "than when alone." Nunquam minus solus quam cum solus.

The Prophet Isaias, describing the sweetness which God gives to those who seek Him in retreat, says: The Lord therefore will comfort Sion, and will comfort all the ruins thereof; and he will make her desert as a place of pleasure, and her wilderness as a garden of the Lord. Joy and gladness shall be found therein, thanksgiving and the voice of praise (Isaiah li. 8).

The Lord well knows how to comfort a soul that withdraws from the world. He compensates a thousandfold for the loss of all the pleasures of the world. He changes solitude into a garden of delights, where the tumult of the world being excluded, the soul thanks and praises God, and finds a very paradise of peace.

Evening Meditation

THE PRACTICE OF THE LOVE OF JESUS CHRIST

"Charity beareth all things"

HE THAT LOVES JESUS CHRIST BEARS ALL THINGS FOR HIM, AND
ESPECIALLY ILLNESS, POVERTY, AND CONTEMPT

I.

Oh, what abundance of merits may be accumulated by patiently enduring an illness!
Almighty God revealed to Father Balthazar Alvarez the great glory He had in store for
a certain nun who had borne a painful sickness with resignation; and told him that she
had acquired greater merit in those eight months of her illness than some other Religious
in many years. It is by the patient endurance of ill-health that we weave a great part, and
perhaps the greater part, of the crown that God destines for us in Heaven. St. Lidwina
had a revelation to this effect. After sustaining many and most cruel disorders, as we
mentioned, she prayed to die a martyr for the love of Jesus Christ; now, as she was one day
sighing after this martyrdom, she suddenly saw a beautiful crown, but as yet incomplete,
and she understood that it was destined for herself; whereupon the Saint, longing to
behold it completed, entreated the Lord to increase her sufferings. Her prayer was heard,
for some soldiers came shortly after and ill-treated her, not only with injurious words,
but with blows and outrage. An Angel then appeared to her with the crown completed
and informed her that those last injuries had added to it the gems that were wanting; and
shortly afterwards she expired.

II.

Ah, yes! to the hearts that fervently love Jesus Christ, pains and ignominies are most
delightful. And thus, we see the holy Martyrs going with gladness to encounter the sharp
prongs and hooks of iron, the plates of glowing steel and axes. The Martyr St. Procopius
thus spoke to the tyrant who tortured him: "Torment me as you like but know at the
same time that nothing is sweeter to the lover of Jesus Christ than to suffer for His sake."
St. Gordiano, Martyr, replied in the same way to the tyrant who threatened him with
death: "Thou threatens me with death; but I am sorry that I can die only once for my
own beloved Jesus." And I ask, did these Saints speak thus because they were insensible to
pain or weak in intellect? No, replies St. Bernard; not insensibility, but love caused this:
Hoc non fecit stupor, sed amor. They were not insensible, for they felt well enough the
torments inflicted on them; but since they loved God, they esteemed it a great privilege
to suffer for God, and to lose all, even life itself, for the love of God.

WEDNESDAY – FIFTH WEEK AFTER PENTECOST

Morning Meditation

THE VANITY OF THE WORLD – THE GOODS OF THIS WORLD ARE FALSE
GOODS

The world! And what is the world but mere show! A scene which quickly passes away!
The fashion of this world passeth away! Death approaches, the curtain falls, the scene
closes, and all comes to an end!

I.

What doth it profit a man, if he gains the whole world and suffer the loss of his own soul?
(Matthew xvi. 26). O great maxim, which has conducted so many souls to Heaven, and
bestowed so many Saints on the Church! What doth it profit to gain the whole world,
which passes away, and lose the soul, which is eternal?

The world! And what is the world but mere show, a scene which quickly passes away!
The fashion of this world passeth away (I Corinthians vii. 31). Death approaches, the
curtain falls, the scene closes, and all comes to an end!

Alas! at the hour of death, how will all worldly things appear to a Christian – those
vessels of silver, those heaps of gold, that rich and vain furniture – when he must leave
them all forever!

O Jesus, grant that henceforward my soul may be wholly Thine! Grant that I may love
no other but Thee. I desire to renounce all things before death tears me away from them.

St. Teresa says: "Nothing ought to be considered of consequence which must come to an end." Let us, therefore, strive to gain that treasure which will not fail with time. What does it avail a man to be happy for a few days (if indeed there can be any happiness without God), if he must be unhappy forever in eternity.

David says that earthly goods, at the hour of death, will seem as a dream to one waking from sleep: As the dream of them that awake (ps. lxxii. 20). What disappointment does he feel who, having dreamt he was a king, on awaking finds himself still as lowly and poor as ever?

O my God, who knows but that this meditation which I am now reading will be the last call for me? Enable me to root out of my heart all earthly affections before I enter into eternity. Grant that I may be sensible of the great wrong I have done Thee, by offending Thee, and by forsaking Thee for the love of creatures. Father, I am not worthy to be called thy son (Luke xv. 21). I am grieved for having turned my back upon Thee; do not reject me, now that I return to Thee.

II.

No position of dignity, no magnificence, no wealth, no nice points of honor, no pastimes, will console a Christian at the hour of death; the love of Jesus Christ, and the little that he has suffered for His love, will alone console him.

Philip II, when dying, said "Oh, that I had been a Lay-Brother in some Monastery, and not a King!" Philip III said "Oh, that I had lived in a desert! Alas, now I shall appear with but little confidence before the tribunal of God!" Thus, at the hour of death, do those express themselves who have been esteemed the most fortunate in this world.

In short, all earthly goods generally bring, at the hour of death, only remorse of conscience and fear of eternal damnation. O God! will the dying sinner say, I have had sufficient light to withdraw myself from worldliness, and yet I have followed the world, and its maxims; and now what sentence will be pronounced upon me? Fool that I have been! I might have been a saint, with the means of grace and the advantages I enjoyed! I might have led a happy life in union with God; and now what have I but remorse of conscience and a dread of damnation! But when will he say this? When the scene is about to close, and himself about to enter into eternity, and at the moment on which will depend his happiness or misery forever.

O Lord, have pity on me! For the past I have not been so wise as to love Thee. From this day forward Thou alone shalt be my only Good: My God and my all! Thou alone deserves all my love, and Thee only will I love.

Spiritual Reading

IV. – THE ADVANTAGE OF A RETREAT MADE IN SOLITUDE AND SILENCE

If, indeed, there were no other satisfaction in solitude than that of knowing the Eternal Truths, that alone would be sufficient to make a Retreat a most desirable thing. The knowledge of the Eternal Truths give the soul a perfect contentment such as is never found in the vanities of the world, which are only lying and deceitful things. Herein consists precisely the happiness which is found in the exercises of a Retreat gone through in solitude and silence. It is then one sees in the clearest light the Christian maxims, the importance of salvation, the ugliness of sin, the value of grace, the love God bears us, the vanity of earthly goods, the foolishness of those who, for the sake of the fleeting joys of the world, fling away eternal goods and prepare for themselves an Eternity of pain and misery.

Hence it comes about that, having convinced himself of these truths, a man takes the most efficacious means to secure his eternal salvation. In a Retreat he disentangles himself from earthly affections and unites himself to God in prayer, by desires of closer union with Him, by repeated offerings of himself, by multiplied acts of sorrow, love, and resignation. He thus finds himself raised so high above all created things that he smiles in pity on those who set such value on the things of this world which he so much despises, knowing how worthless they are, and how unworthy of the love of a heart created to love an infinite Good, which is God. It is certain that one comes out of the Exercises a very different man, and much better than he was when he began them.

It was the opinion of St. John Chrysostom that retirement was a great means of rising to perfection. And a learned author, speaking of the Exercises of a Retreat, says: "Happy, indeed is the man who, fleeing from the noise of the world, allows himself to be led by the Lord to the Spiritual Exercises, into that sweet solitude where he finds and tastes the delights of Paradise." Sermons in the churches are good, but if the hearers do not reflect on what they have heard, the fruit will be little. Reflection will never be made as it should be unless it be made in solitude. As soon as the oyster receives the dew of heaven it shuts itself at once and sinks to the bottom of the sea, and there the pearl is formed. It is beyond all doubt that what makes the fruit of the Exercises perfect is the silent reflection alone with God upon the truths one has heard in a sermon or read in a book. Hence St. Vincent de Paul in his missions never failed to exhort his hearers to make the Exercises in some retired place. One single spiritual maxim well meditated upon is sufficient to make a saint. Thus St. Francis Xavier resolved to give up the world in consequence of the impression made on him by that maxim of the Gospel: What doth it profit a man if he gain the whole world and suffer the loss of his own soul? (Matthew xvi. 26). A young student having once heard a maxim on death, changed his conduct and led a virtuous life. St. Clement of Ancrya was encouraged to suffer for Jesus Christ all the torments inflicted by the tyrant, by thinking of what his mother had taught him: "It is for life eternal we are fighting."

Evening Meditation

THE PRACTICE OF THE LOVE OF JESUS CHRIST
HE THAT LOVES JESUS CHRIST BEARS ALL THINGS FOR HIM, AND ESPECIALLY ILLNESS, POVERTY, AND CONTEMPT

I.

Above all, in time of sickness we should be ready to accept of death, and of that death which God pleases. We must die, and our life must finish in our last illness; but we do not know which will be our last illness. Wherefore in every illness we must be prepared to accept that death God has appointed for us. A sick person says: "Yes, but I have committed many sins, and have done no penance. I should like to live, not for the sake of living, but to make some satisfaction to God before I die." But tell me, how do you know that if you live longer, you will do penance, and not rather do worse than before? At present you can well cherish the hope that God has pardoned you, and what penance can be more satisfactory than to accept of death with resignation, if God wills you are to die? St. Aloysius Gonzaga, at the age of twenty-three, gladly embraced death with this reflection: "At present," he said, "I am, as I hope, in the grace of God. Hereafter I know not what may befall me; so that I now die contentedly if God calls me to the next life." It was the opinion of Blessed John of Avila that everyone, provided he be in proper dispositions, though only moderately good, should desire death, to escape the danger which always surrounds us in this world, of sinning and losing the grace of God.

Besides, owing to our natural frailty, we cannot live in this world without committing at least venial sins; this should be a motive for us to embrace death willingly that we may never offend God any more. Further, if we truly love God, we should ardently long to go to see Him, and love Him with all our strength in Paradise, which no one can do perfectly in this present life; but unless death open to us the door, we cannot enter that blessed region of love. This caused St. Augustine, that loving soul, to cry out: "Oh, let me die, Lord, that I may behold Thee!" O Lord, let me die, otherwise I cannot behold and love Thee face to face.

II.

In the second place we must practice patience in the endurance of poverty. Our patience is certainly very much tried when we are in need of temporal goods. St. Augustine says: "He that has not God, has nothing; he that has God, has all." He who possesses God, and remains united to His will, finds every good. Witness St. Francis, barefooted, clad in sackcloth, and deprived of all things, yet happier than all the monarchs of the world, by simply repeating: Deus meus et omnia! My God and my All! He only is a poor man who has not what he desires; but he that desires nothing, and is contented with his poverty, is in fact very rich. Of such St. Paul says: Having nothing yet possessing all things (2 Corinthians vi. 10). The true lovers of God have nothing, and yet have everything; since, when temporal goods fail them, they exclaim: "My Jesus, Thou alone art sufficient for me!" and with this they rest satisfied. Not only did the Saints maintain patience in poverty, but sought to be despoiled of all, to live detached from all, and united with God alone. If we have not courage to renounce all worldly goods, at all events let us be contented with that state of life in which God has placed us; let our solicitude be not for earthly goods, but for those of Paradise, which are immeasurably greater, and last forever; and let us be fully persuaded of the truth of what St. Teresa says: "The less we have here the more we shall have in Heaven."

Thursday – Fifth Week after Pentecost

Morning Meditation

THE VANITY OF THE WORLD – THE GOODS OF THIS WORLD PASS QUICKLY

Ye great ones of the world who are tormented in the fires of hell, what remains to you now of your honors and your wealth? They answer, weeping: Nothing! Nothing! What advantage hath the boasting of riches brought us? All these things are passed away like a shadow!

I.

Ye great ones of the world who are tormented in the fires of hell, what remains to you now of your honors and your wealth? They answer, weeping: Nothing! Nothing! We have nothing but torments and despair! All is passed but our punishment, which will never end!

At death men will say: What hath pride profited us? or what advantage hath the boasting of riches brought us? All those things are passed away like a shadow (Wis. v. 8). Alas, the remembrance of the good things we have enjoyed in the world will not, at the hour of death, inspire us with confidence, but will fill us with terror and confusion.

Woe to me! How many years have I been in the world, and what have I hitherto done for God? O Lord, have pity on me, and cast me not away from thy face (Psalm l. 18).

The time of death is the time when all worldly things will appear as they really are – vanity, smoke, and dust!

O my God! How frequently have I exchanged Thee for nothing? I should not dare to hope for pardon, were it not that Thou hast died to pardon me. Now will I love Thee above all things and will esteem Thy grace more precious than all the kingdoms of the earth.

Death is compared by St. Paul to a thief (1 Thessalonians v. 4), because it robs us of all things – possessions, relations, beauty, dignity, and even of our own very flesh.

The day of death is also called the day of destruction (Deuteronomy xxxii. 35). Then shall we love all that we have ever acquired, and all that we can hope for from this world. O my Jesus! I am not concerned about the loss of earthly goods, but only lest I should lose Thee, the Infinite Good.

We extol the Saints, who, for the love of Jesus Christ, despise the goods of this earth; and do we continue to be attached to such vanities at the imminent danger of our salvation?

We have a great esteem for the treasures of this life; and why do we make so little account of the treasures of eternity?

Enlighten me, O my God! Make me realize that all creatures are nothing, and that Thou art my All, the Infinite Good. Grant that I may leave all things to possess Thee alone. My God! My God! Thee only do I desire, and besides Thee, nothing in this world!

II.

St. Teresa says that our faults and our attachments to the goods of this earth, arise from a want of Faith. Let us then reanimate our Faith and remember we shall one day have to leave all and go into eternity. And hence let us leave all now, while we can obtain merit by so doing. One day we shall have to leave them all. What are riches, honors, friends? God! God! Let us seek God alone, and God will be our All.

That eminent servant of God, Sister Margaret of St. Ann, daughter of the Emperor Rudolf II, and a discalced Religious used to say: "What will kingdoms avail at the hour of death?"

The death of the Empress Isabella induced St. Francis Borgia to renounce the world, and to give himself entirely to God. At the sight of her corpse, he said to himself: It is thus, then, that the grandeurs and the crowns of this world terminate!

O my God, Thou hast always loved me! Grant that I may be wholly Thine before death overtakes me.

Spiritual Reading

V.—THE ADVANTAGE OF A RETREAT MADE IN SOLITUDE AND SILENCE

To form a true idea of the good produced by a Retreat, read some book on the subject, and see the wonderful conversions brought about by the Exercises. I will mention a few.

Father Maffei tells us there was in Sienna a priest who led a disedifying life. He made a Retreat under the direction of a missionary who happened to be in that town; and not only was he converted, but one day when there was a great multitude in the Church, he went into the pulpit weeping and with a rope round his neck, and there asked pardon for all the scandal he had given. He afterwards became a Capuchin and died a Saint. On his deathbed he made known that all the great graces he had received were due to the Spiritual Exercises.

Father Bartoli relates that a certain German knight, who, having abandoned himself to all kinds of vice, gave his soul to the devil by a document signed in his own blood. He afterwards performed the Spiritual Exercises, and he often fainted from excess of grief. He thenceforth led a life of severe penance till the day of his death.

Father Rossignoli tells us that in Sicily a certain baron's son led so debauched a life that, having tried all means to make him amend, but in vain, his father was obliged to put him in a galley to work with the slaves. But a certain good Religious, moved to compassion, sought out the young man, and by his kind winning manners, induced him to meditate whilst at his work on the great Truths of Eternity. This he did, and soon he made his confession, and so changed his life that his father was glad to receive him back to his house again, and never again had any reason to be displeased with his son.

A young man in Flanders, having made a Spiritual Retreat, gave up his wicked life. Seeing his friends amazed at his conversion, he said to them: "You wonder at my change of life, but I tell you that if the devil himself were capable of making the Spiritual Exercises, he would be converted to penance."

A Religious who had by his bad conduct become insupportable in his Community, was sent by his Superiors to make a Retreat. When he was going away he jestingly said to those about him: "Get ready your Rosary beads to touch me when I return." But the Exercises did indeed change him so completely that he became an example for all the other Religious, and, seeing the change, they all wished to make the Exercises.

Some young men, seeing a number of their friends going to make a Spiritual Retreat, wished to accompany them, not to profit their souls, but in order afterwards to jest about the Exercises. Just the opposite happened; for during the Retreat they were so filled with compunction that they began to sigh and weep for their sins. They made good Confessions and changed their lives.

Evening Meditation

"Charity beareth all things"

HE THAT LOVES JESUS CHRIST BEARS ALL THINGS FOR HIM, AND ESPECIALLY ILLNESS, POVERTY, AND CONTEMPT

I.

St. Bonaventure said that temporal goods were nothing more than a sort of birdlime to hinder the soul from flying to God. And St. John Climacus said that poverty, on the contrary, is a path which leads to God free of all hindrances. Our Lord Himself said: Blessed are the poor in spirit, for theirs is the kingdom of heaven (Matthew v. 8). In the other Beatitudes, the Heaven of the life to come is promised to the meek and to the clean of heart; but to the poor, Heaven (that is heavenly joy) is promised even in this life: theirs is the kingdom of heaven. Yes, for even in the present life the poor enjoy a foretaste of Paradise. By the poor in spirit are meant those who are not merely poor in earthly goods, but who do not so much as desire them, who, having enough to clothe and feed them, live contented, according to the advice of the Apostle: But having food and wherewith to be covered, with these we are content (I Timothy vi. 8). Oh, blessed poverty, exclaimed St. Laurence Justinian, which possesses nothing and fears nothing! Ever joyous and ever in abundance since she turns every inconvenience into advantage for the soul. St. Bernard said: "The avaricious man hungers after earthly things as a beggar, the poor man despises them as a lord." The miser is always hungry as a beggar, because his is never satiated with possessing; the poor man, on the contrary, despises them all as a rich lord, inasmuch as he desires nothing.

II.

One day Jesus Christ thus spoke to St. Angela of Foligno: "If poverty were not of great excellence, I would not have chosen it for Myself, nor have bequeathed it to My Elect." And, in fact, the Saints, seeing Jesus poor, had therefore a great affection for poverty. St. Paul says that the desire of growing rich is a snare of Satan by which he has wrought the ruin of innumerable souls: They that will become rich, fall into temptation, and into the snare of the devil, and into many unprofitable and hurtful desires, which drown men into destruction and perdition (I Tim vi. 9). Unhappy beings who, for the sake of vile creatures of earth, forfeit an Infinite Good, which is God! St. Basil the Martyr was right, when the Emperor Licinius proposed to make him the chief among his priests, if he would renounce Jesus Christ; he was right, I say, to reply: "Tell the emperor that were he to give me his whole kingdom, he would not give me as much as he would rob me of by depriving me of God." Let us be content, then, with God, and with the things He gives us, rejoicing in our poverty, when we stand in need of something we desire, and have it not; for herein consists of our merit. "Not poverty," says St. Bernard, "but the love of poverty, is reckoned a virtue." Many are poor, but from not loving their poverty, they merit nothing; therefore St. Bernard says that the virtue of poverty consists not in being poor, but in the love of poverty.

Friday – Fifth Week after Pentecost

Morning Meditation

THE VANITY OF THE WORLD – DEATH SHOWS US THE VANITY OF THE
WORLD

St. John Chrysostom says: "Go to the tomb, and contemplate the dust and worms and
–sigh!" O the great secret of death! Things the most desirable on this earth lose all their
splendor when viewed from the bed of death.

I.

O the great secret of death! How it brings to an end all worldly desires! How it shows all
worldly grandeur as smoke and deceit! Things the most desired of this earth lose all their
splendor when beheld from the bed of death. The shadow of death obscures the beauty
of all things here below.

Of what profit are riches when nothing remains but a winding-sheet? Of what
advantage bodily beauty, when all is reduced to a heap of worms? Of what avail is
authority, when nothing remains but to be thrown into the grave, and be forgotten by
all?

St. Chrysostom says: "Go to the sepulcher, contemplate dust and worms—and sigh!"
Look on the graves of the dead; see those skeletons gnawed by worms and crumbling into
dust, and say, with a sign: Ah, such must I become, and why do I not think of this? Why
do I not give myself to God? Alas! who knows but that which I am now reading may be
the last call for me?

O my dear Redeemer, I accept of my death, and I accept of it in whatever way it may
please Thee to send it to me; but I beseech Thee, before Thou judges me, to allow me

time to bewail the offences I have committed against Thee. I love Thee, O my Jesus, and I am truly sorry for having despised Thee.

O my God, how many miserable beings, to obtain worldly goods, pleasures, vanities, have lost their souls, and, by losing their souls, have lost all!

Do we believe or not that we must one day die? And that only once? And why do we not leave all, to secure a happy death? Let us leave all, to secure all.

Is it possible we realize that the remembrance of a disorderly life will at the hour of death be an insufferable torment, and still continue to live on in sin?

O my God, I thank Thee for the light Thou affords me. But, O Lord, what have I done? Have I multiplied my sins, and hast Thou increased Thy graces? Woe to me, if I do not avail myself of them!

II.

He who reflects that in a short time he must leave the world will not be attached to it.

Oh, with what peace of soul do those live and die who, despoiled of all things, are contented to say, My God and my all!

Solomon said that all the goods of this earth are only vanity and affliction of spirit; since the more one possesses of the goods of this world, the more he suffers.

St. Philip Neri used to call those fools whose hearts are attached to this world. Fools, because even here they lead miserable lives.

O my God, what now remains of the many sinful deeds of which I have been guilty, but the pain and remorse that torment me, and will torment me still more at the hour of death? Oh, do Thou, O Lord, make haste to pardon me! Thou desire that I should be all Thine, and such do I desire to be. Behold, from this moment, I give myself to Thee, and I desire nothing in return but Thyself.

Let us not imagine that to be detached from all things, to love God alone, is to live an unhappy life. Who on this earth is so contented and happy as the man who loves Jesus Christ with his whole heart? Find me one amongst all the kings of the world, who is happier than the man who gives himself entirely to God.

My soul, if now thou wert to depart out of this world, wouldst thou die satisfied with thy past life? And for what dost thou delay? Is it that the light which God in His mercy now affords thee may only serve to reproach thee at the great accounting day?

O Jesus, I renounce all to give myself to Thee. Thou didst seek me when I fled from Thee; and now that I seek Thee, do not reject me. Thou didst love me when I did not love Thee, nor even desire that Thou shouldst love me; and now that I have no other desire but to love Thee, and to be loved by Thee, cast me not away from Thy face. O my God, I am now convinced that Thou desires to save me, and I desire to work out my salvation to please Thee. I leave all and give my whole self to Thee. Mary, Mother of God, pray to Jesus for me.

Spiritual Reading

VI—THE ADVANTAGE OF A RETREAT MADE IN SOLITUDE AND SILENCE

I could add a thousand other examples, but I shall relate only one more—the case of a nun in the Convent of Torre di Specchi in Rome. She pretended to be a learned woman but led a very imperfect life. When the Spiritual Exercises were being conducted in the convent she began them, but very much against her will. The very first meditation on the "End of Man" made such an impression on her that, weeping, she went to the Spiritual Father, and said: "Father, I wish to become a saint without delay." She wanted to say more, but sobs prevented her. Returning to her cell she wrote out a consecration of her entire self to Jesus Christ, and gave herself up to penance and retirement, and persevered until death.

If we had no other motive for attaching so much importance to the Spiritual Exercises, it would be enough to consider the esteem so many saintly men had for them. St. Charles Borromeo began to lead a perfect life after the first Retreat in Rome. St. Francis de Sales attributed to the Spiritual Exercises the first beginnings of a holy life. Louis of Granada, a man of very great virtue, used to say that a lifetime would not suffice to explain the knowledge of Divine things which he discovered in going through the Spiritual Exercises. Blessed John of Avila called the Exercises a school of heavenly wisdom and exhorted all his spiritual children to make them. Father Louis Blosius, the holy Benedictine, used to say we should give God special thanks for having in these latter times made known to His Church the precious treasure of the Spiritual Exercises of a Retreat.

But if the Exercises are of great help to persons in every state and condition, they are of special help to him who wishes to make a proper choice of a state of life. For I find it laid down that the first end for which the Exercises were instituted was that of making the choice of a state of life, because upon this choice depends on the eternal salvation of each one. We cannot expect that an Angel from Heaven should come to assure us of the state which, according to the will of God, we should choose. It is sufficient to put before us the state we are thinking of choosing, and then to consider the end we have in view in that choice and weigh all the circumstances.

This is the principle reason for which I wish you to make the Exercises in silence; namely, for making the choice of the state of life.

Evening Meditation

THE PRACTICE OF THE LOVE OF JESUS CHRIST

"Charity beareth all things"

HE THAT LOVES JESUS CHRIST BEARS ALL THINGS FOR HIM, AND ESPECIALLY ILLNESS, POVERTY, AND CONTEMPT

I.

This love of poverty should be especially practiced by Religious who have made the Vow of Poverty. "Many Religious," says the great St. Bernard, "wish to be poor; but on the condition of wanting for nothing." "Thus," says St. Francis de Sales, "they wish for the honor of poverty, but not the inconveniences of poverty." To such persons is applicable the saying of the blessed Solomea, a nun of St. Clare: "That Religious will be a laughingstock to Angels and to men, who pretends to be poor, and yet murmurs when in want of anything." Good Religious act differently, they love their poverty above all riches. The daughter of the Emperor Maximilian II, a discalced nun of St. Clare, called Sister Margaret of the Cross, appeared on one occasion before her brother, the Archduke Albert, in a patched habit. He evinced some astonishment at it, as if it were unbecoming her noble birth; but she made him this answer: "My brother, I am more content with this torn garment than all monarchs with their purple robes." St. Mary Magdalen de Pazzi said: "O happy Religious, who, detached from all by means of holy poverty, can say: 'The Lord is the portion of my inheritance!'" My God, Thou art my portion and all my good! St. Teresa, having received a large alms from a certain merchant, sent him word that his name was written in the Book of Life; and that, in token of this, he should lose all his possessions; and the merchant actually failed, and remained in poverty till death. St. Aloysius Gonzaga said that there could be no surer sign of a person's being numbered among the elect than to see him fearing God, and at the same time undergoing crosses and tribulations in this life.

II.

The bereavement of relations and friends by death belongs also, in some measure, to holy poverty; and in this we must especially practice patience. Some people, at the loss of a parent or friend, can find no rest; they shut themselves up to weep in their chamber, and giving free vent to their sorrow, become insupportable to all around them by their want of patience. I would ask these people for whose gratification, or for whose sake, do they thus lament and shed tears? Is it for God's? Certainly not, for God's will is that they should be resigned to His dispensations. For that of the soul departed? By no mean: if the soul be lost, she abhors both you and your tears; if she is saved, and already in Heaven she would have you thank God on her part; if still in Purgatory, she craves the help of your prayers, and wishes you to bow with resignation to the Divine will, and to become a saint, in order that she may one day enjoy your society in Paradise. Of what use, then, is all this weeping? On one occasion the Venerable Father Joseph Caracciolo, the Theatine, was surrounded by his relations, who were all bitterly lamenting the death of his brother, whereupon he said to them: "Come! come! let us keep these tears for a better purpose, to weep over the death of Jesus Christ, Who has been to us a Father, a Brother, a Spouse, and Who died for love of us." On such occasions we must imitate Job, who, on hearing the news of the death of his sons, exclaimed, with full resignation to the Divine will: The Lord gave, and the Lord hath taken away; God gave me my sons, and God hath taken them away. As it hath pleased the Lord, so is it done: blessed be the name of the Lord! It hath pleased God that such things should happen, and so it pleases me; wherefore may He be blessed by me forever (Job i. 21).

Saturday—Fifth Week after Pentecost

Morning Meditation

THE MERCY OF THE BLESSED VIRGIN MARY

"Oh, how many who deserved to be condemned by the justice of the Son, are saved by the mercy of the Mother! For she is God's treasure and the treasurer of all graces, and thus our salvation is in her hands and depends on her."—(Abbot of Celles).

I.

The Blessed Virgin said one day to St. Bridget: I am called, and I truly am, the Mother of Mercy; for such God has made me. And who, but God in His mercy, because He desires our salvation, has given us this advocate to defend us? "Therefore," adds Mary, "miserable will he be, who, while it is in his power, has not recourse to me, who am merciful." Miserable is the man, and miserable for eternity who, though he could, during life, have recommended himself to me, who am so benign and merciful to all, has neglected to have recourse to me, and is lost.

Perhaps, says Bonaventure, we are afraid that in asking Mary's intercession she will refuse it to us? No, says the Saint: "Mary does not refuse, and never has refused pity and aid to any sinner who has invoked her intercession." She has not done so, and she cannot do so, because God has made her the Queen and the Mother of Mercy; and as Queen of Mercy she is bound to attend to the care of the miserable. "Thou," says St. Bernard, "art the Queen of Mercy; and who but the miserable are the subjects of mercy?" Hence the Saint through humility adds: "Since then, O Mother of God, thou art the Queen of Mercy, thou must have a special care of me, who am the most miserable of sinners." As Mother of Mercy, it is her duty to deliver from death her sick children, to whom her mercy makes her a Mother. Hence, St. Basil calls her a public hospital. Public hospitals are erected for the poor; and they who are in the greatest poverty have the best claims to be admitted into them. Hence, according to St. Basil, Mary ought to receive the greatest tenderness and care the greatest sinners who have recourse to her.

O great Mother of God, behold at thy feet a miserable sinner, who has not once, but several times, voluntarily lost Divine grace, which thy Son purchased for him by His death. O Mother of Mercy, I come to thee with a soul covered with wounds and sores; be not angry with me on this account but have the greater pity on me and assist me. I do not ask of thee earthly goods; I ask thee to obtain for me the grace of God and love of thy Son.

II.

But let us not doubt the Mercy of Mary. One day St. Bridget heard the Savior saying to His Mother: "Thou wouldst show compassion to the devil, should he ask it with humility." The haughty Lucifer will never humble himself to ask her prayers; but if he humbled himself to this Divine Mother, and invoked her help, she, by her intercession, would deliver him from hell. By those words, Jesus Christ wished to give us to understand what Mary herself afterwards said to the same St. Bridget—that when a sinner has recourse to her, however enormous his guilt may be, she regards not the sins with which he is charged, but the intention with which he comes. If he come with a sincere desire to amend, she receives him and heals all his wounds. Hence St. Bonaventure says: "Poor sinners, do not despair! Raise your eyes to Mary, and trust in the Mercy of this good Mother." Let us, then, says St. Bernard, ask the grace we have lost, and let us ask it through Mary. The grace which we have lost, she has found, says Richard of St. Laurence; we therefore ought to go to her to recover it. When the Archangel Gabriel announced to the Most Holy Virgin the Divine maternity, he said to her: Fear not, Mary, thou hast found grace (Luke i. 30). But, since Mary was never deprived of grace, but was, on the contrary, always full of grace, how could he say that she had found it? In answer to this question, Cardinal Hugo says that Mary found grace, not for herself, because she had always possessed it, but for us, who have lost it. Hence the same author says that we ought to go to her and say: O Lady, property ought to be restored to him who has lost it; the grace which thou hast found is not thine, for thou hast always possessed it; it is ours, we have lost it through our own fault; thou shouldst then restore it to us. "Let sinners, then, who have lost grace by their sins, run—let them run to the Virgin, and say with confidence: Restore to us our property, which thou hast found."

My Mother Mary, pray for me, and never cease to pray for me. It is through the merits of Jesus Christ and thy intercession that I am to be saved. Thy office is to intercede for sinners: I will, then, say with St. Thomas of Villanova: "O Mary, our advocate, fulfil thy office!" Recommend me to God and defend me. No cause, however desperate, is lost, when defended by thee. Thou, after Jesus, art the hope of sinners; thou art my hope. O Mary, I will not cease to serve thee, to love thee, and to have recourse to thee always. Do not, then, ever cease to pray for me, particularly when thou see me in danger of again losing the grace of God. O Mary, O great Mother of God, have pity on me.

Spiritual Reading

VII—THE ADVANTAGE OF A RETREAT MADE IN SOLITUDE AND SILENCE

When, then, you have entered the Retreat, as I hope you will, I beg of you to follow the advice I now give you.

The sole intention you should have in making these Exercises is that you may know what God will have you to do; and, therefore, in going to that silent Retreat-house, say to yourself: I will hear what the Lord God shall speak in me (Psalm lxxxiv. 9). I go into Retreat to know what the Lord will tell me and what He wishes me to do.

Besides, it is necessary that you have a determined will to obey God and to follow without reserve the vocation He will make known to you.

It is, moreover, necessary that you pray earnestly to the Lord, that He make known to you His will, no matter what the state of life He wishes you to live. But remember that to obtain this light you must ask it with holy indifference. He who prays to God to enlighten him on the choice of a state of life, but does so without this indifference, and, instead of wishing to conform to God's will wishes rather that God should conform to his, is like a pilot who feigns to will, but indeed wills not, that his vessel should advance, since he begins by casting anchor and then hoists the sail! God does not enlighten or speak to such a person. But if you will supplicate God with his holy indifference and the resolution to accomplish His will, He will make you clearly see the state which is best for you. And if you should then feel any repugnance, place before your eyes the hour of your death, and think of the choice you would in that hour wish to have made, and act accordingly.

Take with you to your house of Retreat a book containing the meditations which are commonly made during the Exercises; read these meditations, and let them take the place of sermons, reflecting on them for half an hour in the morning and in the evening.

Bring also with you the Life of some Saint or some other spiritual book for your spiritual reading; and these ought to be your only companions in solitude during the eight days of your Retreat. In order to obtain light and to hear what the Lord will speak to you it is necessary to avoid every distraction: Be still and see that I am God (Psalm xlv. 11). To hear the Divine voice, we must cease all intercourse with the world. To a sick man no remedies will be of any use if he does not take them with the proper precaution, as, for example, avoiding exposure to the cold air, unwholesome food, or too much application of mind. In like manner, in order that the Exercises may be useful for the health of your soul, you must remove hurtful distractions, such as the receiving of visits from friends, messages from without, letters, etc. When St. Francis de Sales was engaged in the Exercises, he laid aside all the letters he received and did not read them until after the Retreat. You must avoid books of amusement and do no study; for you ought then only to study the Crucifix. Therefore, have in your room none but spiritual books, and read not for curiosity's sake, but only for this one end—namely, to help you to follow the state of life which God will make known to you as the one He wishes you embrace.

–Moreover, it is not enough to avoid distractions from without, you must also avoid those from within; for it you should deliberately allow your mind to think on worldly matters, or of your studies, or the like, the Exercises and the solitude will be of little use to you. St. Gregory says: "What will solitude of the body avail if solitude of the heart be wanting?" Peter Ortiz, a minister of the Emperor Charles V, went to make a Retreat at the monastery of Monte Cassino. Having arrived at the gates of the monastery he addressed to his thoughts the words our Lord spoke to His disciples: Sedete hic, donec vadam illuc et orem (Matthew xxvi. 36). "Worldly thoughts, stay you here outside the gates, and when I have ended my Retreat, I shall return to you." When one is engaged in making the Spiritual Exercises, one should occupy the time solely for the good of one's soul without losing or wasting a single moment of it.

Finally, when you are in your Retreat, I would be of you to use the following short prayer: –

O my God, I am that miserable one who in the past despised Thee; but now I esteem and love Thee above everything, nor will I love any other but Thee. Thou wishes me to belong entirely to Thee; to Thee I will belong entirely. Speak, O Lord; for thy servant heareth (I Kings iii. 10). Let me know what Thou wishes from me, and I will do all. Let me especially know in what particular state Thou wishes me to serve Thee: Make thou known to me the way in which I should walk (Psalm cxlii. 8)

During the Exercises recommend yourself also in a special manner to the Divine Mother Mary, praying her to obtain for you the grace to accomplish perfectly the will of her Son.

And do not forget, when you make the Exercises, to recommend me to Jesus Christ, as I will not omit to do so in a particular manner for you, that He may make you a saint, as I wish with all my heart. Your most devoted and obliged servant,

Alphonsus Mary,
Bishop of St. Agatha

Evening Meditation
THE PRACTICE OF THE LOVE OF JESUS CHRIST
"Charity beareth all things"
HE THAT LOVES JESUS CHRIST BEARS ALL THINGS FOR HIM, AND
ESPECIALLY ILLNESS, POVERTY, AND CONTEMPT

I.

In the third place, we must practice patience, and show our love of God by tranquilly submitting to contempt. As soon as a soul delivers herself up to God, He sends her from Himself, or through others, insults and persecution. One day an Angel appeared to the Blessed Henry Suso, and said to him: "Henry, thou hast hitherto mortified thyself in thy own way; henceforth thou shalt be mortified after the pleasure of others." On the day following, as he was looking from a window on the street, he saw a dog shaking and tearing a rag which it held in its mouth; at the same moment a voice said to him: "So hast thou to be torn in the mouths of men." Forthwith the Blessed Henry Suso descended into the street and secured the rag, putting it by to encourage him in his coming trials.

I love Thee with my whole heart, O my dear Redeemer! I love Thee, my Sovereign Good! I love Thee, my own Love, worthy of infinite love! I am grieved at any displeasure I have ever caused Thee, more than for any evil whatever. I promise Thee to receive with patience all the trials Thou mayest send me; but I look to Thee for help to be faithful to my promise, and especially to be enabled to bear in peace the sorrows of my last agony and death.

O Mary, my Queen, vouchsafe to obtain for me a true resignation in all the anguish and trials that await me during life and at death.

II.

Affronts and injuries were the delicacies the Saints earnestly desired and sought for. St. Philip Neri, during the space of thirty years had to put up with much ill-treatment in the house of St. Jerome at Rome; but on this very account he refused to leave it and resisted all the invitations of his sons to come and live with them in the new Oratory, founded by himself, till he received an express command from the Pope to do so. St. John of the Cross was prescribed change of air for an illness which eventually carried him to the grave. Now, he could have selected a more commodious convent, the prior of which was particularly attached to him; but he chose instead a poor convent, whose superior was unfriendly, and who, in fact, for a long time, and almost up to his dying day, spoke ill of him, and abused him in many ways, and even prohibited the others from visiting him. Here we see how the Saints even sought to be despised. St. Teresa wrote this admirable maxim: "Whoever aspires to perfection must beware of ever saying: They had no reason to treat me so. If you will not bear any cross but one which is founded on reason, then perfection is not for you." Whilst St. Peter Martyr was complaining in prison of being confined unjustly, he received that celebrated answer from the Crucifix; our Lord said to him: "And what evil have I done that I suffer and die on this Cross for men?" Oh, what consolation do the Saints derive in all their tribulations from the ignominies Jesus endured! St. Eleazar, on being asked by his wife how he contrived to bear with so much patience the many injuries he had to sustain, and that even from his own servants, replied: "I turn my eyes on the outraged Jesus, and I discover immediately that my affronts are a mere nothing in comparison with what He suffered for my sake; and thus God gives me strength to support all patiently." In fine, affronts, poverty, torments, and tribulations serve only to estrange further from God the soul that does not love Him; whereas, when they befall a soul in love with God, they become an instrument of closer union and more ardent affection: Many waters cannot quench charity (Canticles viii. 7). However great and grievous troubles may be, so far from extinguishing the flames of charity, they only serve to enkindle them the more in a soul that loves nothing else but God.

SIXTH SUNDAY AFTER PENTECOST

Morning Meditation

OUR JOURNEY INTO ETERNITY.–WE ARE ONLY PILGRIMS ON THIS EARTH.

We have not here a lasting city, but we seek one that is to come. In this world we are not citizens, but pilgrims, for we are on our way to Eternity. Man shall go into the house of his eternity.

I.

We do not have here a lasting city, but we seek one that is to come (Hebrews xiii. 14). In this world we are not citizens, but pilgrims, for we are on our way to Eternity: Man shall go into the house of his eternity (Ecclesiastes xii. 5).

Very soon, therefore, we shall have to leave this world. The body must soon go into the grave, and the soul into Eternity.

Would not that traveler be guilty of great folly, who should waste his time and his wealth in building himself a dwelling in a place he must soon leave?

O my God, my soul is eternal; I must, then, either enjoy Thee or lose Thee for Eternity.

In Eternity there are two places of abode–one overflowing with every delight, the other replete with every torment. And these delights and torments will be eternal. If the tree fall to the south, or to the north, in what place soever it shall fall there shall it be (Ecclesiastes xi. 3). If the soul be saved, it will be happy forever; but if it fall into hell, it will remain there to weep and lament as long as God shall be God.

There is no middle state: either a king forever in Heaven, or forever a slave of Lucifer; either blessed forever in Paradise, or in despair forever in hell.

Which of these abodes will fall to the lot of each of us? That which each one voluntarily chooses. Man shall go–Ibit homo. He who goes to hell, goes of his own free will. Every one that is damned, is damned because he wills his own damnation.

O my Jesus, would that I had always loved Thee! Too late have I known Thee! Too late have I loved Thee! O Thou, the God of my heart, and the God that is my portion forever! (Psalm lxxii. 26).

II.

Every Christian, in order to live well, should always keep Eternity before his eyes. Oh, how well regulated is the life of that man who lives and sees all things in the light of Eternity!

If Heaven, Hell, and Eternity were even only doubtful things, surely we ought to do all in our power not to run the risk of being lost forever. But no; they are not doubtful things, but Articles of Faith.

To what will all the greatness of this world come? To a funeral; to a descent into the grave. Blessed in that hour is he who obtains eternal life!

O Jesus! Thou art my life, my riches, my love. Grant me a great desire to please Thee during the remainder of my life; and give me Thy assistance to fulfil it.

The thought of Eternity is sufficient to make a saint. St. Augustine called it the Great Thought. It is this thought that has sent so many young persons into cloisters, so many anchorites into deserts, and so many Martyrs to cruel deaths.

Father John of Avila converted a lady who was attached to the world, by only saying: Consider: Always and Forever!"

Oh, how much depends on the last moment of our lives! On our last breath depends on an Eternity, either of happiness or of misery; a life of eternal bliss, or of eternal woe. Jesus Christ died upon the Cross, in order to secure for us His grace at this last moment.

My dear Redeemer, if then Thou hadst not died for me, I should have been lost forever! I thank Thee, O my Love! I confide in Thee, and I love Thee!

Spiritual Reading

PRAYER, THE GREAT MEANS OF SALVATION.

I have published several spiritual works, the Visits to the Blessed Sacrament, The Passion of Jesus Christ, The Glories of Mary, and, besides, a work against the Materialists and Deists, with other devout little treatises. I have recently brought out a work on the Infancy of our Savior entitled Novena for Christmas; and another entitled Preparation for Death, besides the one on the Eternal Maxims, most useful for meditation and sermons

... But I do not think that I have written a more useful work than the present, in which I speak of prayer as necessary, and a certain means of obtaining salvation, and all the graces which we require for that object. If it were in my power, I would distribute a copy of it to every Catholic in the world, to show him the absolute necessity of prayer for salvation.

I say this, because on the one hand I see that the absolute necessity of prayer is taught throughout the Holy Scriptures, and by all the Holy Fathers of the Church, while, on the other hand, I see that Christians are very careless in their practice of this great means of salvation. And, sadder still, I see that preachers take very little care to speak of it to their flocks, or confessors to their penitents; I see, moreover, that even the spiritual books now popular do not speak sufficiently of it; yet there is nothing which preachers, and confessors and spiritual books should insist upon with more warmth and energy than prayer; not but that they teach many excellent means of keeping ourselves in the grace of God, such as avoiding the occasions of sin, frequenting the Sacraments, resisting temptations, hearing the Word of God, meditation on the Eternal Truths, and other means–all of them, I admit, most useful; but, I say, what profit is there in sermons, meditations, and all the other means pointed out by masters of the spiritual life, if we forget to pray? Has not our Lord declared that He will grant His graces to no one who does not pray? Ask and ye shall receive. Without prayer, in the ordinary course of providence, all the meditations we make, all our resolutions, all our promises, will come to naught. If we do not pray, we shall be always unfaithful to the inspirations of God, and to the promises we make Him. Because, in order actually to do good, to conquer temptations, to practice virtues, and to observe God's law, it is not enough to receive illumination from God, and to meditate and make resolutions, but we require, moreover, the actual assistance of God; and, as we shall see, He does not give this assistance except to those who pray, and pray with perseverance. The light we receive, and the considerations and good resolutions we make, are of use to incite us to the act of prayer when we are in danger and are tempted to transgress God's law; for, then prayer will obtain for us God's help, and we shall be preserved from sin; but if in such moments we do not pray, we shall be lost.

My intention in thus prefacing my book is, that my readers may thank God for giving them an opportunity, by means of this little book, to receive the grace of reflecting more deeply on the importance of prayer; for all adults who are saved, are ordinarily saved by this single means of grace. And therefore, I ask my readers to thank God; for surely it is a great mercy when He gives the light and the grace to pray. I hope, then, that you, my beloved brother, after reading this little work, will never from this day forward, neglect to have continual recourse to God in prayer, whenever you are tempted to offend Him. If ever in times past you have had your conscience burdened with many sins, know that the cause of this has been your neglect of prayer, your not asking God for help to resist the temptations which assailed you. I pray you, therefore, to read my words again and again with the greatest attention; not because I write them, but because this book is a means which God offers you for the good of your salvation, thereby giving you to understand that He wishes you to be saved. And after having read it yourself, induce as many of your friends and neighbors as you can to read it also. Now let us begin in the Name of the Lord.

The Apostle writes to Timothy: I desire, therefore, first of all that supplications, prayers, intercessions and thanksgivings be made (1 Timothy ii. 1). St. Thomas explains that prayer is properly the lifting up of the soul to God. Petition is that particular kind of prayer which begs for determinate objects, but when the thing sought is indeterminate (as when we say, "Incline unto my aid, O God!"), it is called supplication. Obsecration is a solemn adjuration or representation of the grounds on which we dare to ask a favor; as when we say," By Thy Cross and Passion, O Lord, deliver us!" Finally, thanksgiving is the returning of thanks for benefits received, whereby, says St. Thomas, we merit to receive greater favors. Prayer, in a strict sense, says the holy Doctor, means recourse to God; but in its general signification it includes all the kinds just enumerated. It is in this latter sense that the word is used in this book.

We will here treat:

1.–Of the Necessity of Prayer; the Power of Prayer, and the Conditions of Prayer;

2.–We will show that God gives the grace of Prayer to all men.*

Evening Meditation

THE PRACTICE OF THE LOVE OF JESUS CHRIST.

" Charity beareth all things."

HE THAT LOVES JESUS CHRIST BEARS ALL THINGS FOR HIM, AND ESPECIALLY ILLNESS, POVERTY, AND CONTEMPT.

I.

But wherefore does Almighty God load us with so many crosses, and take pleasure in seeing us afflicted, reviled, persecuted, and ill-treated by the world? Is He perchance, a tyrant, whose cruel disposition makes Him rejoice in our suffering? No; God is by no means a tyrant, nor cruel; He is all compassion and love towards us; suffice it to say that He has died for us. He indeed does rejoice at our suffering, because suffering is for our good; inasmuch as by suffering here we are released hereafter from the debt of punishment justly due from us to His Divine justice; He rejoices in our sufferings because they detach us from the sensual pleasures of this world: when a mother would wean her child she puts gall on the breast in order to create a dislike in the child; He rejoices in sufferings because we give Him, by our patience and resignation in bearing them, a token of our love; in fine, He rejoices in them, because they contribute to our increase of glory in Heaven. Such are the reasons for which the Almighty, in His compassion and love towards us, is pleased when we suffer.

I love Thee with my whole heart, O my Redeemer! I love Thee, my sovereign Good! I love Thee, my own Love, worthy of infinite love. I am grieved at any displeasure I have ever caused Thee, more than for any evil whatever. I promise Thee to receive with patience all the trials Thou mayest send me; but I look to Thee for help to be faithful to my promise, and especially to be enabled to bear in peace the sorrows of my last agony and death.

II.

Let us conclude. That we may be able to practice patience to advantage in all our tribulations, we must be fully persuaded that every trial comes from the hands of God, either directly, or indirectly through men; we must therefore render God thanks whenever we are beset with sorrows, and accept, with gladness of heart, of every event, prosperous or adverse, that proceeds from Him, knowing that all happens by His disposition and for our welfare: To them that love God all things work together unto good (Romans viii. 28). In addition to this, it is well in our tribulations to glance a moment at that hell we formerly deserved: for assuredly all the pains of this life are incomparably less than the awful pains of hell. But above all, prayer, by which we gain the Divine assistance, is the great means by which we may suffer patiently all affliction, scorn, and contradictions, and is that which will furnish us with the strength we have not of ourselves. The Saints were persuaded of this; they recommended themselves to God, and so overcame every kind of torments and persecutions.

O Lord, I am fully persuaded that without suffering, and suffering with patience, I cannot win the crown of Paradise. David said: From him is my patience (Psalm lxi. 6). And I say the same; my patience in suffering must come from Thee. I make many resolutions to accept all tribulations in peace; but no sooner are trials at hand than I grow sad and alarmed; and if I suffer, I suffer without merit and without love, because I know not how to suffer them so as to please Thee. O my Jesus, through the merits of Thy patience in bearing so many afflictions for love of me, grant me the grace to bear crosses for the love of Thee!

O Mary, my Queen, vouchsafe to obtain for me a true resignation in all the anguish and trials that await me during life and at death.

Monday--Sixth Week after Pentecost

Morning Meditation

OUR JOURNEY INTO ETERNITY--THE FOLLY OF THOSE WHO DO NOT CONSIDER IT

O my God, the months and years pass! We are hastening towards Eternity and we do not concern ourselves to think about it! And who knows but this may be the last warning I may receive from God!

I.

Either we believe or we do not believe. If we do not believe, we are doing too much for things we regard as fables. But if we do believe, then we do too little to obtain a happy Eternity, and to avoid eternal misery.

Father Vincent Carafa said that if men thoroughly knew the Truths of Eternity, and compared the goods and evils of this life with those of the next, the earth would become a desert, because there would be none at all who would attend to the affairs of this world.

When the last moment is near at hand, how we shall tremble at the thought that on that moment will depend our eternal happiness or misery!

O my God, the months and years pass! We are hastening towards eternity, and we do not concern ourselves to think about it! And who knows but that this year or month may be my last? Who knows but that this may be the last warning I may receive from God?

O my God, I will no longer abuse Thy graces! Behold, I am ready! Make known to me what Thou wouldst have me do, and in all things, I will obey Thee.

And why should we delay after so many lights and calls from God, unless we desire to lament with the damned, saying: The summer is ended, and we are not saved (Jer. viii. 20). Now is the time for reconciliation with God, for after death no remedy will be left.

With good reason did Father John of Avila say that Christians who believe eternal life, and live at a distance from God, ought to be shut up in an asylum as insane.

The business of Eternity is indeed important. It is not whether we shall inhabit a house more or less commodious or lightsome; but whether we shall dwell in a palace of all delights, or in an abyss of the most terrible torments. It is whether we shall be happy with the Saints and Angels or live in despair with the multitude of the enemies of God. And for how many years? For a thousand? No; forever, forever, as long as God shall be God.

If, then, O God, I had died in my sins, should I not have lost Thee forever? If as yet, O Lord, Thou hast not pardoned me, pardon me now, I beseech Thee. I love Thee with all my soul, and I am sorry above every other evil for having offended Thee. I will never lose Thee more. I love Thee with all my heart and will forever love Thee. Have pity on me.

II.

There are many upon whom, during life, it makes little impression to hear of Judgment, Hell, Eternity. But in death what dread and terror do these Truths excite! But, alas! with but little fruit; because then they serve only to increase their remorse and confusion.

St. Teresa used to say to her Religious: "Daughters, one soul, one Eternity!" By which she meant that if the soul is lost, all is lost, and that the soul once lost, is lost forever.

O Lord, wait yet awhile, that I may weep for my sins. Too many years have I spent in displeasing Thee! The time which yet remains to me shall be given all to Thee. Accept of me, that I may serve Thee, O my God, my God!

The Lord waits for us; let us highly prize the time which, in His mercy, He bestows upon us, that we may not have to lament when for us time shall be no more.

O God, what would not a dying man give for another day, or even another hour! Another day or hour in his sound senses! Alas, the time which remains to the dying man is but little adapted to the settling of the affairs of conscience. Giddiness of head, pains of body, oppressions at the chest, hinder the mind from doing anything in a proper manner. Then the soul, as it were, buried in obscurity, is alive to nothing but the distress which overpowers it, and which it cannot alleviate. It longs to have a little time but sees that there is no more time for it.

At what hour you think not, the Son of Man will come (Luke xii. 40). God conceals from us the time of death, that we may always be ready. The time of death is not the time to prepare ourselves to give an account of our souls, but the time when we should find ourselves prepared to do so. St. Bernard said: "In order to die well, we must be ever prepared to die."

O Jesus, too long have I offended Thee! It is surely now time to resolve henceforth to prepare for death. I will no longer abuse Thy patience. I desire to love Thee with all my power. I have very much offended Thee; I desire now to love Thee very much.

Spiritual Reading

PRAYER, ITS NECESSITY

I-IT IS A MEANS NECESSARY FOR SALVATION

One of the errors of Pelagianism was the assertion that Prayer is not necessary for salvation. Pelagius, the impious author of that heresy, said that man will only be damned for neglecting to know the truths necessary to be learned. How astonishing! St. Augustine said: "Pelagius discussed everything except how to pray," though, as the Saint held and taught,--Prayer is the only means of acquiring the science of the Saints, according to the words of St. James: If any man want wisdom, let him ask of God, who giveth to all men abundantly, and upbraided not (James i. 5).

The Scriptures are clear enough in pointing out how necessary it is to pray, if we would be saved. We ought always to pray, and not to faint (Luke xviii. 1). Watch and pray, that ye enter not into temptation (Matthew xxvi. 41). Ask, and it shall be given you (Matthew vii. 7). The words we ought, pray, ask, according to the general consent of Theologians, impose the precept, and denote the Necessity of Prayer. Wickliffe said that these texts are to be understood, not of the necessity of Prayer, but of the necessity of good works, for in his system Prayer was only well-doing; but this was his error and was expressly condemned by the Church. Hence Lessius wrote that it is heresy to deny that Prayer is necessary for salvation in adults, as it is evident from Scripture that Prayer is the means without which we cannot obtain the help necessary for salvation.

The reason of this is clear. Without the assistance of God's grace we can do no good work: Without me, ye can do nothing (John xv. 5). St. Augustine remarks on this passage that our Lord did not say: "Without Me, ye can complete nothing," but "Without Me, ye can do nothing"; giving us to understand, that without grace we cannot even begin to do a good work. Nay more, St. Paul writes, that of ourselves we cannot even have the wish to do good. Not that we are sufficient to think anything of ourselves ... but our sufficiency is from God (2 Corinthians 6). If we cannot even think a good thought, much less can we wish to carry it out. The same thing is taught in many other passages of Scripture: God worketh all in all (1 Corinthians xii. 6). I will cause you to walk in my commandments, and to keep my judgments, and do them (Ezechiel xxxvi. 27). So that, as St. Leo I. says: "Man does no good thing, except that which God, by His grace, enables him to do"; and hence the Council of Trent says: "If any one shall assert that without the previous inspiration of the Holy Ghost, and His assistance, man can believe, hope, Love, or repent, as he ought, in order to obtain the grace of justification, let him be anathema."

The author of the Opus Imperfectum says that God has given to some animals swiftness, to others claws, to others wings, for the preservation of their life; but He has so formed man that God Himself is his only strength. So that man is unable to provide for his own safety, since God has willed that whatever he has, or can have, should come entirely from the assistance of His grace.

But this grace is not given in God's ordinary Providence, except to those who pray for it; according to the celebrated saying of Gennadius, "We believe that no one comes to be saved, except at the invitation of God; that no one who is invited works out his salvation, except by the help of God; that no one merits this help, unless he prays." From these two premises, first, that we can do nothing without the assistance of grace; and secondly, that this assistance is only given ordinarily by God to the man that prays--who does not see that the consequence follows, that prayer is absolutely necessary to us for salvation? And although the first graces that come to us without any co-operation on our part, such as the call to Faith or to penance, are, as St. Augustine says, granted by God even to those who do not pray; yet the Saint considers it certain that the other graces, and specially the grace of perseverance, are not granted except in answer to Prayer: "God gives us some things, as the beginning of Faith, even when we do not pray. Other things, such as perseverance, He has only provided for those who pray."

Hence it is that the generality of Theologians, following St. Basil, St. Chrysostom, Clement of Alexandria, St. Augustine, and other Fathers, teach that Prayer is necessary to adults, not only because of the obligation of the precept, as we have seen, but because Prayer is necessary as a means of salvation. That is to say, in the ordinary course of Providence, it is impossible that a Christian should be saved without recommending himself to God and asking for the graces necessary for salvation. St. Thomas teaches the same: "After Baptism, continual Prayer is necessary for man, in order that he may enter Heaven; for though by Baptism our sins are remitted, there still remain concupiscence to assail us from within, and the world and the devil to assail us from without." The reason, then, which makes us certain of the necessity of Prayer is briefly this: In order to be saved we must fight and conquer: He that strives for the mastery is not crowned except he strive lawfully (2 Timothy 5). But without the Divine assistance we cannot resist the might of so many and such powerful enemies; now this assistance is granted only to Prayer; therefore, without Prayer there is no salvation.

Moreover, that Prayer is the only ordinary means of receiving the Divine gift, is very distinctly proved by St. Thomas in another place, where he says that whatever graces God has from all eternity determined to give us, He will only give them if we pray for them. St. Gregory says the same thing: "Man by Prayer merits to receive that which God had from all eternity determined to give him." Not, says St. Thomas, that Prayer is necessary in order that God may know our necessities, but in order that we may know the necessity of having recourse to God to obtain the help necessary for our salvation, and may thus acknowledge Him to be the Author of all our good. As, therefore, it is God's law that we should provide ourselves with bread by sowing corn, and wine by planting vines, so has He ordained that we should receive the graces necessary to salvation by means of Prayer: Ask and it shall be given you; seek, and ye shall find (Matthew vii. 7).

We, in a word, are merely beggars, who have nothing but what God bestows on us as alms: But I am a beggar and poor (Psalm xxxix. 18). The Lord, says St. Augustine, desires and wills to pour forth His graces upon us, but does not give them except to him who prays. "God wishes to give, but only to him who asks." This is declared in the words, Ask, and it shall be given to you. Whence it follows, says St. Teresa, that he who seeks not, does not receive. As moisture is necessary for the life of plants, to prevent them from drying up, so, says St. Chrysostom, is Prayer necessary for our salvation. Or, as he says in another place, Prayer vivifies the soul as the soul vivifies the body: "As the body without the soul cannot live, so the soul without Prayer is dead and emits an offensive odor." "Graviter olens." He uses these words because the man who omits to recommend himself to God at once begins to be defiled with sins. Prayer is also called the food of the soul, because the body cannot be supported without food; nor can the soul, says St. Augustine, be kept alive without Prayer: "As the flesh is nourished by food, so is man supported by prayers " All these comparisons used by the holy Fathers are intended by them to teach the absolute necessity of Prayer for the salvation of everyone.

Evening Meditation
THE PRACTICE OF THE LOVE OF JESUS CHRIST
"Charity believeth all things"
HE THAT LOVES JESUS CHRIST BELIEVES ALL HIS WORDS
I.

Whoever loves a person believes all that proceeds from the lips of that person; consequently, the more a soul loves Jesus Christ, the more lively and unshaken is her Faith. When the Good Thief beheld our Redeemer, though He had done no ill, suffering death upon the Cross with such patience, he began at once to love Him; under the influence of this love, and of the Divine light which then broke upon his soul, he believed that Jesus was truly the Son of God, and begged not to be forgotten by Him when He should have passed into His Kingdom.

Faith is the foundation of Charity; but Faith afterwards receives its perfection from Charity. His Faith is most perfect whose love of God is most perfect. Charity produces in man not merely the Faith of the understanding, but the Faith of the will also; those who believe only with the understanding, but not with the will, as is the case with sinners who are perfectly convinced of the Truths of the Faith, but do not choose to live according to the Divine Commandments--such as these have a very weak Faith; for had they a more lively belief that the grace of God is a priceless treasure, and that sin, because it robs us of this grace, is the worst of evils, they would assuredly change their lives. If, then, they prefer the miserable creatures of this earth to God, it is because they either do not believe or because their Faith is very weak. On the contrary, he who believes not only with the understanding but also with the will, so that he not only believes in God but has the will to believe in Him, the Revealer of truth, from the love he has for Him, and rejoices in so believing--such a one has a perfect Faith, and consequently seeks to make his life conformable to the truths he believes.

II.

Weakness of Faith, however, in those who live in sin, does not spring from the obscurity of Faith; for though God, in order to make our Faith more meritorious, has veiled the objects of Faith in darkness and secrecy, He has at the same time given us so clear and convincing evidence of their truth, that not to believe them would argue not merely a lack of sense, but sheer madness and impiety. The weakness of the Faith of many persons is to be traced to their wickedness of living. He who, rather than forego the enjoyment of forbidden pleasures, scorns the Divine friendship, would wish there was no law to forbid, and no chastisement to punish, his sin. On this account he strives to blind himself to the eternal truths of Death, Judgment, and Hell, and of Divine justice; and because such subjects strike too much terror into his heart, and are too apt to mix bitterness in his cup of pleasure, he sets his brain to work to discover proofs, which have at least the look of plausibility; and by which he allows himself to be flattered into the persuasion that there is no soul, no God, no hell, in order that he may live and die like the brute beast, without law and without reason.

TUESDAY--SIXTH WEEK AFTER PENTECOST

Morning Meditation

OUR JOURNEY INTO ETERNITY--LET US PROFIT BY THE TIME THAT IS GIVEN US

Walk, says our Divine Lord, while you have the light, for, the night cometh when no man can work. Oh, what a torment for the poor repentant sinner at the end of a careless life when there is no time left him to do all he has left undone!

I.

Oh, what a torment for the poor repentant sinner at the end of a careless life when there is no time left him to do all he left undone! St. Laurence Justinian says that worldlings, in death, would willingly give all their riches to obtain but one more hour of life. But it will be said to them: Time shall be no more (Apocalypse x. 6). It will be intimated to them to depart without delay: Go forth, Christian soul, out of this world!

St. Gregory relates that a certain Crisorius, being at the point of death, cried out to the demons: "Give me time until tomorrow." But they replied, "Fool! thou hast had time, and why didst thou waste it? Now there is no more time for thee."

Ah, my God, how many years have I not wasted! The remainder of my time shall be entirely devoted to Thee. Grant that Thy holy love may abound in me, in whom sin has so long abounded.

St. Bernardine of Sienna said that every moment of time in this life is as precious as God; because at any moment, by an act of love or contrition, we may acquire new degrees of grace.

St. Bernard says that time is a treasure to be found only in this life. In hell, the lamentation of the damned is: "Oh, if one hour were given us!" Oh, if we had but one hour in which to escape from eternal ruin! In Heaven there is no weeping; but if the Blessed could weep, it would be at the thought of having lost so much time in which they might have acquired higher degrees of glory.

My beloved Redeemer, I do not deserve Thy pity; but Thy Passion is my hope. Help me, therefore, and stretch out Thy hand to a miserable sinner, who now desires to become wholly Thine.

And who knows but that a sudden death may surprise us, and deprive us of the time for making up our accounts? The many who have died suddenly did not expect so to die; and if they were in sin, what has become of them for all eternity?

II.

The Saints thought that they did but little, in preparing themselves during their whole lives to secure a good end. Blessed John of Avila, when it was announced to him that he was about to die, said: "Oh, that I had but a little more time to prepare myself!"

And we, why do we delay? Is it that we may make a wicked and most miserable end and leave to others an example of the Divine justice?

No, my Jesus, I will not oblige Thee to abandon me. Tell me what Thou requires of me, and in all things I will do Thy will. Grant that I may love Thee, and I ask for nothing more.

He hath called against me the time (Lamentations i. 15). Let us tremble and let us not so live that God may hereafter, as judge of our ingratitude, call against us the time which, in His mercy, He now bestows upon us. Walk, says our Lord, whilst you have the light (John xii. 35). The night cometh when no man can work (John ix. 4).

St. Andrew Avellino trembled, saying: "Who knows whether I shall be saved or lost?" But speaking thus, he ever united himself the more closely to God. But what are we doing? How is it possible that he who believes he must die and go into Eternity should not give himself wholly to God?

My beloved Redeemer, my crucified Love, I will not wait till my death-hour to embrace Thee; from this moment I embrace Thee, I bind Thee to my heart, and leave all to love

Thee alone, my only Good. O Mary, my Mother, bind me to Jesus, and obtain for me that I may never more separate myself from His love.

Spiritual Reading

PRAYER, ITS NECESSITY

II-WITHOUT PRAYER IT IS IMPOSSIBLE TO RESIST TEMPTATIONS AND TO KEEP THE COMMANDMENTS

Moreover, Prayer is the most necessary weapon of defense against our enemies; he who does not avail himself of it, says St. Thomas, is lost. He does not doubt that the reason of Adam's fall was because he did not recommend himself to God when he was tempted: "He sinned because he had not recourse to the Divine assistance." St. Gelasius says the same of the rebel angels: "Receiving the grace of God in vain, they could not persevere, because they did not pray." St. Charles Borromeo, in a Pastoral letter, observes that among all the means of salvation recommended by Jesus Christ in the Gospel, the first place is given to Prayer; and He has determined that this should distinguish His Church from all false religions, when He calls her "The House of Prayer": My house shall be called a house of prayer (Matthew xxi. 13). St. Charles concludes that Prayer is "the beginning and progress and the completion of all virtues." So that in darkness, distress, and danger, we have no other hope than to raise our eyes to God, and with fervent prayer to beseech His mercy to save us: As we know not what to do, said King Josaphat, we can only turn our eyes to thee (2 Paralipomenon xx. 12). This also was David's practice, who could find no other means of safety from his enemies than continual Prayer to God to deliver him from their snares: My eyes are ever towards the Lord; for he shall pluck my feet out of the snare (Psalm xxiv. 15). So he did nothing but pray. Look thou upon me and have mercy on me; for I am alone and poor (Psalm xxiv. 15). I cried unto thee, O Lord; save me that I may keep thy commandments (Psalm cxviii. 146). Lord, turn Thy eyes to me, have pity on me, and save me; for I can do nothing, and besides Thee there is none that can help me.

And, indeed, how could we ever resist our enemies and observe God's precepts especially since Adam's sin, which has rendered us so weak and infirm, unless we had Prayer as a means whereby we can obtain from God sufficient light and strength to enable us to observe them? It was a blasphemy of Luther's to say that after the sin of Adam the observance of God's law has become absolutely impossible to man. Jansenius also said that there are some precepts which are impossible even to the just, with the power which they actually have, and so far his proposition bears a good sense; but it was justly condemned by the Church for the addition he made to it, when he said that they have not the grace to make the precepts possible. It is true, says St. Augustine, that man, in consequence of his weakness, is unable to fulfil some of God's commands with his present strength and the ordinary grace given to all men; but he can easily, by Prayer, obtain such further aid as he requires for his salvation: "God commands not impossibilities; but by commanding He suggests to you both to do what you can and to ask for what you cannot do; and He helps you, that you may be able" --"Deus impossibilia non jubet; sed jubendo monet, et facere quod possis, et petere quod non possis; et adjuvat ut possis." This is a celebrated text, which was afterwards adopted and made a Dogma of Faith by the Council of Trent. The holy Doctor immediately adds: "Let us see how this is" (i.e. how man is able to do that which he cannot). "By medicine he can do that which his natural weakness renders impossible to him." That is, by Prayer we may obtain a remedy for our weakness; for when we pray, God gives us strength to do that which we cannot do of ourselves.

We cannot believe, continues St. Augustine, that God would have imposed upon us the observance of a law, and then made the law impossible. When, therefore, God shows us that of ourselves we are unable to observe all His commands it is simply to admonish us to do the easier things by means of the ordinary grace which He bestows on us, and then to do the more difficult things by means of the greater help which we can obtain by Prayer. "By the very fact that it is absurd to suppose that God could have commanded us to do impossible things, we are admonished what to do in easy matters, and what to ask for in difficulties." But why, it will be asked, has God commanded us to do things impossible by our natural strength? Precisely for this, says St. Augustine, that we may be incited to pray for help to do that which of ourselves we cannot do. "He commands some things which we cannot do, that we may know what we ought to ask of Him." And in another place: "The law was given that grace might be sought for; grace was given that the law might be fulfilled." The law cannot be kept without grace, and God has given the law with this object, that we may always ask Him for grace to observe it. In another place he says: "The law is good, if it be used lawfully; what then, is the lawful use of the law?" He answers: "When by the law we perceive our own weakness and ask of God the grace to heal us." St. Augustine, then, says: We ought to use the law; but for what purpose? To learn by means of the law, which we find to be above our strength, our own inability to observe it, in order that we may then obtain by prayer the divine aid to cure our weakness.

St. Bernard's teaching is the same: "Who are we, or what is our strength, that we should be able to resist so many temptations? It was certainly this that God intended, that we, seeing our deficiencies, and that we have no other help, should with all humility have recourse to His mercy." God knows how useful it is to us to be obliged to pray, in order to keep us humble, and to exercise our confidence; and He therefore permits us to be assaulted by enemies too mighty to be overcome by our own strength, that by Prayer we may obtain from His mercy aid to resist them; and it is especially to be remarked that no one can resist the impure temptations of the flesh without recommending himself to God when he is tempted. This foe is so terrible that, when he fights with us, he, as it were, takes away all light; he makes us forget all our meditations, all our good resolutions; he makes us also disregard the Truths of Faith, and even almost lose the fear of Divine punishments. For he conspires with our natural inclinations, which drive us with the greatest violence to the indulgence of sensual pleasures. He who in such a moment does not have recourse to God is lost. The only defense against this temptation is Prayer, as St. Gregory of Nyssa says: "Prayer is the bulwark of chastity"; and before him Solomon: And as I knew that I could not otherwise be continent except God gave it, I went to the Lord and besought him (Wis. viii. 21). Chastity is a virtue which we have not strength to practice, unless God gives it to us; and God does not give this strength except to him who asks for it. But whoever prays for it will certainly obtain it.

Hence St. Thomas observes (in contradiction to Jansenius), that we ought not to say that the precept of chastity, or any other, is impossible to us; for though we cannot observe it of our own strength, we can by God's assistance. "It must be said that what we can do with the Divine assistance is not altogether impossible to us." Let no one say that it appears an injustice to order a cripple to walk straight. No, says St. Augustine, it is not an injustice, provided always the means are given him to find the remedy for his lameness, for after this, if he still go lame, the fault is his own. "It is most wisely commanded that man should walk uprightly, so that when he sees that he cannot do so of himself, he may seek a remedy to heal the lameness of sin."

Finally, the same holy Doctor says that he will never know how to live well who does not know how to pray well. "He knows how to live aright who knows how to pray aright"; and, on the other hand, St. Francis of Assisi says that without Prayer you can never hope to find good fruit in a soul. Wrongly, therefore, do these sinners excuse themselves who say that they have no strength to resist temptation. But if you have not this strength, why do you not ask for it? is the reproof which St. James gives them: You have not, because you ask not (James iv. 2). There is no doubt that we are too weak to resist the attacks of our enemies. But, on the other hand, it is certain that God is faithful, as the

Apostle says, and will not permit us to be tempted beyond our strength: God is faithful, who will not suffer you to be tempted above that which you are able; but will make also with the temptation issue, that ye may be able to bear it (1 Corinthians x 13). "He will provide an issue for it," says Primasius, "by the protection of His grace, that you may be able to withstand the temptation." We are weak, but God is strong; when we ask Him for aid, He communicates His strength to us; and we shall be able to do all things, as the Apostle reasonably assured himself: I can do all things in him that strengtheneth me (Philippians iv. 13). He, therefore, who falls has no excuse, says St. Chrysostom, because he has neglected to pray; for if he had prayed, he would not have been overcome by his enemies. "Nor can anyone be excused who, by ceasing to pray, has shown that he did not wish to overcome his enemy."

Evening Meditation

THE PRACTICE OF THE LOVE OF JESUS CHRIST

"Charity believeth all things"

HE THAT LOVES JESUS CHRIST BELIEVES ALL HIS WORDS

I.

And this laxity of morals is the source whence have issued, and still issue daily, so many books and systems of Materialists, Indifferentists, Politicists, Deists, and Naturalists; some among them deny the existence of God, and some Divine Providence, saying that God, after having created men, takes no further notice of them, and is heedless whether they love or hate Him, whether they be saved or lost; others, again, deny the goodness of God, and maintain that He has created numberless souls for hell, becoming Himself their tempter to sin, that so they may damn themselves, and go into everlasting fire, to curse Him there forever!

Oh, ingratitude and wickedness of men! God has created them in His mercy, to make them eternally happy in Heaven; He has poured on them so many lights, benefits, and graces, to bring them to eternal life; for the same end He redeemed them at the price of so many sorrows and sufferings; and yet they strive to deny all, that they may give free rein to their vicious inclinations!

II.

But no; let men strive as they will, the unhappy beings cannot tear themselves away from remorse of conscience, and the dread of the Divine vengeance. On this subject I have lately published a work entitled The Truth of Faith, in which I have clearly shown the inconsistency of all these systems of modern unbelievers. Oh, if they would but once forsake sin, and apply themselves earnestly to the love of Jesus Christ, they would then most certainly cast away all doubts about things of Faith, and firmly believe all the truths that God has revealed!

O my God, let not Thy precious Blood be shed for me in vain! Thou hast promised pardon to him who repents of his sins. O my God, I grieve from the bottom of my heart for the many offences I have committed against Thee. I now love Thee above all things. I will never sin again. No, my God, let me die rather than ever offend Thee.

Wednesday--Sixth Week after Pentecost

Morning Meditation

MORTAL SIN--ITS MALICE

To understand how great is the malice of mortal sin we must first know who God is, and what a wretched being man is who dares to despise Him. Before God all the Saints and Angels are as nothing, and it is a worm of the earth who has the insolence to despise Him!

I.

What is mortal sin? According to St. Thomas and St. Augustine, it is a turning-away from God; an act of contempt for God's grace and love, and a throwing-of of all respect for Him, by which the sinner declares to God's very face: I will not serve Thee! I will act as I please, and, if by so doing, I displease Thee and forfeit Thy friendship, I care not!

To understand how great is the malice of mortal sin, we must first know who God is, and what a wretched being man is who despises Him. Before God all the Saints and Angels are as nothing, and shall a worm of the earth have the insolence to despise Him?

But more than this. Man, by committing sin, not only despises a God of infinite majesty, but a God Who has so loved him as to die for the love of him. An eternity, therefore, would not be sufficient to bewail but one mortal sin.

He who commits mortal sin dishonors God by preferring before Him a whim, a fit of passion, a wretched gratification. A God so great and so good! And so dishonored!

O Lord, if Thou hadst not sacrificed Thyself on the Cross for the love of me, I should lose all hope of pardon; but Thy death gives me confidence. Into thy hands I commend my spirit (Psalm xxx. 6). I commend to Thee my soul for which Thou hast been pleased to shed Thy Blood and sacrifice Thy life; grant that it may love Thee and never more lose Thee. I love Thee, my Jesus, my Love, and my Hope. And how shall I ever be able, after having learned how much Thou hast loved me, to separate myself from Thee, my only Good?

What an affliction it is to us to be injured by one for whom we have done much! God is not capable of grief; but could He grieve, He would die of grief and sorrow at being despised by a creature for whom He gave even His very life.

O my accursed sins, a thousand times do I detest and abhor you! You have caused me to offend my Redeemer, Who has loved me so much!

Unhappy souls, now confined in hell, you who, during life, said that sin was a slight evil, have you not to acknowledge now that all your torments are far less than what you deserved for your sins?

II.

Sin must surely be a great evil since God, Who is Mercy itself, is obliged to punish it with an eternal hell. Yea, more! To satisfy Divine justice for sin, a God was obliged to sacrifice His own life!

O God, we know that hell is the most horrible punishment, and have we no fear of sin, which may cast us into that hell? We know that God has died, in order that He might be able to pardon our sins; and do we still continue to commit sin?

The loss of the least worldly possession makes us uneasy and sad; and does the loss of God distress us not?--a loss that should not fail to overwhelm us with affliction and grief for the remainder of our lives!

I give Thee thanks, O Lord, for having given me time to bewail my offences against Thee. O Jesus, I abhor and hate them. Give me still greater sorrow, still greater love, that I may lament all my sins, not so much on account of the punishment I have deserved for them, as for having offended Thee, my most amiable God.

What disquiet and fears agitate a courtier who is afraid of having offended his prince? And do we, who know for certain that we have displeased God, and forfeited His friendship, live tranquil, without grief or sorrow!

What care do not men take to avoid poison, which destroys only the body? And yet what great negligence in regard to sin which poisons the immortal soul and robs us of God!

Let us not be ensnared by that wile of the devil, by which he suggests to us how easily we can afterwards confess a sin. Oh, how many has the enemy drawn into hell by this stratagem!

O my God, for how many years have I deserved to dwell in hell! Thou hast been waiting for me, that I may forever bless Thy mercy, and love Thee. Yes, my Jesus, I bless Thee and love Thee; and I trust in Thy merits that I shall nevermore be separated from Thy love. But if after so many graces and mercies I again offend Thee, how shall I presume that Thou wilt not abandon me, or ever again forgive me? Permit it not, O Lord, that I ever offend Thee again!

Spiritual Reading

PRAYER, ITS NECESSITY

III-ON INVOKING THE SAINTS AND ON PRAYING TO THE SOULS IN PURGATORY

Here a question arises, whether it is necessary to have recourse to the intercession of the Saints to obtain the grace of God.

1. That it is a lawful and useful thing to invoke the Saints, as intercessors, to obtain for us, by the merits of Jesus Christ, that which we, for our demerits, are not worthy to receive, is a Doctrine of the Church, declared by the Council of Trent. "It is good and useful to invoke them by supplication, and to have recourse to their aid and influence to obtain benefits from God through His Son Jesus Christ."

Such invocation was condemned by the impious Calvin, but most foolishly. For if it is lawful and profitable to invoke living Saints to aid us, and to beseech them to assist us in prayers, as the Prophet Baruch did: And pray ye for us to the Lord our God (Baruch i. 13); and St. Paul: Brethren, pray for us (1 Thessalonians v. 25); and as God Himself commanded the friends of Job to recommend themselves to his prayers, that by the merits of Job He might look favorably on them: Go to my servant Job, ... and my servant Job shall pray for you; his face I will accept (Job xlii. 8); if, then, it is lawful for us to recommend ourselves to the living, how can it be unlawful to invoke the Saints who in Heaven enjoy God face to face? This is not derogatory to the honor due to God, but it is doubling it; for it is honoring the King not only in His Person but in His servants. Therefore, says, St. Thomas, it is good to have recourse to many Saints, "because by the prayers of many we can obtain that which we cannot by the prayers of one." And if anyone objects: But why have recourse to the Saints to pray for us, when they are already praying for all who are worthy of it? The same Doctor answers that no one can be said to be worthy that the Saints should pray for him; but that "he becomes worthy by having recourse to the Saints with devotion."

2. Again, it is disputed whether it is useful to recommend oneself to the Souls in Purgatory. Some say that the Souls in that state cannot pray for us; and these rely on the authority of St. Thomas, who says that those Souls, while they are being purified by pain, are inferior to us, and therefore "are not in a state to pray for us, but rather require our prayers." But many other Doctors, as Bellarmine, Cardinal Gotti, Lessius, and others affirm with great probability that we should piously believe that God manifests our prayers to those Holy Souls, that they may in turn pray for us; and that so the charitable interchange of mutual prayer may be kept up between them and us. Nor do St. Thomas's words present much difficulty; for, as Sylvius and Gotti say, it is one thing not to be in a state to pray, another not to be able to pray. It is true that those Souls are not in a state to pray, because, as St. Thomas says, while suffering they are inferior to us, and rather require our prayers; nevertheless, in this state they are well able to pray, as they are the friends of God. If a father keeps a son whom he tenderly loves in confinement for some fault; if the son then is not in a state to pray for himself, is that any reason why he cannot pray for others? And may he not expect to obtain what he asks, knowing, as he does, his father's affection for him? So the Souls in Purgatory, being beloved by God, and confirmed in grace, have absolutely no impediment to prevent them from praying for us. Still the Church does not invoke them, or implore their intercession, because ordinarily they have no cognizance of our prayers. But we may piously believe that God makes our prayers known to them; and then they, full of charity as they are, most assuredly do not omit to pray for us. St. Catherine of Bologna, whenever she desired any favor, had recourse to the Souls in Purgatory, and was immediately heard. She even testified that by the intercession of the Souls in Purgatory she had obtained many graces which had not been accorded to her by the intercession of the Saints. But here let me make a digression in favor of those Holy Souls.

3. If we desire the aid of their prayers, it is but fair that we should succor them with our prayers and good works. I said it is fair, but I should have said, it is a Christian duty; for Charity obliges us to succor our neighbor when he requires our aid, and we can help him without grave inconvenience. Now it is certain that amongst our neighbors are to be

reckoned the Souls in Purgatory, who, although no longer living in this world, yet have not left the Communion of Saints. "The souls of the pious dead," says St. Augustine, "are not separated from the Church," and St. Thomas says more to our purpose that the Charity which is due to the dead who died in the grace of God is only an extension of the same Charity which we owe to our neighbor while living: "Charity, which is the bond that unites the members of the Church, extends not only to the living, but also to the dead who die in Charity." Therefore, we ought to succor, according to our ability, those Holy Souls as our neighbors; and as their necessities are greater than those of our other neighbors, for this reason our duty to succor them seems also to be greater.

But now, what are the necessities of those holy prisoners? It is certain that their pains are immense. The fire that tortures them, says St. Augustine, is more excruciating than any pain that man can endure in this life: "That fire will be more painful than anything that man can suffer in this life." St. Thomas thinks the same and supposes it to be identical with the fire of hell; " The damned are tormented and the elect purified in the same fire." And this only relates to the pain of sense. But the pain of loss, that is, the privation of the sight of God, which those Holy Souls suffer, is much greater; because not only their natural affection, but also the supernatural love of God, wherewith they burn, draws them with such violence to be united with their Sovereign Good, that when they see the barrier which their sins have put in the way, they feel a pain so acute that, if they were capable of death, they could not live a moment. So that, as St. Chrysostom says, this pain of the deprivation of God tortures them incomparably more than the pain of sense: "The flames of a thousand hells together could not inflict such torments as the pain of loss by itself." So that those Holy Souls would rather suffer every other possible torture than be deprived for a single instant of the union with God for which they long. So St. Thomas says that the pain of Purgatory exceeds anything that can be endured in this life: "The pain of Purgatory must exceed all pain of this life." And Denis the Carthusian relates that a dead person who had been raised to life by the intercession of St. Jerome, told St. Cyril of Jerusalem that all the torments of this earth are refreshing and delightful when compared with the very least pain in Purgatory: "If all the torments of the world were compared with the least that can be had in Purgatory they would appear to be comforts." And he adds that if a man had once felt these torments, he would rather suffer all earthly sorrows that man can endure till the Day of Judgment than suffer for one day the least pain of Purgatory. Hence St. Cyril wrote to St. Augustine: "That as far as regards the infliction of suffering, these pains are the same as those of hell--their only difference being that they are not eternal." Hence we see that the pains of these Holy Souls are excessive, while, on the other hand, they cannot help themselves; because, as Job says: they are in chains, and are bound with the cords of poverty (Job xxxvi. 8). They are destined to reign with Christ; but they are withheld from taking possession of their kingdom till the time of their purgation is accomplished. And they cannot help themselves (at least not sufficiently, even according to those Theologians who assert that they can by their prayers gain some relief) to throw off their chains, until they have entirely satisfied the justice of God. This is precisely what a Cistercian monk said to the sacristan of the monastery: "Help me, I beseech you, with your prayers; for of myself I can obtain nothing." And this is consistent with the saying of St. Bonaventure: "Destitution impedes solvency." That is, those souls are so poor that they have no means of making satisfaction.

Evening Meditation
THE PRACTICE OF THE LOVE OF JESUS CHRIST
"Charity believeth all things"
HE THAT LOVES JESUS CHRIST BELIEVES ALL HIS WORDS
I.

The true lover of Jesus Christ keeps Eternal Truths constantly in view and orders all his actions according to them. Oh, how thoroughly does he who loves Jesus Christ understand the force of that saying of the Wise Man: Vanity of vanities, and all is vanity (Ecclesiastes i. 2)-that all earthly greatness is mere smoke, mire and delusion; that the soul's only welfare and happiness consists in loving its Creator, and in doing His blessed will; that we are, in reality, no more than what we are before God; that it is of no advantage to gain the whole world, if the soul be lost; that all the goods of the world can never satisfy the human heart, that only God Himself can satisfy it; and in fine, that we must leave all in order to gain all.

My beloved Redeemer, O Life of my soul, I firmly believe that Thou art the only Good worthy of being loved! I believe that Thou art the greatest Lover of my soul, since through love alone Thou didst die, overwhelmed with sorrows, for love of me. I believe there is no greater blessing in this world, or in the next, than to love Thee, and to do Thy adorable will. All this I believe most firmly; so that I renounce all things that I may belong wholly to Thee, and that I may possess Thee alone.

II.

Charity believeth, all things. There are other Christians--though not so perverse as the class we have mentioned, who would fain believe in nothing, so that they may give full scope to their unruly passions, and live on undisturbed by the stings of remorse--there are others, I say, who believe indeed, but their Faith is languid; they believe the most holy Mysteries of Religion, the Truths of Revelation contained in the Gospel, the Trinity, the Redemption, the holy Sacraments, and the rest; still they do not believe all. Jesus Christ has said: Blessed are the poor! Blessed are they that hunger! Blessed are they that suffer persecution! Blessed are you when men shall revile you and shall say all manner of evil against you! (Matthew v. 3-11). This is the teaching of Jesus Christ in the Gospel. How, then, can it be said that those believe in the Gospel who say: "Blessed are the rich! Blessed are those who have to suffer nothing! Blessed are those who can have their amusements and pitiable is the man who suffers persecution and ill-treatment from others"? We must certainly say of such as these that either they do not believe the Gospel or that they believe only a part of it. He who believes all the Gospel esteems it his highest fortune, and a mark of Divine favor in this world, to be poor, to be sick, to be humiliated, to be despised and ill-treated by men. Such is the belief, and such the language, of one who believes all that is said in the Gospel and has a real love for Jesus Christ.

Help me, through the merits of Thy sacred Passion, O my Jesus, and make me such as Thou wouldst have me to be. I believe in Thee, O infallible Truth! I trust in Thee, O infinite Mercy! I love Thee, O infinite Goodness! O infinite Love, I give myself wholly to Thee, Who hast given Thyself wholly to me in Thy Passion, and in the Holy Sacrament of the Altar.

And I recommend myself to thee, O Mary, Refuge of sinners, and Mother of God.

Thursday--Sixth Week after Pentecost

Morning Meditation

ABUSE OF DIVINE MERCY

God has pity on those who fear Him, but not on sinners who despise Him. To offend God because He shows us mercy, is to provoke Him in the highest degree to chastise us.

I.

God has pity on those who fear Him but not on sinners who despise Him. To offend God because He shows us mercy is to provoke Him in the highest degree to chastise us.

Again, to offer an insult to God, because God is a forgiving God, is to deride Him; but God is not mocked (Galatians vi. 7).

The devil will say to you: "But who knows? Even with this other sin it may be that you shall yet be saved." But meanwhile, if you sin, you yourself may condemn your soul to hell. Who knows? It may be that as yet you shall be saved; but it may also happen, and more easily happen, that you may be lost. And is the affair of eternal Salvation to be risked on a who knows? If in the meantime death should come upon you! If God should abandon, you after that other sin! What would then become of you?

No, my God, I will never more offend Thee. How many are now suffering in hell for fewer sins than mine? I will no longer be devoted to self but will be Thine and entirely Thine. To Thee I consecrate my whole liberty and my will. I am thine; do thou save me

(Psalm cxviii. 94). Save me from hell, but first save me from sin. I love Thee, my Jesus, I will never more forsake Thee.

The Fathers of the Church say that God has determined the number of sins He will forgive each one. Hence, as we know not this number, we ought to fear lest with everyone more additional sin God should abandon us. This dreadful thought--Who knows whether God will any more pardon me?--ought to be a great restraint upon us and keep us from again offending God: with this fear we should be secure.

II.

He who has been the more favored by God with lights and graces ought to be the more afraid of being abandoned by Him. The Angelic Doctor says that the grievousness of sin increases in proportion to the ingratitude with which sin is committed. Woe, then, to the Christian who, after having been enriched with the graces of God, offends Him mortally!

O my Jesus, while Thou hast shown me numberless mercies, I have repaid them by multiplied offences! Thou hast bestowed favors upon me, and I, in return, have despised Thee! But now I love Thee with my whole heart, and I desire to make amends by my love for all the offences I have committed against Thee. Oh, do Thou enlighten and strengthen me!

Sister Mary Strozzi says that "sin in a religious person strikes Heaven with horror and obliges God to turn away from that soul."

He who has not a great dread of mortal sin is not far from falling into it. Hence it is necessary to fly from dangerous occasions as much as possible.

It is necessary also to fly from all deliberate venial sins. Father Alvarez used to say: "Little voluntary faults do not kill the soul, but they so weaken it that, when there comes a grievous temptation, it will not have strength to resist, and will fall."

St. Teresa has written: "From willful sin, however small it be, may God deliver us!" Because, as the Saint says, a deliberate venial sin does us more harm than all the devils in hell.

No, my Jesus, no, I will no more offend Thee; neither in great things nor in small. Thou hast done too much to oblige me to love Thee. I desire rather to die than to give Thee the least offence. Thou dost not deserve insult; but rather all my love, and I desire to love Thee with all my strength. Give me Thy assistance.

Spiritual Reading
PRAYER, ITS NECESSITY

IV-ON INVOKING THE SAINTS AND ON PRAYING TO THE SOULS IN PURGATORY AND HELPING THEM BY OUR PRAYERS

Since it is certain, and even of Faith, that by our suffrages, and chiefly by our prayers, as particularly recommended and practiced by the Church, we can relieve those Holy Souls, I do not know how to excuse that man from sin who neglects to give them some assistance, at least by his prayers. If a sense of duty will not persuade us to succor them, let us think of the pleasure it will give Jesus Christ to see us endeavoring to deliver His beloved spouses from prison, in order that He may have them with Him in Paradise. Let us think of the store of merit which we can lay up by practicing this great act of Charity; let us think, too, that those Souls are not ungrateful, and will never forget the great benefit we do them in relieving them of their pains, and in obtaining for them, by our prayers, anticipation of their entrance into glory; so that when they are there they will never neglect to pray for us. And if God promises mercy to him who practices mercy towards his neighbor--Blessed are the merciful, for they shall obtain mercy (Matthew v. 7)--he may reasonably expect to be saved who remembers to assist those Souls so afflicted, and yet so dear to God. Jonathan, after having saved the Hebrews from ruin by a victory over their enemies was condemned to death by his father, Saul, for having tasted some honey against his express commands; but the people came before the king, and said: Shall Jonathan then die, who hath wrought this great salvation in Israel? (1 Kings xiv. 45). So may we expect, that if any of us ever obtains, by his prayers, the liberation of a Soul from Purgatory, that Soul will say to God: "Lord, suffer not him who has delivered me from my torments to be lost." And if Saul spared Jonathan's life at the request of his people, God will not refuse the salvation of a Christian to the prayers of a Soul which is His own spouse. Moreover, St. Augustine says that God will cause those who in this life have succored those Holy Souls, when they come to Purgatory themselves, to be most succored by others. I may here observe that, in practice, one of the best suffrages is to hear Mass for them, and during the Holy Sacrifice to recommend them to God by the infinite merits of Jesus Christ. The following form may be used: Eternal Father, I offer Thee this Sacrifice of the Body and Blood of Jesus Christ, with all the pains which He suffered in His life and death; and by the merits of His Passion, I recommend to Thee the Souls in Purgatory, and especially that of, etc. And it is a very charitable act to recommend, at the same time, the souls of all those who are in their agony.

4. Whatever doubt there may be whether or not the Souls in Purgatory can pray for us, and therefore whether or not it is useful to recommend ourselves to their prayers, there

can be no doubt whatever with regard to the Saints. For it is certain that it is most useful to have recourse to the intercession of the Saints canonized by the Church, who are already enjoying the vision of God. To suppose that the Church can err in canonizing is a sin, or is heresy, according to St. Bonaventure, Bellarmine, and others; or at least very near to heresy, according to Suarez, Azorius, Gotti, etc.: because the Sovereign Pontiff, according to St. Thomas, is guided by the infallible influence of the Holy Ghost in an especial way when canonizing the Saints.

But to return to the question just proposed; are we obliged to have recourse to the intercession of the Saints? I have no wish to undertake to decide this question; but I cannot omit the exposition of the teaching of St. Thomas. In several places above quoted, and especially in his Book of Sentences, he expressly lays it down as certain that everyone is bound to pray; because (as he asserts) in no other way can the graces necessary for salvation be obtained from God, except by Prayer: "Every man is bound to pray, from the fact that he is bound to procure spiritual good for himself, which can only be got from God; so it can only be obtained by asking it of God." Then, in another place of the same Book, he proposes the exact question, "Whether we are bound to pray to the Saints to intercede for us?" And he answers as follows--in order to catch his real meaning, we will quote the entire passage: "According to Dionysius, the order which God has instituted for His creatures requires that things which are remote may be brought to God by means of things which are nearer to Him. Hence, as the Saints in Heaven are nearest of all to Him, the order of His law requires that we who remaining in the body are absent from the Lord, should be brought to Him by means of the Saints; and this is affected by the Divine Goodness pouring forth His gifts through them. And as the path of our return to God should correspond to the path of the good things which proceed from Him to us, it follows that, as the benefits of God come down to us by means of the suffrages of the Saints, we ought to be brought to God by the same way, so that a second time we may receive His benefits by the mediation of the Saints. Hence it is that we make them our intercessors with God, and, as it were, our mediators, when we ask them to pray for us." Note well the words--"The order of God's law requires"; and especially note the last words--"As the benefits of God come down to us by means of the suffrages of the Saints, in the same way we must be brought back to God, so that a second time we may receive His benefits by the mediation of the Saints." So that, according to St. Thomas, the order of the Divine law requires that we mortals should be saved by means of the Saints, in that we receive by their intercession the help necessary for our salvation. He then puts the objection that it appears superfluous to have recourse to the Saints, since God is infinitely more merciful than they, and more ready to hear us. This he answers by saying: God has so ordered not on account of any want of clemency on His part, but to keep the right order which He has universally established, of working by means of second causes. "It is not for want of mercy, but to preserve the aforesaid order in the creation."

In conformity with this doctrine of St. Thomas, the Continuator of Tourneley says with Sylvius, that although God only is to be prayed to as the Author of grace, yet we are bound to have recourse also to the intercession of the Saints, so as to observe the order which God has established with regard to our salvation, which is, that the inferior should be saved by imploring the aid of the superior. "By the law of nature, we are bound to observe the order which God has appointed; but God has appointed that the inferior should obtain salvation by imploring the assistance of his superior."

Evening Meditation

THE PRACTICE OF THE LOVE OF JESUS CHRIST

"Charity hopeth all things"

HE THAT LOVES JESUS CHRIST HOPES FOR ALL THINGS FROM HIM

I.

Hope increases Charity, and Charity increases Hope. Hope in the Divine goodness undoubtedly gives an increase to our love of Jesus Christ. St. Thomas says that in the very moment when we hope to receive some benefit from a person, we begin also to love him. On this account, the Lord forbids us to put our trust in creatures: Put not your trust in princes. Further, He pronounces a curse on those who do so: Cursed be the man that trusteth in man (Jeremiah xvii. 5). God does not wish us to trust in creatures, because He does not wish us to fix our love upon them. Hence St. Vincent de Paul said: "Let us beware of reposing too much confidence in men; for when God beholds us thus leaning on them for support, He Himself withdraws from us. On the other hand, the more we trust in God, the more we shall advance in His holy love": I have run the way of thy commandments, when thou didst enlarge my heart (Psalm cxviii. 32). Oh, how rapidly does that soul advance in perfection who has her heart dilated with confidence in God! She flies rather than runs; for by making God the foundation of all her Hope she flings aside her own weakness, and borrows the strength of God Himself, which is communicated to all who place confidence in Him: They that hope in the Lord shall renew their strength, and they shall take wings as eagles, they shall run and not be weary, they shall walk and not faint (Isaiah xl. 31). The eagle is the bird that soars nearest the sun; in like manner, the soul that has God for her trust becomes detached from the earth, and more and more united to God by love.

II.

Now as Hope increases the love of God, so does love help to increase hope; for charity makes us the adopted sons of God. In the natural order we are the work of His hands; but in the supernatural order we are made sons of God, and partakers of the Divine nature through the merits of Jesus Christ; as the Apostle St. Peter writes: That by these you may be made partakers of the divine nature (2 Peter i. 4). And if Charity makes us the sons of God, it consequently makes us heirs of Heaven, according to St. Paul: And if sons, heirs also (Romans viii. 17). Now a son claims the right of abiding under the paternal roof; an heir is entitled to the property; and thus Charity increases the Hope of Paradise; so that the souls that love God cry out incessantly: Thy kingdom come! Thy kingdom come!

Friday–Sixth Week after Pentecost

Morning Meditation

VENIAL SIN

Venial sin is, unfortunately regarded as a slight evil. Is that called a slight evil which is an offence against God!

A man will go on committing venial sins, and foolishly says: "It will be enough for me to be saved!" But I answer: By continuing that course you will not be saved! For, as St. Gregory says, the soul never remains where it falls, but descends much lower.

I.

Venial sin is, unfortunately, regarded as a slight evil. Is that called a slight evil which is an offence against God!

A man will go on committing venial sins, and foolishly says: "It will be enough for me to be saved!" But I answer: By continuing that course you will not be saved! For, as St. Gregory says, the soul never remains where it falls, but descends much lower.

St. Isodore writes that he who makes no account of venial sins is permitted by the Almighty to fall into mortal sins, in punishment of his little love of God. And our Lord Himself said to the Blessed Henry Suso that those who have not a horror of venial sins expose themselves to much greater dangers than they are aware of; because it thus becomes much more difficult for them to persevere in grace.

The Council of Trent teaches that we cannot persevere in grace without the special assistance of God; but he is quite undeserving of such special assistance who offends God by voluntary venial sins, and without a thought of amendment. Chastise me not, O Lord, as I have deserved! Remember not the many offences I have committed against Thee and deprive me not of Thy light and assistance. I desire to amend; I desire to be Thine. O Omnipotent God, accept of me and change me! This is my hope.

Our Lord said to Blessed Angela de Foligno: "Those who have been enlightened by Me to aim at perfection, but who debase their souls and walk in the ordinary way, will be abandoned by me."

He who serves God but is not afraid of offending Him by venial gratifications, would seem to think that God deserves no better. He declares, in fact, that God is not deserving of so much love as to oblige us to prefer His pleasure to our own satisfaction.

Habitual defects, says St. Augustine, are a kind of leprosy, which renders the soul so disgusting that God deprives it of His loving embraces.

I see, O Lord, that Thou hast not yet abandoned me, as I have deserved; strengthen me, therefore, to shake off my tepidity. I desire never more deliberately to offend Thee. I desire to love Thee with my whole soul. O Jesus, help me! In Thee do I confide.

II.

St. Francis de Sales says that it is an artifice of Satan: to bind souls first with a hair, that he may afterwards bind them with a chain, and make them slaves. Let us. therefore, be on our guard not to be entangled by any passion. A soul that is entangled by passion is either lost or in great danger of being lost.

"The devil," said Mary Victoria Strada, "when he cannot have much is content with little, but by that little he gains much in the end."

Our Lord declares that the lukewarm are loathsome and disgusting to Him: Because thou art lukewarm...I will begin to vomit thee out of my mouth (Apocalypse iii. 16). This means abandonment by God.

Tepidity is a kind of fever, which is scarcely perceived, but if neglected becomes fatal; inasmuch as tepidity renders the soul insensible to remorse of conscience.

O Jesus, do not cast me off, as I have deserved! Look not on my ingratitude, but on the sufferings, Thou hast endured for my sake. I am sorry for all my offences against Thee. I love Thee, O my God, and from this day forward I desire to do all in my power to please Thee. O Love of my soul! I have much offended Thee; grant that for the remainder of my life I may love Thee very much. O Mary, my hope, succor me by thy holy intercession.

Spiritual Reading

PRAYER, ITS NECESSITY

V-THE INTERCESSION OF THE BLESSED VIRGIN

If it be true that the intercession of the Saints is necessary for us, much more is it true of the intercession of the Mother of God, whose prayers are certainly of more value in His sight than those of all the rest of the inhabitants of Heaven together. For St. Thomas says that the Saints, in proportion to the merits by which they have obtained grace for themselves, are able also to save others; but that Jesus Christ, and so also His Mother, have merited so much grace, that They can save all men. "It is a great thing in any Saint that he should have grace enough for the salvation of many besides himself; but if he had enough for the salvation of all men, this would be the greatest of all; and this is the case with Christ, and with the Blessed Virgin." And St. Bernard speaks thus to Mary: "Through thee we have access to thy Son, O discoverer of grace and Mother of salvation, that through thee He may receive us, Who through thee was given to us." These words signify, that as we have access to the Father only by means of the Son, Who is the Mediator of Justice, so we have access to the Son only by means of the Mother, who is mediator of grace, and who obtains for us, by her intercession, the gifts which Jesus Christ has merited for us. And therefore St. Bernard says, in another place, that Mary has received a twofold fullness of grace. The first was the Incarnation of the Eternal Word, Who was made Man in her most holy womb; the second in that fullness of grace which we receive from God by means of her prayers. Hence the Saint adds: "God has placed the fullness of all good in Mary, that if we have any hope, any grace, any salvation, we may know that it overflows from her who ascendeth abounding with delights. She is a garden of delights, whose odors spread abroad and abound, that is, the gifts of graces." So that whatever good we have from God, we receive all by the intercession of Mary. And why so? Because, says St. Bernard, it is God's will: "Such is His will, Who would have us receive everything through Mary." But the more precise reason is deduced from the expression of St. Augustine, that Mary is justly called our Mother because she co-operated by her charity in the birth of the faithful to the life of grace, by which we become members of Jesus Christ, our Head: "But clearly she is the Mother of His members (which we are), because she co-operated by her charity in the birth of the faithful in the Church, and they are members of that Head." Therefore, as Mary co-operated by her charity in the spiritual birth of the faithful, so also God willed that she should co-operate by her intercession to make them enjoy the life of grace in this world, and the life of glory in the next; and therefore the Church makes us salute her and give her absolutely the titles of "our Life, our Sweetness, and our Hope."

Hence St. Bernard exhorts us to have continual recourse to the Mother of God, because her prayers are certain to be heard by her Son: "Go to Mary, I say, without hesitation; the

Son will hear the Mother." And then he adds: "My children, she is the ladder of sinners, she is my chief confidence, she is the whole ground of my hope." He calls her "ladder", because, as you cannot mount the third step except you put your foot on the second, nor can you arrive at the second except by the first, so you cannot come to God except by means of Jesus Christ, nor can you come to Christ except by means of His Mother. Then he calls her "his greatest security, and the whole ground of his hope"; because, as he affirms, God wills that all the graces which He gives us should pass through the hands of Mary. And he concludes by saying that we ought to ask all the graces which we desire through Mary; because she obtains whatever she seeks, and her prayers cannot be rejected. "Let us seek grace, and let us seek it through Mary; because what she seeks she finds, and she cannot be disappointed." The following Saints teach the same as St. Bernard: St. Ephrem "We have no other confidence than from thee, O purest Virgin!" St. Ildephonsus: "All the good things that the Divine Majesty has determined to give, He has also decreed to commit to thy hands; for to thee are entrusted the treasures and the ornaments of grace." St. Germanus: "If thou desertest us, what will become of us, O life of Christians?" St. Peter Damien: "In thy hands are all the treasures of the mercies of God." St. Antoninus: "He who seeks graces without her, attempts to fly without wings." St. Bernardine of Sienna "Thou art the dispenser of all graces; our salvation is in thy hands." In another place, he not only says that all graces are transmitted to us by means of Mary, but he also asserts that the Blessed Virgin, from the time she became Mother of God, acquired a certain jurisdiction over all the graces that are given to us. "Through the Virgin the vital graces are transfused from Christ, the Head, into His mystical body. From the time when the Virgin Mother conceived in her womb the Word of God, she obtained a certain jurisdiction (if I may so speak) over every temporal procession of the Holy Ghost; so that no creature could obtain any grace from God except by the dispensation of His sweet Mother." And he concludes: "Therefore all gifts, virtues, and graces are dispensed through her hands to whom she wills, and as she wills." St. Bonaventure says the same: "Since, the whole Divine nature was in the womb of the Virgin, I do not fear to teach that she has a certain jurisdiction over all the streams of grace; for her womb was, as it were, an ocean of the Divine nature, whence all the streams of grace must emanate." On the authority of these Saints many Theologians have piously and reasonably defended the opinion that there is no grace given to us except by means of the intercession of Mary; so Mendoza, Vega, Paciucchelli, Segneri, Poire, Crasset, and others, as also the learned Alexander Natalis, who says: "Since it is from God we expect all good things, He wishes us to ask them through the intercession of the Virgin Mother, when, as is fitting, we invoke her." And he quotes in confirmation the passage of St. Bernard: Such is His Will, Who has determined that we should receive all through Mary." Contenson says the same, in a comment on the words addressed by Jesus on the Cross to St. John, Behold thy mother (John xix. 27); as though He said: "No one shall be partaker of My Blood except by the intercession of My Mother. My Wounds are Fountains of grace; but their stream shall flow to no one, except through the channel of Mary. O My disciple John, I will love you as you love her."

Besides it is certain that if God is pleased when we have recourse to the Saints, He will be much more pleased when we avail ourselves of the intercession of Mary, that she by her merits may compensate for our unworthiness, according to the words of St. Anselm: "that the dignity of the intercessor may supply for our poverty. So that to invoke the Virgin is not to distrust God's Mercy but to fear our own unworthiness." St. Thomas, speaking of her dignity, says it is, in a sense, infinite. "From the fact that she is the Mother of God she has a certain infinite dignity."

CONCLUSION

Let us conclude this point by giving the gist of all that has been said hitherto.

He who prays is certainly saved. He who does not pray is certainly damned. All the Blessed (except infants) have been saved by Prayer. All the damned have been lost through not praying. If they had prayed they would not have been lost. And this is, and will be, their greatest torment in hell, to think how easily they might have been saved, only by asking God for His graces. But now for these miserable ones the time for Prayer is over.

Evening Meditation
THE PRACTICE OF THE LOVE OF JESUS CHRIST
"Charity hopeth all things."
HE THAT LOVES JESUS CHRIST HOPES FOR ALL THINGS FROM HIM
I.

The Lord God loves those who love Him: I love them that love me (Proverbs viii. 17). He showers down His graces on those that seek Him by love: The Lord is good ... to the soul that seeketh him (Lamentations 25). Consequently, the soul that loves God most has the greatest hope in His goodness. This confidence produces that imperturbable tranquility in the Saints which makes them always joyful and full of peace, even amid the severest trials; for their love of Jesus Christ, and the conviction they have of His liberality towards those who love Him, leads them to trust solely in Him; and thus they find a lasting repose. The sacred spouse abounded with delights, because she loved none but her Spouse, and leaned entirely on Him for support; and she was full of contentment, since she well knew how generous her Beloved is towards all that love Him; so that of her it is written: Who is this that cometh up from the desert, flowing with delights, leaning upon her beloved? (Canticles viii. 5). These words of the Wise Man are most true: All good things came to me together with her (Wisdom vii. 11). With Charity all blessings are introduced into the soul.

II.

The primary object of Christian Hope is God, Whom the soul enjoys in the Kingdom of Heaven. But we must not suppose that the hope of enjoying God in Paradise is any obstacle to Charity; since the hope of Paradise is inseparably connected with Charity, which there receives its full and complete perfection. Charity is that infinite treasure, spoken of by the Wise Man, which makes us the friends of God: An infinite treasure to men, which they that use become the friends of God (Wisdom vii. 14). The angelic Doctor, St. Thomas, says that friendship is founded on the mutual communication of goods; for as friendship is nothing more than a mutual love between friends, it follows that there must be a reciprocal interchange of the goods which each possesses. Hence the Saint says: "If there be no communication, there is no friendship." On this account Jesus Christ says to His disciples:

I have called you friends, because all things whatsoever I have heard of my Father I have made known to you (Jo. xv. 15). Since He had made them His friends, He had communicated all His secrets to them.

SATURDAY--SIXTH WEEK AFTER PENTECOST

Morning Meditation

THE MERCY OF THE BLESSED VIRGIN TOWARDS SINNERS WHO INVOKE HER

Mary is called the Mother of Mercy, because, like a mother, she cannot see her children in danger of being lost without giving them her assistance. She is so solicitous about the relief of the miserable that she appears to desire nothing with greater ardor than to comfort them.

I.

Consider that Mary is so merciful an advocate she not only assists all who have recourse to her, but also goes in search of the miserable in order to defend and save them. Behold how she invites us all, and encourages us to hope for every good, if we have recourse to her. In me is all hope of life and virtue. Come over to me, all ye who desire me (Ecclesiasticus xxiv. 25-26). In explaining this passage, the devout Pelbart says: "She invites all, the just and sinners." The devil, according to St. Peter, goes about continually seeking whom he may devour (1 Peter v. 8). But this Divine Mother, says Bernard de Eustis, goes about seeking whom she may save. Mary is called the Mother of Mercy; because, like a mother, she cannot see her children in danger of being lost without giving them assistance. Mary pities all our miseries, and constantly seeks our salvation. And, asks St. Germanus, who, after Jesus, has greater care of our salvation, than thou, O Mother of Mercy? St. Bonaventure says that Mary is so solicitous about the relief of the miserable that she appears to desire nothing with greater ardor than to comfort them.

She certainly assists us as often as we have recourse to her, but this, adds Richard of St. Victor, is not enough for her; she anticipates our supplications, and obtains aid for us before we ask her prayers. Moreover, the same author says that Mary is so full of mercy that, as soon as she sees misery, she instantly obtains relief, and cannot behold anyone in distress without coming to his assistance. It was thus she acted when she lived on this earth, as we learn from what happened at the marriage of Cana in Galilee; where, when the wine failed, she did not wait to be asked, but taking pity on the affliction and shame of the spouses, asked her Son to console them, saying: They have no wine (John ii. 3). Thus she induced Him to change, by miracle, water into wine. But, says St. Bonaventure, if Mary's compassion for the afflicted was so great while she was in this world, her pity for us is certainly much greater now that she is in Heaven, where she has a better knowledge of our miseries, and greater compassion for us. Novarino adds: If Mary, unasked, shows such readiness to afford relief, how much more careful will she be to console those who ask her prayers!

II.

Ah! let us never cease to have recourse in all our necessities to the Divine Mother, who is always ready to obtain relief for all who pray to her. "You will find her ever ready to assist," says Richard of St. Laurence. And Bernardine de Bustis adds that she desires more ardently to obtain graces for us than we do to receive them. Hence, he says that, whenever we have recourse to her, we shall always find her hands full of grace and mercies. According to St. Bonaventure, Mary's desire for our welfare and salvation is so great that she feels offended not only with those who do her a positive injury but also with those who neglect to ask favors from her. And, on the other hand, the Saint affirms that they who invoke Mary's intercession (that is, with a determination to amend their lives) are saved. Hence he calls her the salvation of those who invoke her. Let us, then, always have recourse to the Divine Mother, and always say to her with the holy Doctor: "In thee, O Lady, have I hoped; may I not be confounded forever." No, O Lady, O Mother of God, O Mary, I shall not be lost after having placed my hopes in thee after Jesus.

Spiritual Reading

PRAYER, ITS POWER

I-ITS POWER AND EXCELLENCE WITH GOD

Our prayers are so dear to God that He has appointed the Angels to present them to Him as soon as they come forth from our mouths. "The angels," says St. Hilary, "preside over the prayers of the faithful, and offer them daily to God." This is that smoke of the incense of the prayers of the saints (Apocalypse viii. 3), which St. John saw ascending to God from the hands of Angels. This he saw in another place represented by golden phials full of sweet odors, very acceptable to God. But to understand better the value of prayers in God's sight it is sufficient to read both in the Old and New Testaments the innumerable promises which God makes to the man that prays. Cry to me, and I will hear thee (Jeremiah xxxii. 3). Call upon me, and I will deliver thee (Psalm xlix. 15). Ask, and it shall be given you; seek, and you shall find; knock and it shall be opened unto you. He shall give good things to them that ask him (Matthew vii. 7, 11). Everyone that asketh receiveth, and he that seeketh findeth (Luke xi. 10). Whatsoever they shall ask, it shall be done to them by my father (Matthew xviii. 19). All things whatsoever you ask when you pray, believe that you shall receive, and they shall come unto you (Mark xi. 24). If you shall ask me anything in my name, that will I do (John xiv. 14). You shall ask whatever you will, and it shall be done unto you (John xv. 7). Amen, amen, I say unto you, if you ask the Father anything in my name, he will give it you (John xvi. 23). There are many similar texts, but it would take too long to quote them.

God wills us to be saved; but for our greater good He wills us to be saved as conquerors. While, therefore, we remain here, we must live in a continual warfare; and if we would be saved, we have to fight and conquer. "No one can be crowned without victory," says St. Chrysostom. We are very feeble, and our enemies are many and mighty; how shall we be able to stand against them, or to defeat them? Let us take courage, and say with the Apostle, I can do all things in him who strengtheneth me (Philippians iv. 13). By Prayer we can do all things; for by this means God will give us that strength which we want. Theodoret says that Prayer is omnipotent; it is but one, yet it can do all things: "Prayer, though one, can do all things." And St. Bonaventure asserts that by Prayer we may obtain every good and escape every evil: "By Prayer, the possession of every good, the liberation from every evil." St. Laurence Justinian says that by means of Prayer we build for ourselves a strong tower, where we shall be secure from all the snares and assaults of our enemies: "By the exercise of Prayer man is able to erect a citadel for himself." "The powers of hell are mighty," says St. Bernard, "but Prayer is stronger than all the devils." Yes, for by Prayer the soul obtains God's help, which is stronger than any created power. Thus David encouraged himself in his fears: Praising I will call upon the Lord, and I shall be saved from my enemies (Psalm xvii. 4). For, as St. Chrysostom says, "Prayer is a strong weapon, a defense, a port, and a treasure." It is a weapon sufficient to overcome every assault of the devil; it is a defense to preserve us in every danger; it is a port where we may be safe in every tempest; and it is at the same time a treasure which provides us with every good.

II--POWER OF PRAYER AGAINST TEMPTATION

God knows the great good which it does us to be obliged to pray, and therefore permits us, as we have already shown (The Necessity of Prayer, p. 66) to be assaulted by our enemies, in order that we may ask Him for the help which He offers and promises us. But as He is pleased when we run to Him in our dangers, so is He displeased when He sees us neglectful of Prayer. As the king, says St. Bonaventure, would think it faithlessness if an officer, when attacked, did not ask him for reinforcements, so God thinks Himself betrayed by the man who, when he finds himself surrounded by temptations, does not run to Him for assistance. For He desires to help us; and only waits to be asked, and then gives abundant succor. This is strikingly shown by Isaias, when, on God's part, he told King Achaz to ask some sign to assure himself of God's readiness to help him: Ask thee a sign of the Lord thy God (Isaiah vii. 11). The impious king answered: I will not ask, and I will not tempt the Lord (Isaiah vii. 12). He trusted in his own power to overcome his enemies without God's aid. And for this the Prophet reproved him: Hear ye, therefore, O house of David; is it a small thing for you to be grievous to men, that you are grievous to my God also? (Isaiah vii. 13), which means that that man is grievous and offensive to God who will not ask Him for the graces which He offers.

Come to me, all you that labour and are burdened, and I will refresh you (Matt. xi. 28). "My poor children," says our Saviour, "though you find yourselves assailed by enemies, and oppressed with the weight of your sins, do not lose heart, but have recourse to Me in Prayer, and I will give you strength to resist; and I will give you a remedy for all your misfortunes." In another place He says, by the mouth of Isaias: Come and accuse me, saith the Lord; if your sins be as scarlet, they shall be made white as snow (Isaiah i. 18). O men, come to me; though your consciences are horribly defiled, yet come; I even give you leave to reproach Me (so to speak), if, after you have recourse to Me, I do not give you grace to become white as snow.

What is Prayer? It is, as St. Chrysostom says, "the anchor of those tossed on the sea, the treasure of the poor, the cure of diseases, the safeguard of health." It is a secure anchor for him who is in peril of shipwreck; it is a treasury of immense wealth for him who is poor;

it is a most efficacious medicine for him who is sick; and it is a certain preservative for him who would keep himself in health. What does Prayer effect? Let us hear St. Laurence Justinian: "It pleases God, it gets what it asks, it overcomes enemies, it changes men." It appeases the wrath of God Who pardons all who pray with humility. It obtains every grace that is asked for; it vanquishes all the strength of the tempter; it gives sight to the blind; it changes the weak into strong, and sinners into Saints. Let him who wants light ask it of God, and it shall be given. As soon as I had recourse to God, says Solomon, He granted me wisdom: I called upon God, and the spirit of wisdom came upon me (Wisdom vii. 7). Let him who wants fortitude ask it of God and it shall be given. For how, in fact, did the Martyrs obtain strength to resist tyrants, except by Prayer, which gave them force to overcome dangers and death? "He who uses this great weapon," says St. Chrysostom, "knows not death, leaves the earth, enters Heaven, lives with God." He falls not into sin; he loses affection for the earth; he makes his abode in Heaven; and begins even in this life to enjoy the conversation of God. Why then should you disquiet such a man by saying: How do you know that you are written in the Book of Life? How do you know whether God will give you efficacious grace and the gift of perseverance? Be nothing solicitous, says St. Paul, but in everything by prayer and supplication, with thanksgiving, let your petitions be made known unto God (Philippians iv. 6). Drive from you all those cares which only lessen your confidence and make you more tepid and slothful in walking in the Way of Salvation. Pray and seek always, make your prayers known to God, and thank Him for having promised to give you the gifts you desire whenever you ask for them, namely, efficacious grace, perseverance, salvation, and everything you may desire. The Lord has given us our post in the battle against powerful foes; but He is faithful in His promises and will never allow us to be assaulted more violently than we can resist: God is faithful, who will not suffer you to be tempted above that which you are able (1 Corinthians x. 13). He is faithful, since He instantly succors the man who invokes Him. The learned Cardinal Gotti writes that God is bound, when we are tempted and fly to His protection, to give us, by the grace prepared and offered to all, the strength by which we not only can, but will actually resist for we can do all things in Him who strengthens us by His grace if we humbly ask for it. We can do all things with God's help, which is granted to everyone who humbly seeks it; so that we have no excuse when we allow ourselves to be overcome by a temptation. We are conquered solely by our own fault because we do not pray. By Prayer all the snares and power of the devil are easily overcome. "By prayer all hurtful things are put to flight," says St. Augustine.

Evening Meditation

THE PRACTICE OF THE LOVE OF JESUS CHRIST

"Charity hopeth all things"

HE THAT LOVES JESUS CHRIST HOPES FOR ALL THINGS FROM HIM

I.

St. Francis de Sales says: "If by a supposition of what is impossible, there could be an infinite Good (that is a God) to whom we belonged in no way whatever, and with Whom we could have no union or communication, we should certainly esteem Him more than ourselves; so that we might feel a great desire of being able to love Him; but we should not actually love Him, because love is built upon union; for love is a friendship, and the foundation of friendship is to have things in common; and its end is union." Thus St. Thomas teaches us that Charity does not exclude the desire of the reward prepared for us in Heaven by Almighty God; on the contrary, it makes us look to it as the chief object of our love, for such is God, Who constitutes the bliss of Paradise; for friendship implies that friends mutually rejoice in one another.

The Spouse in the Canticles refers to this reciprocal interchange of goods when she says: My beloved to me and I to him (Canticles ii. 16). In Heaven the soul belongs wholly to God and God belongs wholly to the soul, according to the measure of her capacity and of her merits.

II.

From the persuasion the soul has of her own nothingness in comparison with the infinite attractions of Almighty God, and aware consequently that the claims of God on her love are beyond measure greater than her own can be on the love of God, she is far more anxious to procure the Divine pleasure than her own enjoyment; so that she is more gratified by the pleasure she affords Almighty God by giving herself entirely to Him, than by God's giving Himself entirely to her; but at the same time she is delighted when God thus gives Himself to her, inasmuch as she is thereby animated to give herself up to God with a greater intensity of love. She indeed rejoices at the glory which God imparts to her, but for the sole purpose of referring it back to God Himself, and of thus doing her utmost to increase the Divine glory. At the sight of God in Heaven the soul cannot help loving Him with all her strength; on the other hand, God cannot hate anyone that loves Him: but if (supposing what is impossible) God could hate a soul that loves Him, and if a beatified soul could exist without loving God, she would much rather endure all the pains of hell on condition of being allowed to love God as much as He should hate her, than to live without loving God, even though she could enjoy all the delights of Paradise. So it is; for that conviction which the soul has of God's boundless claims upon her love gives her a greater desire to love God than to be loved by Him.

SEVENTH SUNDAY AFTER PENTECOST

Morning Meditation

DEATH–THE WORLDLING AT THE APPROACH OF DEATH

What will be the terror of the poor worldling when he reflects: In a short time, I shall be no more! And I know not whether I shall be happy or miserable for eternity! O God, what consternation will the bare words, Judgment, Hell, Eternity, strike into the souls of poor worldlings!

I.

We must die. Sooner or later we must all die. In every age houses and cities are filled with new inhabitants, and their predecessors are consigned to the grave.

We are born but to die–born with a halter, as it were, about our necks. However long, then, our life may be, a day, an hour, will come which will be our last, and this hour is already determined.

I thank Thee, O God, for the patience with which Thou hast borne with me. Oh, that I had died rather than have ever offended Thee! But since Thou givest me time to repair the past, make known to me what Thou requires of me, and I will obey Thee in all things.

In a few years neither I who write nor thou who readest will be living on this earth. As we have heard the bell toll for others, so will others one day hear it toll for us. As we now read the names of others inscribed in the lists of the dead, so will others read our names.

In a word, there is no alternative; we must all die. And, what is more terrible, we can die but once; and if once lost, we shall be lost forever.

What will be your alarm when it is announced to you that you must receive the Last Sacraments, and that there is no time to be lost! Then will you see your relatives and friends leave your room, and none remain but your confessor and those who are to attend you in your last moments.

O Jesus, I will not wait until death to give myself to Thee. Thou hast said that Thou knowest not how to reject the soul that seeks Thee: Seek and you shall find (Matthew vii. 7).

Now, therefore, O Jesus, do I seek Thee; grant that I may find Thee. I love Thee, O infinite Goodness! Thee alone do I desire, and besides Thee, nothing more.

In the midst of his schemes and worldly projects the man of the world shall hear it said to him: "My brother, you are fatally ill, and must prepare to die." He would wish to put his accounts in order; but alas! the terror and confusion which agitate him render him incapable of doing anything.

Whatever he sees or hears adds to his pain and distress. All worldly things are now thorns to him: the remembrance of past pleasures, his vanities, his successes, the friends who have withdrawn him from God, vain apparel; all are thorns, and all alarm and torment him.

What will be his terror when he reflects: "In a short time I shall be no more; and I know not whether I shall be happy, or miserable, for eternity!" O God, what consternation will the bare words, Judgment, Hell, Eternity, strike into the souls of poor dying worldlings!

My Redeemer, I believe that Thou hast died for me. From Thy precious Blood do I hope for salvation. I love Thee, O infinite Goodness! And I am grieved for having offended Thee. O Jesus, my Hope, my Love, have pity on me.

II.

Consider that poor worldling now seized with his last illness. He who but a little while ago went about slandering, threatening, and ridiculing others, is suddenly struck down and deprived of his strength and bodily senses, so that he can no longer speak, or see, or hear.

Alas, the unhappy man thinks now no more of his worldly projects, or his schemes of vanity; the thought of the account which he must soon render to God alone occupies his mind. His relatives are weeping and sighing, or in sad silence around him, and his confessor is there to assist him.

Physicians consult together. Everything increases his alarm. In such a state, he thinks no longer of his amusements; he thinks only of the news which has been brought him–his malady is fatal!

But there is no help for it, and in this state of confusion, in this tempest of pain, affliction, and fear, he must prepare himself to depart out of this world. But how is he to prepare himself in so short a time and his mind so troubled? But it matters not! There is no remedy; he must depart! What is done is done!

O God, what shall my end be? No, I desire not to die in so great uncertainty as to my salvation. I will change my life. O Jesus! help me, for I am resolved to love Thee henceforward with my whole heart. Unite me to Thyself, and never suffer me to be separated from Thee.

Spiritual Reading

PRAYER, ITS POWER

III–GOD IS ALWAYS READY TO HEAR OUR PRAYER

St. Bernardine of Sienna says that Prayer is a faithful ambassador, well known to the King of Heaven, and having access to His audience chamber, and able by his importunity to induce the merciful Heart of the King to grant every aid to us His wretched creatures, groaning in the midst of our conflicts and miseries in this valley of tears. Isaias also assures us, that as soon as the Lord hears our prayers He is moved with compassion towards us, and does not leave us to cry long to Him, but instantly replies, and grants us what we ask: Weeping, thou shalt not weep; he will surely have pity upon thee: at the voice of thy cry as soon as he shall hear, he will answer thee (Isaiah xxx. 19). In another place He complains of us by the mouth of Jeremias: Am I become a wilderness to Israel, or a late ward springing land? Why then have my people said, we are revolted, we will come to thee no more? (Jeremiah ii. 31). Why do you say that you will no more have recourse to Me? Has My mercy become to you a barren land, which can yield you no fruits of grace? or a tardy soil, which yields its fruit too late? So has our loving Lord assured us that He never neglects to hear us, and to hear us instantly when we pray; and so does He reproach those who neglect to pray through diffidence of being heard.

If God were to allow us to present our petitions to Him once a month, even this would be a great favor. The kings of the earth give audience a few times a year, but God gives continual audience. St. Chrysostom writes that God is always waiting to hear our prayers, and that a case never occurred when He neglected to hear a petition offered to Him with the proper dispositions. And again, he says that when we pray to God, before we have finished recounting to Him our petitions, He has already heard us: "It is always obtained, even while we are yet praying." We even have the like promise from God: As they are yet speaking, I will hear (Isaiah lxv. 24). The Lord, says David, stands near to everyone who prays, to console, to hear, and to save him: The Lord is nigh to all them that call upon him; to all that call upon him in truth (that is, as they ought). He will do the will of them that fear him; and he will hear their prayer and will save them (Psalm cxliv. 18, 19). It was in this that Moses gloried, saying: There is no other nation so great, that has gods so nigh them, as our God is present to all our petitions (Deuteronomy iv. 7). The gods of the Gentiles were deaf to those who invoked them, for they were wretched fabrications, which could do nothing. But our God, Who is Almighty, is not deaf to our prayers, but always stands near the man who prays, ready to grant him all the graces which he asks: In what day soever I shall call upon thee, behold I shall know that thou art my God (Psalm lv. 10). Lord, says the Psalmist, hereby do I know that Thou art my God, all goodness and mercy, in that, whenever I have recourse to Thee, Thou dost instantly help me.

IV–THE POWER OF PRAYER TO OBTAIN GREAT THINGS FOR US.

We are so poor that we have nothing; but if we pray we are no longer poor. If we are poor, God is rich; and God, as the Apostle says, is all liberality to him that calls for His aid: Rich unto all who call upon Him (Romans x. 12). Since therefore (as St. Augustine exhorts us), we have to do with a Lord of infinite power and infinite riches, let us not go to Him for little and valueless things, but let us ask some great thing of Him: "You seek from the Almighty–seek something great." If a man went to a king to ask some trumpery coin, like a farthing, methinks that man would but insult the king. On the other hand, we honor God, we honor His mercy, and His liberality, when, though we see how miserable we are, and how unworthy of any kindness, we yet ask for great graces, trusting in the goodness of God, and in His faithfulness to His promises of granting to the man who prays whatever grace he asks: You shall ask whatsoever you will, and it shall be done unto you (John xv. 7). St. Mary Magdalen de Pazzi said that "God feels Himself so honored and is so delighted when we ask for His grace, that He is, in a certain sense, grateful to us; because when we do this we seem to open to Him a way to do us a kindness, and to satisfy His nature, which is to do good to all. "And let us be sure that, when we seek God's grace, He always gives us more than we ask: If any of you want wisdom, let him ask of God, who giveth to all men abundantly, and upbraideth not (James i. 5). Thus speaks St. James, to show us that God is not like men, parsimonious of His goods. Men, though rich and liberal, when they give alms, are always somewhat niggardly, and generally give less than what is asked of them, because their wealth, however great it be, is always finite, so that the more they give the less they have. But God, when He is asked, gives His good things abundantly, that is, with a generous hand, always giving more than is asked, because His wealth is infinite, and the more He gives the more He has to give: For thou, O Lord, art sweet and mild; and plenteous in mercy to all that call upon thee (Psalm lxxxv. 5).

On this point, then, we have to fix all our attention, namely, to pray with confidence, feeling sure that by Prayer all the treasures of Heaven are thrown open to us. "Let us attend to this," says St. Chrysostom, "and we shall open Heaven to ourselves." Prayer is a treasure; he who asks most receives most. St. Venture says that every time a man has recourse to God by fervent Prayer he gains good things that are of more value than the whole world: "A man gains any day more by devout prayer than the whole world is worth." Some devout souls spend a great deal of time in reading, and in meditating, but pay little attention to petition. There is no doubt that Spiritual Reading and Meditation on the Eternal Truths are very useful things; "but", says St. Augustine, "it is of much more use to pray." By reading and meditating we learn our duty; but by Prayer we obtain the grace to do it. "It is better to pray than to read: by reading we know what we ought to do; by prayer we receive what we ask." What is the use of knowing our duty and then not doing it, but to make us more guilty in God's sight? Read and meditate as we like, we shall never satisfy our obligations, unless we ask of God the grace to fulfil them.

And, therefore, as St. Isidore observes, the devil is never busier to distract us with the thoughts of worldly cares than when he perceives us praying and asking God for grace: "Then mostly does the devil insinuate thoughts, when he sees a man praying." And why? Because the enemy sees that at no other time do we gain so many treasures of heavenly goods as when we pray. This is the chief fruit of Mental Prayer, to ask God for the graces which we need for perseverance and for eternal salvation; and chiefly for this reason is it that Mental Prayer is morally necessary for the soul, to enable it to preserve itself in the grace of God. For if a person neglects in the time of Meditation to ask for the help necessary for perseverance he will not do so at any other time; for without Meditation, he will not think of asking for it, and will not even think of the necessity of asking for it. On the other hand, he who makes his Meditation every day will easily see the needs of his soul, its dangers, and the necessity for his praying; and so he will pray, and will obtain the graces which will enable him to persevere and save his soul. Father Segneri said of himself that when he began to meditate, he aimed rather at exciting affections than at making petitions. But when he came to know the immense utility of Prayer, he more and more applied himself, in his long mental prayer, to making petitions.

I will cry like a young swallow, said the devout King Ezechias (Isaiah xxxviii. 14). The young of the swallow do nothing but cry to their mother for help and food; so should we all do, if we would preserve our life of grace. We should be always crying to God for aid to avoid the death of sin, and to advance in His holy love. Father Rodriguez relates that the Ancient Fathers who were our first instructors in the spiritual life held a conference to determine which was the exercise most useful and most necessary for salvation; and that they determined it was to repeat over and over again the short prayer of David, Incline unto my aid, O God (Psalm lxix. 2). "This," says Cassian, "is what everyone ought to do who wishes to be saved: he ought to be always saying, My God, help me! My God, help me!" We ought to do this the first thing when we awake in the morning; and then to continue doing it in all our needs, and when attending to our business, whether spiritual or temporal; and most especially when we find ourselves troubled by any temptation or passion. St. Bonaventure says that at times we obtain a grace by a short prayer sooner than by many other good works: "Sometimes a man can soon obtain by a short prayer what he would with difficulty obtain by pious works." St. Ambrose says that he who prays while he is praying obtains what he asks, because the very act of prayer is the same as receiving: He who asks of God, while he asks receives; for to ask is to receive." Hence St. Chrysostom wrote that "there is nothing more powerful than a man who prays," because such a one is made partaker of the power of God. To arrive at perfection, says St. Bernard, we must meditate and pray: by Meditation we see what we want; by Prayer we receive what we want. "Let us mount up by Meditation and Prayer: the one points out what may be deficient, the other obtains it."

CONCLUSION

In conclusion, to save one's soul without Prayer is most difficult, and (as we have seen) in the ordinary course of God's Providence, even impossible. But by praying our salvation is made secure, and very easy. It is not necessary in order to save our souls to go among the heathen and give up our life as martyrs. Nor is it necessary, like the hermits, to retire into the desert, and eat nothing but herbs. What does it cost us to say, My God, help me! Lord, assist me! Have mercy on me! Is there anything easier than this? And this little will be enough to save us, if we are diligent in doing it. St. Laurence Justinian specially exhorts us to oblige ourselves to say a prayer at least when we begin any action: "We must endeavor to offer a prayer at least in the beginning of every work." Cassian attests that the principal exhortation of the Ancient Fathers was to have recourse to God with short but frequent prayers. St. Bernard says: "Let no one undervalue his prayer, for God does not undervalue it ... He will give either what we ask or what He knows to be better". And let us understand that if we do not pray we have no excuse, because the grace of Prayer is given to everyone. It is in our power to pray whenever we will, as David says of himself: With me is prayer to the God of my life; I will say to God, thou art my support (Psalm xli. 9). On this point I shall later speak at length, and I will make it quite clear that God gives to all men the grace of Prayer in order that thereby they may obtain every help, and even more than they need, for keeping the Divine Law and for persevering till death. At present I will only say that if we are not saved the whole fault will be ours; and we shall have to answer for our own failure because we did not pray.

Evening Meditation

THE PRACTICE OF THE LOVE OF JESUS CHRIST

"Charity hopeth all things"

HE THAT LOVES JESUS CHRIST HOPES FOR ALL THINGS FROM HIM

I.

Charity hopeth all things. St. Thomas, with the Master of the Sentences, defines Christian Hope to be a "sure expectation of eternal happiness." Its certainty arises from the infallible promise of God to give eternal life to His faithful servants. Now Charity, by taking away sin, at the same time takes away all obstacles to our obtaining the happiness of the Blessed; hence the greater our Charity the greater also and firmer is our Hope; Hope, on the other hand, can in no way interfere with the purity of love, because, according to the observation of St. Denis the Areopagite, love tends naturally to union with the object beloved; or, as St. Augustine asserts in stronger terms, love itself is like a chain of gold that links together the hearts of the lover and the loved. "Love is as it were a kind of bond uniting two together." And as this union can never be affected at a distance, the person that loves always longs for the presence of the object of his love. The Sacred Spouse languished in the absence of her Beloved and entreated her companions to acquaint Him with her sorrow, that He might come and console her with His presence: I adjure you, O daughters of Jerusalem, if you find my beloved, that you tell him that I languish with love (Canticles v. 8). A soul that loves Jesus Christ exceedingly cannot but desire and hope, if she remains on earth, to go without delay and be united to her beloved Lord in Heaven.

Thus, we see that the desire to go and see God in Heaven, not so much for the delight we shall experience in loving God, as for the pleasure we shall afford God by loving Him, is pure and perfect love. Neither is the joy of the Blessed in Heaven any hindrance to the purity of their love; such joy is inseparable from their love; but they take far more satisfaction in their love of God than in the joy that it affords them. Someone will, perhaps, say: But the desire of a reward is rather a love of concupiscence than a love of friendship.

We must therefore make a distinction between temporal rewards promised by men, and the eternal rewards of Paradise promised by God to those who love Him: the rewards given by man are distinct from and independent of their own persons, since they do not bestow themselves, but only their goods, when they would remunerate others; on the contrary, the principal reward which God gives to the Blessed is the gift of Himself: I am thy reward exceeding great (Genesis xv.1). Hence to desire Heaven is the same thing as to desire God, Who is our last end.

Monday--Seventh Week after Pentecost

Morning Meditation

DEATH--THE FINAL PREPARATIONS

At the approach of death the Crucifix will be presented to you, and you will be admonished that Jesus Christ must be your only refuge, your only consolation. To those who have had but little love for Jesus Crucified, this will bring fear rather than encouragement. O my God, assist me by Thy graces to change my life!

I.

If you were about to die, what would you not give for another year, or another month? Resolve, therefore, to do now what you will not be able to do when the hour of your death comes.

Who knows but that this year, or this very month, or even this very day may be your last?

You would not wish to die in the state in which you now are; and will you dare to continue to live in this state? You lament over those who die suddenly, because they have no time to prepare for death; and you have this precious time, and will you not prepare?

O my God, I will not force Thee to cast me away! I thank Thee for the mercies which Thou hast bestowed upon me; assist me by Thy grace to change my life. I see that Thou desirest to save me; and I desire to be saved that I may praise and love Thee for all eternity.

At the approach of death the Crucifix will be presented to you, and you will be admonished that Jesus Christ must be your only refuge and consolation. To those who have had but little love for Jesus Crucified, this will bring fear rather than encouragement. On the contrary, what a consolation will it be to those who have left all for the love of Jesus!

My beloved Jesus, Thou shalt be my only love in life and in death! My God and my All!

II.

For the dying whose consciences are in a bad state, how terrible will be the sole mention of Eternity! They will not hear anything else spoken of but their malady, physicians, remedies; and if the affairs of their soul be mentioned they soon grow weary, change the subject, and beg of you to let them be at rest!

The sinner will exclaim: "Oh, that I had time to amend my life!" But it will be said to him: Depart out of this world. "Call in additional medical aid," he will answer; "and try other remedies". But of what avail will these be? His hour is come; he must depart and go into Eternity.

To him who loves God how consoling will it be to hear it said: Depart! He will not be terrified but rejoice at the thought of being soon out of all danger of losing his sovereign and only Good.

Let thy place be this day in peace, and thy abode in holy Sion. What a joyful announcement to him who dies in a well-grounded certainty of being in the grace of God!

O Jesus, in Thy precious Blood I place my hope, that Thou wilt conduct me into that place of peace, where I shall be able to say: O God of my heart, I have now no longer any fear of losing Thee!

Have compassion, O Lord, on his sighs: have compassion on his tears. My God, I will not wait until the hour of death to bewail my offences against Thee; I now detest and abhor them, and am sorry for them with my whole heart, and would willingly die of sorrow for having committed them. I love Thee, O infinite Goodness! I desire to live and to die in sorrow and in love.

Remember, O Lord, he is thy creature; not made by strange gods, but by thee, the only living and true God. O my God, Thou Who hast created me for Thyself, cast me not away from Thy face. If I have despised Thee, I now love Thee more than myself, and I desire to love Thee alone.

He who has had but little love for Jesus Christ will tremble at the coming of the Holy Viaticum; but he, on the contrary, who has loved only Jesus, will be filled with confidence and love, when he beholds his Lord at hand to accompany him in his passage into Eternity.

While Extreme Unction is being administered, the devil will remind the dying man of all the sins committed by means of the senses. Let us therefore hasten to weep for them before the approach of death.

When he has received all the Sacraments, his relatives and friends will retire, and he will be left alone in the presence of the Crucifix.

O Jesus, when all have abandoned me, do not Thou depart from me! In thee, O Lord have I hoped, let me never be confounded (Psalm xxx. 2).

Spiritual Reading

PRAYER, CONDITIONS OF PRAYER

I-THAT THE PRAYER BE OFFERED FOR ONESELF OR FOR THINGS NECESSARY FOR SALVATION

Amen, amen, I say to you, if you ask the Father anything in my name, he will give it you (John xvi. 23). Jesus Christ, then, has promised that whatever we ask the Father in His Name, the Father will give us. But always with the understanding that we ask under the proper conditions. Many seek, says St. James, and obtain not, because they seek improperly: Ye ask and receive not, because ye ask amiss (James iv. 3). So St. Basil, following out the argument of the Apostle, says: "You sometimes ask and receive not, because you have asked badly; either without faith, or lightly, or you have requested things not fit for you, or you have not persevered." "Faithlessly" (infideliter), with little faith or confidence; "lightly" (leviter), that is, with little desire for the grace you ask; "things not fit for you", that is, things not conducive to your salvation; or, you have left off praying. Hence St. Thomas reduces to four in number the conditions required to make Prayer efficacious. These four Conditions are:

A.--That the Prayer be offered for oneself.

B.--For things necessary for salvation.

C.--Piously.

D.--With Perseverance.

A.-THAT THE PRAYER BE OFFERED FOR ONESELF.

The First Condition, then, of Prayer is that you make it for yourself. The Angelic Doctor holds that one man cannot ex condigno (i.e. by title of justice) obtain for another eternal life; and, consequently, not even those graces which are requisite for his salvation, for, as he says, the promise is made not to others, but only to those that pray: He will give to you.

There are, nevertheless, many Theologians, Cornelius a Lapide, Sylvester, Tolet, Habert, and others, who hold the opposite doctrine, on the authority of St. Basil, who teaches that Prayer, by virtue of God's promise, is infallibly efficacious, even for those for whom we pray, provided they put no positive impediment in the way. And they support their doctrine by Scripture: Pray for one another, that you may be saved; for the continual prayer of the just man availeth much (James v. 16). Pray for them that persecute and calumniate you (Luke vi. 28). And better still, on the text of St. John: He that knoweth his brother to sin a sin which is not to death, let him ask, and life shall be given to him who sinneth not unto death (1 John v. 16). St. Ambrose, St. Augustine, the Venerable Bede, and others explain the words who sinneth not unto death to mean the sinner who does not intend to remain obstinate till death, since for such a one a very extraordinary grace would be required. But for other sinners, who are not guilty of such malice, the Apostle promises their conversion to him who prays for them: Let him ask, and life shall be given him for him that sinneth.

Besides, it is quite certain that the prayers of others are of great use to sinners, and are very pleasing to God. The Lord complains of His servants who do not recommend sinners to Him, as He once complained to St. Mary Magdalen de Pazzi, to whom He said one day: See, my daughter, how many Christians are in the devil's hands; if My elect did not deliver them by their prayers they would be devoured. But God specially requires this of Priests and Religious. The same Saint used to say to her nuns: "My sisters, God has not separated us from the world that we should only do good for ourselves but also that we should appease Him in behalf of sinners" and God one day said to her: "I have given to you, My chosen spouses the City of Refuge (i.e. the Passion of Jesus Christ), that you may have a place where you may obtain help for My creatures. Therefore, have recourse to it, and thence stretch forth a helping hand to My creatures who are perishing, and even lay down your lives for them." For this reason, the Saint, inflamed with holy zeal, used to offer God the Blood of the Redeemer fifty times a day in behalf of sinners, and was quite consumed with the desire she had for their conversion. She used to say: What pain it is, O Lord, to see how one could help Thy creatures by giving one's life for them and not be able to do so! In every exercise she recommended sinners to God; and it is written in her Life that she scarcely passed an hour in the day without praying for them. Frequently too, she arose in the middle of the night and went before the Blessed Sacrament to pray for them; and yet for all this, when she was once found bathed in tears, on being asked the cause, she answered, "Because I seem to myself to do nothing for the salvation of sinners." She went so far as to offer to endure even the pains of hell for their conversion, provided that in that place she might still love God; and often God gratified her by inflicting on her grievous pains and infirmities for the salvation of sinners. She prayed especially for Priests, seeing that their good life was the occasion of salvation to others, while their bad life was the cause of ruin to many; and therefore, she prayed God to visit their faults upon her, saying: "Lord, make me die and return to life again as many times as is necessary to satisfy Thy justice for them!" And it is related in her Life that the Saint, by her prayers, did indeed release many souls from the hands of Lucifer.

I wished to speak rather particularly of the zeal of this Saint; but, indeed, no souls that really love God neglect to pray for poor sinners. For how is it possible for a person who loves God, and knows what love He has for our souls, and what Jesus Christ has done and suffered for their salvation, and how our Savior desires us to pray for sinners--how is it possible, I say, that he should be able to look with indifference on the numbers of poor souls who are living without God, and are slaves of hell, without being moved to importune God with frequent prayers to give light and strength to those wretched beings, so that they may rise from the miserable state of perdition in which they are slumbering? True it is that God has not promised to grant our requests when those for whom we pray put a positive impediment in the way of their conversion; but still, God of His goodness has often deigned, at the Prayer of His servants, to bring back the most blind and obstinate sinners to a state of salvation by means of extraordinary graces. Therefore, let us never omit, when we say or hear Mass, when we receive Holy Communion, when we make our Meditation or the Visit to the Blessed Sacrament, to recommend poor sinners to God. And a learned author says that he who prays for others will find that his prayers for himself are heard much sooner. But this is a digression. Let us now return to the examination of the other conditions that St. Thomas lays down as necessary for the efficacy of Prayer.

B.-THAT WE PRAY FOR THINGS NECESSARY FOR SALVATION.

The Second Condition assigned by the Saint is that we ask those favors which are necessary for salvation; because the promise annexed to Prayer was not made with reference to temporal favors, which are not necessary for the salvation of the soul. St. Augustine, explaining the words of the Gospel, whatever ye shall ask in my name, says that what is in any way detrimental to salvation is not asked in the Name of the Savior. Sometimes, says the same Father, we seek some temporal favors, and God does not hear us; but He does not hear us because He loves us and wishes to be merciful to us. The physician knows better than the patient what is good for the sick man. The physician who loves his patient will not allow him to have those things that he sees would do him harm. Oh, how many, if they had been sick or poor would have escaped those sins which they commit in health and affluence! And, therefore when men ask God for health or riches, He often denies them because He loves them, knowing that these things would be to them an occasion of losing His grace, or at any rate of growing tepid in the spiritual life. Not that we mean to say that it is any defect to pray to God for the necessaries of this present life, so far as they are not inconsistent with our eternal salvation, as the Wise Man said: Give me only the necessaries of life (Proverbs xxx. 8). Nor is it a defect, says St. Thomas, to have anxiety about such goods, if it is not inordinate. The defect consists in desiring and seeking these temporal goods, and in having an inordinate anxiety about them, as if they were our highest good. Therefore, when we ask of God these temporal favors, we ought always to ask them with resignation, and with the condition if they will be useful to our souls; and when we see that God does not grant them, let us be certain that He then denies them to us for the love He bears us, and because He sees that they would be injurious to the salvation of our souls.

It often happens that we pray God to deliver us from some dangerous temptation, and yet that God does not seem to hear us but permits the temptation to continue troubling us. In such a case let us understand that God permits even this for our greater good. It is not temptation nor bad thoughts that separate us from God, but our consent to the evil. When a soul in temptation recommends itself to God, and by His aid resists, oh, how it then advances in perfection, and unites itself more closely to God! And this is the reason why God does not hear it. St. Paul earnestly prayed to be delivered from the temptation of impurity: There was given me a sting of my flesh, an angel of Satan to buffet me; for which thing thrice I besought the Lord that it might depart from me. But God answered him that it was enough to have His grace: My grace is sufficient for thee (2 Corinthians xii. 7). So that even in temptation we ought to pray with resignation, saying: Lord, deliver me from this trouble, if it is expedient to deliver me; and if not at least give me help to resist. And here comes in what St. Bernard says, that when we beg any grace of God, He gives us either that which we ask or some other thing more useful to us. He often leaves us to be buffeted by the waves to try our faithfulness, and for our greater profit. He would seem to be deaf to our prayers. But no; let us be sure that God then really hears us, and secretly aids us, and strengthens us by His grace to resist all the assaults of our enemies. See how

He Himself: assures us of this by the mouth of the Psalmist: Thou calledst upon me in affliction, and I delivered thee: I heard thee in the secret place of tempest; I proved thee at the waters of contradiction (Psalm lxxx. 8).

The other considerations assigned by St. Thomas to Prayer are, that it is to be made piously and perseveringly; by piously he means with humility and confidence --by perseveringly, continuing to pray until death. We must now speak distinctly of each of these three conditions which are the most necessary for Prayer, namely, of Humility, Confidence, and Perseverance.

Evening Meditation

THE PRACTICE OF THE LOVE OF JESUS CHRIST

"Charity hopeth all things"

HE THAT LOVES JESUS CHRIST HOPES FOR ALL THINGS FROM HIM

I.

I wish here to propose a doubt which may rise in the mind of one who loves God and strives to conform himself in all things to His blessed will. If it should be ever revealed to such an one that he was to be eternally lost, would be obliged to bow to it with resignation in order to practice conformity with the will of God? St. Thomas says no; and further, that he would sin by consenting to it, because he would be consenting to live in a state that involves sin, and is contrary to the last end for which God created him; for God did not create souls to hate Him, but to love Him in Heaven: so that He does not wish the death even of the sinner, but that all should be converted and saved. The holy Doctor says that God wishes no one to be damned except through sin; and therefore, a person, by consenting to his damnation, would not be acting in conformity with the will of God, but with the will of sin. But suppose that God, foreseeing the sin of a person, should have decreed his damnation, and that this decree should be revealed to him, would he be bound to coincide in it? In the same passage the Saint says, by no means; because such a revelation must not be taken as an irrevocable decree, but made merely by way of communication, as a threat of what would follow if he persists in sin.

II.

But let everyone banish such baneful thoughts from his mind, as only calculated to cool his confidence and love. Let us love Jesus Christ as much as possible here below; let us always be sighing to go hence, and to behold Him in Paradise, that we may there love Him perfectly; let us make it the grand object of all our hopes to go thither to love Him with all our strength. We are commanded even in this life to love God with our whole strength:

Thou shalt love the Lord thy God with thy whole heart, with thy whole soul, and with all thy strength (Luke x. 27); but the angelical Doctor says that man cannot perfectly fulfil this precept upon earth; only Jesus Christ, Who was both God and Man, and the most holy Mary, who was full of grace and free from Original sin, perfectly fulfilled it. But we miserable children of Adam, infected as we are with sin, cannot love God without some imperfection; and it is in Heaven alone, when we shall meet God face to face, that we shall love Him, nay more, that we shall be necessitated to love Him with all our strength.

TUESDAY–SEVENTH WEEK AFTER PENTECOST

Morning Meditation

DEATH–THE LAST AGONY

A cold sweat spreads itself over the sick man; his eyes grow dim; his pulse intermittent; his extremities become cold and he is stretched out on his bed like a corpse. He is now rapidly passing into Eternity.

O moment of death, upon which will depend an Eternity of happiness, or an Eternity of woe!

I.

A cold sweat spreads itself over the sick man, his eyes become dim, his pulse intermittent, his extremities become cold, he stretches himself out like a corpse, and his agony begins. He is already rapidly passing into Eternity.

His breath fails, the breathing is scarcely noticeable, and death is at hand. The priest lights a blessed candle and places it in his hand and begins to repeat for him acts suitable for the soul's immediate departure. O light, enlighten now our souls, for then thou wilt be of but little service to us when the time has gone for repairing the evil we have done!

O God, how guilty will our offences, and how empty will the vanities of this world appear in the light of the last candle!

The dying man expires; and in the same moment in which he breathes his last, time for him is ended, and Eternity begins. O moment which will decide an Eternity of happiness or an Eternity of woe!

O Jesus, mercy! Pardon me and so unite me to Thee that I may not at my last moment be able to lose Thee forever.

The soul being departed, the priest says to the bystanders: He is dead! Yes, he is dead–Requiescat in pace! May he rest in peace! He rests in peace if he has died in peace with God; but if not, he will never enjoy peace so long as God shall be God.

As soon as he is dead the news spreads around. One says: He was an honest man, but not very devout. Another: I wonder is he saved? His relatives and friends, to save their feelings, will not hear him spoken of, and wish those who mention him to speak of something else!

Thus, he who was the center of conversation has become an object of horror for all. Go into his house, he is no longer there. His rooms, his bed, his furniture, are divided amongst others. And where is he? His body is in the grave, his soul in Eternity!

II.

If you wish to see the dead man, open that grave; he is no longer in the bloom of health, no longer feasting, but a heap of corruption, in which are engendered multitudes of worms. These will soon eat away the lips and the cheeks, so that in a little while nothing more will remain but a fetid skeleton, which, in time, will fall to pieces, the head from the trunk, and the bones from one another.

See, then, to what it will one day be reduced, this body of ours, on account of which we so often offend God!

O Saints of God, you remembered this, and kept your bodies in subjection by mortification! Now your bones are venerated upon altars, and your souls are enjoying the sight of God, waiting for the day of final reward when your bodies will become your companions in glory, as they were formerly your companions in suffering.

Were I now in Eternity, what should I not wish to have done for God?

St. Camillus of Lellis, looking on the graves of the dead, was accustomed to say: "Oh, if these were alive, what would they not now do for eternal life? And I who am alive, what am I doing?"

O Lord, do not cast me away with the reprobate on account of my ingratitude! Others have offended Thee in the midst of darkness and ignorance, but I have offended Thee in the midst of light. Thou didst fully enlighten me to know the wrong I did in committing sin; and yet I closed my eyes to Thy lights, trampled on Thy graces, and turned my back upon Thee. Be not thou a terror unto me: Thou art my hope in the day of affliction (Jeremiah xvii. 17).

Spiritual Reading

PRAYER, CONDITIONS OF PRAYER

II.-THAT WE PRAY PIOUSLY.

(a) WITH HUMILITY.

The Lord does not indeed regard the prayers of His servants, but only of His servants who are humble. He hath had regard to the prayer of the humble (Psalm ci. 18). Others he does not regard, but rejects them: God resisteth the proud, and giveth grace to the humble (James iv. 6). He does not hear the prayers of the proud who trust in their own strength; but for that reason, leaves them to their own feebleness; and in this state, deprived of God's aid, they must certainly perish. David had thus to lament: Before I was humbled, I offended (Psalm cxviii. 67). I sinned because I was not humble. The same thing happened to St. Peter, who, though he was warned by our Lord that all the disciples would abandon Him on that night–All you shall be scandalized in me this night (Matthew xxvi. 31)–nevertheless, instead of acknowledging his own weakness, and begging our Lord's aid against his unfaithfulness, was too confident in his own strength, and said that though all should abandon Him he would never leave Him: Although all shall be scandalized in thee, I, will never be scandalized (Matthew xxvi. 33). And although our Savior again foretold to him, in a special manner, that in that very night, before the cock-crow, he should deny Him three times; yet, trusting in his own courage, he boasted, saying, Yea, though I should die with thee, I will not deny thee (Matthew xxvi. 35). But what was the result? Scarcely had the unhappy man entered the house of the High Priest when he was accused of being a disciple of Jesus Christ, and three times did he deny with an oath that he had ever known Him: And again, he denied with an oath, I know not the man (Matthew xxvi. 72). If Peter had humbled himself and had asked our Lord for the grace of constancy, he would not have denied Him.

We ought all to feel that we are standing on the edge of a precipice, suspended over the abyss of all our sins, and supported only by the thread of God's grace. If this thread fails us, we shall certainly fall into the gulf, and shall commit the most horrible wickedness. Unless the Lord had been my helper, my soul had almost dwelt in hell (Psalm xciii. 17). If God had not succored me I should have fallen into a thousand sins and now I should be in hell. So said the Psalmist, and so ought each of us to say. This is what St. Francis of

Assisi meant when he said that he was the worst sinner in the world. But, my Father, said his companion, what you say is not true; there are many in the world who are certainly worse than you are. Yes, what I say is but too true, answered St. Francis, because if God did not keep His hand over me, I should commit every possible sin.

It is of Faith, that without the aid of grace we cannot do any good work, nor even think a good thought. "Without grace men can do no good whatever, either in thought or in deed," says St. Augustine. As the eye cannot see without light, so, says the holy Father, man can do no good without grace. The Apostle had said the same thing before him: Not that we are sufficient to think anything of ourselves, as of ourselves; but our sufficiency is from God (2 Corinthians iii. 5). And David had said it before St. Paul: Unless the Lord build the house, they labor in vain that build it (Ps. cxxvi. 1). In vain does man weary himself to become a saint, unless God lends a helping hand: Unless the Lord keep the city, he watcheth in vain that keepeth (Psalm cxxvi. 1). If God does not preserve the soul from sins, in vain will it try to preserve itself by its own strength: and therefore did the holy Prophet protest: I will not trust in my bow (Psalm xliii. 7). I will not trust in my arms, but only in God, Who alone can save me.

Hence, whoever finds that he has done any good, and does not find that he has fallen into greater sins than those which are commonly committed, let him say with St. Paul: By the grace of God I am what I am (1 Corinthians xv. 10); and for the same reason, he ought never to cease to be afraid of falling in every occasion of sin: Wherefore, he that thinketh himself to stand, let him take heed lest he fall (1 Corinthians x. 12). St. Paul wishes to warn us that he who feels himself secure of not falling is in great danger of falling; and he assigns the reason in another place, where he says: If any man think himself to be something, whereas he is nothing, he deceiveth himself (Galatians vi. 3). So that St. Augustine wrote wisely, the presumption of stability renders many unstable; no one will be so firm as he who feels himself infirm. If a man says he has no fear, it is a sign that he trusts in himself, and in his good resolutions; but such a man, with his pernicious self-confidence, deceives himself, because, through trust in his own strength he neglects to fear; and through not fearing he neglects to recommend himself to God, and thus he will certainly fall. And so, for like reasons, we should all abstain from noticing with any vain-glory the sins of our neighbors; but rather we should esteem ourselves as worse in ourselves than they are, and should say: Lord, if thou hadst not helped me, I should have done worse. Otherwise, to punish us for our pride, God will permit us to fall into worse and more shameful sins. For this cause St. Paul instructs us to labor for our salvation: With fear and trembling work out your salvation (Philippians ii. 12). Yes, for he who has a great fear of falling distrusts his own strength, and therefore places his confidence in the Lord, and has recourse to Him in dangers; and God will aid him, and so he will vanquish his temptations, and will be saved. St. Philip Neri, walking one day through Rome, kept saying: "I am in despair!" A certain Religious rebuked him, and the Saint thereupon said: "My father, I am in despair of myself; but I trust in God". So must we do, if we would be saved; we must always live in despair of doing anything by our own strength; and in so doing we shall imitate St. Philip, who used to say to God the first moment he awoke in the morning: "Lord, keep Thy hands over Philip this day; for if not, Philip will betray Thee."

This then, we may conclude with St. Augustine, is all the grand science of a Christian—to know that he is nothing and can do nothing. "This is all knowledge, to know that man is nothing." For then he will never neglect to furnish himself, by Prayer to God, with that strength which he has not of himself and which he needs in order to resist temptation, and to do good. Thus, with the help of God, Who never refuses anything to the man who prays to Him in humility, he will be able to do all things: The prayer of him that humbleth himself shall pierce the clouds, and he will not depart until the Most High behold (Ecclesiasticus xxxv. 21). The prayer of a humble soul penetrates the heavens and presents itself before the throne of God, and departs not without God's looking on it and hearing it. And though the soul be guilty of any number of sins, God never despises a heart that humbles itself: A contrite and humbled heart, O God, thou wilt not despise (Psalm 1. 19): God resisteth the proud, but giveth grace to the humble (James iv. 6). As the Lord is severe with the proud, and resists their prayers, so He is kind and liberal to the humble. This is precisely what Jesus Christ said one day to St. Catherine of Sienna: Know, my daughter, that a soul that perseveres in humble Prayer gains every virtue.

It will be of use to introduce here the advice which the learned and pious Palafox, Bishop of Osma, gives to spiritual persons who desire to become Saints. It occurs in a note to the 18th Letter of St. Teresa, which she wrote to her confessor, to give him an account of all the grades of supernatural prayer with which God had favored her. On this the Bishop writes that these supernatural graces which God deigned to grant to St. Teresa, as He had also done to other Saints, are not necessary to arrive at sanctity, since many souls have become Saints without them; and, on the other hand, many who had received them have, after all, been damned. Therefore he says it is superfluous, and even presumptuous, to desire and to ask for these supernatural gifts, when the true and only way to become a Saint is to exercise ourselves in virtue and in the love of God; and this is done by means of Prayer, and by corresponding to the inspirations and assistance of God, Who wishes nothing so much as to see us Saints. For this is the will of God, your sanctification (1 Thessalonians iv. 3).

Hence Bishop Palafox, speaking of the grades of supernatural Prayer mentioned in St. Teresa's Letter, namely, the Prayer of Quiet, the Sleep or Suspension of the Faculties, the Prayer of Union, Ecstasy or Rapture, Flight and Impulse of the Spirit, and the Wound of Love, says, very wisely, that as regards the Prayer of Quiet, what we ought to ask of God is that He would free us from attachment to earthly goods, and the desire of them, which give no peace, but bring disquiet and affliction to the soul: Vanity of vanities, as Solomon called them, and vexation of spirit (Ecclesiastes i. 2, 14). The heart of man will never find true peace if it does not empty itself of all that is not God, to leave itself all free for His love, that He alone may possess the whole of it. But this the soul cannot do of itself; it must obtain it of God by repeated prayers. As regards the Sleep and Suspension of the Faculties, we ought to ask God for grace to keep them asleep to all that is temporal, and only awake to consider God's goodness and to set our hearts upon His love and eternal happiness, As regards the Union of the Faculties, let us pray Him to give us grace not to think, nor to seek, nor to wish anything but what God wills; since all sanctity and the perfection of love consists in uniting our will to the will of God. As regards Ecstasy and Rapture, let us pray God to draw us away from the inordinate love of ourselves and of creatures, and to draw us entirely to Himself. As regards the Flight of the Spirit, let us pray Him to give us grace to live altogether detached from this world, and to be as the swallows, that do not settle on the ground even to feed, but take their food flying. So should we use our temporal goods, but only as is necessary for the support of life, but always flying, without settling on the ground to look for earthly pleasures. As regards Impulse of Spirit, let us pray Him to give us courage and strength to do violence to ourselves, whenever it is necessary for resisting the assaults of our enemies, for conquering our passions, and for accepting sufferings even in the midst of desolation and dryness of spirit. Finally, as regards the Wound of Love, as a wound by its pain perpetually renews the remembrance of what we suffer, so ought we to pray God to wound our hearts with His holy love in such a way that we shall always be reminded of His goodness and of the love which He has borne us; and thus we should live in continual love of Him, and should be always pleasing Him with our works and our affections. But none of these graces can be obtained without Prayer; while with Prayer, provided it be humble, confident, and persevering, everything is obtained.

Evening Meditation

THE PRACTICE OF THE LOVE OF JESUS CHRIST
"Charity hopeth all things"
HE THAT LOVES JESUS CHRIST HOPES FOR ALL THINGS FROM HIM

I.

Behold, then, the scope of all our desires and aspirations, of all our thoughts and ardent hopes; to go and enjoy God in Heaven, to love Him with all our strength, and to rejoice in the enjoyment of God. The Blessed certainly rejoice in their own felicity in that kingdom of delights; but the chief source of their happiness, and that which absorbs all the rest, is to know that their beloved Lord possesses an infinite happiness; for they love God incomparably more than themselves. Each one of the Blessed has such a love for Him that he would willingly forfeit all happiness, and undergo the cruelest torments, rather than that God should lose, if it were possible for Him to lose, even the least particle of His happiness. Hence the sight of God's infinite happiness, and the knowledge that it can never suffer diminution for all eternity, constitutes his Paradise. This is the meaning of what our Lord says to every soul on whom He bestows the possession of eternal glory: Enter into the joy of thy Lord (Matthew xxv. 21). It is not the joy that enters into the blessed soul, but the soul that enters into the joy of God, since the joy of God is the object of the joy of the Blessed. Thus, the good of God will be the good of the Blessed; the riches of God will be their riches, and the happiness of God will be their happiness.

II.

In the instant that a soul enters Heaven and sees by the light of glory the infinite beauty of God face to face, she is at once seized and all consumed with love. The happy soul is then as it were lost and immersed in that boundless ocean of the goodness of God. Then it is that she quite forgets herself, and, inebriated with Divine love, thinks only of loving her God: They shall be inebriated with the plenty of thy house (Psalm xxxv. 9). As one intoxicated no longer thinks of himself, so a soul in bliss can only think of loving and affording delight to her beloved Lord; she desires to possess Him entirely, and she does in fact possess Him, without fear of losing Him anymore; she desires to give herself wholly to Him at every moment, and every moment she offers herself to God without reserve, and God receives her in His loving embraces, and so holds her, and shall hold her in the same fond embraces for all eternity.

WEDNESDAY–SEVENTH WEEK AFTER PENTECOST

DEATH–THE DEATH OF THE JUST

Precious in the sight of the Lord is the death of his saints. That word–Proficiscere! Depart!–which brings such terror to worldlings alarms not the just. To them it is not painful to leave all earthly goods, for God has been their only Treasure; nor honors, for they always despised them; nor friends and relatives, for they loved them only in God.

I.

Precious in the sight of the Lord is the death of his saints (Psalm cxv. 15). St. Bernard says that the death of the just is called precious because it is the end of labor and the gate of life. To the Saints death is a reward because it is the end of sufferings, pains, struggles, and the fear of losing God.

That word Proficiscere! Depart!–which brings such terror to worldlings, alarms not the just. To them it is not painful to leave all worldly goods, for God has been their only Treasure: nor honors, for they always despised them: nor relatives, for they have loved them only in God. Hence, as they frequently repeated in life, so now with redoubled joy do they exclaim in death, My God and my All!

Nor do the pains of death afflict them; they rejoice in offering to God the last moments of life in testimony of their love for Him, uniting the sacrifice of their lives to the sacrifice Jesus Christ offered of His life on the Cross for the love of them.

Oh, what a consolation for the Saints is the thought that now the time is over when they could have offended God, and were in constant danger of losing Him! Oh, what joy to be able then to embrace the Crucifix, and to say: In peace, in the self same, I will sleep and I will rest! (Psalm iv. 9).

The devil will endeavor at that time to disquiet us by the sight of our sins; but if we have wept for them, and have loved Jesus Christ with our whole heart, Jesus will console us. God is more desirous for our salvation than the devil is for our perdition.

II.

Moreover, death is the gate of life. God is faithful and will indeed at that supreme moment console those who have loved Him. Even in the sorrows of death He will bestow upon them a foretaste of Heaven. In the acts of confidence, of love of God, in the desire soon to behold Him, they will begin to taste that peace which they will enjoy throughout Eternity. What joy, in particular, will the Holy Viaticum afford to those who can say, with St. Philip Neri: "Behold my Love! Behold my Love!"

We should therefore fear not death but sin, which alone makes death so terrible. A great servant of God, Father Colombiere, said: "It is morally impossible for one who in life has been faithful to God to die an unhappy death."

He who loves God desires death, which will unite him eternally to God. It is a sign of but little love for God not to desire soon to behold Him.

Let us, therefore, now accept death and the loss of worldly things. We may do this now meritoriously, but then, it must be done forcibly and with danger of being lost. Let us live as though every day were to be the last of our lives. Oh, how well does he live who lives with the remembrance of death ever present to his mind!

O my God, when will the day arrive in which I shall see Thee and love Thee face to face? I do not deserve it; but Thy Wounds, O my Redeemer, are my hope. I will say to Thee with St. Bernard: Thy wounds are my merits. And hence I will have confidence and will also say to Thee with St. Augustine: O that I may die, Lord, that I may behold Thee! O Mary, my Mother, in the Blood of Jesus Christ, and in thy holy intercession, do I hope to be saved, and to go to praise thee, thank thee, and love thee forever in Heaven!

Spiritual Reading

PRAYER, CONDITIONS OF PRAYER

III.-CONFIDENCE-ITS EXCELLENCE AND NECESSITY.

The principal instruction that St. James gives us, if we wish by Prayer to obtain grace from God, is that we pray with a confidence that feels sure of being heard, and without hesitating: Let him ask in faith, nothing wavering (James i. 6). St. Thomas teaches that as Prayer receives its power of meriting from Charity, so it receives from Faith and Confidence its power of being efficacious to obtain. St. Bernard teaches the same, saying that it is our confidence alone which obtains for us the Divine mercies. God is much pleased with our confidence in His mercy, because we then honor and exalt that infinite Goodness which it was His object in creating us to manifest to the world: Let all those, O my God, says the Royal Prophet, who hope in thee be glad, for they shall be eternally happy, and Thou shalt dwell in them (Psalm v. 12). God protects and saves all those who confide in Him: He is the protector of all that hope in him (Psalm xvii. 31). Thou who savest them that trust in thee (Psalm xvi. 7). Oh, the great promises that are recorded in the Scriptures to all those who hope in God! He who hopes in God will not fall into sin: None of them that trust in him shall offend (Psalm xxxiii. 23). Yes, says David, because God has His eyes turned to all those who confide in His Goodness to deliver them by His aid from the death of sin. Behold, the eyes of the Lord are on them that fear him, and on them that hope for his mercy to deliver their souls from death (Psalm xxxii. 18). And in another place God Himself says: Because he hoped in me, I will deliver him; I will deliver him and I will glorify him (Psalm xc. 14). Mark the word because. Because he confided in Me, I will protect him, I will deliver him from his enemies, and from the danger of falling; and finally, I will give him eternal glory. Isaias says of those who place their hope in God: They that hope in the Lord shall renew their strength; they shall take wings as the eagles; they shall run and not be weary; they shall walk and not faint (Isaiah xl. 31). They shall cease to be weak as they are now and shall gain from God a great strength; they shall not faint; they shall not even feel weary in walking the way of salvation, but they shall run and fly as eagles; in silence and in hope shall your strength be (Isaiah xxx. 15). All our strength, the Prophet tells us, consists in placing all our confidence in God, and in being silent; that is, in reposing in the arms of His Mercy, without trusting to our own efforts, or to human means.

And when did it ever happen that a man had confidence in God and was lost? No one hath hoped in the Lord and hath been confounded (Ecclesiasticus 11). It was this confidence that assured David that he would not perish: In thee, O Lord, have I trusted; I shall not be confounded forever (Ps. xxx. 2). Perhaps, then, says St. Augustine, God could be a deceiver, Who offers to support us in dangers if we lean upon Him, and then withdraws Himself if we have recourse to Him? "God is not a deceiver, that He should offer to support us, and then when we lean upon Him should slip away from us." David calls the man happy who trusts in God: Blessed is the man that trusteth in thee (Psalm lxxxiii. 13). And why? Because, says he, he who trusts in God will always find himself surrounded by God's Mercy. Mercy shall encompass him that hopeth in the Lord (Psalm xxxi. 10). So that he shall be surrounded and guarded by God on every side in such a way that he shall be prevented from losing his soul.

It is for this cause that the Apostle recommends us so earnestly to preserve our confidence in God; for (he tells us) it will certainly obtain from Him a great remuneration: Do not therefore lose your confidence, which hath a great reward (Hebrews x. 35). As is our confidence, so shall be the graces we receive from God: if our confidence is great, great too will be the graces: "Great faith merits great things." St Bernard writes that divine Mercy is an inexhaustible fountain, and that he who brings to it the largest vessel of confidence shall take from it the largest measure of gifts: "Neither, O Lord, dost Thou put the oil of mercy into any other vessel than that of confidence." The Prophet had long before expressed the same thought: Let thy mercy, O Lord be upon us, as we have hoped in thee (Psalm xxxii. 22). This was well exemplified in the Centurion to whom our Savior said, in praise of his confidence: Go and as thou hast believed, so be it done unto thee (Matthew viii. 13). And our Lord revealed to St. Gertrude that he who prays with confidence does Him in a manner such violence that He cannot but hear him in everything he asks. "Prayer," says St. John Climacus, "does a pious violence to God." It does Him a violence, but a violence which He likes, and which pleases Him.

Let us go, therefore, according to the admonition of St. Paul, with confidence to the throne of grace, that we may obtain mercy, and find grace in seasonable aid. (Hebrews iv. 16). The throne of grace is Jesus Christ, Who is now sitting on the right hand of the Father; not on the throne of justice, but of grace, to obtain pardon for us all if we fall into sin, and help to enable us to persevere if we are enjoying His friendship. To this throne we must always have recourse with confidence; that is to say, with that trust which springs from faith in the goodness and truth of God, Who has promised to hear him who prays to Him with confidence, but with a confidence that is both sure and stable. On the other hand, says St. James, let not the man who prays with hesitation think that he will receive anything: For he who wavereth is like a wave of the sea which is moved and carried about by the wind. Therefore, let not that man think he shall receive anything of the Lord (James i. 6). He will receive nothing, because the diffidence which agitates him is unjust towards God and will hinder His Mercy from listening to his prayers: "Thou hast not asked rightly, because thou hast asked doubtingly," says St. Basil; thou hast not received grace, because thou hast asked it without confidence. David says that our confidence in God ought to be as firm as a mountain, that is, not moved by every gust of wind: They who trust in the Lord, shall be as Mount Sion; he shall not be moved forever (Psalm cxxiv. 1). And it is this that Our Lord recommends to us, if we wish to obtain the graces which we ask: Whatsoever you ask when you pray, believe that you shall receive, and they shall come unto you (Mark xi. 24). Whatever grace you require, be sure that it will be given to you, and so you shall obtain it.

Evening Meditation

THE PRACTICE OF THE LOVE OF JESUS CHRIST

"Charity hopeth all things"

HE THAT LOVES JESUS CHRIST HOPES FOR ALL THINGS FROM HIM

I.

In this manner the soul is wholly united to God in Heaven and loves Him with all her strength; her love is most perfect and complete, and though necessarily finite, since a creature is not capable of infinite love, it nevertheless renders her perfectly happy and contented, so that she desires nothing more. On the other hand, Almighty God communicates Himself, and unites Himself wholly to the soul, filling her with Himself proportionately to her merits; and this union is not merely by means only of His gifts, lights, and loving attractions, as is the case during the present life, but by His own very Essence. As fire penetrates iron, and seems to change it into itself, so does God penetrate the soul and fill her with Himself; and though she never loses her own being, yet she becomes so penetrated and absorbed by that immense ocean of the Divine substance that she remains, as it were, annihilated, and as if she ceased to exist. The Apostle prayed for this happy lot for his disciples when he said: That you may be filled unto all the fullness of God (Ephesians iii. 19).

II.

And this is the end which the goodness of God has appointed for us in the life to come. Hence the soul can never enjoy perfect repose on earth; because it is only in Heaven that she can obtain perfect union with God. It is true that the lovers of Jesus Christ find peace in the practice of perfect conformity with the will of God; but they cannot in this life find complete repose. This is only obtained when our last end is obtained; that is, when we see God face to face, and are consumed with His Divine love; but until the soul has reached this end, she is ill at ease, and groans and sighs, saying: Behold, in peace is my bitterness most bitter (Psalm xxxviii. 17).

Thursday--Seventh Week after Pentecost

THE PARTICULAR JUDGMENT

Picture to yourself the state to which you will be reduced when death comes, and you are in your last agony, and scarcely another hour of life remains. You are about to appear before your Judge, Jesus Christ, to give an account of your whole life. Nothing in that hour will alarm you so much as a bad conscience. Put your accounts in order, therefore, before the coming of that great accounting day.

I.

Picture to yourself the state to which you will be reduced when death comes, and you are in your last agony, and scarcely another hour of life remains. You are about to appear before your Judge, Jesus Christ, to give an account of your whole life. Nothing in that hour will alarm you so much as a bad conscience. Put your accounts in order, therefore, before the coming of that great accounting day.

When you are on the point of entering into Eternity, remorse for past sins, diffidence, increased by the suggestions of the devil, and uncertainty as to your future lot --oh, how all this will cast the soul into a tempest of confusion and fear! Let us therefore now unite ourselves to Jesus Christ, and to Mary, that at that decisive moment they may not abandon us.

How terrified shall we be at the thought that in a few moments we shall be judged by Jesus Christ! St. Mary Magdalen de Pazzi, being ill, was asked by her director why she trembled, and she answered: "How terrible is the thought of having to appear before Christ as our Judge!"

O Jesus, remember that I am one of those whom Thou hast redeemed with Thy Blood. We beseech thee, therefore, help Thy servants, whom Thou hast redeemed with Thy precious blood!

It is the common opinion among divines that in the same place and at the very moment in which the soul departs it is judged by Jesus Christ. So that at one and the same moment the trial is gone through and the sentence passed and put into execution.

O fatal moment, in which the lot of each one is decided for a happy or a miserable Eternity!

The Venerable Father da Ponte, when he considered the Judgment, trembled to such a degree as to shake the room in which he was.

O Jesus, if Thou wert to judge me now, what would become of me? Eternal Father, look upon the face of thy Christ (Psalm lxxxiii. 10). I sincerely repent of all the sins I have committed against Thee; look on the Blood, the Wounds of Thy Son, and have pity on me.

II.

The soul goes forth and leaves the body, but sometimes it is still doubtful whether the person is alive or dead. The soul enters Eternity. The priest sprinkles the corpse with holy water and repeats the prayer of the Church: "Come to his assistance, all ye Saints of God meet him, ye Angels of the Lord." But if the soul be lost, the Saints and Angels can no longer assist it.

Jesus will come to judge us appearing with the same Wounds that He received for us in His Passion. These Wounds will be a source of great consolation to penitents, who with sorrow shall have bewailed their sins during life but will be a source of great terror to sinners who shall have died in their sins.

O God, what anguish for a man to behold Jesus for the first time, and as his indignant Judge! It will be more terrible than hell itself.

Man will then behold the majesty of the Judge; he will see how much He suffered for his love; he will see God's many mercies towards him, the many and great means He afforded him of working out his salvation; he will see the vanity of all worldly things, and the greatness of those which are eternal; he will see, in a word, all these truths, but--too late! Then there will be no more time to repair past errors. What is done is done.

My beloved Redeemer, grant that when I first behold Thee, I may find Thee appeased; and for this end give me now light and strength to reform my life. I desire to love Thee always. If hitherto I have despised Thy graces, I now esteem them above all the kingdoms of the world.

Spiritual Reading

PRAYER, CONDITIONS OF PRAYER
IV.-CONFIDENCE; THE FOUNDATION OF ONE'S CONFIDENCE.

But, someone will say, on what am I, a miserable sinner, to found this certain confidence of obtaining what I ask? On what? On the promise made by Jesus Christ: Ask, and you shall receive (Jo. xvi. 24). "Who will fear to be deceived, when the Truth promises?" says St. Augustine. How can we doubt that we shall be heard, when God, Who is Truth itself, promises to give us that which we ask of Him in Prayer? "We should not be exhorted to ask," says the same Father, "unless He meant to give." This is the very thing to which He exhorts us so strongly, and which is repeated so often in the Scriptures--pray, ask, seek, and you shall obtain what you desire: You shall ask whatever you will, and it shall be done unto you (John xv. 7). And in order that we may pray to Him with due confidence our Savior has taught us, in the "Our Father," that when we have recourse to Him for the graces necessary for salvation (all of which are included in the Petitions of the Lord's Prayer) we should call Him, not Lord, but Father--Our Father--because it is His will that we should ask God for grace with the same confidence with which a son, when in want, or sick, asks food or medicine from his own father. If a son is suffering hunger, he has only to make his case known to his father and his father will forthwith provide him with food; and if he has received a bite from a venomous serpent, he has only to show his father the wound, and the father will immediately apply whatever remedy he has.

Trusting, therefore, in God's promises, let us always pray with confidence; not vacillating, but stable and firm, as the Apostle says: Let us hold fast the confession of our hope without wavering: for he is faithful that hath promised (Hebrews x. 23). As it is perfectly certain that God is faithful to His promises, so ought our confidence also be perfectly certain that He will hear us when we pray. And although sometimes, when we are in a state of aridity, or disturbed by some fault we have committed, we perhaps do not feel while praying that sensible confidence which we would wish to experience, yet, for all this, let us force ourselves to pray, and to pray without ceasing, for God will not refuse us. Nay, rather He will hear us more readily, because we shall then pray with more distrust of ourselves and confiding only in the goodness and faithfulness of God, Who has promised to hear the man who prays to Him. Oh, how God is pleased in the time of our tribulations, of our fears, and of our temptations to see us hope against hope; that is, in spite of the feeling of diffidence which we then experience because of our desolation! This is what the Apostle praised in the Patriarch Abraham, who against hope believed in hope (Romans iv. 18).

St. John says that he who reposes a firm trust in God will certainly become a saint: And every one that hath this hope in him sanctifieth himself, as he also is holy (1 John iii. 3). For God gives abundant graces to them that trust in Him. By this confidence it was that so many Martyrs and Virgins, and even children, in spite of the dread of the torments which their persecutors prepared for them, overcame both their tortures and their persecutors.

Sometimes, I say, we pray, but it seems to us that God will not hear us. Ah! let us not then neglect to persevere in Prayer and to hope; let us then say with Job: Although he should kill me, I will trust in him (Job xiii. 15). O my God! though Thou shouldst drive me from Thy presence, I will not cease to pray, and to hope in Thy Mercy. Let us do so, and we shall obtain what we want from God. So did the Canaanite woman, and she obtained all that she wished from Jesus Christ. This woman had a daughter possessed of a devil and prayed our Savior to deliver her: Have mercy on me, my daughter is grievously tormented by a devil (Matthew xv. 22). Our Lord answered her that He was not sent for the Gentiles, of whom she was one, but for the Jews. She, however, did not lose heart, but renewed her prayer with confidence: Lord, Thou canst console me Thou must console me. Lord help me! (Matthew xv. 25). Jesus answered: It is not good to take the children's bread and to cast it to the dogs. (Matthew xv. 26). But she replied: Yea, Lord; for even the whelps eat of the crumbs that fall from the table of their masters (Matthew xv. 27). Then our Savior, seeing the great confidence of this woman, praised her, and did what she asked, saying: O woman, great is thy faith; be it done to thee as thou wilt (Matthew xv. 28). For who, says Ecclesiasticus has ever called on God for aid, and has been neglected and left unaided by Him? Or who hath called upon him and he hath despised him? (Ecclesiasticus ii. 12).

St. Augustine says that Prayer is a key which opens heaven to us; the same moment in which our Prayer ascends to God, the grace which we ask for descends to us: "The Prayer of the Just is the key of heaven; the petition ascends, and the mercy of God descends." The royal Prophet says that our supplications and God's Mercy are united together: Blessed be God, who has not turned away my prayer, nor his mercy from me (Psalm lxv. 20. And hence the same St. Augustine says that when we are praying to God we ought to be certain that God is listening to us "When you see that your prayer is not removed from you, be sure that His Mercy is not removed from you." And for myself, I speak the truth, I never feel greater consolation nor a greater confidence of my salvation than when I am praying to God and recommending myself to Him. And I think that the same thing happens to all other believers. All the other signs of our salvation are uncertain and unstable, but that God hears the man who prays to Him with confidence is an infallible truth, as it is infallible that God cannot fail in His promises.

When we find ourselves weak and unable to overcome any passion, or any great difficulty in fulfilling that which God requires of us, let us take courage and say, with the Apostle: I can do all things in him that strengtheneth me (Philippians iv. 13). Let us not say, as some do; I cannot; I distrust myself. With our own strength certainly we can do nothing; but with God's help we can do everything. If God said to some one: Take this mountain on your shoulders and carry it, for I am helping you, would not the man be a fool or impious if he answered: I will not take it, for I have not strength to carry it? And thus, when we know how miserable and weak we are and when we find ourselves most encompassed with temptations, let us not lose heart, but let us lift up our eyes to God, and say, with David: The Lord is my helper; and I will despise my enemies. (Psalm cxvii. 7). With the help of my Lord, I shall overcome and laugh to scorn all the assaults of my foes. And when we find ourselves in danger of offending God, or in any other critical position, and are too confused to know what is best to be done, let us recommend ourselves to God, saying: The Lord is my light and my salvation; whom shall I fear? (Psalm xxvi. 1). And let us be sure that God will then certainly give us light and will save us from every evil.

Evening Meditation

THE PRACTICE OF THE LOVE OF JESUS CHRIST

"Charity hopeth all things"

HE THAT LOVES JESUS CHRIST HOPES FOR ALL THINGS FROM HIM

I.

Yes, O my God, I live in peace in this valley of tears, because such is Thy will; but I cannot help feeling unspeakable bitterness at finding myself at a distance from Thee, and not yet perfectly united with Thee, Who art my center, my All, and the fulness of my repose! For this reason, the Saints, though they were all inflamed with the love of God, did nothing but sigh after Paradise. David cried out: Woe is me, that my sojourning is prolonged! (Psalm cxiv. 5). I shall be satisfied when thy glory shall appear (Psalm xvi. 15).

St. Paul said of himself: Having a desire to be with Christ (Philippians i. 23). St. Francis of Assisi said:

"I look for such a need of bliss That all my pain seems happiness."

These were all so many acts of perfect Charity. The angelic Doctor teaches us that the highest degree of Charity which a soul can reach upon this earth is to desire intensely to go and be united with God, and to enjoy Him in Heaven. But, as we have already seen, this enjoyment of God in Heaven does not consist so much in the fruition of the delights there lavished on her by Almighty God, as in the pleasure she takes in the happiness of God Himself Whom she loves incomparably more than herself.

O God, my Creator and my Redeemer, Thou hast created me for Heaven; Thou hast redeemed me from hell to bring me into Heaven; and I have so many times, in Thy very face, renounced my claim to Heaven by my sins, and have remained contented in seeing myself doomed to hell! But blessed forever be Thy infinite mercy, which, I hope, has pardoned me, and many a time rescued me from perdition. Ah, my Jesus, would that I had never offended Thee! Would that I had always loved Thee! I rejoice that at least I still have time to do so. I love Thee! O Love of my soul, I love Thee with my whole heart; I love Thee more than myself! I see plainly that Thou wishest to save me, that I may be able to love Thee for all eternity in that kingdom of love. I thank Thee and beseech Thee to help me for the remainder of my life, in which I wish to love Thee most ardently, that I may ardently love Thee in eternity.

II.

The Holy Souls in Purgatory feel no pain more acutely than that of their yearning to possess God, from Whom they remain still at a distance. And this sort of pain will afflict those especially who in their lifetime had but little desire of Paradise. Blessed Cardinal Bellarmine also says that there is a certain place in Purgatory called career honoratus, or prison of honor, where certain souls are not tormented with any pains of sense, but merely with the pain of privation of the sight of God. Examples of this are related by St. Gregory, Venerable Bede, St. Vincent Ferrar, and St. Bridget; and this punishment is not for the commission of sin, but for coldness in desiring Heaven. Many souls aspire to perfection, but for the rest, they are very indifferent whether they go to enjoy the sight of God or continue on earth. But eternal life is an inestimable good that has been purchased by the death of Jesus Christ; and God punishes such souls as have been remiss during life in their desires to obtain it.

Ah, my Jesus, when will the day arrive that shall free me from all danger of losing Thee, and consume me with love, by unveiling before my eyes Thy infinite beauty, so that I shall be under the necessity of loving Thee? Oh, sweet necessity! Oh, happy and dear and most desired necessity, which shall relieve me from all fear of evermore displeasing Thee and shall oblige me to love Thee with all my strength! My conscience alarms me, and says: "How canst thou presume to enter Heaven?" But, my dearest Redeemer, Thy merits are all my hope. O Mary, Queen of Heaven, thy intercession is all-powerful with God; in thee I put my trust!

FRIDAY--SEVENTH WEEK AFTER PENTECOST

FIRST FRIDAY OF JULY

Morning Meditation

THE AMIABLE HEART OF JESUS

The Heart of Jesus is all pure, all holy, all full of love towards God and towards us. Every perfection, every virtue reigns in this Heart. This is the Heart in which God Himself finds all His delight. O amiable Heart of Jesus, Thou dost well deserve the love of all hearts.

I.

He who shows himself amiable in everything must necessarily make himself loved. Oh, if we only applied ourselves to discover all the good qualities by which Jesus Christ renders Himself worthy of our love, we should all be under the happy necessity of loving Him. And what heart among all hearts can be found more worthy of love than the Heart of Jesus Christ? A Heart all pure, all holy, all full of love towards God and towards us; because all Its desires are for the Divine glory and our good. This is the Heart in which God finds all His delight. Every perfection, every virtue reigns in this Heart;--a most ardent love for God, His Father, united to the greatest humility and respect that can possibly exist; a sovereign confusion for our sins, which He has taken upon Himself, united to the extreme confidence of a most affectionate Son; a sovereign abhorrence of our sins, united to a lively compassion for our miseries; an extreme sorrow, united to a perfect conformity to the Will of God; so that in Jesus is found everything that is most amiable.

O my amiable Redeemer, what object more worthy of love could the Eternal Father command me to love than Thee? Thou art the Beauty of Paradise, Thou art the Love of Thy Father, Thy Heart is the throne of all virtues. O amiable Heart of my Jesus, Thou dost well deserve the love of all hearts; poor and wretched is that heart which loves Thee not! Thus miserable, O my God, has my heart been during all the time in which it has not loved Thee. But I will not continue to be thus wretched; I love Thee, I will always continue to love Thee, O my Jesus. O my Lord, I have hitherto forgotten Thee, and now what can I expect? That my ingratitude will oblige Thee to forget me entirely and forsake me forever? No, my Savior, do not permit it. Thou art the object of the love of God; and shalt Thou not, then, be loved by a miserable sinner such as I am, who have been so favored and loved by Thee? O lovely flames that burn in the amiable Heart of my Jesus, enkindle in my poor heart that holy fire which Jesus came down from Heaven to kindle on earth. Consume and destroy all the impure affections that dwell in my heart and prevent it from being entirely His.

II.

Some are attracted to love others by their beauty, others by their innocence, others by living with them, others by devotion. But if there were a person in whom all these and other virtues were united, who could help loving him? If we heard that there was in a distant foreign country a prince who was handsome, humble, courteous, devout, full of charity, affable to all, who rendered good to those who did him evil; then, although we knew not who he was, and though he knew not us, and though we were not acquainted with him, nor was there any possibility of our ever being so, yet we should be enamored of him, and should be constrained to love him. How is it, then, possible that Jesus Christ, Who possesses in Himself all these virtues, and in the most perfect degree, and Who loves us so tenderly, how is it possible that He should be so little loved by men, and should not be the only object of our love? O my God, how is it that Jesus, Who alone is worthy of love, and Who has given us so many proofs of the love that He bears us, should be alone, as it were, the unlucky One with us, Who cannot succeed in making us love Him; as if He were not sufficiently worthy of our love! This is what caused floods of tears to St. Rose of Lima, St. Catherine of Genoa, St. Teresa, St. Mary Magdalen de Pazzi, who, on considering the ingratitude of men, exclaimed, weeping: "Love is not loved! Love is not loved!"

O my God, grant that I may exist only to love Thee, and Thee alone, my dearest Savior! If at one time I despised Thee, Thou art now the only object of my love. I love Thee, I love

Thee, I love Thee, and I will never love any but Thee! My beloved Lord, do not disdain to accept the love of a heart which has once afflicted Thee by its sins. Let it be Thy glory to exhibit to the Angels a heart now burning with the love of Thee, which hitherto shunned and despised Thee. Most holy Virgin Mary, my hope, do thou assist me, and beseech Jesus to make me, by His grace, all that He wishes me to be.

Spiritual Reading

PRAYER, CONDITIONS OF PRAYER

V.--THE PRAYER OF SINNERS

But I am a sinner, you will say, and in the Scriptures I read: God doth not hear sinners (John ix. 31). St. Thomas answers, with St. Augustine: "That is the word of a blind man not yet perfectly enlightened, and therefore it is not authoritative." Besides, St. Thomas adds, it is true of the petition which the sinner makes, "so far as he is a sinner," that is, when he asks from a desire of continuing to sin; as, for instance, if he were to ask assistance to enable him to take revenge on his enemy, or to execute any other bad intention. The same holds good for the sinner who prays God to save him, but has no desire to quit the state of sin. There are some unhappy people who love the chains with which the devil keeps them bound like slaves. The prayers of such men are not heard by God, because they are rash and abominable. For what greater temerity can there be than for a man to ask favors of a prince whom he not only has often offended, but whom he intends to offend still more? And this is the meaning of the Holy Spirit, when He says that the Prayer of him who turns away his ears so as not to hear what God commands is detestable and odious to God: He who turneth away his ears from learning the law, his prayer shall be an abomination (Proverbs xxviii. 9). To these people God says: You need not pray to Me, for I will turn My eyes from you, and will not hear you: When you stretch forth your hands, I will turn away my eyes from you; and when you multiply prayer, I will not hear (Is. i. 15). Such, precisely, was the prayer of the impious King Antiochus, who prayed to God, and made great promises, but insincerely, and with a heart obstinate in sin; the sole object of his Prayer being to escape the punishment that impended over him; therefore God did not hear his Prayer, but caused him to die devoured by worms: Then this wicked man prayed to the Lord, of whom he was not like to obtain mercy (2 Maccabees ix. 13).

But there are others who sin through frailty, or by the violence of some great passion, and who groan under the yoke of the enemy, and desire to break the chains of death and to escape from their miserable slavery, and for this they ask the assistance of God--the Prayer of these, if it is persevering, will certainly be heard by God Who says: For every one that asketh receiveth, and he that seeketh findeth (Matthew vii. 8). "Everyone, whether he be a just man or a sinner," says the Author of the Opus Imperfectum. And in St. Luke, our Lord, when speaking of the man who gave all the loaves he had to his friend, not so much on account of his friendship as because of the other's importunity, says: If he shall continue knocking, I say to you, although he will not rise and give him because he is his friend, yet because of his importunity he will rise and give him as many as he needeth. And so I say unto you, Ask, and it shall be given you (Luke xi. 8, 9). So that persevering Prayer obtains Mercy from God, even for those who are not His friends. "That which is not obtained through friendship," says St. Chrysostom, "is obtained by Prayer." He even says that Prayer is valued more by God than friendship: "Friendship is not of such avail with God as Prayer; that which is not effected by friendship is effected by Prayer." And St. Basil doubts not that even sinners obtain what they ask, if they persevere in praying: "Sinners obtain what they seek, if they seek perseveringly." St. Gregory says the same: "The sinner shall also cry, and his Prayer shall reach to God." So, likewise, St. Jerome, who says that even the sinner can call God his Father, if he prays to Him to receive him back as a son, after the example of the Prodigal Son, who called Him Father: Father, I have sinned (Luke xv. 21), even though he had not as yet been pardoned. And St. Augustine: "If God does not hear sinners, in vain would that Publican have said, God be merciful to me, a sinner" (Luke xviii. 13). But the Gospel assures us that the Publican did by his Prayer obtain forgiveness: This man went down into his house justified (Luke xviii. 14).

But St. Thomas, who examines this point more minutely than others, does not hesitate to affirm that even a sinner is heard if he prays; for though his Prayer is not meritorious, yet it has the power of impetration --that is, of obtaining what is asked; because impetration is not founded on God's justice, but on His goodness. "Merit," he says, "depends on justice; impetration, on grace." Thus did Daniel pray: Incline, O my God, thine ear and hear ... For it is not for our justifications do we present our prayers before thy face, but for the multitude of thy mercies (Daniel ix. 18). Therefore, when we pray, says St. Thomas, it is not necessary to be the friends of God to obtain the grace we ask for: "Prayer itself makes us of the family of God." Moreover, St. Bernard uses a beautiful explanation of this, saying that the Prayer of a sinner to escape from sin arises from the desire to return to the grace of God. Now this desire is a gift which is certainly given by no other than God Himself. "To what end, therefore," says St. Bernard, "would God give to a sinner this holy desire, unless He meant to hear him?" And indeed, in the Holy Scriptures themselves there are multitudes of instances of sinners who have been delivered from sin by Prayer. Thus was

King Achab delivered; thus King Manasses; thus King Nabuchodonosor; and thus the good Thief. O wonderful thing, the mighty power of Prayer! Two sinners are dying on Calvary by the side of Jesus Christ: one, because he prays, Remember me, is saved! The other because he does not pray is damned!

And, in fine, St. Chrysostom says, "No man has with sorrow asked favors from Him without obtaining what he wished." But why should we cite more authorities, and give more reasons to demonstrate this point, when Our Lord Himself says: Come to me, all you that labor and are burdened, and I will refresh you (Matt. xi. 28). The burdened, according to Saints Augustine, Jerome, and others, are sinners in general, who groan under the load of their sins, and who, if they have recourse to God, will surely, according to His promise, be refreshed and saved by His grace. Ah, we cannot desire to be pardoned so much as He longs to pardon us. "Thou dost not," says St. Chrysostom, "so much desire thy sins to be forgiven as He desires to forgive thy sins." And he goes on to say: "There is nothing which Prayer cannot obtain, though a man were guilty of a thousand sins, provided it be fervent and unremitting." And let us mark well the words of St. James: If any of you wanteth wisdom, let him ask of God, who giveth to all abundantly, and upbraideth not (James i. 5). All those, therefore, who pray to God, are infallibly heard by Him, and receive grace in abundance: He giveth to all abundantly. But you should particularly remark the words which follow, and upbraideth not. This means that God does not do as men, who, when a person that has formerly done them an injury comes to ask a favor, immediately upbraid him with his offence. God does not do so to the man who prays, even though he were the greatest sinner in the world, when he asks for some grace conducive to his eternal salvation. Then He does not upbraid him with the offences he has committed; but, as though he had never displeased Him, He instantly receives him, He consoles him, He hears him, and enriches him with an abundance of His gifts. To crown all, our Savior, in order to encourage us to pray says: Amen, amen, I say to you, if you ask the Father anything in my name, he will give it you (John xvi. 23). As though He had said: Courage, O sinners, do not despair; do not let your sins turn you away from having recourse to My Father, and from hoping to be saved by Him if you desire it. You have not now any merits to obtain the graces which you ask for, for you only deserve to be punished; still do this: go to My Father in My Name, through My merits ask all the favors you want, and I promise and swear to you--Amen, amen, I say to you (which according to St. Augustine is a species of oath) that whatever you ask, My Father will grant. O God, what greater comfort can a sinner have after his fall than to know for certain that whatever he asks from God in the Name of Jesus Christ will be given to him!

I say all, but I mean only that which has reference to his eternal salvation, for with respect to temporal goods, we have already shown that God, even when asked, sometimes does not give them, because He sees that they would injure the soul. But so far as relates to spiritual goods, His promise to hear us is not conditional, but absolute; and therefore St. Augustine tells us that those things which God promises absolutely we should demand with absolute certainty of receiving. And how, says the Saint, can God ever deny us anything, when we ask Him for it with confidence? How much more does He not desire to dispense to us graces than we to receive them! "He is more willing to be munificent in His benefits to thee than thou art desirous to receive them."

St. Chrysostom says that the only time when God is angry with us is when we neglect to ask Him for His gifts: "He is only angry when we do not pray." And how can it ever happen that God will not hear a soul who asks Him for what is according to His own Heart? When the soul says to Him: Lord, I ask Thee not for goods of this world,--riches, pleasures, honors; I ask Thee only for Thy grace: deliver me from sin, grant me a good death, give me Paradise, give me Thy holy love (which is the grace which St. Francis de Sales says we should seek more than all others), give me resignation to Thy will; how is it possible that God should not hear? What petitions wilt Thou, O my God, ever hear, says St. Augustine, if Thou dost not hear those which are made after Thy own Heart? But, above all, our confidence ought to revive when we pray to God for spiritual graces, as Jesus Christ says: If you, being evil, know how to give good gifts to your children, how much more will your Father from heaven give the good Spirit to them that ask him! (Luke xi. 13). If you, who are so attached to your own interests, so full of self-love, cannot refuse your children that which they ask, how much more will your heavenly Father, Who loves you better than any earthly father, grant you His spiritual goods when you pray for them!

Evening Meditation

THE PRACTICE OF THE LOVE OF JESUS CHRIST

"Charity endureth all things"

HE THAT LOVES JESUS CHRIST WITH A STRONG LOVE DOES NOT CEASE TO LOVE HIM IN THE MIDST OF TEMPTATIONS AND DESOLATIONS

It is not the pains of poverty, of sickness, of dishonor and persecution which in this life most afflict souls that love God, but temptation and desolation of spirit. Whilst a soul is in the enjoyment of the loving presence of God, she is so far from grieving at all the afflictions and outrages of men that she is rather comforted by them, as they afford her an opportunity of showing God a token of her love; they serve, in short, as fuel to enkindle her love more and more. But to find herself solicited by temptations to forfeit the Divine grace, or in the hour of desolation to dread having already lost it --oh, these are torments too cruel to bear for one who loves Jesus Christ with all her heart! However, the same love supplies her with strength to endure all patiently, and to pursue the way of perfection, on which she has entered. And oh, what progress do those souls make by means of these trials which God is pleased to send them to prove their love!

Temptations are the most grievous trials that can happen to a soul that loves Jesus Christ; she accepts with resignation of every other evil, as calculated only to bind her in closer union with God; but temptations to commit sin would drive her, as we said above, to a separation from Jesus Christ, and on this account they are more intolerable to her than all other afflictions. We must know, however, that although no temptation to evil can ever come from God, but only from the devil or our own corrupt inclinations: For God is not a tempter of evils, and he tempteth no man (James i. 13); nevertheless, God does at times permit His most cherished souls to be the most grievously tempted. And in the first place, in order that from temptation the soul may better learn her own weakness, and the need she has of the Divine assistance not to fall. Whilst a soul is favored with heavenly consolations, she feels as if she were able to vanquish every assault of the enemy, and to achieve every undertaking for the glory of God. But when she is strongly tempted and is almost reeling on the edge of the precipice, and just ready to fall, then she becomes better acquainted with her own misery and with her inability to resist, if God does not come to her rescue. So it fared with St. Paul, who tells us that God had suffered him to be troubled with a temptation to sensual pleasure in order to keep him humble after the revelations with which God has favored him: And lest the greatness of the revelations should exalt me, there was given me a sting of my flesh, an angel of Satan, to buffet me (2 Corinthians xii. 7).

Saturday--Seventh Week after Pentecost

MARY IS THE HOPE OF SINNERS

One of the titles which is the most encouraging for poor sinners and under which the Church teaches us to invoke Mary, in the Litany of Loretto, is that of "Refuge of sinners." Therefore a devout author exhorts all sinners to take refuge under the mantle of Mary: "Fly, O Adam and Eve, and all you, their children, who have outraged God, fly and take refuge in the bosom of this good Mother, for know you not that she is your only city of refuge?"

I.

In the first Chapter of the Book of Genesis we read that God made two great lights; a greater light to rule the day; a lesser light to rule the night (Genesis i. 16). Cardinal Hugo says that "Christ is the greater light to rule the just, and Mary the lesser to rule sinners"; meaning that the sun is a figure of Jesus Christ, Whose light is enjoyed by the just who live in the clear day of Divine grace; and that the moon is a figure of Mary, by whose means those who are in the night of sin are enlightened. Since Mary is this auspicious luminary, and is so for the benefit of poor sinners, should anyone have been so unfortunate as to fall into the night of sin, what is he to do? Innocent III replies, "Whoever is in the night of sin, let him cast his eyes on the moon, let him implore Mary." Since he has lost the light of the sun of justice by losing the grace of God, let him turn to the moon, and beseech

Mary; and she will certainly give him light to see the misery of his state, and strength to leave it without delay. St. Methodius says that "by the prayers of Mary well nigh countless sinners are converted."

II.

One of the titles which is the most encouraging to poor sinners, and under which the Church teaches us to invoke Mary, in the Litany of Loretto, is that of "Refuge of Sinners." In Judea in ancient times there were cities of refuge in which criminals who fled there for protection were exempt from the punishments which they had deserved. Nowadays those cities are not so numerous; there is but one, and that is Mary, of whom the Psalmist says: Glorious things are said of thee, O city of God (Psalm lxxxvi. 3). But this city differs from the ancient ones in this respect--that in these ancient cities all kinds of criminals did not find refuge, nor was the protection extended to every class of crime; but under the mantle of Mary all sinners, without exception, find mercy for every sin that they may have committed, provided only that they go there to seek this protection. "I am the city of refuge," says St. John Damascene, in the name of our Queen, "to all who fly to me." And it is sufficient to have recourse to her, for whoever has the good fortune to enter this city need not speak to be saved. Assemble yourselves, and let us enter into the fenced city, and let us be silent there (Jeremiah viii. 14), to speak in the words of the Prophet Jeremias. This city, says Blessed Albert the Great, is the most holy Virgin fenced in with grace and glory. And let us be silent there, that is, continues an interpreter, "because we dare not invoke the Lord, whom we have offended, she will invoke and ask." For if we do not presume to ask our Lord to forgive us, it will suffice to enter this city and be silent, for Mary will speak and ask all we may require. And for this reason a devout author exhorts all sinners to take refuge under the mantle of Mary, exclaiming: "Fly, O Adam and Eve, and all you, their children, who have outraged God; fly, and take refuge in the bosom of this Good Mother; know you not that she is our only city of refuge?"--the only hope of sinners.

Spiritual Reading

PRAYER, CONDITIONS OF PRAYER

VI.-PERSEVERANCE.

Our Prayers, then, must be humble and confident; but this is not enough to obtain final perseverance, and thereby eternal life. Individual prayers will obtain the individual graces which they ask of God; but unless they are persevering, they will not obtain final perseverance, which, as it is the accumulation of many graces, requires many Prayers that are not to cease till death. The grace of salvation is not a single grace, but a chain of graces, all of which are at last linked with the grace of final perseverance. Now, to this chain of graces there ought to correspond another chain (as it were) of our prayers; if we, by neglecting to pray, break the chain of our prayers, the chain of graces will be broken too; and as it is by this that we have to obtain salvation, we shall not be saved.

It is true that we cannot merit final Perseverance as the Council of Trent teaches: "It cannot be had from any other source but from Him Who is able to confirm the man who is standing, that he may stand with perseverance." Nevertheless, says St. Augustine, this great gift of Perseverance can in a manner be merited by our prayers; that is, can be obtained by praying: "This gift, therefore, can be suppliantly merited (suppliciter emereri potest), that is, can be obtained by supplication." And Father Suarez adds that the man who prays infallibly obtains it. But to obtain it, and to save ourselves, says St. Thomas, a persevering and continual Prayer is necessary: "After Baptism continual Prayer is necessary to a man in order that he may enter Heaven." And before this our Savior Himself had told us over and over again: We ought always to pray, and not to faint (Luke xviii. 1). Watch ye, therefore, praying at all times, that you may be accounted worthy to escape all these things that are to come, and to stand before the Son of Man (Luke xxi. 36). The same had been previously said in the Old Testament: Let nothing hinder thee from praying always (Ecclesiasticus xviii. 22). Bless God at all times, and desire him to direct thy ways (Tobit iv. 20). Hence the Apostle inculcated on his disciples never to neglect Prayer: Pray without ceasing (1 Thessalonians v. 17). Be instant in prayer, watching in it with thanksgiving (Colossians iv. 2). I will, therefore, that men pray in every place (1 Timothy 8). God does indeed wish to give us Perseverance, says St. Nilus, but He will only give it to him who prays for it perseveringly: "He willeth to confer benefits on him who perseveres in prayer." Many sinners by the help of God's grace come to be converted, and to receive pardon. But then because they neglect to ask for perseverance, they fall again, and lose all.

Nor is it enough, says Bellarmine, to ask the grace of Perseverance once, or a few times; we ought always to ask it, every day till our death, if we wish to obtain it: "It must be asked day by day, that it may be obtained day by day." He who asks it one day, obtains it for that one day; but if he does not ask it the next day, the next day he will fall.

And this is the lesson which our Lord wished to teach us in the Parable of the man who would not give the loaves to his friend who asked him for them, until he had become importunate in his demand: Although he will not rise and give him because he is his friend, yet because of his importunity, he will rise and give him as many as he needeth (Luke xi. 8). Now if this man, solely to deliver himself from the troublesome importunity of his friend, gave him even against his own will the loaves for which he asked, "how much more," says St. Augustine, "will the good God give, Who both commands us to ask, and is angry if we ask not!" God, then, does indeed wish to give us eternal life, and therein all graces; but He wishes also that we should never omit to ask Him for them, even to the extent of being troublesome. Cornelius a Lapide says on the text just quoted, "God wishes us to be persevering in Prayer to the extent of importunity." Men of the world cannot bear the importunate; but God not only bears with them, but wishes us to be importunate in praying to Him for graces, and especially for Perseverance. St. Gregory says that " God wills to be called upon, He wills to be forced, He wills to be conquered by importunity ... Happy violence, by which God is not offended, but appeased!"

So that to obtain Perseverance we must always recommend ourselves to God morning and night, at Meditation, at Mass, at Communion, at all times; especially in time of temptation, when we must keep repeating: Lord, help me! Lord, assist me! Keep Thy hand upon me; leave me not; have pity upon me! Is there anything easier than to say: Lord, help me, assist me! The Psalmist says: With me is prayer to the God of my life (Psalm 9). On which the Gloss is as follows: "A man may say, I cannot fast, I cannot give alms; but if he is told to pray, he dare not say I cannot." For there is nothing easier than to pray. But we must never cease praying; we must (so to speak) continually do violence to God, that He may assist us always--a violence which is delightful and dear to Him. This violence is agreeable to God," says Tertullian; and St. Jerome says that the more persevering and importunate our Prayers are, so much the more are they acceptable to God: "Prayer, even though it is importunate, is more acceptable."

Blesseth is the man that heareth me, and that watcheth daily at my gates (Proverbs viii. 34). Happy is that man, says God, who listens to Me, and watches continually with holy prayers at the gates of My Mercy. And Isaias says: Blessed are all they that wait for him (Isaiah xxx. 18). Blessed are they who till the end wait (in Prayer) for their salvation from God. Therefore, in the Gospel Jesus Christ exhorts us to pray; but how? Ask, and ye shall receive; seek, and ye shall find; knock, and it shall be opened to you (Luke xi. 9). Would it not have been enough to have said, ask? Why add seek and knock? No, it was not superfluous to add them; for thereby our Savior wished us to understand that we ought to do as the poor who go begging. If they do not receive the alms they ask, they do not cease asking; they return to ask again; and if the master of the house does not show himself anymore, they set to work to knock at the door till they become troublesome. That is what God wishes us to do: to pray, and to pray again, and never leave off praying, that He would assist us and succor us, that He would enlighten us and strengthen us, and never allow us to forfeit His grace. The learned Lessius says that the man cannot be excused from mortal sin who does not pray when he is in sin, or in danger of death; or, again, if he neglects to pray for any notable time, as (he says) for one or two months, but this is not understood to refer to the time of temptations; because whoever finds himself assailed by any grievous temptation without doubt sins mortally if he does not have recourse to God at once, to ask for assistance to resist it; seeing that otherwise he places himself in a proximate, nay, in a certain occasion of sin.

But someone will say: Since God can give and wishes to give me the grace of Perseverance, why does He not give it to me all at once, when I ask Him?

The Holy Fathers assign many reasons. God does not grant it at once, but delays it:

(1) That He may prove our confidence.

(2) And, further, says St. Augustine, that we may long for it more vehemently. Great gifts, he says, should be greatly desired; for good things soon obtained are not held in the same estimation as those which have been long looked for: "God wills not to give quickly, that you may learn to have great desire for great things; for things long desired are all the more pleasant when obtained; but things soon given are cheapened."

(3) Again, the Lord does so that we may not forget Him; if we were already secure of persevering and of being saved, and if we had not the continual need of God's help to preserve us in His grace and to save us, we should soon forget God. Want makes the poor keep resorting to the houses of the rich; so God, to draw us to Himself, as St. Chrysostom says, and to see us often at His feet, in order that He may thus be able to do us greater good, delays giving us the complete grace of salvation till the hour of our death: "It is not because He rejects our prayers that He delays, but by this contrivance He wishes to make us careful, and to draw us to Himself." Again, He does so in order that we, by persevering in Prayer, may unite ourselves closer to Him with the sweet bonds of love: "Prayer," says the same St. Chrysostom, "which accustoms us to converse with God, is no slight bond of love with Him." This continual recourse to God in Prayer, and this confident expectation of the graces we desire--oh, what a great incentive to inflame us with love, and what a firm chain to bind us more closely to God!

But how long have we to pray? Always, says the same Saint, till we receive favorable sentence of eternal life: that is to say, till our death: "Do not leave off till you receive." And he adds: "If you say, I will not give up till I have received, you will assuredly receive." The Apostle writes that many run for the prize, but that he only receives it who runs till he wins: Know you not that they who run in the race, all run indeed, but one receiveth the prize? So run that you may obtain (1 Corinthians ix. 24). It is not, then, enough for salvation to simply pray; but we must pray always, that we may at last receive the crown which God promises but promises only to those who are constant in Prayer till the end.

So that if we wish to be saved, we must do as David did, who always kept his eyes turned to God, to implore His aid against being overcome by his enemies: My eyes are ever towards the Lord, for he shall pluck my feet out of the snare (Psalm xxiv. 15). As the devil does not cease continually spreading snares to devour us, as St. Peter writes: Your adversary, the devil, as, a roaring lion, goeth about, seeking whom he may devour (1 Peter v. 8); so ought we ever to stand with our arms in our hands to defend ourselves against such a foe, and to say, with the royal Prophet, I will pursue after my enemies; and I will not turn again till they are consumed (Psalm xvii. 38). I will never cease fighting till I see my enemies conquered. But how can we obtain this victory, so important for us and so difficult? "By most persevering prayers," says St. Augustine--only by prayers, and those most persevering; and till when? As long as the fight shall last. "As the battle is never over," says St. Bonaventure, "so let us never give over asking for Mercy." As we must be always in the combat, so should we be always asking God for aid not to be overcome. Woe, says the Wise Man, to him who in this battle leaves off praying: Woe to them that have lost patience (Ecclesiasticus 16). We may be saved, the Apostle tells us, but on this condition, if we hold fast the confidence and the glory of hope unto the end (Hebrews iii. 6); if we are constant in praying with confidence until death.

Let us, then, take courage from the Mercy of God, and His promises, and say with the same Apostle: Who, then shall separate us from the love of Christ? Shall tribulation, distress, or danger, or persecution, or the sword? (Romans viii. 35). Who shall succeed in estranging us from the love of Jesus Christ? Tribulation, perhaps or the danger of losing the goods of this world? The persecutions of devils or men? The torments inflicted by tyrants? In all these we overcome (it is St. Paul who encourages us), because of Him that hath loved us (Romans viii. 37). No, he says, no tribulation, no misery, danger, persecution, or torture, shall ever be able to separate us from the love of Jesus Christ; because with God's help we shall overcome all, if we fight for love of Him Who gave His life for us.

Father Hippolitus Durazzo, the day when he resolved to relinquish his dignity of prelate at Rome, and to give himself entirely to God by entering the Society of Jesus (which he afterwards did), was so afraid of being faithless by reason of his weakness that he said to God: "Forsake me not, Lord, now that I have given myself wholly to Thee! For pity's sake do not forsake me!" But he heard the whisper of God in his heart: "Rather should I say to thee: Do not thou forsake Me!" And so at last the servant of God, trusting in His goodness and help, concluded, "Then, O my God, Thou wilt not leave me, and I will not leave Thee."

Finally, if we wish not to be forsaken by God, we ought never cease praying to Him not to leave us. If we do this, He will certainly always assist us, and will never allow us to perish, or be separated from His love. And to this end let us not only take care always to ask for final Perseverance, and the graces necessary to obtain it, but let us, at the same time, always by anticipation, ask God for grace to go on praying; for this is precisely that great gift which He promised to His Elect by the mouth of the Prophet: And I will pour out upon the house of David, and upon the inhabitants of Jerusalem, the spirit of grace and of prayers (Zachariah xii. 10). Oh, what a great grace is the spirit of Prayer; that is, the grace which God confers on a soul to enable it to pray always! Let us, then, never neglect to beg God to give us this grace, and this spirit of continual Prayer; because if we pray always, we shall certainly obtain from God Perseverance and every other gift which we desire, since His promise of hearing whoever prays to Him cannot fail. For we are saved by hope (Romans viii. 24). With this hope of always praying we may reckon ourselves saved. "Confidence," says the Venerable Bede, "will give us a broad entrance into this City." This hope will give us a safe passage into the City of Paradise.

Evening Meditation

THE PRACTICE OF THE LOVE OF JESUS CHRIST

"Charity endureth all things"

HE THAT LOVES JESUS CHRIST WITH A STRONG LOVE DOES NOT CEASE TO LOVE HIM IN THE MIDST OF TEMPTATIONS AND DESOLATIONS

I.

God permits temptations with a view to detach us more thoroughly from this life; and to kindle in us a desire to go and behold Him in Heaven. Hence pious souls, finding themselves attacked day and night by so many enemies, come at length to feel a loathing for life, and exclaim: "Woe is me, that my sojourning is prolonged! (Psalm cxix. 5). And they sigh for the moment when they can say: The snare is broken and we are delivered (Psalm cxxiii. 7). The soul would willingly wing her flight to God; but as long as she lives upon this earth she is bound by a snare which detains her here below, where she is continually assailed with temptations; this snare is only broken by death; so that the souls that love God sigh for death, which will deliver them from all danger of losing Him.

Almighty God, moreover, allows us to be tempted, to make us richer in merits, as it was said to Tobias: And because thou wast acceptable to God, it was necessary that temptations should prove thee (Tobit xii. 13). Thus a soul need not imagine herself out of God's favor because she is tempted, but should make it rather a motive of hope that God loves her. It is a delusion of the devil to lead some pusillanimous persons to suppose that temptations are sins that contaminate the soul. It is not bad thoughts that make us lose God, but the consenting to them; let the suggestions of the devil be everso violent, let those filthy imaginations which overload our minds be ever so lively, they cannot cast the least stain on our souls, provided only we yield no consent to them; on the contrary, they make the soul purer, stronger, and dearer to Almighty God. St. Bernard says that every time we overcome a temptation, we win a fresh crown in Heaven: "As often as we conquer, so often are we crowned." An Angel once appeared to a Cistercian monk, and put a crown into his hands, with orders that he should carry it to one of his fellow-Religious, as a reward for the temptation that he had lately overcome. Neither must we be disturbed if evil thoughts do not forthwith disappear from our minds but continue obstinately to persecute us; it is enough if we detest them and do our best to banish them.

God is faithful, says the Apostle; He will not allow us to be tempted above our strength: God is faithful, who will not suffer you to be tempted above that which you are able; but will make also with the temptation issue, that you may be able to bear it (1 Corinthians x. 13).

II.

So far from losing anything by temptations, a person derives great profit from them. On this account God frequently allows the souls dearest to Him to undergo the severest temptations, that they may turn them into a source of greater merit on earth, and of greater glory in Heaven. Stagnant waters soon grow putrid; a soul at ease, without any struggle or temptation, stands in great danger of perishing from some self-conceit of her own merit. She perhaps imagines herself to have already attained to perfection, and therefore has little to fear; and consequently takes little pains to recommend herself to God and to secure her salvation; but when, on the contrary, she is agitated by temptations, and sees herself in danger of rushing headlong into sin, then she has recourse to God; she goes to the Divine Mother; she renews her resolution rather to die than to sin; she humbles herself, and casts herself into the arms of the Divine mercy: in this manner, as experience shows us, the soul acquires fresh strength and closer union with God.

This must not, however, lead us to seek after temptations; on the contrary, we must pray God to deliver us from temptations, and from those more especially by which God foresees we should be overcome; and this is precisely the object of that petition of the Our Father: Lead us not into temptation. But when, by God's permission, we are beset with temptations, we must then, without being either alarmed or discouraged by those foul thoughts, rely wholly on Jesus Christ, and beseech Him to help us; and He, on His part, will not fail to give us the strength to resist. St. Augustine says: "Throw thyself on Him, and fear not; He will not withdraw to let thee fall."

EIGHTH SUNDAY AFTER PENTECOST

OUR ETERNAL SALVATION DEPENDS UPON OURSELVES

What joy will he experience at the Judgment when he hears these welcome words: Well done, thou good and faithful servant! Enter thou into the joy of thy Lord! But it is written: What things a man shall sow, those also shall he reap. Let us weigh well what things we have hitherto been sowing, and let us do now what we shall then wish to have done.

I.

What great consolation he will enjoy at the Judgment hour who, for the love of Jesus Christ, has been detached from all worldly things; who has loved contempt, and mortified the body; who, in a word has loved only God!

What joy will he experience in hearing these welcome words: Well done, thou good and faithful servant! Enter thou into the joy of thy Lord! Be glad and rejoice, for now thou art saved, and there is no longer any fear of being lost.

On the contrary, the soul which leaves this life in a state of sin, will, even before Jesus condemns it, condemn itself, and declare itself deserving of hell.

O Mary, my powerful advocate, pray to Jesus for me. Help me, now that thou art able to help me. For then thou wouldst have to see me perish and not be able to assist me.

What things a man shall sow, those also shall he reap (Gal. vi. 8). Let us consider what things we have hitherto been sowing and let us do now what we shall then wish to have done.

If now, within an hour, we had to stand for judgment, how much should we be willing to give to purchase another year? And how are we going to employ the years which remain for us?

II.

The Abbot Agatho, after long years of penance, when he thought of Judgment, would say: "What will become of me when I shall be judged?" And holy Job exclaimed: What shall I do when God shall rise to judge? And when he shall examine, what shall I answer him? (Job. xxxi. 14). And what shall we answer when Jesus Christ calls us to account for the graces He has bestowed upon us, and for the bad use we have made of them?

O my God, deliver not up to beasts the souls that confess to thee (Psalm lxxiii. 19). I do not deserve pardon, but Thou wouldst not have me to lose confidence in Thy mercy. Save me, O Lord, and raise me up from the mire of my miseries. I desire to amend my life, do Thou assist me.

The cause to be decided at the hour of our death will be one that will involve eternal happiness or eternal misery. Hence we should be most careful in using our utmost endeavors to secure success. Each one, considering this, should say to himself: Yes, this is true. Why, therefore, do I not leave all things to give myself entirely to God? Seek ye the Lord, while he may be found (Is. lv. 6). The sinner who thinks to find God at the Judgment after death will not find Him. But in life he who seeks Him, finds Him.

O Jesus, if hitherto I have despised Thy love, I now seek for nothing but to love Thee and to be loved by Thee. Grant that I may find Thee, O God of my soul!

Spiritual Reading

PRAYER

GOD WISHES ALL MEN TO BE SAVED.

Taking, then, for granted that Prayer is necessary for the attainment of Eternal Life, as we have proved, we ought, consequently, to take for granted also that everyone has Divine assistance to enable him actually to pray, without need of any further special grace; and that by Prayer he may obtain all the other graces necessary to enable him to persevere in keeping the Commandments, and thus gain Eternal Life; so that no one who is lost can ever excuse himself by saying that it was through want of the aid necessary for his salvation. For as God, in the natural order, has ordained that man should be born naked, and in want of several things necessary for life, but then has given him hands and intelligence to clothe himself and provide for his other needs; so, in the supernatural order, man is born unable to obtain salvation by his own strength; but God in His goodness grants to everyone the grace of Prayer, by which he is able to obtain all other graces which he needs in order to keep the Commandments and to be saved.

But before I come to treat this point, I must first establish Two Preliminary Propositions:

FIRST PRELIMINARY PROPOSITION.
GOD WISHES ALL MEN TO BE SAVED, AND THEREFORE CHRIST DIED TO SAVE ALL MEN.

(a) God wishes all men to be saved.

God loves all things that He has created: For thou lovest all things that are, and hatest none of the things which thou hast made (Wisdom xi. 25). Now love cannot be idle: "All love has a force of its own, and cannot be idle," says St. Augustine. Hence love necessarily implies benevolence, so that the person who loves cannot help doing good to the person beloved whenever there is an opportunity: "Love persuades a man to do those things which he believes to be good for him whom he loves," says Aristotle. If, then, God loves all men, He must, in consequence, will that all should obtain Eternal salvation, which is the one and sovereign good of man, seeing that it is the one end for which he was created: You have your fruit unto sanctification; and the end life everlasting (Romans vi. 22).

This doctrine, that God wishes all men to be saved, and that Jesus Christ died for the salvation of all, is now a certain doctrine taught by the Catholic Church, as theologians in common teach, for example, Petavius, Gonet, Gotti, and others, besides Tourneley, who adds, that it is a doctrine all but of Faith.

1.–Proved from Decision of the Church.

With reason, therefore, were the Predestinarians condemned, who, among their errors, taught that God does not will all men to be saved, as Hincmar, Archbishop of Rheims, testifies of them: "The ancient Predestinarians asserted that God does not will all men to be saved, but only those who are saved." These persons were condemned, first in the Council of Arles, A.D. 475, which pronounced "anathema to him that said that Christ did not die for all men, and that He does not will all to be saved." They were next condemned in the Council of Lyons, A.D. 490, where Lucidus was forced to retract, and also to proclaim, "I condemn the man who says that Christ did not suffer for the salvation of all men." So also in the ninth century, Gottschalk, who renewed the same error, was condemned by the Council of Quercy, A.D. 853, in the third Article of which it was decided, "God wills all men, without exception, to be saved, although all men be not saved." These men were justly condemned, precisely because they taught that God does not will all men to be saved; since from the proposition that those whom God wills to be saved are infallibly saved, it would logically follow that God does not will even all the faithful to be saved, let alone all men.

This was also clearly expressed by the Council of Trent, in which it was said that Jesus Christ died, "that all might receive the adoption of sons," and again it says: "But though He died for all, yet all do not receive the benefits of His death." The Council, then, takes for granted that the Redeemer died not only for the elect, but also for those who, through their own fault, do not receive the benefit of Redemption. Nor is it of any use to affirm that the Council only meant to say that Jesus Christ has given to the world a ransom sufficient to save all men; for in this sense we might say that He died also for the devils. Moreover, the Council of Trent intended here to reprove the errors of those innovators, who, not denying that the Blood of Christ was sufficient to save all, yet asserted that in fact it was not shed and given for all. This is the error which the Council intended to condemn when it said that our Savior died for all. Further, in Chapter VI, it says that sinners are put in a fit state to receive justification by hope in God through the merits of Jesus Christ: "They are raised to hope, trusting that God will be merciful to them through Christ." Now, if Jesus Christ had not applied to all the merits of His Passion, then, since no one (without a special revelation) could be certain of being among the number of those to whom the Redeemer had willed to apply the fruit of His merits, no sinner could entertain such hope, not having the certain and secure foundation which is necessary for hope; namely, that God wills all men to be saved, and will grant pardon to all sinners made worthy of it by the merits of Jesus Christ.

2.–Proved from the celebrated text of St. Paul.

On the other hand, both the Scriptures and all the Fathers assure us that God sincerely and really wishes the salvation of all men and the conversion of all sinners, as long as they are in this world. For this we have, first of all, the express words of St. Paul: Who will have all men to be saved, and to come to the knowledge of the truth (1 Timothy ii. 4). The sentence of the Apostle is absolute and decisive–God wills all men to be saved. These words in their natural sense declare that God truly wills all men to be saved; and it is a certain rule received in common by all, that the words of Scripture are to be interpreted in the literal sense, except in the sole case where the literal sense is repugnant to Faith and morals. St. Bonaventure writes precisely to our purpose when he says: "We must hold that when the Apostle says, God wills all men to be saved, it is necessary to grant that He does will it."

It is true that St. Augustine and St. Thomas mention different interpretations which have been given to this text, but both these Doctors understand it to mean a real will of God to save all, without exception.

And concerning St. Augustine, we shall see just now that this was his true opinion; so that St. Prosper protests against attributing to him the idea that God did not sincerely wish the salvation of all men, and of each individual, as an aspersion on the holy Doctor. Hence the same St. Prosper, who was a most faithful disciple of his, says: "It is most sincerely to be believed and confessed that God wills all men to be saved; since the Apostle (whose very words these are) is particular in commanding that prayers should be made to God for all."

The argument of the Saint is clear, founded on St. Paul's words in the above-cited passage: I desire, therefore,... that supplications, prayers ... be made for all men (1 Timothy ii. 1); and then he adds: For this is good and acceptable in the sight of God our Savior, who will have all men to be saved (1 Timothy ii. 3, 4). So the Apostle wishes us to pray for all, exactly in the sense that God wishes the salvation of all. St. Chrysostom uses the same argument: "If He wills all to be saved, surely we ought to pray for all. If He desires all to be saved, do you also be of one mind with Him." And if in some passages in his controversy with the Semi-Pelagians, St. Augustine seems to have held a different interpretation of this text, saying that God does not will the salvation of each individual, but only of some, Petavius well observes that here the holy Father speaks only incidentally, not with direct intention; or at any rate, that he speaks of the grace of that absolute and victorious will (voluntas absoluta et victrix) with which God absolutely wills the salvation of some persons, and of which the Saint elsewhere says, "The will of the Almighty is always invincible."

Let us hear how St. Thomas uses another method of reconciling the opinion of St. Augustine with that of St. John Damascene, who holds that antecedently God wills all and each individual to be saved: "God's first intention is to will all men to be saved, that as Good He may make us partakers of His goodness: but after we have sinned, He wills as Just to punish us." On the other hand, St. Augustine (as we have seen) seems in a few passages to think differently. But St. Thomas reconciles these opinions and says St. John Damascene spoke of the antecedent will of God, by which he really wills all men to be saved, while St. Augustine spoke of the consequent will. He then goes on to explain the meaning of antecedent and consequent will: "Antecedent will is that by which God wills all to be saved; but when all the circumstances of this or that individual are considered, it is not found to be good that all men should be saved; for it is good that he who prepares himself, and consents to it, should be saved; but not good that he who is unwilling and resists... And this is called the consequent will, because it presupposes a foreknowledge of a man's deeds, not as a cause of the act of will, but as a reason for the thing willed and determined." ...

And again: "God, by His most liberal will, gives grace to everyone that prepares himself–who wills all men to be saved; and therefore the grace of God is wanting to no man, but as far as He is concerned He communicates it to everyone." ... And St. Thomas again, and more distinctly, declares what he means by antecedent, and consequent will: "A judge antecedently wishes every man to live, but he consequently wishes a murderer to be hanged; so God antecedently wills every man to be saved, but He consequently wills some to be damned; in consequence, that is, of the exigencies of His justice."

I have no intention here of blaming the opinion that men are predestined to glory previously to the provision of their merits; I only say that I cannot understand how those who think that God, without any regard to their merits, has elected some to eternal life, and excluded others, can therefore persuade themselves that He wills all to be saved; unless, indeed, they mean that this will of God is not true and sincere, but rather a hypothetical or metaphorical will...

It is certain that the happiness of a creature consists in the attainment of the end for which he was created. It is likewise certain that God creates all men for eternal life. If, therefore, God, having created certain men for eternal life, had thereupon, without regard to their sins, excluded them from it, He would in creating them have utterly hated them without cause, and would have done them the greatest injury they could possibly suffer in excluding them from the attainment of their end, that is, of the glory for which they had been created: "For," says Petavius in a passage which we abridge, "God cannot feel indifferent whether He loves or hates His creatures, especially men, whom He either loves to eternal life or hates to damnation. Now it is the greatest evil that can befall man to be alienated from God and to be reprobate; wherefore, if God wills the everlasting destruction of any man's soul, He does not love him, but hates him with the greatest hatred possible in that kind which transcends the natural order." ... "Wherefore," Petavius concludes, "if God loves every man with a love which is antecedent to his merits, He does not hate his soul, and therefore He does not desire the greatest evil to him." If, then, God loves all men, as is certain, we ought to hold that He wills all to be saved, and that He has never hated any one to such a degree that He has willed to do him the greatest evil, by excluding him from glory previously to the prevision of his demerits.

I say, however, and repeat again and again, that I cannot understand it; for this matter of predestination is so profound a mystery, that it made the Apostle exclaim: Oh, the depth of the riches of the wisdom and the knowledge of God! How incomprehensible his judgments, and how unsearchable his ways! For who hath known the mind of the Lord? (Romans xi. 33, 34). We ought to submit ourselves to the will of God, Who has chosen to leave this mystery in obscurity in His Church, that we all may humble ourselves under the deep judgments of His Divine Providence. All the more, because Divine grace, by which alone men gain eternal life, is dispensed more or less abundantly by God entirely gratuitously, and without any regard to our merits. So that to save ourselves it will always be necessary for us to throw ourselves into the arms of the Divine Mercy, in order that God may assist us with His grace to obtain salvation, trusting always in His infallible promises to hear and save the man who prays to Him.

But let us return to our point, that God sincerely wills all men to be saved.

3.–There are other texts which prove the same thing.

As I live, saith the Lord, I desire not the death of the wicked, but that the wicked may turn from his way and live (Ezechiel xxxiii. 11). He says that not only does He not will the death, but that He wills the life of a sinner; and He swears, as Tertullian observes, in order that He may be more readily believed in this: "When moreover He swears, saying, as I live, He desires to be believed."

Further, David says: For wrath is in his indignation, and life in his will (Ps. xxix. 6). If He chastises us, He does it because our sins provoke Him to indignation; but as to His will, He wills not our death but our life; Life in his will. St. Basil says concerning this text, that God wills all to be made partakers of life. David says elsewhere: Our God is the God of salvation; ... of the Lord are the issues from death (Psalm lxvii. 21). On this Bellarmine says: "This is proper to Him; this is His nature; our God is a saving God, and His are the issues from death–that is, liberation from death"; so that it is God's proper nature to save all, and to deliver all from eternal death.

Our Lord says: Come to me, all ye that labor and are burdened, and I will refresh you (Matthew xi. 28). If He calls all to salvation, then He truly wills all to be saved. Again, St. Peter says: He willeth not that any should perish, but that all should return to penance (2 Peter iii. 9). He does not will the damnation of anyone, but He wills that all should do penance, and so be saved.

Again the Lord says: Behold I stand at the gate and knock. If any man shall open to me the door I will come in to him. Why will you die, O house of Israel? Return ye and live (Ezechiel xviii. 31, 32). What is there that I ought to do more to my vineyard, that I have not done to it? (Isaiah v. 4). How often would I have gathered together thy children, as the hen gathereth her chickens under her wings, and thou wouldst not! (Matthew xxiii. 37). How could the Lord have said that He stands knocking at the hearts of us sinners? How exhort us so strongly to return to His arms? How reproach us by asking what more He could have done for our salvation? How say that He has willed to receive us as children, if he had not a true will to save all men? Again, St. Luke relates that our Lord, looking on Jerusalem from a distance, and contemplating the destruction of its people because of sin, wept: Seeing the city, he wept over it (Luke xix. 41). Why did He weep then, says Theophylact (after St. Chrysostom), seeing the ruin of the Jews, unless it was because He really desired their salvation? How, then, after so many attestations of our Lord, in which He makes known to us that He wills to see all men saved, how can it ever be said that God does not will the salvation of all? "But if these texts of Scripture," says Petavius, "in which God has testified His will in such clear and often-repeated expressions, nay even with tears and with an oath, may be abused and distorted to the very opposite sense—namely, that God determined to send all mankind (except a few) to perdition, and never had a will to save them, what dogma of Faith is so clear as to be safe from similar injury and cavil?" ... And Cardinal Sfondrati adds: "Those who think otherwise seem to me to make God a mere stage-god; like those people who pretend to be kings in a play, when indeed they are anything but kings."

4.–Proved from the general consent of the Fathers.

Moreover, this truth, that God wills all men to be saved, is confirmed by the general consent of the Fathers. There can be no doubt that all the Greek Fathers are unanimous in saying that God wills all and each individual to be saved. So, St. Justin, St. Basil, St. Gregory, St. Cyril, St. Methodius, and St. Chrysostom, all adduced by Petavius. But let us see what the Latin Fathers say.

St. Jerome: "God wills to save all; but since no man is saved without his own will, God wills us to will what is good, that when we have willed, He may also will to fulfil His designs in us." And in another place: "God therefore willed to save those who desire (to be saved); and He invited them to salvation that their will might have its reward; but they would not believe in Him."

St. Hilary: "God would have all men to be saved, and not those alone who are to belong to the number of the elect, but all absolutely, so as to make no exception."

St. Paulinus: "Christ says to all: Come to me, etc.; for He, the Creator of all men, so far as He is concerned, wills every man to be saved."

St. Ambrose: "Even with respect to the wicked He had to manifest His will (to save them), and therefore He could not pass over His betrayer, that all might see that in the election even of the traitor He exhibits His desire to save all ... and, so far as God is concerned, He shows to all that He was willing to deliver all." ...

St. Chrysostom asks: "Why then are not all men saved, if God wills all to be saved?" And he answers: "Because every man's will does not coincide with God's will, and He forces no man."

St. Augustine: "God wills all men to be saved, but not so as to destroy their free will." He says the same thing in several other places to which we shall refer later.

Evening Meditation

THE PRACTICE OF THE LOVE OF JESUS CHRIST

"Charity endureth all things"

HE THAT LOVES JESUS CHRIST WITH A STRONG LOVE DOES NOT CEASE TO LOVE HIM IN THE MIDST OF TEMPTATIONS AND DESOLATIONS

I.

Let us come now to the means which we have to employ in order to vanquish temptations. Spiritual masters prescribe a variety of means; but the most necessary, and the safest, of which only I will here speak, is to have immediate recourse to God with all humility and confidence, saying: "Incline unto my aid, O God; O Lord make haste to help me!" This short prayer will enable us to overcome the assaults of all the devils of hell; for God is infinitely more powerful than all of them. Almighty God knows well that of ourselves we are unable to resist the temptations of the infernal powers; and on this account the most learned Cardinal Gotti remarks that "whenever we are assailed, and in danger of being overcome, God is obliged to give us strength enough to resist as often as we call upon Him for it."

And how can we doubt of receiving help from Jesus Christ, after all the promises He has made us in the Holy Scriptures? Come to me, all you that labor and are heavy laden, and I will refresh you (Matt. xi. 28). Come to Me, ye who are wearied in fighting against temptations, and I will restore your strength. Call upon me in the day of trouble: I will deliver thee, and thou shalt glorify me (Ps. xlix. 15). When thou seest thyself troubled by thine enemies, call upon Me, and I will bring thee out of danger, and thou shalt praise Me. Then shalt thou call, and the Lord shall hear: thou shalt cry, and He shall say, Here I am (Isaiah lviii. 9). Then shalt thou call upon the Lord for help, and He will hear thee: thou shalt cry out, Quick, O Lord, help me! and He will say to thee, Behold, here I am; I am present to help thee. Who hath called upon him and he despised him? (Ecclesiasticus ii. 12). And who, says the Prophet, has ever called upon God, and God has despised him and given him no help? David felt sure of never falling a prey to his enemies, whilst he could have recourse to God. He says: Praising, I will call upon the Lord: and I shall be saved from my enemies (Psalm xvii. 4). For he well knew that God is close to all who invoke His aid: The Lord is nigh unto all them that call upon him (Ps. cxliv. 18). And St. Paul adds that the Lord is by no means sparing, but lavish of graces towards all that pray to Him: Rich unto all that call upon him. (Romans x. 12).

II.

Oh, would to God that all men had recourse to Him whenever they are tempted to offend Him; they would then certainly never commit sin! They unhappily fall, because, led away by the cravings of their vicious appetites, they prefer to lose God, the Sovereign Good, then to forego their wretched short-lived pleasures. Experience gives us manifest proofs that whoever calls on God in temptation does not fall; and whoever fails to call on Him, as surely falls and this is especially true of temptations to impurity. Solomon himself said that he knew very well that he could not be chaste unless God gave him the grace to be so; and therefore, he invoked Him by prayer in the moment of temptation: And as I knew that I could not otherwise be continent, except God gave it ... I went to the Lord and besought him (Wisdom viii. 21). In temptations against purity (and the same holds good with regard to those against Faith), we must take it as a rule never to stay and combat the temptation hand to hand; but we must endeavor immediately to get rid of it indirectly by making a good act of the love of God or of sorrow for our sins, or else by applying ourselves to some indifferent occupation calculated to distract us. As soon as we discover a thought of evil tendency, we must disown it immediately, and, so to speak, close the door in its face, and deny it all entrance into the mind, without tarrying in the least to examine its object or errand. We must cast away these foul suggestions as quickly as we would shake off a hot spark from the fire.

Monday--Eighth Week after Pentecost

Morning Meditation

THE GENERAL JUDGMENT

When all shall be gathered together in the Valley of Josaphet, what a glorious appearance will the Saints make who in this world were so much despised! And what a horrible appearance will so many of those great ones of earth, and kings, and princes make, who will on that day stand condemned!

I.

O ye foolish worldlings! I look forward to your appearance in the Valley of Josaphet. There you will change your sentiments! There you will bewail your folly! But to no purpose.

And you, who are hard tried in this world, be of good heart. On that last day all your pains will be changed into the delights and enjoyments of Paradise: Your sorrow shall be turned into joy (John xvi. 20).

What a glorious appearance will the Saints then make who in this world were so much despised! And what a horrible appearance will so many of those nobles and kings and princes make, who will stand condemned on that day!

My crucified and despised Jesus, I embrace Thy Cross. What is the world, what are pleasures, what are honors? O my God, Thee only do I desire; Thee alone and nothing more!

What horror will not the reprobate in that day experience at being rejected by Jesus Christ in that terrible sentence, publicly pronounced: Depart from me, ye cursed! (Matthew xxv. 41).

O my Jesus, I also at one time deserved such a sentence. But now I hope that Thou hast pardoned me. Oh, do not suffer me to be any more separated from Thee. I love Thee, and I hope to love Thee forever.

O what joy, on the other hand will the Elect experience when they hear Jesus Christ inviting them to partake of the bliss of Heaven in those sweet words: Come ye blessed!

My beloved Redeemer, I hope in Thy precious Blood that I also shall be numbered among those happy souls, and embracing Thy feet, love Thee for all eternity in Heaven!

II.

Let us, then, reanimate our Faith, and reflect that one day we shall meet in that Valley of Judgment and be placed either on the right hand with the Elect, or on the left with the reprobate. Let us cast ourselves at the foot of the Crucifix and look into the state of our souls; and if we find them unprepared to appear before Jesus Christ, the Divine Judge, let us apply a remedy now whilst we have time. Let us detach ourselves from everything which is not God and unite ourselves to Jesus Christ as much as we are able, by Meditation, the Holy Communion, mortification of the senses, and, above all, by Prayer. The use of these means which God affords us for our salvation will be a sure sign of our predestination.

O my Jesus and my Judge, I do not wish to lose Thee, but I wish to love Thee forever. I love Thee, my Lord, I love Thee; and thus I hope to be able to address Thee when I shall first behold Thee as my Judge. I now say to Thee: Lord, if Thou desirest to chastise me, as I have deserved, chastise me, but do not deprive me of Thy love; grant that I may always love Thee, and may be always loved by Thee, and then do with me what Thou wilt.

Spiritual Reading

PRAYER

(b) Therefore Christ died to save all men.

That Jesus Christ, therefore, died for all and for each individual is clear, not only from the Scriptures, but from the writings of the Fathers. Great, certainly, was the ruin which the sin of Adam occasioned to the whole human race; but Jesus Christ, by the grace of Redemption, repaired all the evils which Adam brought upon us. Hence the Council of Trent has declared that Baptism renders the soul pure and immaculate; and that the concupiscence which remains in it is not for its harm, but to enable it to gain a higher crown, if it resists so as not to consent to sin: "For in those who have been regenerated God hates nothing ... they are made innocent, immaculate, pure, and beloved of God ... But this holy Synod confesses and declares that concupiscence or the fuel (of sin) remains in baptized persons; but as it was left for our probation, it cannot injure those who do not consent to it; nay rather, he who contends lawfully (against it) shall be crowned." Thus, as St. Leo says, "we have gained greater things by the grace of Christ than we had lost through the envy of the devil." The gain which we have made by the Redemption of Jesus Christ is greater than the loss which we suffered by the sin of Adam. The Apostle plainly declared this when he said: Not as the offence, so also the gift ... And where sin abounded, grace did more abound (Romans v. 15, 20). Our Lord says the same: I am come that they may have life and have it more abundantly (John x. 10). David and Isaias had predicted it: With him is plentiful redemption (Psalm cxxix. 7) She hath received of the hand of the Lord double for all her sins (Isaiah xl. 2). Cornelius a Lapide interprets these words and says: "God has so forgiven iniquities through Christ that men have received double--that is, very much greater good, instead of the punishment of sin which they deserved."

Now, our Savior, as I have said, died for all, and offered the work of His Redemption to the Eternal Father for the salvation of each one, according to the testimony of the Holy Scriptures and the Fathers of the Church.

1.--The Testimony of Holy Scriptures.

The Son of Man came to save that which was lost (Matthew xviii. 11). Who gave himself a redemption for all (1 Timothy ii. 6). Christ died for all, that they also who live may not now live to themselves, but to him who died for them (2 Corinthians v. 15). For therefore we labor and are reviled, because we hope in the living God, who is the Savior of all men, especially of the faithful (1 Timothy iv. 10). And he is the propitiation for our sins; and not for ours only, but also for those of the whole world (1 John ii. 2). For the charity of Christ presseth us, judging this that, if one died for all, then all were dead (2 Corinthians v. 14). Now, to speak only of this last text, I ask, how could the Apostle ever have concluded that all were dead because Christ died for all, unless he had been certain that Christ had really died for all? And the more so seeing that St. Paul uses this truth as an argument for the love which it should kindle in us towards our Savior. But by far the best proof of the desire and wish which God has to save all men is found in that other text of St. Paul: He that spared not his own son but delivered him for us all. The force of this passage is increased by what follows: How hath he not also with him given us all things? (Romans viii. 32). If God has given us all things, how can we henceforth fear that He has denied us election to glory if we fulfil the condition of corresponding to His grace? And if He has given us His Son, says Cardinal Sfondrati, how will He deny us the grace to be saved? "Here he clearly instructs us" (he is speaking of St. Paul) "that God assures us that He will not refuse us the less after He has given the greater; that He will not deny us grace to save ourselves, after giving us His Son that we might be saved." And in truth, how could St. Paul have said that God, in giving us His Son, has given us all things, if the Apostle had believed that God had excluded many from the glory which is the one good and the one end for which they were created? Has, then, God given all things to these "many" and yet denied them the best thing--namely, eternal happiness, without which (as there is no middle way) they cannot but be eternally miserable? Or are we to believe another thing still more unseemly, as a certain learned author well observes--namely, that God gives to all the grace to attain glory, but then refuses to allow many to enter on its enjoyment; that He gives the means and refuses the end!

2.--Proved from the teaching of the Holy Fathers.

Besides the testimony of the Scripture, all the holy Fathers agree in saying that Jesus Christ died to obtain eternal salvation for all men.

St. Jerome: "Christ died for all; He was the only One Who could be offered for all, because all were dead in sin."

St. Ambrose: "Christ came to cure our wounds; but since all do not search for the remedy ... therefore He cures those who are willing; He does not force the unwilling." In another place: "He has provided for all men the means of cure, that whoever perishes may lay the blame of his death on himself, because he would not be cured when he had a remedy; and that, on the other hand, the Mercy of Christ to all may be openly proclaimed, Who wills that all men should be saved." And more clearly still in another place: "Jesus did not write His will for the benefit of one, or of few, but of all; we are all inscribed therein as His heirs; the legacy is in common, and belongs by right to all; the universal heritage belonging wholly to each." Mark the words, "We are all inscribed as heirs; the Redeemer has written us all down as heirs of heaven."

St. Leo: "As Christ found no one free from guilt, so He came to deliver all."

St. Augustine, on the words of St. John, For God did not send his son ... to judge the world, but that the world may be saved by him (John 17), says: "So as far as it lies with the Physician, He came to heal the sick man." Mark the words, "as far as it lies with the Physician." For God, as far as He is concerned, effectually wills the salvation of all, but (as St. Augustine goes on to say) cannot heal the man who will not be healed: "He heals universally, but He heals not the unwilling. For what can be happier for thee, than, as thou hast thy life in thy hands, so to have thy health depend on thy will?" When he says: "He heals," he speaks of sinners who are sick, and unable to get well by their own strength; when he says "universally," he declares that nothing is wanting on God's part for sinners to be healed and saved. Then when he says, "as thou hast thy life in thy hands, so thy health depends on thy will," he shows that God, for His part, really wills us all to be saved; otherwise, it would not be in our power to obtain health and eternal life. In another place: "He Who redeemed us at such a cost, wills not that we perish, for He does not purchase in order to destroy, but He redeems in order to give life." He has redeemed us all, to save us all. And the Saint encourages all to hope for eternal bliss, in that celebrated sentence: "Let human frailty raise itself; let it not say 'I shall never be happy' ... It is a greater thing that Christ has done, than that which He has promised. What has He done? He has died for thee. What has He promised? That thou shalt live with Him."

Some have pretended to say that Jesus Christ offered His Blood for all, in order to obtain grace for them, but not salvation. But Petrocorensis will not hear of this opinion, of which he says: "O disputatious trifling! How could the Wisdom of God will the means of salvation, without willing its end?" St. Augustine, moreover, speaking against the Jews, says: "Ye acknowledge the Side which ye pierced, that it has opened both by you and for you." If Jesus Christ had not really given His Blood for all, the Jews might have answered St. Augustine that it was quite true the side of our Savior had been opened by them, but that it was not opened for them.

In like manner St. Thomas has no doubt that Jesus Christ died for all; whence he deduces that He wills all to be saved: "Christ Jesus is Mediator between God and men; not between God and some men, but between God and all men; and this would not be unless He willed all to be saved." This is confirmed, as we have already said, by the condemnation of the fifth Proposition of Jansenius, who said: "It is semi-Pelagianism to assert that Christ died or shed His Blood for all men." The sense of this, according to the context of the other Condemned Propositions, and according to the principles of Jansenius, is as follows:--Jesus Christ did not die to merit for all men the graces sufficient for salvation, but only for the predestined. Therefore the contrary, and the Catholic belief is as follows:--It is not semi-Pelagianism, but it is right to say that Jesus Christ died to merit not only for the predestinate, but for all, even for the reprobate, grace sufficient to obtain eternal salvation in the ordinary course of Providence.

Further, that God truly, on His part, wills all men to be saved, and that Jesus Christ died for the salvation of all, is proved to us by the fact that God imposes on us all the precept of Hope. The reason is clear. St. Paul calls Christian Hope the anchor of the soul, secure and firm: Who have fled for refuge to hold fast the hope set before us which we have as an anchor of the soul, sure and firm (Hebrews vi. 18, 19). Now in what could we fix this sure and firm anchor of our hope, except in the truth that God wills all to be saved? And if Jesus Christ had not died for the salvation of all, how could we have a sure ground to hope for salvation through the merits of Jesus Christ, without a special revelation? But St. Augustine had no doubt when he said: "All my hope, and the certainty of my Faith, is in the Precious Blood of Christ, which was shed for us and for our salvation." Thus the Saint placed all his hope in the Blood of Jesus Christ; because the Faith assured him that Christ died for all. But we shall have a better opportunity later of examining this question of hope when we come to establish the principal point--namely, that the Grace of Prayer is given to all.

CHILDREN WHO DIE WITHOUT BAPTISM.
A difficulty answered.

Here it only remains for us to answer the objection which is drawn from children being lost when they die before Baptism, and before they come to the use of reason. If God wills all to be saved, it is objected, how is it that these children perish without any fault of their own, since God gives them no assistance to attain eternal salvation? There are two answers to this objection, the second more correct than the first. I will state them briefly.

First, it is answered that God, by His antecedent will, wishes all to be saved, and therefore has granted universal means for the salvation of all. But these means at times fail of their effect, either by reason of the unwillingness of some persons to avail themselves of them, or because others are unable to make use of them, on account of secondary causes (such as the death of children), causes the course of which God is not bound to change, after having disposed the whole according to the just judgment of His general Providence. All this is gathered from the teaching of St. Thomas. Jesus Christ offered His merits for all men, and instituted Baptism for all; but the application of this means of salvation, so far as relates to children who die before the use of reason, is not prevented by the direct will of God, but by a merely permissive will; because as He is the general Provider of all things, He is not bound to disturb the general order to provide for the particular order.

The second answer is that not to be blessed is not the same as to perish, for eternal happiness being a gift entirely gratuitous, the privation of it is not a punishment. The opinion, therefore, of St. Thomas, is very just, that children who die in infancy have neither the pain of sense nor the pain of loss. They have not the pain of sense, he says, "because pain of sense corresponds to conversion to creatures; and in Original Sin there is not conversion to creatures and therefore pain of sense is not due to Original Sin." Original Sin does not imply an act in the infant deserving of punishment. Objectors oppose to this the teaching of St. Augustine, who in some place shows his opinion to be that children are condemned even to the pain of sense. But in another place he declares that he was very uncertain on this point. These are his words: "When I come to the punishment of infants, I find myself, believe me, in great straits; nor can I by any means find an answer." And in another place he writes that it may be said that such children receive neither reward nor punishment: "Nor need we fear that there cannot be a middle sentence between reward and punishment; since their life was midway between sin and good works." This was directly affirmed by St. Gregory Nazianzen: "Children will be sentenced by the just Judge neither to the glory of Heaven nor to punishment." St. Gregory of Nyssa was of the same opinion: "The premature death of children shows that they who have thus ceased to live will not be in pain and unhappiness."

And as far as relates to the pain of loss, although these children are excluded from glory, nevertheless St. Thomas, who had reflected most deeply on this point, teaches that no one feels pain for the want of that good which he is not capable of acquiring; so that as no man grieves that he cannot fly, or no private citizen that he is not emperor, so these children feel no pain at being deprived of the glory of which they have never been made capable; since they could never pretend to it by nature, or by their own merits. St. Thomas adds, in another place, a further reason which is, that the supernatural knowledge of glory comes only by means of actual Faith, which transcends all natural knowledge; so that children can never feel pain for the privation of that glory of which they never had a supernatural knowledge. He further says that such children will not only not grieve for the loss of eternal happiness, but will, moreover, have pleasure in their natural gifts; and will even in some way enjoy God, so far as is implied in natural knowledge, and in natural love: "Rather will they rejoice in this, that they will participate much in the Divine Goodness, and in natural perfections." And he immediately adds that although they will be separated from God, as regards the union of glory, nevertheless, "they will be united with Him by participation of natural gifts; and so will even be able to rejoice in Him with a natural knowledge and love."

Evening Meditation

THE PRACTICE OF THE LOVE OF JESUS CHRIST
"Charity endureth all things"
HE THAT LOVES JESUS CHRIST WITH A STRONG LOVE DOES NOT CEASE TO LOVE HIM IN THE MIDST OF TEMPTATIONS AND DESOLATIONS

I.

If the impure temptation has already forced its way into the mind, and plainly pictures its object to the imagination, to stir the passions, then, according to the advice of St. Jerome, we must burst forth into these words: "O Lord, thou art my helper." As soon, says the Saint, as we feel the sting of concupiscence, we must have recourse to God, and say: "O Lord, do Thou assist me"; we must invoke the most holy Names of Jesus and Mary, which possess a wonderful efficacy in the suppression of temptations of this nature. St. Francis de Sales says that no sooner do children espy a wolf than they instantly seek refuge in the arms of their father and mother, and there they remain out of all danger. Our conduct must be the same; we must flee without delay for succor to Jesus and Mary, by earnestly calling upon them. I repeat that we must instantly have recourse to them, without giving a moment's audience to, or disputing with, the temptation. It is related in the 4th paragraph of the Book of Sentences of the Fathers, that one day St. Pacomius heard the devil boasting that he had frequently got the better of a certain monk on account of his lending ear to him, and not turning instantly to call upon God. He heard another devil, on the contrary, utter this complaint: As for me, I can do nothing with my monk, because he never fails to have recourse to God, and always defeats me.

II.

Should the temptation, however, obstinately persist in attacking us, let us beware of becoming troubled or angry at it; for this might put it in the power of our enemy to overcome us. We must, on such occasions, make an act of humble resignation to the will of God, Who thinks fit to allow us to be tormented by these abominable temptations; and we must say: O Lord, I deserve to be molested with these filthy suggestions, in punishment of my past sins, but Thou must help to free me. And as long as the temptation lasts, let us never cease calling on Jesus and Mary. It is also very profitable, in the like importunity of temptations, to renew our firm promise to God of suffering every torment, and a thousand deaths, rather than offend Him; and at the same time, we must invoke His Divine assistance. And even should the temptation be of such violence as to put us in imminent risk of consenting to it, we must then redouble our prayers, hasten into the presence of the Blessed Sacrament, cast ourselves at the foot of the Crucifix, or of some image of our Blessed Lady, and there pray with increased fervor, and cry out for help with groans and tears. God is certainly ready to hear all who pray to Him; and it is from Him alone, and not from our own exertions, that we must look for strength to resist; but sometimes Almighty God wills these struggles and then He makes up for our weakness and grants us the victory.

TUESDAY--EIGHTH WEEK AFTER PENTECOST

Morning Meditation

REMORSE OF CHRISTIANS IN HELL

The greatest torment the damned will have to suffer in hell will be from themselves; from their own remorse of conscience. Their worm dieth not. Alas, what a cruel worm will it be to Christians who are lost in hell, to remember for what trifles they have damned their souls!

I.

The greatest torment the damned will have to suffer in hell will be from themselves; from their own remorse of conscience. Their worm dieth not. Alas, what a cruel worm will it be to Christians who are lost in hell, to remember for what trifles they have damned their souls! Have we, then, they will say, for such trifling, transitory, and poisonous gratifications, lost Heaven and God for ever and condemned ourselves to this prison of eternal torments? We had the happiness of being of the true Faith; but, forsaking God, we led miserable lives, to be succeeded by another life still more miserable in this pool of fire! God favored us with so many lights, so many means of salvation, and we miserably chose to damn ourselves!

O my Jesus, thus should I now have been bewailing my misery in hell if Thou hadst let me die when I was in sin. I thank thee for the mercies Thou hast shown me and detest all the sins that I have committed against Thee. Had I been in hell, I could no longer have loved Thee; but since I can still love Thee, I desire to love Thee with all my heart. I love Thee, my God, my Love, my All!

What does our past life appear at present but as a dream, a moment? But what will a life on earth of forty or fifty years appear to the damned, when, after hundreds and thousands of millions of years have passed away, they find that their eternity is only commencing?

How will those miserable pleasures for which they have sacrificed their salvation appear to them then? They will say: "Have we, then, for these accursed gratifications, which were scarcely tasted before they were ended, have we condemned ourselves to burn forever in this furnace of fire, abandoned by all, and for all eternity?"

II.

Another subject of remorse will be the thought of the little they were required to do in order to be saved. They will say: "Had we pardoned those injuries; had we overcome that human respect, had we avoided those occasions, we should not have now been lost."

It would not have cost us much to avoid those conversations; to deprive ourselves of those accursed gratifications; to yield that point of honor? Whatever it would have cost us, we should have been willing to do everything to obtain salvation; but we were not willing, and now there is no remedy for our eternal ruin. Had we frequented the Sacraments; had we not neglected Meditation; had we recommended ourselves to God, we should not have fallen into sin. We frequently proposed to do this, but we did it not. We sometimes began a good course, but we did not persevere in it, and hence we are lost forever!

O God of my soul, how many times have I promised to love Thee, and have again turned my back upon Thee? Oh, by that love with which Thou didst die for me on the Cross, grant me sorrow for my sins, grant me grace to love Thee, and ever to have recourse to Thee in the time of temptation!

Spiritual Reading

PRAYER

SECOND PRELIMINARY PROPOSITION.

GOD GIVES TO ALL MEN THE GRACES NECESSARY FOR SALVATION WHEREBY ONE MAY BE SAVED THAT CORRESPONDS WITH THEM.

If, then, God wills all to be saved, it follows that He gives to all that grace and those aids which are necessary for the attainment of salvation, otherwise it could never be said that He has a true will to save all. The effect of God's antecedent will, says St. Thomas, by which He wills the salvation of all men, is "that order of nature the purpose of which is our salvation, and likewise those things which conduce to that end, and which are offered to all in common, whether by nature or by grace." It is certain, in contradiction to the blasphemies of Luther and Calvin, that God does not impose a law that is impossible to be observed. On the other hand, it is certain, that without the assistance of grace the observance of the law is impossible, as Innocent I declared against the Pelagians when he said: "It is certain that as we overcome by the aid of God, so without His aid we must be overcome." Pope Celestine declared the same thing. Therefore if God gives to all men a law they can keep, it follows that He also gives to all men the grace necessary to observe it, whether immediately, or mediately by means of Prayer, as the Council of Trent has most clearly defined: "God does not command impossibilities; but by commanding He admonishes you both to do what you can and to ask for that which is beyond your power, and by His help enables you to do it." Otherwise, if God refused us both the proximate and remote grace to enable us to fulfil the law, either the law would have been given in vain, or sin would be necessary, and if necessary would be no longer sin, as we shall presently prove at some length.

1.--Teaching of the Fathers of the Greek Church.

And this is the general opinion of the Greek Fathers:

St. Cyril of Alexandria says: "But if a man endowed as others, and equally with them, with the gifts of Divine grace, has fallen by his own free will, how shall Christ be said not to have preserved even him, since He delivered the man inasmuch as He gave him the aids to avoid sin?" How, says the Saint, can that sinner blame Jesus Christ? St. John Chrysostom asks: "How is it that some are vessels of wrath, others vessels of mercy?" And he answers, "Because of each person's free will; for, since God is very good, He manifests equal kindness to all." Then, speaking of Pharaoh, whose heart is said in Scripture to have been hardened, he adds: "If Pharaoh was not saved, it must all be attributed to his will, since no less was given to him than to those who were saved." And in another place, speaking of the petition of the mother of the sons of Zebedee, on the words It is not mine to give (Matthew xx. 23), he observes: "By this Christ wished to show that it was not simply his to give, but that it also belonged to the combatants to take; for if it depended only on Him, all men would be saved."

St. Isidore of Pelusium: "For God wills seriously, and in all ways, to assist those who are wallowing in vice, that He may deprive them of all excuse."

St. Cyril of Jerusalem: "God has opened the gate of eternal life, so that, as far as He is concerned, all may gain it without anything to hinder them."

But the doctrine of these Greek Fathers does not please Jansenius, who has the temerity to say that they have spoken most imperfectly on the question of Grace: "None have spoken on Grace more imperfectly than the Greeks."

On the question of Grace, then, are we not to follow the teaching of the Greek Fathers, who were the first masters and columns of the Church? But perhaps the doctrine of the Greeks, especially in this important matter, was different from that of the Latin Church? On the very contrary, it is certain that the true doctrine of Faith came from the Greek to the Latin Church; so that, as St. Augustine said, when writing against Julian, who opposed to him the authority of the Greek Fathers, there can be no doubt that the Faith of the Latins is the same as that of the Greeks. Whom, then, are we to follow? Shall we follow Jansenius, whose errors have already been condemned as heretical by the Church; who had the temerity to say that even the just have not the grace requisite to enable them to keep certain precepts; and that man acquires merits and demerits, even though he acts through necessity, provided he is not forced by violence? These, and other errors as well, spring from his most false system.

2.--Teaching of the Fathers of the Latin Church.

But since the Greek Fathers do not satisfy Jansenius, let us see what the Latins say on this subject. They in no wise differ from the Greeks.

St. Jerome says: "Man can do no good work without God, Who, in giving free will, did not refuse His grace to aid every single work." Mark the words, "did not refuse His grace for every single work." St. Ambrose: "He would never come and knock at the door unless He wished to enter; it is our fault that He does not always enter." St. Leo: "Justly does He insist on the command, since He furnishes beforehand aid to keep it." St. Hilary: "Now the grace of justification has abounded through one gift to all men." Innocent I: "He gives to man daily remedies; and unless we put confidence in them and depend upon them we shall never be able to overcome human errors."

St. Augustine: "It is not imputed to you as a sin that you are unwillingly ignorant, but that you neglect to learn that of which you are ignorant. Nor is it imputed as a sin that you do not bind up your wounded limbs, but (mark this) that you despise Him Who is willing to cure you. These are your own sins; for no man is deprived of the knowledge of how to seek with benefit to himself." In another place: "Therefore if the soul is ignorant what it is to do, it proceeds from this, that it has not yet learned; but it will receive this knowledge if it has made a good use of what it has already received; for it has received this that it can piously and diligently seek, if it will." Mark the words: "it has received power to seek piously and diligently." So that everyone receives at least the remote grace to seek; and if he makes good use of this, he will receive the proximate grace to perform that which at first he could not do. St. Augustine founds all this on the principle that no man sins in doing that which he cannot help; therefore, if a man sins in anything, he sins in that he might have avoided it by the grace of God, which is wanting to no man: "Who sins in that which cannot in any way be avoided? But a man does sin, therefore it might have been avoided." "But only by His aid, Who cannot be deceived," says the Saint in another place--an evident reason, which makes it clear (as we shall show when we speak of the sin of the obstinate) that if the grace necessary to observe the Commandments were wanting, there would be no sin.

St. Thomas teaches the same in several places. In one place, in explaining the text, Who wills all men to be saved (1 Timothy ii. 4), he says, "and therefore grace is wanting to no man, but (as far as God is concerned) is communicated to all, as the sun is present even to the eyes of the blind." So that as the sun sheds its light upon all, and only those are deprived of it who voluntarily blind themselves to its rays, so God communicates to all men grace to observe the Law; and men are lost simply because they will not avail themselves of it. In another place: "It belongs to Divine Providence to provide all men with what is necessary to salvation, if only there be no impediment on man's part." If, then, God gives all men the graces necessary for salvation, and if actual grace is necessary to overcome temptations, and to observe the Commandments, we must necessarily conclude that He gives all men either immediately or mediately, actual grace to do good; so that no further grace is necessary to enable them to put in practice the means (such as Prayer) of obtaining actual proximate grace. In another place, on the words of St. John's Gospel, No man cometh to me, etc. (John vi. 44), he says: "If the heart of man be not lifted up, it is from no defect on the part of Him Who draws it, Who as far as He is concerned, never fails; but from an impediment caused by him who is being drawn."

Scotus says the same: "God wills to save all men, so far as rests with Him, and with His antecedent will, by which He has given them the ordinary gifts necessary to salvation." The Council of Cologne (1536) says: "Although no one is converted except he is drawn by the Father, yet let no one pretend to excuse himself on the plea of not being drawn. He stands at the gate and knocks by the internal and the external word."

3.--Testimony of Holy Scripture.

Nor did the Fathers speak without warrant of the Holy Scriptures; God in several places most clearly assures us that He does not neglect to assist us with His grace, if we are willing to avail ourselves of it either for perseverance, if we are in a state of justification, or for conversion, if we are in sin.

I stand at the gate and knock; if any man shall hear my voice and open to me the door, I will come in to him (Apocalypse 20). Bellarmine reasons well on this text that our Lord Who knows that man cannot open without His grace, would knock in vain at the door of his heart, unless He had first conferred on him the grace to open when he will. This is exactly what St. Thomas teaches in explaining the text; he says that God gives everyone the grace necessary for salvation, that he may correspond to it if he will: "God by His most liberal will gives grace to everyone that prepares himself: Behold I stand at the door and knock. And therefore, the grace of God is wanting to no one but, "as far as in it lies, communicates itself to all men." In another place he says: "It pertains to God's Providence to provide everyone with what is necessary to salvation." Yes, says St. Augustine, "For He Who comes and knocks at the door always wishes to enter; it is through us that He does not always go in, nor always remain."

What is there that I ought to do more to my vineyard that I have not done to it? Was it that I expected that it should bring forth grapes; and it hath brought forth wild grapes? (Isaiah v. 4). Bellarmine says on these words: "If He had not given the power to bring forth grapes, how could God say I expected? And if God had not given to all men the grace necessary for salvation, He could not have said to the Jews, What is there that I ought to have done more? for they could have answered that if they had not yielded fruit, it was for lack of necessary assistance. Bellarmine says the same on the words of our Lord: How often would I have gathered together thy children, and thou wouldst not? (Matthew xxiii. 37). "How did He wish to be sought for by the unwilling, if He does not help them that they may be able to will."

We have received thy mercy, O God, in the midst of thy temple (Psalm xlvii. 10). On this St. Bernard observes: "Mercy is in the midst of the temple, not in any hole or corner, because there is no acceptance of persons with God (Romans 11); it is placed in public, it is offered to all, and no one is without it, except he who refuses it."

Or despisest thou the riches of his goodness? Knowest thou not that the benignity of God leadeth thee to penance? (Romans ii. 4). You see that it is through his own malice that the sinner is not converted, because he despises the riches of the Divine Goodness, which calls him, and never ceases to move him to conversion by God's grace. God hates sin, but at the same time never ceases to love the sinful soul while it remains on earth, and always gives it the assistance it requires for salvation: But thou sparest all because they are thine, O Lord, who lovest souls (Wisdom xi. 27). Hence we see, says Bellarmine, that God does not refuse grace to resist temptations to any sinner, however obstinate and blinded he may be: "Assistance to avoid new sin is always at hand for all men, either immediately or mediately (i.e. by means of Prayer), so that they may ask further aid from God, by the help of which they will avoid sin." Here we may quote what God says by Ezechiel: As I live, saith the Lord God, I desire not the death of the wicked, but that the wicked turn from his way and live (Ezechiel xxxiii. 11). St. Peter says the same: He beareth patiently for your sakes, not willing that any should perish, but that all should return to penance (2 Peter 9). If, therefore, God wishes that all should actually be converted, it must necessarily be held that He gives to all the grace which they need for actual conversion.

Evening Meditation

THE PRACTICE OF THE LOVE OF JESUS CHRIST

"Charity endureth all things"

HE THAT LOVES JESUS CHRIST WITH A STRONG LOVE DOES NOT CEASE TO LOVE HIM IN THE MIDST OF TEMPTATIONS AND DESOLATIONS

I.

It is an excellent practice also, in the moment of temptation, to make the Sign of the Cross on the forehead and breast. It is also of great service to reveal the temptation to our spiritual director. St. Philip Neri used to say that a temptation made known is half-conquered. Here it will be well to remark, what is unanimously admitted by all Theologians, even of the rigorist school, that persons who have during a considerable period of time been leading virtuous lives, and living habitually in the fear of God, whenever they are in doubt, and are not certain whether they have given consent to a grievous sin, ought to be perfectly assured that they have not lost the Divine grace; for it is morally impossible that the will, confirmed in her good purposes for a considerable lapse of time, should on a sudden undergo such a total change as at once to consent to a mortal sin without clearly knowing it. The reason of it is that mortal sin is so horrible a monster that it cannot possibly enter a soul by which it has long been held in abhorrence, without her being fully aware of it. We have proved this at length in our Moral Theology. St. Teresa says: No one is lost without knowing it; and no one is deceived without the will to be deceived.

II.

Wherefore, with regard to certain souls of delicate conscience, and solidly rooted in virtue, but at the same time timid and molested with temptations (especially if they be against faith or chastity), the director will find it sometimes expedient to forbid them to reveal or mention their temptations at all, for if they have to mention them, they are led to consider how such thoughts got into their minds, and whether they paused to dispute with them, or took any complacency in them, or gave any consent to them; and so, by this too great reflection, those evil imaginations make a still deeper impression on their minds and disturb them the more. And I find that St. Jane de Chantal acted precisely in this manner. She relates of herself that she was for several years assailed by the most violent storms of temptation, but had never spoken of them in confession, since she was not conscious of ever having yielded to them; and in this she had only followed faithfully the rule received from her director. She says: "I never had a full conviction of having consented"; these words give us to understand that the temptations did produce in her some agitation from scruples; but in spite of these she resumed her tranquility on the strength of the obedience imposed by her confessor, not to confess similar doubts. With this exception, it will be generally found an admirable means of quelling the violence of temptations to lay them open to our director, as we have said above.

WEDNESDAY-EIGHTH WEEK AFTER PENTECOST

CHRISTIANS IN HELL KNOW THEY HAVE BEEN GIVEN ALL THE GRACES NECESSARY FOR SALVATION

What cruel swords of anguish and remorse for the damned will the lights, the calls, and all the other graces be which they received from God to repent and be saved! They will say: "We might have become saints and happy for ever in Heaven, but now, alas, we must be forever miserable in hell!"

I.

What cruel swords of anguish for the damned will the lights, the calls, and all the other graces be which they received from God! They will say: "We might have been saints and happy for ever in Heaven; but now we must be forever miserable in hell!"

The greatest torment of the damned will be to reflect that they are lost through their own fault, their own will, notwithstanding that Jesus Christ died to save them. "God," they will say, "gave His life for our salvation and we fools, of our own free will, have cast ourselves into this furnace of fire to burn forever! Heaven lost! God lost! Ourselves eternally miserable!"

Such will be the eternal lamentations of the damned.

O my God, despised and forsaken by me, grant that I may find Thee whilst time yet remains for me to repent. For this end, grant me, O my Redeemer, to share in that sorrow which overwhelmed Thee in the Garden of Gethsemani for my sins. I am sorry above every evil for having offended Thee. Receive me into Thy favor, O Jesus, now that I promise to love Thee, and to love no other but Thee.

Represent to yourself a sick man in great pain and suffering, who has none to pity him, but many to load him with injuries, to reproach him with his disorders, and to ill-treat him with great rage. The damned are treated far worse. They suffer all kinds of torments, without the slightest compassion from anyone. But, at least, cannot the damned love God Who justly punishes them? Ah, no; while they know that God is sovereignly amiable, they are constrained to hate Him. This is hell, not to be able to love the Sovereign Good, which is God.

If the damned could resign themselves to the Divine will, as pious souls in their sufferings are now able to do, hell would no longer be hell. But no; the damned shall rage like wild beasts under the scourge of Divine justice, and their rage shall serve but to increase their torments. If, then, O Jesus, I were in hell, I should be incapable of loving Thee, but have to hate Thee forever! And what evil hast Thou done me, for which I should hate Thee? Thou hast created me, Thou hast died for me; Thou hast bestowed upon me many special graces. These are the evils which Thou hast done me. Chastise me as Thou pleasest, but do not deprive me of the power of loving Thee. I love Thee, my Jesus, and I desire ever to love Thee.

II.

Consider the terror of the soul on its first entrance into hell: "Am I, then, really damned?" it will ask, "or is it all a hideous dream?" It will think whether there can be any remedy; but will find that there can be no remedy—none, for all eternity!

Millions of ages will pass away, as many ages as there are drops of water in the sea, or grains of sand on the earth, or leaves upon the trees; and hell will still be hell, eternity will still be only commencing!

At least, may not the damned be able to flatter themselves, saying: "Who knows but that hell may one day come to an end?" No, for in hell there can be no who knows? The damned will be most certain that all the torments which they suffer every moment will continue throughout eternity. O my God, do men believe in hell and yet commit sin?

All the greater will the torment of those be who often meditated on hell, and yet by sin condemned themselves to its torments. Ah, let us not lose time, but let us renounce sin and give ourselves to Jesus Christ! All that we can do to avoid hell will be but little. Let us be persuaded of this and tremble; he that trembles not will not be saved.

O my Jesus, Thy Precious Blood, Thy Death, are my hope! Let others abandon me, but do not Thou abandon me! I see that Thou hast not as yet abandoned me, since Thou still invites me to pardon, if I will but repent of my sins, and Thou still offers me Thy grace and Thy love if I will but love Thee. Yes, my Jesus, my Life, my Treasure, my Love, I will ever bewail my offences against Thee, and will ever love Thee with my whole heart. My God, if I have lost Thee, I will lose Thee no more. Tell me what Thou requires of me, and I will endeavor to comply with Thy will in all things; grant that I may live and die in Thy grace, and then dispose of me as Thou pleases. O Mary, my hope, be thou my protectress, and suffer me never again to lose my God.

Spiritual Reading

PRAYER

GOD GIVES THE GRACE OF SALVATION EVEN TO OBSTINATE SINNERS.

I know well that there are theologians who maintain that God refuses to certain obstinate sinners even sufficient grace. And, among others, they avail themselves of a passage of St. Thomas which says: "But although they who are in sin cannot through their own power help putting or interposing an obstacle to grace, unless they are aided by antecedent grace, as we have shown; nevertheless, this also is imputed to them as a sin, because this defect is left in them from previous sin—as a drunken man is not excused from murder committed in that drunkenness which was incurred by his own fault. Besides, although he who is in sin has it not in his own power that he may altogether avoid sin, yet he has power at this present moment to avoid this or that sin, as has been said; so that whatever he commits, he commits voluntarily, and therefore it is properly imputed to him as sin." From this they gather that St. Thomas intends to say that sinners can indeed avoid particular sins, but not all sins; because in punishment for sins previously committed, they are deprived of all actual grace.

But we answer that here St. Thomas is not speaking at all of actual, but of habitual or sanctifying grace, without which the sinner cannot keep himself long from falling into new sins, as he teaches in several places. So that, in the first place, the intention of St. Thomas is not to prove that some sinners are deprived of all actual grace, and therefore, being unable to avoid all sin, they fall, and are all the same worthy of punishment; but his intention is to prove against the Pelagians that a man who remains without sanctifying grace cannot abstain from sinning. And this is the teaching of the Thomists in their comments on this passage.

And it is impossible that the holy Doctor could have meant otherwise, since he elsewhere teaches that, on the one hand, God's grace is never wanting to any one; and, on the other hand, that there is no sinner so lost and abandoned by grace as not to be able to lay aside his obstinacy, and to unite himself to the will of God, which he certainly could not do without the assistance of grace: "During this life there is no man who cannot lay aside obstinacy of mind, and so conform to the Divine will."

In another place St. Thomas observes, on the text of St. Paul, Who will have all men to be saved: "Therefore the grace of God is wanting to no man; but, as far as it is concerned, it communicates itself to all."

Cardinal Gotti, confuting those who say that God keeps ready at hand the aids necessary for salvation, but as a matter of fact does not give them to all, asks: Of what use would it be to a sick man if the physician only kept the remedies ready, and then would not apply them? Then he concludes (quite to the point of our argument) that we must necessarily say: "God not only offers, but also confers on every individual, even on infidels and hardened sinners, help sufficient to observe the Commandments, whether it be proximate or remote."

Bellarmine makes a sound distinction on this point, and says that for avoiding fresh sins every sinner has at all times sufficient assistance, at least mediately: "The necessary and sufficient assistance for the avoidance of sin is given by God's goodness to all men at all times, either immediately or mediately ... We say or mediately because it is certain that some men have not that help by which they can immediately avoid sin, but yet they have the help which enables them to obtain from God greater safeguards, by the assistance of which they will avoid sin." But as to the grace of conversion, he says that this is not given at every single moment to the sinner; but that no one will be ever so far left to himself "as to be surely and absolutely deprived of God's help through all this life, so as to have no hope of salvation."

And so say the theologians who follow St. Thomas. Thus Soto: "I am absolutely certain, and I believe that all the holy Doctors who are worthy of the name were always most positive, that no one was ever deserted by God in this mortal life." And the reason is evident; for if the sinner were quite abandoned by grace, either his sins afterwards committed could no longer be imputed to him, or he would be under an obligation to do that which he had no power to do; but it is a positive rule of St. Augustine that there is never a sin in that which cannot be avoided: "No one sins in that which can by no means be avoided." This is in harmony with the teaching of the Apostle: But God is faithful who will not suffer you to be tempted above that which you are able; but will also make with temptation issue, that you may be able to bear it (1 Corinthians x. 13). And Primasius explains: "God will so order the issue that we shall be able to endure," that is, in temptation He will strengthen you with the help of His grace, so that you may be able to bear it. St. Augustine and St. Thomas go so far as to say that God would be unjust and cruel if He obliged any one to a command which he could not keep. St. Augustine says: "It is the deepest injustice to reckon any one guilty of sin for not doing that which he could not do." And St. Thomas: "God is not crueler than man; but it is reckoned cruelty in a man to oblige a person by law to do that which he cannot fulfil; therefore we must by no means imagine this of God." "It is, however, different," he says, "when it is through his own neglect that he has not the grace to be able to keep the Commandments." This is the case when a man neglects to avail himself of the remote grace of Prayer, in order to obtain the proximate grace to enable him to keep the law, as the Council of Trent teaches: "God does not command impossibilities but by commanding admonishes you to do what you can, and to ask for that which is beyond your power, and by His help enables you to do it."

Other Fathers have taught the same doctrine. So St. Jerome: "We are not forced by necessity to be either virtuous or vicious; for where there is necessity, there is neither condemnation nor crown." Tertullian: "For a law would not be given to him who had it not in his power to observe it duly." Marcus the Hermit: "Hidden grace assists us; but it depends on us to do or not to do according to our strength." So also St. Irenaeus, St. Cyril of Alexandria, St. Chrysostom, and others.

From all this several Theologians conclude that to say that God refuses to any one sufficient help to enable him to keep the Commandments would be contrary to the Faith, because in that case God would oblige us to impossibilities. So F. Nunez teaches: "God never refused aid sufficient to keep the Commandments, otherwise they could not be in any way fulfilled; and thus we should have the heresy of Luther back again, that God has obliged men to impossibilities." And in another place: "It is of Faith (so that the opposite doctrine is a manifest heresy) that every man, while he is alive, can do penance for his sins." And Father Ledesma: "It is a certain truth of Faith that that is not sin which is not in the free power of man."

Nor is it right to say that if the sinner is deprived of grace, he is deprived of it by his own fault and therefore though he is deprived of grace, yet he sins. For Cardinal Gotti well replies to this that God can justly punish the sinner for his previous faults, but not for future transgressions of precepts which he is no longer able to fulfil. If a servant, he says, were sent to a place, and if he, through his own fault, fell into a pit, his master might punish him for his carelessness in falling, and even for his subsequent disobedience, if means, such as a rope or ladder, were given him to get out of the pit, and he would not avail himself of them. But supposing that his master did not help him to get out, he would be a tyrant if he ordered him to proceed and punished him for not proceeding. Hence he concludes: "When, therefore, a man has by sin fallen into the ditch, and becomes unable to proceed on his way to eternal life, though God may punish him for this fault, and also if he refuses the offer of grace to enable him to proceed; yet if God chose to leave him to his own weakness, He cannot without injustice oblige him to proceed on his way, or punish him for not proceeding."

Moreover, our opponents adduce many texts of Scripture where this abandonment is apparently expressed: Blind the heart of this people ... lest they see with their eyes ... and be converted, and I heal them (Isaiah vi. 10). We would have cured Babylon, but she is not healed; let us forsake her (Jeremiah. li. 9). Add thou iniquity upon their iniquity, and let them not come into thy justice (Psalm lxviii. 28). For this cause God delivered them up to shameful affections. He hath mercy on whom he will; and whom he will he hardeneth (Romans i. 26; ix. 18), and others similar. But we can answer all these objections, and it is the answer usually given, that in the Holy Scriptures God is often said to do what He only permits (that is, does not prevent); so that if we would not blaspheme with Calvin, and say that God positively destines and determines some persons to sin, we must say that God permits some sinners, in penalty of their faults, to be, on the one hand, assailed by vehement temptations (which is the evil from which we pray God to deliver us when we say Lead us not into temptation) (Matthew vi. 13), and, on the other hand, that they remain morally abandoned in their sin. Thus it is their conversion, and the resistance they make to temptation, although neither impossible nor desperate, is yet, through their faults and bad habits, very difficult; for, in such a state of laxity, they have only very rare and weak desires and attempts to resist their bad habits, and to regain the way of salvation. And this is the imperfect obstinacy of the hardened sinner which St. Thomas describes: "He is hardened who cannot easily co-operate in his escape from sin; and this is imperfect obstinacy, because a man may be obstinate in this life if he has a will so fixed upon sin that no impulses towards good arise, except very weak ones." On the one hand the mind is obscured, the will is hardened against God's inspirations, and attached to the pleasures of sense, so as to despise and feel disgust for spiritual things, and the sensual passions and appetites reign in the soul through the bad habits that have been acquired. While on the other hand the illuminations and the callings of God are, by its own fault, rendered scarcely efficacious to move the soul, which has so despised them, and made so bad a use of them that it even feels a certain aversion towards them because it does not want to be disturbed in its sensual gratifications. All these things constitute moral abandonment; and when a sinner has once fallen into it, it is only with the utmost difficulty that he can escape from his miserable state and bring himself to live a well-regulated life.

In order to escape and pass at once from such a miserable state to a state of salvation, a great and extraordinary grace would be requisite; but God seldom confers such a grace on these obstinate sinners. To some He gives it, says St. Thomas, and chooses them for vessels of Mercy, as the Apostle calls them, in order to make known His Goodness; but to others He justly refuses it, and leaves them in their unhappy state, in order to show forth His Justice and Power: "Sometimes," says the Angel of the Schools, "out of the abundance of His Goodness He gives His assistance even to those who put a hindrance in the way of His grace, and converts them ... And just as He does not enlighten all the blind, nor cure all the sick, so neither does He assist all who place an impediment to His grace, so as to convert them ... This is what the Apostle means when He says that God, to show forth his anger, and to make his power known, endured with much patience the vessels of wrath, fitted for destruction, that he might show the riches of his glory upon the vessels of mercy, which he hath prepared unto glory (Romans ix. 22, 23)." Then he adds: "But since out of the number of those who are involved in the same sins there are some to whom God gives the grace of conversion, while others He endures, or allows to follow the ordinary course we are not to inquire the reason why He converts some and not others. For the Apostle says: Has not the potter power over the clay, to make of the same mass one vessel to honor, and another to dishonor? (Romans ix. 21)."

To bring this point to a conclusion—we do not deny that there is such a thing as the moral abandonment of some obstinate sinners, so that their conversion is morally impossible, that is to say, very difficult. And this concession is abundantly sufficient for the laudable object which our opponents have in defending their opinion, which is to restrain evil-doers, and to induce them to enter into themselves before they come to fall into such a deplorable state. But then it is cruelty, as Petrocorensis well says, to take from them all hope, and entirely to shut against them the way of salvation, by the doctrine that they have fallen into so complete an abandonment as to be deprived of all actual grace to enable them to avoid fresh sins, and to be converted. Even sinners have the means of

Prayer, a grace not refused to any man while he lives, as we shall prove, whereby they can afterwards obtain abundant help for placing themselves in a state of salvation. The fear of total abandonment would not only lead them to despair, but also to give themselves up more completely to their vices, in the belief that they were altogether destitute of grace, and that they had no hope left of escaping eternal damnation.

Evening Meditation

THE PRACTICE OF THE LOVE OF JESUS CHRIST

"Charity endureth all things"

HE THAT LOVES JESUS CHRIST WITH A STRONG LOVE DOES NOT CEASE TO LOVE HIM IN THE MIDST OF TEMPTATIONS AND DESOLATIONS

I.

But, I repeat, the most efficacious and the most necessary of all remedies against temptation, is that remedy of remedies, namely to pray to God for help, and to continue praying as long as the temptation continues. Almighty God will frequently have decreed success, not to the first prayer, but to the second, third, or fourth. In short, we must be thoroughly persuaded that all our welfare depends on prayer: our change of life depends on prayer; our victory over temptations depends on prayer; on prayer depends on our obtaining Divine love, together with perfection, perseverance, and eternal salvation. There may be some who, after the perusal of my spiritual works, will accuse me of tediousness in so often recommending the importance and necessity of having continual recourse to God by prayer. But I seem to myself to have said not too much but far too little. I know that day and night we are all assailed with temptations from the infernal powers, and that Satan lets slip no occasion of causing us to fall. I know that, without the Divine help, we have not strength to repel the assaults of the devils; and that therefore the Apostle exhorts us to put on the armor of God: Put you on the armor of God, that you may be able to stand against the deceits of the devil. For our wrestling is not against flesh and blood; but against principalities and powers, against the rulers of the world of this darkness (Ephesians vi. 11, 12). And what is this armor with which St. Paul warns us to clothe ourselves in order to conquer our enemies? Behold in what it consists: By all prayer and supplication, praying at all times in the spirit, and in the same watching with all instance (Ephesians vi. 18). This armor is constant and fervent prayer to God, that He may help us to gain the victory. I know, moreover, that in every page of the Holy Scriptures, both in the Old and New Testament, we are repeatedly admonished to pray: Call upon me, and I will deliver thee (Psalm xlix. 15). Cry to me and I will hear thee (Jeremiah xxxiii.

3). We ought always to pray and not to faint (Luke xviii. 1). Ask, and you shall receive (Matt. vii. 7). Watch and pray (Mark xiii. 33). Pray without ceasing (1 Thessalonians v. 17). So that I think, far from having spoken too much on prayer, I have not said enough.

II.

I would urge it on all preachers to recommend nothing so much to the people as prayer; on confessors, to insist on nothing so earnestly with their penitents as prayer; on spiritual writers, to treat of no subject more copiously than on prayer. But it is a source of grief to my heart, and it seems to me a chastisement of our sins, that so many preachers, confessors, and authors speak so little of prayer. There is no doubt that sermons, meditations, communions, and mortifications are great helps in the spiritual life; but if we fail to call upon God by prayer in the moment of temptation, we shall fall, in spite of all the sermons, meditations, communions, penances, and virtuous resolutions. If, then, we really wish to be saved, let us aways pray, and commend ourselves to Jesus Christ, and most of all when we are tempted; and let us not only pray for the grace of holy perseverance, but at the same time for the grace to pray always. Let us, likewise, take care to recommend ourselves to the Divine Mother, who, as St. Bernard says, is the dispenser of graces: "Let us seek for graces, and let us seek them through Mary." For the same Saint assures us that it is the will of God, that not a single grace should be dealt to us except through the hands of Mary: "God has willed us to receive nothing that has not passed through the hands of Mary."

O Jesus, my Redeemer, I trust in Thy Blood, that Thou has forgiven me all my offences against Thee; and I fondly hope to come one day to bless Thee for it eternally in Heaven: The mercies of the Lord I will sing forever. I plainly see now that I have over and over again fallen in times past from the want of entreating Thee for holy perseverance. I earnestly beg Thee at this present moment to grant me perseverance: Never suffer me to be separated from Thee. And I propose to make this prayer to Thee always; but especially when I am tempted to offend Thee. I indeed make this resolution and promise; but what will it profit me thus to resolve and promise if Thou dost not give me the grace to run and cast myself at Thy feet? By the merits, then, of Thy Sacred Passion, oh, grant me this grace, in all my necessities to have recourse to Thee. O Mary, my Queen and my Mother, I beseech thee, by thy tender love for Jesus Christ, to procure me the grace of always fleeing for succor, as long as I live, to thy blessed Son and to thee.

THURSDAY--EIGHTH WEEK AFTER PENTECOST

Morning Meditation
OUR INGRATITUDE TOWARDS JESUS CHRIST

O ye sons of men, why do you not love Jesus Christ? Tell me, what more could He have done to make you love Him? If the vilest of mankind had suffered for us the torments Jesus Christ suffered, could we help giving him all our affection and showing him our gratitude?

I.

O my Jesus, what greater proof of Thy love couldst Thou have given me, than the sacrificing of Thy life upon the disgraceful gibbet of the Cross, to make satisfaction for my sins, and to conduct me with Thee into Paradise?

He humbled himself, becoming obedient unto death, even to the death of the cross (Philippians ii. 8). The Son of God, therefore, for the love of man, obedient to His Eternal Father, Whose will it was that He should die for our salvation, humbled Himself to die, and to die on a Cross! And are there men to be found who believe this and love not such a God!

O Jesus, how much has it cost Thee to make me understand Thy burning love for me; and I have basely repaid Thee with ingratitude. Oh, accept me now and suffer me to love Thee, since I will no more abuse Thy love. I love Thee, my Sovereign Good, and desire to love Thee forever. Remind me continually of the pains Thou didst suffer for me, that I may never forget the love I owe Thee.

O God, the Passion of Jesus Christ is spoken of, and is listened to as though it were a fable, or story about the sufferings and death of someone unknown to us, or something that did not concern us at all!

O ye sons of men, why do ye not love Jesus Christ? Tell me, what more could our Blessed Redeemer have done to make us love Him than to die in the midst of humiliations and torments?

If the vilest of mankind had suffered for us the torments Jesus Christ suffered, could we help giving him our affection and showing him our gratitude?

But, my Jesus, why do I speak of the ingratitude of others and not rather of my own? What has hitherto been my conduct towards Thee? Alas, I have repaid Thy love only with offences against Thee!

Pardon me, O Jesus! From this day, I desire to love Thee, and to love Thee much. I should be too ungrateful, if, after so many favors and mercies, I loved Thee but little.

II.

Let us reflect that this Man of Sorrows, nailed to the disgraceful wood of the Cross, is our true God, and suffers and dies there for no other motive but for love of us.

Do we, then, believe that Jesus Christ crucified is our God, and really dies for us, and can we love aught but Jesus crucified?

O beautiful flames of love which consumed the life of my Savior on Calvary, come and consume in me all worldly affections! Cause me ever to burn with love for such a God, Who was pleased to die and to sacrifice Himself entirely for the love of me.

What a spectacle for the Angels of Heaven to behold the Divine Word fastened to a gibbet, and dying for the salvation of us, His miserable creatures!

O my Savior, Thou hast not refused me Thy Blood and Thy life, and shall I refuse Thee the affection of my heart? Shall I refuse Thee anything Thou askest of me? No, my Jesus! Thou hast given Thy whole Self to me, and I will give my whole self without reserve to Thee.

Spiritual Reading

PRAYER

GOD GIVES TO ALL MEN THE GRACE TO PRAY.

We have proved that God wishes all men to be saved, and that, as far as He is concerned, He gives to all the graces necessary for their salvation. We say, moreover, that all men have given to them the grace to enable them actually to pray without needing a further grace, and by Prayer to obtain all further aid necessary for the observance of the Commandments and for salvation. But it must be remarked that when we say, "without needing a further grace," we do not mean that the common grace gives the power of Prayer without the aid of assisting grace, since, to exercise any act of piety, besides the exciting grace, there is undoubtedly required the assisting or co-operating grace. But we mean that the common grace gives every man the power of actual Prayer, without a further preventing grace to determine, physically or morally, the will of man to exercise the act of Prayer. We will therefore:

First mention the famous Theologians who teach this doctrine as certain;

Secondly, examine the proofs of this doctrine

(a) from Scripture,

(b) the Council of Trent,

(c) and the Fathers;

Thirdly, examine the theological arguments which prove it.

I.-THE FAMOUS THEOLOGIANS WHO TEACH THIS DOCTRINE.

It is held by Isambert, Cardinal du Perron, Alphonsus le Moyne, and others whom we shall presently quote, and especially by Honoratus Tourneley, who treats the matter fully. All these authors prove that every man, by means of the ordinary sufficient grace alone, can actually pray without need of further aid, and by Prayer can obtain all the graces requisite for the performance of the most difficult things.

It was also held by Cardinal Noris, who proves the proposition that man, when the Commandment urges, can pray if he will; and he proves it in this way: Assuming that, in order to keep the Commandments and to be saved, Prayer is necessary, as we proved in the beginning when we spoke of the Necessity of Prayer, this learned author says that everyone has the proximate power of Prayer, in order that by Prayer he may obtain the proximate power to do good; and therefore all can pray with only the ordinary grace, without other assistance. Otherwise, he argues, if, to obtain the proximate power for the act of Prayer we require another power, we should still want another power of grace to obtain this power, and so on ad infinitum, and it would no longer be in the power of man to co-operate in his salvation.

The same author held it as certain that in the present state all men have the assistance sine qua non, i.e., ordinary grace, which, without need of further assistance, produces Prayer, by which we can then obtain efficacious grace to enable us to observe the Law. And hence we can easily understand the axiom universally received in the Schools: "Facienti quod in se est, Deus non denegat gratiam." To him who does what in him lies, God does not refuse His grace. That is, to the man who prays, and thus makes good use of the sufficient grace which enables him to do such an easy thing as to pray, God does not refuse the efficacious grace to enable him to execute difficult things.

Thus also, Louis Thomassin, who says that "sufficient grace," to be really sufficient, ought to give a man the proximate and ready power to execute a good act. But if, to perform such an act, another grace--namely, efficacious grace--is needed, and a man has not, at least, mediately, this efficacious grace which is necessary for salvation, how can it be said that the "sufficient grace" gives him this proximate and ready power? But Saint Thomas says: "God does not neglect to do that which is necessary to salvation." It is true, of course, that God is not bound to give us His grace, because what is gratis is not of obligation; but, on the other hand, supposing that He gives us Commandments, He is obliged to give us the assistance necessary for observing them. And as God does oblige us actually to observe every precept whenever it applies, so ought He also actually to supply us (at least mediately or remotely) with the assistance necessary for the observance of the precept, without the necessity of a further grace which is not common to all. Hence Thomassin concludes that to reconcile the proposition that sufficient grace is enough for a man's salvation with the statement that efficacious grace is requisite to observe the whole Law, it is necessary to say that sufficient grace is enough to pray, and to perform similar easy acts, and that by means of these we then obtain efficacious grace to fulfil the difficult acts. And this is without doubt in conformity with the doctrine of St. Augustine, who teaches: "By the very fact that it is most firmly believed that the just and good God does not command impossibilities, we are admonished both what to do in easy things, and in difficult things what to ask for." On this passage Cardinal Noris observes: "Therefore, we are able to do easy or less perfect works without asking God for further help; for which, however, we must pray in more difficult works." Thomassin also brings forward the authority of St. Bonaventure, Scotus, and others on this subject, and says that all these considered sufficient graces to be truly sufficient, whether the will consents to them or not. And this he demonstrates in four parts of his book, adducing the authorities of the Schoolmen for a long series of years beginning from the year 1100.

Habert, Bishop of Vabres and Doctor of the Sorbonne, who was the first to write against Jansenius, says: "We think, first, that sufficient grace has only a contingent or mediate connection with the actual effect of the complete consent... We think, further, that 'sufficient grace' is a grace that disposes for efficacious grace, since from a good use of it God afterwards grants to the created will the grace that performs the complete effect." He had said before that "all Catholic Doctors have professed, and do profess, that a real inward grace is given, which is capable of persuading the will to consent to good, though, on account of the free resistance of the will, it sometimes does not persuade it thus to consent"; and for this doctrine he quotes Gamaches, Duval, Isambert, Perez, Le Moyne, and others. Then he proceeds: "The assistance, therefore, of sufficient grace disposes us for the reception of efficacious grace, and is in some sort efficacious, namely, of an incomplete effect, obtained first remotely, then more nearly, and at last proximately --such as is an Act of Faith, Hope, Love ... and amongst all these, of Prayer. Hence the famous Alphonsus Le Moyne taught that this sufficient grace was the grace of asking or of Prayer, of which St. Augustine so often speaks." So that, according to Habert, the difference between efficacious and sufficient grace is that the former produces its effect completely while the latter produces it either contingently (that is, sometimes, but not always), or mediately (that is, by means of Prayer). Moreover, he says that sufficient grace, according to the good use we make of it, prepares us to obtain efficacious grace; hence he calls sufficient grace " in some sort efficacious" (secundum quid), because of its effect commenced but not completed. Lastly, he says that sufficient grace is the grace of Prayer, of which it is in our power to avail ourselves, as St. Augustine teaches. So that a man has no excuse if he does not do that which he already has sufficient grace to enable him to perform, seeing that without further assistance he has the sufficient grace either to act, or at least obtain more help to enable him to act. And Habert asserts that this was the common doctrine of the Sorbonne.

Charles du Plessis d'Argentre, another Theologian of the Sorbonne, quotes more than a thousand Theologians who teach expressly that with sufficient grace easy works are accomplished, and that a man who makes use of it obtains thereby more abundant assistance for his thorough conversion. And precisely in this sense, as we have already explained, he says the celebrated axiom of the Schools is to be understood: "To those who do what is in their power" (by means of sufficient grace) "God does not deny grace"; that is, more abundant and efficacious grace.

The learned Dionysius Petavius proves at great length that man works with simple sufficient grace; and he even says that it would be monstrous to assert the contrary, and that this is the doctrine not only of Theologians, but also of the Church. Hence, he says, the grace of observing the precepts follows Prayer; and that the gift of Prayer is given by

God at the time when He imposes the precept. So that as the Law is imposed upon all, the gift of Prayer is given to all.

The author of the Theology for the Use of the Seminary of Peterkau says that with sufficient grace alone a " man can act well, and sometimes does act well"; so that "there is nothing to hinder that, of two persons furnished with equal graces, one should perform the easier acts (which very often precede full conversion), the other should not." And this, he says, is in conformity with the doctrine of St. Augustine, and also of St. Thomas and his first disciples, notably Father Bartholomew Medina, who says that sometimes a man is converted with sufficient grace alone. And I find that also Father Louis of Granada asserts this to be the common doctrine of Theologians: "Theologians reckon two kinds of assistance--one sufficient, the other more than sufficient; by the former men are sometimes converted and sometimes refuse to be converted." And he adds: "And Theologians define how universally this assistance is open to men." "Thus," says the Theology of Peterkau, a man can perform some acts of piety, such as pray to God humbly, with the aid of sufficient grace alone, and sometimes actually does perform them, and so prepares himself for further graces." This, it adds, is the order of God's Providence with regard to graces, "that the succeeding should follow the good use of the former." And it concludes that thorough conversion and final perseverance "are infallibly obtained by Prayer, for which the sufficient grace which is given to everyone abundantly suffices..."

Richard of St. Victor similarly teaches that there is a sufficient grace to which a man sometimes consents and which he sometimes resists.

Dominic Soto asks: "Why of two persons whom God is most ready and desirous to convert, one is drawn by grace, and the other is not?" And he answers: "No other reason can be given, except that one consents and co-operates, while the other does not co-operate." ...

Cardinal Gotti in one place of his Theology apparently agrees with us; for when discussing how it is that a man can persevere if he will, when it is not in his power to have the special assistance which is requisite for perseverance, he says that although this special assistance is not in a man's power, "yet it is said to be in a certain sense in a man's power, because he can by the grace of God ask for it and obtain it; and in this way it may be said to be in a man's power to have the assistance necessary for perseverance because it can be obtained by prayer." But to verify the proposition that it is in a man's power to persevere, it is necessary to grant both that he can, without needing any further grace, obtain by Prayer the assistance requisite for perseverance; also, that with only the sufficient grace common to all, without need of any special grace he can actually pray, and by Prayer obtain perseverance; otherwise it could not be said that every man had the grace necessary for perseverance, at least remotely or mediately, by means of Prayer.

But if Cardinal Gotti did not so understand it, at any rate this is what St. Francis de Sales teaches when he says that the grace of actual Prayer is given to everyone who will avail himself of it, and thence concludes that perseverance is in the power of everybody. The Saint says this clearly in his Treatise on the Love of God, where, after proving that constant Prayer is necessary to obtain from God the gift of final perseverance, he adds, that as the gift of Prayer is freely granted to all those who will consent to the heavenly inspirations, it is consequently in our power to persevere.

Cardinal Bellarmine teaches the same thing. He says: "Assistance, then and there sufficient for salvation, is given mediately or immediately to all men ... We say mediately or immediately, because to those who have the use of reason we believe that holy inspirations are given by God, and that by these they have immediately the exciting grace, by which, if they will acquiesce in it, they can be disposed to be justified, and at last to obtain salvation."

Evening Meditation

"Charity endureth all things"

HE THAT LOVES JESUS CHRIST WITH A STRONG LOVE DOES NOT CEASE TO LOVE HIM IN THE MIDST OF TEMPTATIONS AND DESOLATIONS

I.

St. Francis de Sales says: "It is a mistake to estimate devotion by the consolations which we feel. True devotion in the way of God consists in having a determined will to execute all that is pleasing to God." Almighty God is wont to make use of aridities to draw closer to Him His most cherished souls. Attachment to our own inordinate inclinations is the greatest obstacle to true union with God. When, therefore, God intends to draw a soul to His perfect love, He endeavors to detach her from all affection to created goods. Thus His first care is to deprive her of temporal goods, of worldly pleasures, of property, honors, friends, relations, and bodily health; by the like means, that is, of losses, troubles, neglect, bereavements, and infirmities, He extirpates by degrees all earthly attachment, in order that the affections may be set on Him alone.

II.

With a view to produce a longing for spiritual things God regales the soul at first with great consolations, with an abundance of tears and tenderness. She is thus easily weaned from the gratifications of sense, and seeks further to mortify herself with works of penance, fasts, cilices, and disciplines. At this stage the director must keep a check on her, and not allow her to practice mortifications--at least not all those for which she asks permission --because, under the spur of this sensible devotion, a soul might easily ruin her health by indiscretion. It is a subtle artifice of the devil, when he beholds a person giving himself up to God, and receiving the consolations and caresses which God generally gives to beginners, to do his utmost to plunge him into the performance of such immoderate penances as utterly to destroy his health; so that afterwards, because of bodily weakness, he not only gives up the mortifications, but prayer, Communion, and all exercises of devotion, and eventually sinks back into his old way of living. On this account, the director should be very sparing in allowing mortifications to those who are only just entering upon the spiritual life, and who desire to practice bodily mortifications. Let him exhort them to practice rather interior mortification by bearing patiently with affronts and contradictions, by obedience to superiors, by bridling the curiosity to see, to hear, and the like; and let him tell them that, when they have acquired the good habit of practicing these interior mortifications, they will then be sufficiently perfect to proceed to the external. It would be, of course, a serious error to say, as some say, that external mortifications are of little or no use. Without doubt, interior mortification is most requisite for perfection; but it does not follow from this that external mortifications are unnecessary. St. Vincent de Paul declared that the person who did not practice external mortifications would be mortified neither interiorly nor exteriorly. And St. John of the Cross declared that the director who despised external mortifications was unworthy of confidence, even though he should work miracles.

Friday--Eighth Week after Pentecost

Morning Meditation

THE LOVE OF JESUS FOR US DEMANDS OUR LOVE

My soul, consider thy God crucified and dying on Calvary. See how much He suffers, and say to Him: Why, O Jesus, why dost Thou love me so much, and why art Thou so much tormented and afflicted on the Cross? Oh, Thou wouldst be less afflicted didst Thou love me less!

I.

My soul, consider thy God crucified and dying on Calvary. See how much He suffers, and say to Him: Why, O Jesus, why dost Thou love me so much, and why art Thou so much tormented and afflicted on the Cross? Oh, Thou wouldst be less afflicted, didst Thou love me less!

Ah, my dear Redeemer, what a multitude of sorrows, ignominies, and afflictions torment Thee upon the Cross! Thy most sacred body hangs from three nails and rests only on Thy Wounds; the people who surround Thee deride and blaspheme Thee; and Thy immaculate soul is much more afflicted than Thy body. Tell me, why dost Thou suffer so much? Thou answerest me: I suffer all for the love of thee; remember, then, the affection I have borne thee, and love Me.

Yes, my Jesus, I will love Thee. And whom shall I love, if not my God Who dies for me? Hitherto I have despised Thee, but now my greatest grief is the remembrance of my offences against Thee, and I desire nothing but to be entirely Thine. O my Jesus, pardon me, and draw my heart to Thee; pierce and inflame it through and through with Thy love.

Let us consider how loving were the sentiments with which Jesus Christ presented His hands and feet to be nailed to the Cross, offering at the same time His Divine life to His Eternal Father for our salvation. My beloved Savior, when I think how much my soul cost Thee, I cannot despair of pardon. However great and numerous my sins, I will not despair of being saved, since Thou hast already superabundantly satisfied for me. My Jesus, my Hope, and my Love, as much as I have offended thee, so much will I love Thee: I have exceedingly offended Thee, I desire also to love Thee exceedingly. Thou Who givest me this desire, help me.

Eternal Father, look on the face of thy Christ (Psalm. lxxxiii. 10). Behold Thy dying Son upon the Cross; look on that livid countenance, that head crowned with thorns, those hands pierced with nails, that body all bruised and wounded; behold the Victim sacrificed for me, Whom I now present to Thee, and have pity on me!

II.

He hath loved us and washed us from our sins in his own blood (Apocalypse i. 5). Why should we fear that our sins will hinder us from becoming saints, when Jesus Christ has made for us a bath of His own Blood to wash our souls of every stain? It is sufficient that we repent of our sins and desire to amend.

Jesus, on the Cross, had us in His thoughts, and there prepared for us all those graces and mercies He now bestows upon us, with as much love as though He had to save only the soul of one of us in particular.

O my Savior, Thou didst foresee upon the Cross the offences I should commit against Thee, and instead of punishments Thou didst prepare for me lights, loving calls, and pardon. O my Jesus, shall I ever again, after so many graces, offend Thee and separate myself from Thee? O my Lord, permit it not! Grant that I may die rather than cease to love Thee. I will say to Thee, with St. Francis de Sales: "Either to die, or to love! Either to love, or to die!"

Spiritual Reading

PRAYER

GOD GIVES TO ALL MEN THE GRACE TO PRAY.

II.-FURTHER PROOFS.

(a) From Holy Scripture.

We have first the authority of the Apostle St. Paul, who assures us that God is faithful, and will not permit us to be tempted beyond our strength, since He always gives us assistance (either immediate or mediate, by means of Prayer) to resist the assaults of our enemies: God is faithful, who will not suffer you to be tempted above that which you are able; but will make also with temptation issue, that you may be able to bear it (1 Corinthians x. 13). Jansenius says that this text refers only to the predestined, but this comment of his is completely unfounded; for St. Paul is writing to all the faithful of Corinth, whom he certainly did not consider to be all predestined. So that St. Thomas has good reason for understanding it generally of all men, and for saying that God would not be faithful if He did not grant us, so far as in Him lies, those graces by means of which we can obtain salvation. It is proved, moreover, by all those texts in which God exhorts us to be converted, and to have recourse to Him for the graces necessary for our salvation and promises to hear us when we have recourse to Him. Wisdom preacheth aloud ... saying, O children, how long will ye love childishness, and fools covet those things which are hurtful to themselves ...? Turn ye at my reproof; behold, I will utter my spirit to you ... Because I called, and you refused ... I also will laugh in your destruction and will mock (Proverbs i. 22-26).

This exhortation, Turn ye, would be simple mockery, says Bellarmine, if God did not give to sinners at least the mediate assistance of Prayer for their conversion. Besides, we find in the passage, Behold, I will utter my spirit to you, mention made of the internal grace by which God calls sinners, and gives them actual assistance for conversion, if they will accept it. And again: Come to me, all you that labor and are heavy laden, and I will refresh you (Matthew xi. 28). Come and accuse me, saith the Lord; if your sins be as scarlet, they shall be made white as snow (Isaiah. i. 18). Ask, and it shall be given you (Matthew vii. 7). And so on in innumerable other texts already quoted. Now, if God did not give every one grace actually to have recourse to Him and actually to pray to Him, all these invitations and exhortations would be vain.

(b) From the Council of Trent.

It is clearly proved from the words of the Council of Trent. I beg the reader to give his best attention to this proof, which, if I am not mistaken, is perfectly decisive. There were innovators who asserted that man was deprived of free-will by the sin of Adam, and that the will of man at present has no share in good actions, but is induced to receive them passively from God, without producing them itself; and hence they inferred that the observance of the Commandments was impossible to those who were not efficaciously moved and predetermined by grace to avoid evil and to do good. Against this error the Council pronounced sentence in words borrowed from St. Augustine: "Deus impossibilia non jubet; sed jubendo monet, et facere quad possis, et petere quod non possis; et adjuvat ut possis." "God does not command impossible things; but by commanding, admonishes you both to do what you can, and to pray for what you cannot do; and He helps you so that you may be able ..."

So that, according to the Council, the Divine precepts are possible to all men, at least by the assistance of Prayer, by which greater help may be obtained to enable men to observe them. If, therefore, God has imposed His Commandments on all men, and has rendered their observance possible to all, at least mediately by means of Prayer, we must necessarily conclude that all men have the grace to enable them to pray, for the Commandments would not be possible to them without this grace. And as God grants to Prayer actual grace to do good, and thereby renders all His Commandments possible, so also He gives all actual grace to pray; for if there were any man who had not actual grace to pray to God, the Commandments would be impossible, as he could by no means, not even by Prayer, obtain the assistance necessary for their observance.

This being laid down, it cannot be said that the words, God admonishes you to do what you can, and to ask for what you cannot do, are only to be understood of the power to pray, not of actual Prayer; because, we reply, if the common and ordinary grace gave only the power to pray but not the power of actually Praying, the Council would not have said: "He admonishes you to do what you can, and to ask for what you cannot do," but rather, He admonishes you that you can do, and that you can pray. Moreover, if the Council had not intended to declare that everyone can observe the Precepts, or can pray to obtain grace to observe them, and had not meant to speak of actual grace, it would not have said "He admonishes," because this word properly refers to actual operation, and denotes not the instruction of the mind, but the movement of the will to do that good which it can actually do. When, therefore, the Council said: "He admonishes you to do what you can, and to ask for what you cannot do," it most clearly expressed, not only possible operation and possible Prayer, but actual operation and actual Prayer. For if man had need of another extraordinary grace, which as yet he has not, in order actually to work or actually to pray, how could God admonish him to do or to ask that which he cannot actually either do or ask without efficacious grace? Father Fortuanto Brescia speaks wisely on his point: "If the actual grace of Prayer were not given to all, but if for Prayer we had need of efficacious grace, which is not common to all, Prayer would be impossible to many who are without this efficacious grace; so that it could not be rightly said that 'God admonishes you to ask for that which you cannot do', because He would then admonish us to do a thing requiring a grace which we did not possess. Therefore, God's admonition to do and to pray must be understood of actual operation and Prayer, without need of a further extraordinary grace." And this is exactly what St. Augustine means when he says: "Hence we are admonished in easy things what to do, and in difficult things what to pray for"; for he supposes that though all have not grace, to enable them to do difficult things, all have at least grace to pray, because Prayer is an easy thing for everybody, as he also propounds in the words afterwards adopted by the Council of Trent: "God admonishes you to do what you can, and to ask for what you cannot do."

To recapitulate the argument: the Council says that God does not impose impossible Commands, because He either gives assistance to observe them, or gives the grace of Prayer to obtain that assistance, which He always grants when it is prayed for. Now, if it could ever be true that God does not give all men grace, at least the mediate grace of Prayer, actually to observe all His Precepts, Jansenius' Proposition would be true, that even the just man is without grace to enable him actually to observe some of the Commandments.

I do not know how else the text of the Council of Trent which I have cited, can be understood and explained, unless "sufficient grace" gives to all men the power of actually praying without the "efficacious grace" which our opponents supposed to be necessary for the actual performance of any pious work. And supposing the necessity of a further grace for actual Prayer, I cannot understand how this other text of the same Council can be true: "God does not leave those who have been once justified by His grace, unless they first leave Him." If, I argue, the ordinary sufficient grace would not be enough for actual Prayer, but that for this purpose efficacious grace, which is not common to all men, should be required, it would follow that when the just man would be tempted to commit his first mortal sin, and God would not give him efficacious grace at least to enable him to pray, and so obtain strength to resist, his succumbing to temptation might be said to result rather from the just man being abandoned by God than that he had abandoned God, seeing that he was left without the efficacious grace necessary to enable him to resist.

(c) From the Holy Fathers.

In the next place, our opinion is proved from the words of the holy Fathers.

St. Basil says: "When, however, any one is allowed to fall into temptation, it must issue that he may be able to endure it, and to ask in Prayer that the will of God may be done." The Saint, then, teaches that when God permits a man to be tempted, He does it in order that the man may resist by asking for the Divine Will, i.e., the grace to overcome. He therefore supposes that when a man has not sufficient assistance to overcome the temptation, he at least has the actual and common grace of Prayer, by which he may obtain whatever further grace he needs.

St. John Chrysostom says that God gave a law which would make the wounds manifest, in order that men may desire a physician. And again: "Nor can anyone be excused who, by ceasing to pray, has voluntarily abstained from overcoming his adversary." If such a man had not the grace necessary for actual Prayer, whereby he might obtain grace to resist, he might excuse himself when he is overcome.

So also St. Bernard: "Who are we, or what is our strength? This is what God wanted, that we, seeing our weakness, and that we have no other help, should with all humility have recourse to His Mercy." God, then, has imposed on us a Law impossible by our own strength, in order that we should go to Him, and by Prayer obtain strength to observe it; but if to any one was denied the grace of actual Prayer, to him the Law would be utterly impossible. "Many persons," says the same St. Bernard, "complain that they are deserted by grace; but grace could much more justly complain of being deserted by them."

But no Father is more clear on this point than St. Augustine, and that in many places. In one place he says: "The Pelagians think themselves very learned when they say, 'God would not command that which He knows man could not do.' Who is ignorant of this? But God does command some things that we cannot do, in order that we may know that for which we ought to ask Him."

Again: "It is not reckoned your fault, if you are ignorant without wishing to be so, but only if you neglect to inquire into that of which you are ignorant; nor that you do not cure your wounded members, but that you despise Him Who is willing to heal you. These are your own sins; no man is deprived of the knowledge of how to seek with advantage." So that, according to St. Augustine, no one is deprived of the grace of Prayer, whereby he may obtain grace for his conversion; otherwise, if this grace were wanting, it could not be his fault if he were not converted.

Again St. Augustine says: "What else, then, is shown us but that it is God that gives the power to ask, and to seek, and to knock, Who commands us to do these things?"

Again: "Once for all, receive this and understand it. Art thou not yet drawn? Pray that thou mayest be drawn."

Again the Saint says: "That the soul, then, knows not what it should do comes from this, that it has not yet received it; but will receive this also, if it has made a good use of what it has received; and it has received power to seek piously and diligently if it will."

Mark the words "it has received power to seek diligently and piously." Everyone, then, has the grace necessary for Prayer, and if he makes a good use of this, he will receive grace to do that which before he was unable to do immediately. Again: "Let the man who may be willing, but may not be able to do what he wills, pray that he may have such a measure as suffices for fulfilling the Commandments; thus is he assisted so as to be able to do what is commanded."

Again St. Augustine says: "He gives us Commandments for this reason, that when we have tried to do what we are commanded, and are wearied through our infirmity, we may know how to ask the help of grace." Here the Saint supposes that with ordinary grace we are not able to do difficult things, but can by means of Prayer obtain the aid necessary to accomplish them ... When, therefore, St. Augustine says that man is unable to fulfil the whole Law, and that Prayer is the only means given him to obtain help to fulfil it, he certainly supposes that God gives every man the grace of actual Prayer without need of a further extraordinary aid, not common to all men ...

But there are two texts of St. Augustine which have particular bearing on the point.

The first is this: "It is certain that we can keep the Commandments if we will; but since the will is prepared by God, we must ask Him that we may have such a will as is sufficient to enable us to perform what we will." Here he says that it is certain we could observe the Law if we would; on the other hand, he says that in order to will to do so, and actually to do so, we must pray. Therefore, all men have grace given them to pray, and by Prayer to obtain the abundant grace which enables us to keep the Commandments; otherwise, if for actual Prayer, efficacious grace, which is not common to all, were requisite, those to whom it was not given would not be able to keep the Commandments, nor to have the will to keep them.

The second text is that in which the holy Doctor answers the monks of Adramyttiurn, who spoke thus: If grace is necessary, and if we can do nothing without it, why blame us when we cannot act, and have not grace to act? You should rather pray God for us, that He may give us this grace. St. Augustine answers: You must be blamed, not because you do not act when you have not strength, but because you do not pray to obtain strength. "He who will not be admonished, and says, ' Do you rather pray for me,' must on that very account be admonished to do it (i.e. to pray) for himself." Now if the Saint did not believe that every man had grace to pray (if he so will) without need of further aid, he never could have said that these people were to be blamed for not praying; for they could have answered that if they were not to be blamed for not doing a thing when they had not special grace to enable them to do it, so they could not be blamed for not praying when they had not special grace for actual Prayer. This is what St. Augustine elsewhere says: "Let them not deceive themselves who say: ' Why are we commanded to abstain from evil and do good if it is God Who works in us both to will and to do it?' " And he answers that when men do good they should thank God for it, Who gives them strength to do it; " but when they do it not," he says, "let them pray that they may receive that which as yet they have not." Now, if these people had not even the grace for the act of Prayer, they might answer " Why are we commanded to pray if God does not work in us to make us pray?" How are we to have the will to pray if we do not receive the grace necessary for actual Prayer?

St. Thomas is not speaking of Prayer expressly, but assumes the certainty of our Proposition, when he says: "It belongs to God's Providence to provide every individual with what is necessary for salvation, provided he puts no impediment in the way." Since, then, it is true, on the one hand, that God gives to all men the graces necessary for salvation, and, on the other, that we require for Prayer the grace which enables us actually to pray, and thereby to obtain further and greater assistance to enable us to do that which we cannot compass with ordinary grace--it follows, necessarily, that God gives all men sufficient grace actually to pray if they will, without need of efficacious grace.

Here we may add the answer of Bellarmine to the heretics who inferred from the text, No one can come to me, unless my Father draw him (John vi. 44), that no one could go to God who was not properly drawn by Him. "We answer," he says, "that the only conclusion from this text is that all men have not the efficacious grace to make them really believe; but we cannot conclude that all men have not at least the assistance which confers the possibility of believing, or, at any rate, the possibility of asking for grace."

Evening Meditation

THE PRACTICE OF THE LOVE OF JESUS CHRIST

"Charity endureth all things"

HE THAT LOVES JESUS CHRIST WITH A STRONG LOVE DOES NOT CEASE TO LOVE HIM IN THE MIDST OF TEMPTATIONS AND DESOLATIONS

I.

The soul, then, in the commencement of her conversion to God, tastes the sweetness of those sensible consolations with which God seeks to allure her, and by them to wean her from earthly pleasures; she breaks off her attachment to creatures, and becomes attached to God. Still, her attachment is imperfect, inasmuch as it is fostered more by that sensibility of spiritual consolations than by the real wish to do what is pleasing to God; and she deceives herself by believing that the greater the pleasure she feels in her devotions, the more she loves Almighty God. The consequence of this is that if this food of spiritual consolation is stopped, by her being taken from her ordinary exercises of devotion, and employed in other works of obedience, charity, or duties of her state, she is disturbed, and takes it greatly to heart: and this is a universal defect in our miserable human nature, to seek our own satisfaction in all that we do. Or again, when she no longer finds this sweet relish of devotion in her exercises, she either forsakes them or lessens them, and continuing to lessen them from day to day, she at length omits them entirely. And this misfortune befalls many souls who, when called by Almighty God to love Him, enter upon the way of perfection, and as long as spiritual sweetness lasts, make a certain progress; but alas! when this is no longer tasted, they leave off all, and resume their former ways. But it is of the highest importance to be fully persuaded that the love of God and perfection, do not consist in feelings of tenderness and consolation, but in overcoming self-love and in following the Divine Will. St. Francis de Sales says: "God is as worthy of our love when He afflicts us as when He consoles us."

I do love Thee, my Sovereign Good; I love Thee with my whole heart; I love Thee more than myself; I love Thee, and have no other desire than to love Thee. I own that this my good-will is the pure effect of Thy grace; but do Thou, O my Lord, perfect Thy own work; withdraw not Thy helping hand till death! Oh, never for a moment leave me in my own hands; give me strength to vanquish temptations and to overcome myself; and for this end give me grace always to have recourse to Thee!

II.

Amid these consolations, it requires no remarkable degree of virtue to forego sensible delights, and to endure affronts and contradictions. The soul in the midst of these sweetnesses can endure all things; but this endurance comes far more frequently from those sensible consolations than from the strength of true love of God. On this account the Lord, with a view to give her a solid foundation in virtue, retires from her, and deprives her of that sensible devotion, that He may rid her of all attachment to self-love, which was fed by such consolations. And hence it happens that whereas formerly she felt a joy in making acts of offering, of confidence, and love, now that the stream of consolation is dried up she makes these acts with a coldness and painful effort, and finds a weariness in the most pious exercises, in her prayers, spiritual readings, and Communions; she even finds in them nothing but darkness and fears, and all seems lost to her. She prays and prays again, and is overwhelmed with sadness, because God seems to have abandoned her.

O Jesus, my Hope, my Love and only Love of my soul, I deserve not Thy consolations and sweet visitations; keep them for those innocent souls who have always loved Thee; sinner that I am, I do not deserve them, nor do I ask for them: this only do I ask, give me grace to love Thee, to accomplish Thy adorable will during my whole life, and then dispose of me as Thou pleasest! Unhappy me! far other darkness, other terrors, other abandonments would be due to the outrages I have done Thee: hell were my just award, where, separated from Thee forever, and totally abandoned by Thee, I should shed tears eternally, without ever being able to love Thee more. But no, my Jesus, I accept of every punishment; only spare me this. Thou art deserving of an infinite love; Thou hast placed me under an excessive obligation of loving Thee; oh, no, I cannot trust myself to live and not love Thee!

Saturday-Eighth Week After Pentecost

MARY IS THE HOPE OF ALL SINNERS

St. Basil of Seleucia remarks that "if God granted to some who were only His servants such power that not only their touch, but even their very shadows, healed the sick who were placed for this purpose in the streets, how much greater power must we suppose He has granted to her who was not only His servant but His Mother!"

I.

St. Ephrem, addressing this Blessed Virgin, says: "Thou art the only advocate of sinners, and of all who are unprotected." And then he salutes her in the following words: "Hail, refuge and hospital of sinners!"--true refuge, in which alone they can hope for reception and liberty. And an author remarks that this was the meaning of David when he said: For he hath hidden me in his tabernacle (Psalm xxvi. 5). And truly what can this tabernacle of God be unless it is Mary, who is called by St. Germanus "a tabernacle made by God, into which He alone entered to accomplish the great work of the Redemption of man."

St. Basil of Seleucia remarks that "if God granted to some who were only His servants such power that not only their touch but even their shadows healed the sick who were placed for this purpose in the public streets, how much greater power must we suppose that He has granted to her who was not only His handmaid but His Mother?" We may indeed say that our Lord has given us Mary as a public hospital, in which all who are sick, poor, and destitute can be received. But now I ask, in hospitals erected expressly for the poor, who have the greatest claim to admission? Certainly the most infirm, and those who are in the greatest need.

And for this reason, should any one find himself devoid of merit and overwhelmed with spiritual infirmities, that is to say, sin, he can thus address Mary: O Lady, thou art the refuge of the sick poor; reject me not, for as I am the poorest and the most infirm of all, I have the greatest right to be welcomed by thee.

II.

Let us, then, cry out with St. Thomas of Villanova: "O Mary, we poor sinners know no other refuge than thee, for thou art our only hope, and on thee we rely for our salvation." Thou art our only advocate with Jesus Christ; to thee do we all turn.

In the Revelations of St. Bridget, Mary is called the "Star preceding the sun," giving us thereby to understand, that when devotion towards the Divine Mother begins to manifest itself in a soul that is in a state of sin, it is a certain mark that before long God will enrich it with His grace. The glorious St. Bonaventure, in order to revive the confidence of sinners in the protection of Mary, places before them the picture of a tempestuous sea into which sinners have already fallen from the ship of Divine grace; they are already dashed about on every side by remorse of conscience and by fear of the judgments of God; they are without light or guide, and are on the point of losing the last breath of hope and falling into despair; then it is that our Lord, pointing out Mary to them, who is commonly called the "Star of the Sea", raises His voice and says: "O poor lost sinners, despair not! Raise up your eyes, and cast them on this beautiful star; breathe again with confidence, for it will save you from this tempest, and will guide you into the port of salvation." St. Bernard says the same thing: "If thou wouldst not be lost in the tempest, cast thine eyes on the star, and call upon Mary."

Spiritual Reading

PRAYER

GOD GIVES TO ALL THE GRACE TO PRAY.

III-THEOLOGICAL REASONS THAT JUSTIFY THIS DOCTRINE.

Let us now proceed, in the third and last place, to examine the reasons of this opinion. Petavius, with Duval and other Theologians, asks: Why does God impose on us commands which we cannot keep with the common and ordinary grace? Because, he answers, He wishes us to have recourse to Him in Prayer. This is the general teaching of the Fathers, as we have seen above. Hence, he infers that we ought to hold it as certain that every man has grace actually to pray, and by Prayer to obtain greater grace to enable him to do that which is impossible to him with the ordinary grace; otherwise God would have imposed an impossible law. This reason is very strong.

Another reason is that if God imposes on all men the duty of actual observance of His Commandments, we must necessarily suppose that He also gives to all men the grace necessary for this actual observance, at least mediately by means of Prayer. In order, therefore, to uphold the reasonableness of the Law, and the justice of the punishment of the disobedient, we must hold that every man has sufficient power, at least mediately by means of Prayer, for the actual performance of what is prescribed, and that he is able to pray without any unusual and additional grace; otherwise, if he had not this mediate or remote power of actually keeping the Commandments, it could never be said that all men had from God sufficient grace for the actual observance of the Law.

Tomassin and Tourneley bring forward many other reasons for this opinion; but I pass them over for one that seems to me demonstrative. It is founded on the Precept of Hope, which obliges us all to hope in God with confidence for Eternal Life; and I say: If we were not certain that God gives us all grace to enable us actually to pray, without our being in need of another particular and unusual grace, no one without a special revelation could hope for salvation as he ought. But I must first explain the grounds of this argument.

The Virtue of Hope is so pleasing to God that He has declared that He feels delight in those who trust in Him: The Lord taketh pleasure in them that hope in his mercy (Psalm cxlvi. 11): And he promises victory over his enemies, perseverance in grace and eternal glory, to the man who hopes, and that because he hopes: Because he hoped in me, I will deliver him; I will protect him ... I will deliver him and I will glorify him (Psalm xc. 14). Preserve me, for I have put my trust in thee (Psalm xv. 1). He will save them because they have hoped in him (Psalm xxxvi. 40). No one hath hoped in the Lord, and hath been confounded (Ecclesiasticus 11). And let us be sure that the heavens and the earth will fail, but the promises of God cannot fail: Heaven and earth shall pass away, but my words shall not pass away (Matthew. xxiv. 35). St. Bernard, therefore, says that all our merit consists in reposing all our confidence in God: "This is the whole merit of man, if he places all his hope in Him." The reason is that he who hopes in God honors Him much: Call upon me in the day of trouble, I will deliver thee, and thou shalt glorify me (Psalm xlix. 15). He honors the power, the mercy, and the faithfulness of God; since he believes that God can and will save him; and that He cannot fail in His promises to save the man who trusts in Him. And the Prophet assures us that the greater our confidence is, the greater will be the measure of God's mercy poured out upon us: Let thy mercy, O Lord, be upon us, as we have hoped in thee (Psalm xxxii. 22).

Now, as this Virtue of Hope is so pleasing to God, He has willed to impose it upon us by a Precept that binds under mortal sin, as all Theologians agree, and as is evident from many texts of Scripture. Trust in him, all ye congregations of people (Psalm lxi. 9). Ye that fear the Lord, hope in him (Ecclesiasticus. ii. 9). Hope in thy God always (Osee xii. 6). Hope perfectly in that grace which is offered to you (1 Peter i. 13). This Hope of Eternal Life ought, then, to be sure and firm in us, according to the definition of St. Thomas: "Hope is the certain expectation of Beatitude." And the sacred Council of Trent has expressly declared: "All men ought to place and repose a most firm Hope in the help of God; for God, unless they fail to correspond to His grace, as He has begun the good work, will also finish it, working in them both to will and to perform." And speaking of himself, St. Paul had already said: I know whom I have believed, and I am certain that he is able to keep that which I have committed unto him (2 Timothy i. 12). And herein is the difference between Christian hope and worldly hope. Worldly hope need only be an uncertain expectation; nor can it be otherwise; for it is always doubtful whether the man who has promised a favor may not hereafter change his mind, if he has not already changed it. But the Christian Hope of Eternal Salvation is certain on God's part; for He can and will save us and has promised to save those who obey His Law, and to this end has promised us all necessary graces to enable us to observe this Law, if we ask for them. It is true that Hope is accompanied by fear, as St. Thomas says; but this fear does not arise from God's side, but from our own, since we may at any time fall by not corresponding as we ought and by putting an impediment in the way of grace by our sins. For this reason then, did the Council of Trent condemn those innovators, who, because they entirely deprive man of free will, say that every believer must have an infallible certitude of perseverance and salvation. This error was condemned by the Council; because, as we have said, to obtain salvation our correspondence is necessary, and this correspondence of ours is uncertain and fallible. Hence God wills that we should, on the one hand, always fear for ourselves, lest, trusting in our own strength, we should fall into presumption, but, on the other, that we should be always certain of His good will, and of His assistance to save us, provided always that we ask Him for it, so that we may always have a sure confidence in His goodness. St. Thomas says that we ought to look with certainty to receive from God Eternal happiness, confiding in His power and mercy, and believing that He can and will save us. "Whoever has Faith, is certain of God's power and mercy."

Now, as the Hope of our salvation which we place in God ought to be certain (according to the definition of St. Thomas--"the certain expectation of beatitude") it follows that the motive of our Hope must also be certain; for if the foundation of our Hope were uncertain, and open to a doubt, we could not with any certainty hope and expect to receive salvation, and the means necessary for it from the hands of God. St. Paul insists on our being firm and immovable in our Hope, if we would be saved: If so ye continue in the faith, grounded and settled, and immovable from the hope of the Gospel, which you have heard (Colossians i. 23). This he confirms in another place where he says that our Faith ought to be as immovable as an anchor securely fixed, since it is grounded on the promises of God Who cannot deceive: And we desire that every one of you show forth the same carefulness to the accomplishing of hope unto the end. That by two immutable things, in which it is impossible for God to lie, we may have the strongest comfort, who have fled for refuge to hold fast the hope set before us, which we have as an anchor of the soul, sure and firm (Hebrews vi. 11-19). Hence St. Bernard says that our Hope cannot be uncertain, as it rests on God's promises: "Nor does this expectation seem to us vain, or this Hope doubtful, since we rely on the promises of the Eternal Truth." In another place St. Bernard says of himself that his hope depends on three things--the love which induced God to adopt us as His children, the truth of His promises, and His power to fulfil them: "Three things I see in which my Hope consists--the love of adoption, the truth of the promise, the power to fulfil."

And therefore the Apostle, St. James, declares that the man who desires the grace of God must ask for it, not with hesitation, but with the confident certainty of obtaining it: Let him ask in faith, nothing wavering (James i. 6). For if he asks with hesitation, he shall obtain nothing: For he that wavereth is like the wave of the sea, that is moved and carried about by the wind; therefore, let not that man think that he shall receive anything of the Lord (James i. 6, 7). And St. Paul praises Abraham because he in nothing doubted God's promise, knowing that when God promises, He cannot fail to perform: In the promise also of God he staggered not by distrust; but was strengthened in faith, giving glory to God; most fully knowing that whatsoever he has promised, he is able also to perform (Romans iv. 20-21). Hence, also, Jesus Christ tells us that we shall then receive all the graces that we desire when we ask them with a sure belief of receiving them: Therefore, I say to you, all things whatsoever you ask when ye pray, believe that you shall receive them, and they shall come unto you (Mark xi. 24). In a word, God will not hear us, unless we have a sure confidence of being heard.

Now, my argument is this. Our Hope of salvation, and of receiving the means necessary for its attainment, must be certain on God's part. The foundations of this certainty are, as we have seen, the Power, the Mercy, and the Fidelity of God; and of these the strongest and most certain is God's infallible Fidelity to the promise which He has made on account of the merits of Jesus Christ, to save us, and to give us the graces necessary for our salvation; for, as Giovenino well observes, though we might believe God to be infinite in Power and Mercy, nevertheless we could not feel confident expectation of God saving us, unless He had surely promised to do so. But this promise is on condition that we correspond with God's grace and pray, as is clear from the Scriptures: Ask, and ye shall receive. If ye ask the Father anything in my name, he will give it you. He will give good things to those that ask him. We ought always to pray. Ye have not, because ye ask not. If anyone wanteth wisdom let him ask of God; and from many other texts which we have already quoted. Wherefore it is that the Fathers and Theologians maintain, as we have shown, that Prayer is a necessary means of Salvation.

Now, if we were not certain that God gives to all men grace to enable them actually to pray, without need of a further special grace and one not common to all, we could have no certain and firm foundation for a certain Hope of salvation in God, but only an uncertain and conditional foundation. When I have the assurance that by Prayer I shall obtain Eternal Life, and all the graces necessary to attain it; and when I know that God will give to me what he gives to all men, namely, the grace of actual Prayer, if I so will, then I have a sure foundation for hoping in God for salvation, if I fail not on my part. But when I am in doubt whether or not God will give me that particular grace which He does not give to all, but which is necessary for actual Prayer, then I have not a certain foundation for my Hope of salvation, but only a doubtful and uncertain one, since I cannot be sure that God will give me this special grace, without which I cannot pray, as He refuses it to so many. And in this case the uncertainty would be not only on my part, but also on God's part; and so Christian Hope would be destroyed, which, according to the Apostle, ought to be immovable, firm, and secure. I say in all truth, I cannot see how a Christian can fulfil the precept of Hope--hoping, as he ought, with sure confidence for salvation from God, and for the graces necessary for its attainment--unless he holds it as an infallible truth that God commonly gives to every individual the grace actually to pray, if he chooses, without any further special assistance.

So that to conclude, our System or opinion (held by so many Theologians, and by our humble Congregation) well agrees--

(a) On the one hand, with the doctrine of grace intrinsically efficacious, by means of which we infallibly, though freely, act virtuously.

It cannot be denied that God can easily, with His Omnipotence, incline and move men's hearts freely to will that which He wills, as the Scriptures teach: The heart of the king is in the hand of the Lord: whithersoever he will, he shall turn it (Proverbs xxi. 1); I will put my spirit in the midst of you, and I will cause you to walk in my commandments (Ezechiel xxxvi. 27); My counsel shall stand, and all my will shall be done (Isaiah xlvi. 10); He changeth the heart of the princes of the people of the earth (Job xii. 24); May the God of peace make you perfect in every good work, that you may do his will; working in you that which is well pleasing in his sight, through Jesus Christ (Hebrews xiii. 21).

And it cannot be denied that St. Augustine and St. Thomas have taught the opinion of the efficaciousness of grace in itself, by its own nature. This is evident from many passages, and specially from the following:

St. Augustine says: "Yet God did not this, except by the will of the men themselves; since He, no doubt, has the most almighty and absolute power of inclining the hearts of men." Again: "Almighty God works in the hearts of men that He may do by their means that which He has willed to do through them." Again: "Although they all do what is right in the service of God, yet He causes them to do what He commands." Again: "It is certain that it is we who act when we act; but He causes us to act, by bestowing most efficacious powers on the will, according to His words, I will cause you to walk in my commandments (Ezechiel xxxvi. 27). Again, on the text, For it is God that worketh in you, both to will and to accomplish according to his good will (Philippians ii. 13), St. Augustine says: We therefore will; but God worketh in us even to will."

Again: "God knows how to work in men's hearts, not so as to make them believe against their will, which is impossible, but so as to make them willing instead of unwilling." Again: "He works in the hearts of men not only true revelations, but also good-will." Again: "The acts of our will have just so much power as God wishes them to have." So also St. Thomas: "God infallibly moves the will by the efficacy of the moving power, which cannot fail." Again: "Love has the character of impeccability, from the power of the Holy Spirit, Who infallibly works whatever He will; hence it is impossible that these two things should be at the same time true--that the Holy Spirit wills to move a person to an act of love, and that at the same time the person should lose love by an act of sin." Again: "If God moves the will to do anything, it is impossible to say that the will is not moved to it."

(b) On the other hand, our teaching is quite consonant to the doctrine of truly sufficient grace being given to all, by corresponding to which a man will gain efficacious grace; while by not corresponding, but resisting, he will deservedly be denied this efficacious grace. And thus all excuse is taken away from those sinners who say that they have not strength to overcome their temptations; because if they had prayed, and made use of the ordinary grace which is given to all men, they would have obtained strength, and would have been saved. If, on the contrary, a person does not admit this ordinary grace by which everyone is enabled at least to pray, without needing a further special unusual grace, and by Prayer to obtain further assistance to enable him to fulfil the Law, I do not know how he can explain all those texts of Scripture, in which souls are exhorted to return to God, to overcome temptation, and to correspond to the Divine invitation: Return, ye transgressors, to the heart (Isaiah xlvi. 8); Return and live: Be converted and do penance (Ezechiel xviii. 30, 32); Loose the bonds from off thy neck (Is. lii. 2); Come to me, all you that labor and are burdened (Matthew xi. 28); Resist, strong in faith (1 Peter v. 9); Walk whilst you have the light (Jo. xii. 35). I cannot tell, I say, supposing it were true that the grace of Prayer were not given to all to enable them thereby to obtain the further assistance necessary for salvation, how these texts could be explained. And I do not know how the Sacred Writers could so forcibly exhort all men, without any exception, to be converted, to resist the enemy, to walk in the way of virtue, and, for this end, to pray with confidence and perseverance, if the grace of doing well, or at least of praying, were not granted to all, but only to those who have the gift of efficacious grace. And I cannot see where would be the justice of the reproof given to all sinners, without exception, who resist grace and despise the Voice of God: You always resist the Holy Ghost (Acts vii. 51). Because I called and you refused; I stretched out my hand and there was none that regarded; you have despised all my counsel, and have neglected my reprehensions (Proverbs i. 24-25). If sinners were without even the remote grace of Prayer, and that, too, an efficacious grace, which our opponents consider necessary for actual Prayer, I cannot see how all these reproofs could be justly made against them.

Evening Meditation

THE PRACTICE OF THE LOVE OF JESUS CHRIST

"Charity endureth all things"

HE THAT LOVES JESUS CHRIST WITH A STRONG LOVE DOES NOT CEASE TO LOVE HIM IN THE MIDST OF TEMPTATIONS AND DESOLATIONS

I.

Let us come now to the practice of what we are to do on our part in the like circumstances. When Almighty God in His mercy deigns to console us with His loving visitations, and to let us feel the presence of His grace, it is not good to reject the Divine consolations, as some false mystics advise: let us thankfully receive them, but let us beware of settling down on them, and seeking delight in those feelings of spiritual tenderness. St. John of the Cross calls this a "spiritual gluttony," which is faulty and displeasing to God. Let us strive in such moments to banish from our mind the sensible enjoyment of these sweetnesses: and let us be especially on our guard against supposing that these favors are a token of our standing better with God than others; for such a thought of vanity would oblige God to withdraw Himself from us altogether, and to leave us in our miseries. We must certainly at such times return most fervent thanks to God, because such spiritual consolations are signal gifts of the Divine bounty to our souls, far greater than all the riches and honors of this world. But let us not seek then to regale ourselves on these sensible sweetnesses, but let us rather humble ourselves by the remembrance of the sins of our past life. For the rest, we must consider this loving treatment as the pure result of the goodness of God; and that perhaps, it is sent in order that we may be strengthened by these consolations to endure with patience and resignation some great tribulation soon to befall us. We should, therefore, take the occasion of offering ourselves to suffer every pain, internal or external, that may happen to us--every illness, every persecution, every spiritual desolation--saying: O my Lord, I am here before Thee; do with me, and with all that belongs to me, whatever Thou wilt; grant me the grace to love Thee and perfectly to accomplish Thy holy will, and I ask no more!

II.

When a soul is morally certain of being in the grace of God, although she may be deprived of worldly pleasures, as well as of those which come from God, she nevertheless rests satisfied with her state, conscious, as she is, of loving God and of being loved by Him. But God wishes to see her purified and divested of all sensible satisfaction, in order to unite her entirely to Himself by means of pure love and so He puts her in the crucible of desolation, which is more painful to bear than the most severe trials, whether internal or external; she is left in uncertainty as to whether she is in the grace of God or, not, and in the dense darkness that shrouds her, there seems no prospect of her evermore finding God. Almighty God, moreover, will sometimes permit the soul to be assailed by violent sensual temptations, accompanied by irregular movements of the lower nature, or perhaps by thoughts of unbelief, of despair, and even of hatred of God, when she imagines herself cast off by Him, and that He no longer hears her prayers. And as, on the one hand, the suggestions of the devil are vehement, and the motions of concupiscence are excited, and, on the other, the soul finds herself in this great darkness, she can no longer sufficiently distinguish whether she properly resists or yields to the temptations, though her will resolutely refuses all consent. Her fears of having lost God are thus very much increased; and from her fancied infidelity in struggling against the temptations, she thinks herself deservedly abandoned by God. The saddest of all calamities seems to have befallen her--to be able no longer to love God, and to be hated by Him. St. Teresa passed through all these trials, and declares that during them solitude had no charms for her, but on the contrary filled her with horror, while prayer was changed for her into a perfect hell.